FROM
Montrose
TO
Culloden

4

~Tales of a Scottish Grandfather~

FROM
Montrose
TO
Culloden

Bonnie Prince Charlie
& Scotland's Romantic Age

Sir Walter Scott

Introduction by
GEORGE GRANT

CUMBERLAND HOUSE
NASHVILLE, TENNESSEE

Introduction copyright © 2001 by George Grant

Published by
CUMBERLAND HOUSE PUBLISHING, INC.
431 Harding Industrial Drive
Nashville, Tennessee 37211
www.cumberlandhouse.com

Cover design by Unlikely Suburban Design, Nashville, Tennessee

Library of Congress Cataloging-in-Publication Data

Scott, Walter, Sir, 1771–1832.
[Tales of a grandfather]
Tales of a Scottish grandfather / Sir Walter Scott ; introduction by George Grant.
   p. cm.
Includes index.
Originally published: London : Routledge, 1828.
Contents: v. 4. From Montrose to Culloden : Bonnie Prince Charlie & Scotland's Romantic age.
ISBN 1-58182-147-6 (v. 4 : pbk. : alk. paper)
1. Scotland—History. I. Title.
DA761.S55 2001
941.1—dc21   00-065775

ISBN 978-1-68442-186-2 (hc)

CONTENTS

INTRODUCTION

S IR Walter Scott (1771–1832) created the genre of historical fiction in a series called the Waverley Novels. In his phenomenally popular works, readers entered into the lives of both great and ordinary people caught up in violent, dramatic changes in history.

To some degree Scott's work shows the influence of the Scottish Enlightenment. So, for instance, he believed every person was basically decent regardless of class, religion, politics, or ancestry. In fact, tolerance is a major theme in his historical works—he was the first novelist to portray peasant characters sympathetically and realistically, and he was equally just to merchants and soldiers. But the novels also expressed his belief in the need for social progress that would not reject the traditions of the past. Thus, he drew on his great Scottish legacy of Calvinism, Covenantalism, and Communitarianism.Clearly, his early influences included long evenings of storytelling by his elders and varied readings in poetry, history, and drama, as well as fairy tales and grand romances.

In his introduction to *The Fortunes of Nigel*, Scott remarked, "But no one shall find me rowing against the stream. I care not who knows it; I write for the general amusement." Nevertheless, the works were serious literary and intellectual efforts. In his portraits of Scotland, England, and the Continent from medieval times to the eighteenth century, he showed a keen knowledge of political and traditional forces and of their influences on individuals. Indeed, Scott wrote frequently about the conflicts between different cultures. *Ivanhoe* (1791) dealt with the struggle between Normans and Saxons. *The Talisman* (1825) described the conflict between Christians and Muslims in the Crusades. But it was for his Scottish novels that he was best known—and most beloved. They have generally garnered the highest praise from critics and common readers alike. They deal with the cataclysmic clashes between the new commercial English culture and the older Scottish clan culture. A number of critics rank *Old Mortality* (1816), *The Heart of Midlothian* (1819), and *St Ronan's Well* (1824) as Scott's best novels. But several other works in the Waverley series also claim adherents, including *Antiquary* (1816), *Rob Roy* (1817), *A Legend of Montrose* (1819), and *Quentin Dunward* (1823).

James Fenimore Cooper in America, Honoré de Balzac in France, and Charles Dickens and William Makepeace Thackeray in England were among the many who learned from Scott's panoramic studies of the interplay between social trends and individual character. In Great Britain, he created an enduring interest in Scottish traditions, and throughout the Western world he encouraged the cult of the Middle Ages, which strongly characterized romanticism.

But besides his novels—to say nothing of the ideas they spawned and the enthusiasms they inculcated—his vast and ornate estate over-looking the Tweed River remains a lasting testimony to the faith, vision, and passion of this remarkable man who almost single-handedly wrenched Scotland out of the dregs of self-immolation. Abbotsford became a combination folly, museum, and world-view proclamation of the great man's quirkiness, amiability, generosity, chivalry, virtue, family pride, and national integrity.

It was a combination of those two elements of the great man—the passion to retell the tales of his homeland in his historical novels and the passion to collect artifacts of his Scottish legacy at Abbotsford—that seemed to come together in the last great project he undertook at the end of his life: writing *Tales of a Scottish Grandfather*.Particularly in this fourth and final volume, which details the heroic saga of Bonnie Prince Charlie and the Jacobite Risings of the eighteenth century, Scott remains the consummate storyteller while at the same time assembling the historical materials like a true archivist.Indeed, it represents the very height of his mastery and the very depth of his passion.

George Grant

FROM
Montrose
TO
Culloden

LXVI

The Hanoverian Ascent

1714-1715

THE period of Queen Anne's demise found the Jacobites, for a party who were both numerous and zealous, uncommonly ill prepared and irresolute. They had nursed themselves in the hope that the dark and mysterious conduct of Oxford was designed to favour his purpose of a counter-revolution; and the more open professions of Bolingbroke, which reached the Jacobites of Scotland through the medium of the Earl of Mar, were considered as pointing more explicitly to the same important end.

But they were mistaken in Oxford's purpose, who only acted towards them as it was in his nature to do towards all mankind, and so regulated his conduct as to cause the Jacobites to believe he was upon their side, while, in fact, his only purpose was to keep factions from breaking into extremities, and to rule all parties, by affording hopes to each in their turn, which were all to be ultimately found delusive.

Bolingbroke, on the other hand, was more sanguine and decided, both in opinion and action; and he would probably have been sufficiently active in his measures in behalf of King James had he possessed the power of maturing them. But being thus mocked by the cross fate which showed him the place of his ambition at one moment empty, and in the next all access to it closed against him, he was taken totally unprepared; and the Duke of Ormond, Sir William Windham, and other leaders of the Jacobite party, shared the same disadvantage. They might, indeed, have proclaimed King James the Third in the person of the Chevalier de St. George, and trusted to their influence with the Tory landed gentlemen, and with the populace, to effect a universal insurrection. Some of them even inclined to this desperate measure; and the celebrated Dr. Atterbury, Bishop of Rochester, offered to go to Westminster in his rochet and lawn sleeves, and himself to perform the ceremony. This, however, would have been commencing a civil war, in which, the succession of the House of Hanover being determined by the existing law, the insurrectionists must have begun by incurring the guilt of high treason, without being assured of any force by which they might be protected. Upon the whole, therefore, the Jacobites, and those who wished them well, remained, after the Queen's death, dejected, confused, and anxiously watchful of circumstances, which they did not pretend to regulate or control.

On the contrary the Whigs, acting with uncommon firmness and unanimity, took hold of the power which had so lately been possessed by their opponents, like troops who seize in action the artillery of their enemy, and turn it instantly against them. The privy counsellors who were of that party, imitating the determined conduct of the Dukes of Somerset and Argyle, repaired to the Council, without waiting for a summons, and issued instant orders for the proclamation of King George, which were generally obeyed without resistance. The assembled Parliament recognised King George I. as the sovereign entitled to succeed, in terms of the act regulating the destination of the crown. The same proclamation took place in Ireland and Scotland without opposition; and thus the King took legal and peaceable possession of his kingdom. It appeared, also, that England's most powerful, and, it might seem, most hostile neighbour, Louis XIV., was nowise disposed to encourage any machinations which could disturb the Elector of Hanover's accession to the crown. The Chevalier de St. George had made a hasty journey to Paris, upon learning the tidings of Queen Anne's death; but far from experiencing a reception favourable to his views on the British crown, he was obliged to return to Lorraine, with the sad assurance that the monarch of France was determined to adhere to the Treaty of Utrecht, by an important article of which he had recognised the succession of the House of Hanover to the crown of Great Britain. It is more than probable, as before hinted, that there had been, during the dependence of the treaty, some private understanding, or perhaps secret agreement with Bolingbroke, which might disarm the rigour of this article. But it was evident that the power of the minister with whom such an engagement had been made if indeed it existed in any formal shape, was now utterly fallen; and the affairs of Britain were, soon after King George's accession, entrusted to a ministry who had the sagacity to keep the French King firm to his engagement, by sending to Paris an ambassador, equally distinguished for talents in war and in diplomacy and for warm adherence to the Protestant line.

This eminent person was John Dalrymple, the second Earl of Stair, whose character demands particular notice amongst the celebrated Scotsmen of this period. He was eldest surviving son of the first Earl, distinguished more for his talents than his principles, in the reigns of King William and Queen Anne; infamous for his accession to the massacre of Glencoe, and unpopular from the skill and political talent which he displayed in favour of the Union, in carrying which through the Scottish Parliament he was a most useful agent. According to the prejudiced observations of the common people, ill fortune seemed to attend his house. He died suddenly during the dependence of the Union treaty, and vulgar report attributed his death to suicide, for which, however, there is no evidence but that of common fame.

A previous calamity of a cruel nature had occurred, in which John, his second son, was the unfortunate agent. While yet a mere boy, and while playing with firearms, he had the great misfortune to shoot his elder brother, and kill him on the spot. The unhappy agent in this melancholy affair was sent off by the ill-fated parents, who could not bear to look upon him, to reside with a clergyman, in Ayrshire, as one who was for ever banished from his family. The person to whose care he was committed was fortunately a man of sound sense, and a keen discriminator of character. The idea he formed of the young exile's powers of mind induced him, by a succession of favourable reports, mixed with intercession, warmly to solicit his pupil's restoration to the family of which he afterwards became the principal ornament. It was long before he could effect a reconciliation; and the youth, when this was accomplished, entered into the army with the advantages of his rank, and those arising out of early misfortune, which had compelled him to severe study. He was repeatedly

distinguished in the wars of Marlborough, and particularly at Rami-
lies, Oudenarde, and Malplaquet. Lord Stair rose in rank in proportion to his military reputation, but was deprived of his command
when the Tory ministers, in the latter end of Queen Anne's reign, new
modelled the army to the exclusion of the Whig officers. Upon the
accession of George I. he was appointed a lord of the bedchamber, a
privy counsellor, and commander of the Scottish forces in the absence
of the Duke of Argyle. Shortly after that great event, the Earl of Stair
was, as we have already mentioned, sent to Paris, where he held for
several years the situation of ambassador extraordinary, and where his
almost miraculous power of acquiring information enabled him to
detect the most secret intrigues of the Jacobites, and to watch, and
even overawe, the conduct of the court of France, who, well disposed
as they were to encourage privately the undertakings of the Chevalier
St. George, which public faith prevented them from countenancing
openly, found themselves under the eye of the most active and acute
of statesmen, from whom nothing seemed to remain concealed; while
his character for courage, talent, and integrity, made it equally impossible to intimidate, deceive, or influence him. It may be added that his
perfect knowledge of good breeding, in a nation where manners are
reduced almost to a science,[1] enabled Lord Stair to preserve the good-
will and favour of those with whom he treated, even while he insisted
upon topics the most unpalatable to the French monarch and his ministers, and that in a manner the most courteous in style, though most
unyielding in purpose. It may be believed that large sums in secret
service money were lavished in this species of diplomacy. Lord Stair
was always able, by his superior information, to counteract the plots
of the Jacobites, and, satisfied with doing so, was often desirous of
screening from the vengeance of his own court the misguided individuals who had rashly engaged in them. It was owing to the activity of
this vigilant diplomatist that George I. owed, in a great measure, the
neutrality of France, which was a very important addition to the security of his new throne.

To return to our history:—George I., in the fifty-fifth year of his
age, thus quietly installed in his British dominions, landed at Greenwich on the 17th of September 1714, six weeks after the death of his

---

[1] Voltaire records the admiration of Louis XIV. at Lord Stair's tact in at once entering the
royal carriage, when his Majesty, who stood beside it, bid him do so, without hesitating
to take precedence of the Sovereign.

predecessor, Queen Anne. The two great parties of the kingdom seemed in appearance equally disposed to receive him as their rightful monarch; and both submitted to his sway, though with very different hopes and feelings.

The triumphant Whigs were naturally assured of King George's favour towards those who had always shown themselves friendly to his title to the throne; and confident of the merit they might claim, were desirous of exerting their influence to the utter disgrace, discomfiture, and total suppression, of their political opponents.

The Tories, on the other hand, thought it still possible, while renouncing every plan of opposing the accession of King George, to present themselves before him in such a manner as might command regard; for the number, quality, and importance of a party which comprised a great majority of the established clergy, the greater part of both the universities, many, if not the largest portion of the lawyers, and the bulk of the proprietors of the soil, or what is called the landed interest, rendered their appearance imposing. Though dejected and humbled, therefore, by their fall from power, they consoled themselves with the idea that they were too numerous and too important to be ill received by a sovereign whose accession they had not opposed, and whom, on the contrary, they had shown themselves willing to acknowledge in the capacity of their monarch, disproving, as they might be disposed to think, by their dutiful demonstrations, any rumours which might have reached his Majesty of the disaffection of many among them to his person.

It would certainly have been the best policy of the newly enthroned monarch to have received and rewarded the services of the Whigs, without lending himself to the gratification of their political enmities. There was little policy in taking measures which were likely to drive into despair, and probably into rebellion a large party among his subjects; and there might have been more wisdom, perhaps, as magnanimity, in overlooking circumstances which had occurred before his accession—in receiving the allegiance and dutiful professions of the Tories, without attaching any visible doubts to their sincerity—in becoming thus the King of Great Britain, instead of the chief of a party—and by stifling the remembrance of old feuds, and showing himself indifferently the paternal ruler of all his subjects, to have convinced any who remained disaffected, that if they desired to have another prince they had at least no personal reason for doing so.

We cannot, however, be surprised that George I., a foreign prince, totally unacquainted with the character of the British nation, their peculiar constitution, and the spirit of their parties,—which usually appear, when in the act of collision, much more violent and extravagant than they prove to be when a cessation of hostilities takes place,—should have been disposed to throw himself into the arms of the Whigs, who could plead their sufferings for having steadily adhered to his interest; or that those who had been his steady adherents should have found him willingly inclined to aid them in measures of vindictive retaliation upon their opponents, whom he had some reason to regard as his personal enemies. It was a case in which to forgive would have been politic as well as magnanimous; but to resent injuries, and revenge them, was a course natural to human feeling.

The late ministers seemed for a time disposed to abide the shock of the enmity of their political rivals. Lord Oxford waited on the King at his landing, and, though coldly received, remained in London till impeached of high treason by the House of Commons, and committed to the Tower. Lord Bolingbroke continued to exercise his office of Secretary of State until he was almost forcibly deprived of it. An impeachment was also brought against him. His conscience probably pleaded guilty, for he retired to France, and soon after became Secretary to the Chevalier de St. George. The Duke of Ormond, a nobleman of popular qualities, brave, generous, and liberal, was in like manner impeached, and in like manner made his escape to France. His fate was peculiarly regretted, for the general voice exculpated him from taking any step with a view to selfish aggrandisement. Several of the Whigs themselves, who were disposed to prosecute to the uttermost the mysterious Oxford and the intriguing Bolingbroke, were inclined to sympathise with the gallant and generous cavalier who had always professed openly the principles on which he acted. Many other distinguished persons of the Tory party were threatened with prosecutions, or actually subjected to them; which filed the whole body with fear and alarm, and inclined some of the leaders amongst them to listen to the desperate counsels of the more zealous Jacobites, who exhorted them to try their strength with an enemy who showed themselves implacable, and not to submit to their ruin without an effort to defend themselves. A large party of the populace all through the country, and in London itself, renewed the cry of "High Church for ever," with which were mingled the names of Ormond and Oxford, the principal persons under prosecution. Among the clergy there were found many who, out of zeal for their order, encouraged the lower classes in their disorderly proceedings; in which they burnt and destroyed the meeting-houses of dissenters, pillaged the houses of their ministers, and committed all those irregularities by which an English mob is distinguished, but whose vehemence of sentiment generally evaporates in such acts of clamour and violence.

There were, however, deeper symptoms of disaffection than those displayed in the empty roar and senseless ravage of the populace. Bolingbroke and Ormond, who had both found refuge at the court of the Pretender to the crown, and acknowledged his title, carried on a secret correspondence with the Tories of influence and rank in England, and encouraged them to seek, in a general insurrection for the cause of James III., a remedy for the evils with which they were threatened, both personally and as a political party. But England had been long a peaceful country. The gentry were opulent, and little disposed to risk, in the event of war, their fortunes and comforts. Strong assistance from France might have rendered the proposal of an insurrection more acceptable; but the successful diplomacy of Lord Stair at the court of Louis destroyed all hopes of this, unless on a pitifully small scale. Another resource occurred to the Jacobite leaders which might be attained by instigating Scotland to set the example of insurrection. The gentry in that country were ready for war, which had been familiar to them on many occasions during the lives of their fathers and their own. They might be easily induced to take arms—the Highlanders, to whom war was a state preferable to peace, were sure to take the field with them—the Border counties of England were most likely to catch the flame, from the disposition of many of the gentry there,—and the conflagration, it was expected, might in the present humour of the nation, be extended all over England. To effect a rising therefore, in Scotland, with a view to a general insurrection throughout Great Britain, became the principal object of those who were affected by, or who resented, the prosecutions directed with so much rigour against the members of Queen Anne's last ministry.

John, eighteenth Lord Erskine, and eleventh Earl of Mar, whom we have repeatedly mentioned as Secretary of State during the last years of Queen Anne, and as the person to whom the distribution of money among the Highland clans, and the general management of Scottish affairs, was entrusted by her Ministry, was naturally considered as the person best qualified to bring his countrymen to the desired point. Mar had not felt any difficulty in changing from the Whig principles which he professed at the time of the Union,—on which occasion he was one of the Scottish Secretaries of State,—to the Tory principles of Bolingbroke, which he now professed. We do him, therefore, no wrong in supposing that he would not have sturdily rejected any proposal from the court of George I. to return to the party of Whig and Low Church. At least it is certain, that when the heads of the Tory party had determined to submit themselves to George I., Lord Mar, in following the general example, endeavoured to distinguish himself by a display of influence and consequence which might mark him as a man whose adherence was worth securing, and who was, at the same time, willing to attach himself to the new sovereign. In a letter addressed to King George while in Holland, and dated 30th August 1714, the Earl expresses great apprehension that his loyalty or zeal for the King's interests may have been misrepresented to his Majesty, because he found himself the only one of Queen Anne's servants whom the Hanoverian ministers at the court of London did not visit. His Lordship then pleads the loyalty of his ancestors, his own services at the Union, and in passing the Act of Succession; and, assuring the King that he will find him as faithful a subject and servant as any of his family had been to the preceding Royal race, or as he himself had been to the late Queen, he conjures him not to believe any misrepresentations of his conduct, and concludes with a devout prayer for the quiet and peaceful reign of the monarch, in disturbing which he himself was destined to be the prime instrument.

But it was not only on his individual application that the Earl of Mar expected indemnity, and perhaps favour, at the court of George I. He desired also to display his influence over the Highlanders, and for that purpose procured a letter, subscribed by a number of the most influential chiefs of the clans, addressed to himself, as having an estate and interest in the Highlands, conjuring him to assure the Government of their loyalty to his sacred Majesty, King George, and to protect them, and the heads of other clans who, from distance, could not attend at the signing of the letter, against the misrepresentations to which they might be exposed; protesting, that as they had been ready to follow Lord Mar's directions in obeying Queen Anne, so they would be equally forward to concur with him in faithfully serving King George.[1] At the same time, a

---

[1] The Highland chiefs who adhibited their signatures to this letter, were MacLean of MacLean; Macdonnell of Glengarry; Mackenzie of Fraserdale; Cameron of Lochiel; Macleod of Contulick; Macdonald of Keppoch; Grant of Glenmoristown; Macintosh of Macintosh; Chisholm of Comar; Macpherson of Cluny; and Sir Donald Macdonald.

loyal address of the clans to the same effect, drawn up by Lord Grange, brother to Mar, was forwarded to and placed in the hands of the Earl, to be delivered to the King at his landing. Lord Mar attended at Greenwich accordingly, and doubtless expected a favourable reception, when delivering to the new monarch a recognition of his authority on the part of a class of his subjects who were supposed to be inimical to his accession, and were certainly best prepared to disturb his new reign. Lord Mar was, however, informed that the King would not receive the address of the clans, alleging it had been concocted at the court of the Pretender; and he was at the same time commanded to deliver up the seals, and informed that the King had no further occasion for his services.

On the policy of this repulse it is almost unnecessary to make observations. Although it might be very true that the address was made up with the sanction of the Chevalier de St. George and his advisers, it was not less the interest of George I. to have received with the usual civility the expressions of homage and allegiance which it contained. In a similar situation King William did not hesitate to receive, with apparent confidence, the submission of the Highland clans, though it was well understood that it was made under the express authority of King James II. A monarch whose claim to obedience is yet young, ought in policy to avoid an immediate quarrel with any part of his subjects who are ready to profess allegiance as such. His authority is, like a transplanted tree, subject to injury from each sudden blast, and ought, therefore, to be secured from such until it is gradually connected by the ramification of its roots incorporating themselves with the soil in which it is planted. A sudden gust may in the one case overturn what in the other can defy the rage of a continued tempest. It seems at least certain, that in bluntly, and in a disparaging manner, refusing an address expressing allegiance and loyalty, and affronting the haughty courtier by whom it was presented, King George exposed his government to the desperate alternative of civil war, and the melancholy expedient of closing it by bringing many noble victims to the scaffold, which during the reign of his predecessors had never been stained with British blood shed for political causes. The impolicy, however, cannot justly be imputed to a foreign prince, who, looking at the list of Celtic names, and barbarously unpronounceable designations which were attached to the address, could not be supposed to infer from thence that the subscribers were collectively capable of bringing into the field, on the shortest notice, ten thousand men, who, if not regular soldiers, were accustomed to a sort of discipline which rendered them equal to such. There were many around the King who could have informed him on this subject; and to their failing to do so the bloodshed and concomitant misfortunes of the future civil war must justly be attributed.

The Earl of Mar, thus repulsed in his advances to the new monarch, necessarily concluded that his ruin was determined on; and, with the desire of revenge, which was natural at least, if not justifiable, he resolved to place himself at the head of the disaffected party in Scotland, encouraging them to instant insurrection, and paying back the contumely with which his offer of service had been rejected by endangering the throne of the Prince at whose hands he had experienced such an insult.

It was early in August 1715 that the Earl of Mar embarked at Gravesend, in the strictest incognito, having for his companions Major-General Hamilton and Colonel Hay, men of some military experience. They sailed in a coal-sloop, working, it was said, their passage, the better to maintain their disguise, landed at Newcastle, hired a vessel there, and then proceeded to the small port of Elie, on the eastern shore of Fife, a county which then abounded with friends to the Jacobite cause. The state of this province in other respects offered facilities to Mar. It is a peninsula, separated from Lothian by the Firth of Forth, and from the shire of Angus by that of Tay; and as it did not, until a very late period, hold much intercourse with the metropolis, though so near it in point of distance, it seemed like a district separated from the rest of Scotland, and was sometimes jocosely termed the "Kingdom of Fife." The commonalty were, in the beginning of the eighteenth century, almost exclusively attached to the Presbyterian persuasion; but it was otherwise with the gentry, who were numerous in this province to a degree little known in other parts of Scotland. Its security during the long wars of former centuries had made it early acquainted with civilisation. The value of the soil on the seacoasts, at least, had admitted of great subdivision of property, and there is no county of Scotland which displays so many country-seats within so short a distance of each other. These gentlemen were, as we have said, chiefly of the Tory persuasion, or, in other words, Jacobites; for the subdivision of politicians termed *Whimsicals* or *Tories attached to the House of Hanover*, could hardly be said to exist in Scotland, though well known in South Britain. Besides their tenants the Fife lairds were most of them men who had not much to lose in civil broils, having to support an establishment considerably above the actual rents of their estates, which were, of course, impaired by increasing debts; they were, therefore, the less unwilling to engage in dangerous enterprises. As a party affecting the manners of the ancient Cavaliers, they were jovial in their habits, and cautious to omit no opportunity of drinking the King's health; a point of loyalty which, like virtue of other kinds, had its own immediate reward. Loud and bold talkers, the Jacobites had accustomed themselves to think they were the prevailing party; an idea which those of any particular faction, who converse exclusively with each other, are usually found to entertain. Their want of knowledge of the world, and the total absence of newspapers, save those of a strong party leaning, whose doctrines or facts they took care never to correct by consulting any of an opposite tendency, rendered them at once curious and credulous. This slight sketch of the Fife lairds may be applied, with equal justice, to the Jacobite country gentleman of that period in most counties of Scotland. They had virtues to balance their faults and follies. The political principles they followed had been handed down to them from their fathers; they were connected, in their ideas, with the honour of their country; and they were prepared to defend them with a degree of zeal which valued not the personal risks in which the doing so might place life and property. There were also individuals among them who had natural talents improved by education. But, in general, the persons whom the Earl of Mar was now desirous to stir up to some sudden act of mutiny were of that frank and fearless class who are not guilty of seeing far before them. They had already partaken in the general excitation caused by Queen Anne's death, and the approaching crisis which was expected to follow that important event. They had struggled with the Whig gentry, inferior in number, but generally more alert and sacacious in counsel and action, concerning the addresses of head-courts, and the seats on the bench of justices. Many of them had commissioned swords, carabines, and pistols, from abroad. They had bought up horses fit for military service; and some had taken into their service additional domestics, selecting in preference men who had served in some of the dragoon regiments which had been reduced in consequence of the peace of Utrecht. Still, notwithstanding these preparations for a rising, some of the leading men in Fife, as elsewhere, were disposed to hesitate before engaging in the irretrievable step of rebellion against the established government. Their reluctance was overcome by the impatience of the majority, excited by the flattering though premature rumours which were actively circulated by a set of men who might be termed the Intelligencers of the faction.

It is well known that in every great political body there are persons, usually neither the wisest, the most important, or most estimable, who endeavour to gain personal consequence by pretending peculiar access to information concerning its most intimate concerns, and who are equally credulous in believing, and indefatigable in communicating, whatever rumours are afloat concerning the affairs of the party whom they encumber by adhering to. With several of these Lord Mar communicated, and exalted their hopes to the highest pitch by the advantageous light in which he placed the political matters which he wished them to support, trusting to the exaggerations and amplifications with which they were sure to retail what he had said.

Such agents, changing what had been stated as probabilities into certainties, furnished an answer to every objection which could be offered by the more prudent of their party. If any cautious person objected to stir before the English Jacobites had shown themselves serious—some one of these active vouchers was ready to affirm that everything was on the point of a general rising in England, and only waited the appearance of a French fleet with ten thousand men, headed by the Duke of Ormond. Did the listener prefer an invasion of Scotland,—the same number of men, with the Duke of Berwick at their head, were as readily promised. Supplies of every kind were measured out, according to the desire of the auditors; and if any was moderate enough to restrain his wish to a pair of pistols for his own use, he was assured of twenty brace to accommodate his friends and neighbours. This kind of mutual delusion was every day increasing; for as those who engaged in the conspiracy were interested in obtaining as many proselytes as possible, they became active circulators of the sanguine hopes and expectations by which they, perhaps, began already to suspect that they had been themselves deceived.

It is true, that looking abroad at the condition of Europe, these unfortunate gentlemen ought to have seen that the state of France at that time was far from being such as to authorise any expectations of the prodigal supplies which she was represented as being ready to furnish, or, rather, as being in the act of furnishing. Nothing was less likely than that that kingdom, just extricated from a war in which it had been nearly ruined, by a peace so much more advantageous than they had reason to expect, should have been disposed to afford a pretext for breaking the treaty which had pacified Europe, and for renewing against France the confederacy under whose pressure she had nearly sunk. This was more especially the case, when, by the death of Louis XIV., whose ambition and senseless vanity had cost so much blood, the government devolved on the Regent Duke of Orleans. Had Louis survived, it is probable that, although he neither did nor dared to have publicly adopted the cause of the Chevalier de St. George, as was indeed evident by his refusing to receive him at his court; yet the recollection of his promise to the dying James II., as well as the wish to embarrass England, might have induced him to advance money, or give some underhand assistance to the unhappy exile. But, upon Louis's death, the policy of the Duke of Orleans, who had no personal ties whatever with the Chevalier de St. George, induced him to keep entire good faith with Britain—to comply with the requisitions of the Earl of Stair—and to put a stop to all such preparations in the French ports as the vigilance of that minister had detected, and denounced as being made, for the purpose of favouring the Jacobite insurrection. Thus, while the Chevalier de St. George was represented as obtaining succours in arms, money, and troops, from France to an amount which that kingdom could hardly have supplied, and from her inferiority in naval force certainly must have found it difficult to have transported into Britain, even in Louis's most palmy days, the ports of that country were even closed against such exertions as the Chevalier might make upon a small scale by means of big private resources.

But the death of Louis XIV. was represented in Scotland as rather favourable than otherwise to the cause of James the Pretender. The power of France was now wielded, it was said, by a courageous and active young prince, to whose character enterprise was more natural than to that of an aged and heartbroken old man, and who would, of course, be ready to hazard as much, or more, in the cause of the Jacobites, than the late monarch had so often promised. In short, the death of Louis the Great, long the hope and prop of the Jacobite cause, was boldly represented as a favourable event during the present crisis.

Although a little dispassionate inquiry would have dispelled the fantastic hopes, founded on the baseless rumour of foreign assistance, yet such fictions as I have here alluded to, tending to exalt the zeal and spirits of the party, were circulated because they were believed, and believed because they were circulated; and the gentlemen of Stirlingshire, Perth, Angus, and Fifeshire, began to leave their homes and assemble in arms, though in small parties, at the foot of the Grampian Hills, expecting the issue of Lord Mar's negotiations in the Highlands.

Upon leaving Fifeshire, having communicated with such gentlemen as were most likely to serve his purpose, Mar proceeded instantly to his own estates of Braemar, lying along the side of the river Dee, and took up his residence with Farquharson of Invercauld. This gentleman was chief of the clan Farquharson, and could command a very considerable body of men. But he was vassal to Lord Mar for a small part of his estate, which gave the Earl considerable influence with him; not, however, sufficient to induce him to place himself and followers in such hazard as would have been occasioned by an instant rising. He went to Aberdeen to avoid importunity on the subject, having previously declared to Mar that he would not take arms until the Chevalier de St. George had actually landed. At a later period he joined the insurgents.

Disappointed in this instance, Mar conceived that as desperate resolutions are usually most readily adopted in large assemblies, where men are hurried forward by example, and prevented from retreating or dissenting by shame, he should best attain his purpose in a large convocation of the chiefs and men of rank who professed attachment to the exiled family. The assembly was made under pretext of a grand hunting match, which, as maintained in the Highlands, was an occasion of general rendezvous of a peculiar nature. The lords attended at the head of their vassals, all, even Lowland guests, attired in the Highland garb, and the sport was carried on upon a scale of rude magnificence. A circuit of many miles was formed around the wild desolate forests and wildernesses, which are inhabited by the red deer, and is called the *tinchel*. Upon a signal given, the hunters who compose the tinchel begin to move inwards, closing the circle, and driving the terrified deer before them, with whatever else the forest contains of wild animals who cannot elude the surrounding sportsmen. Being in this manner concentrated and crowded together, they are driven down a defile, where the principal hunters lie in wait for them, and show their dexterity by marking out and shooting those bucks which are in season. As it required many men to form the tinchel, the attendance of vassals on these occasions was strictly insisted upon. Indeed, it was one of the feudal services required by the law, attendance on the superior at *hunting* being as regularly required as at *hosting*, that is, joining his banner in war; or *watching* and *warding*, garrisoning, namely, his castle in times of danger.

An occasion such as this was highly favourable; and the general love of sport, and well-known fame of the forest of Braemar for game of every kind, assembled many of the men of rank and influence who resided within reach of the rendezvous, and a great number of persons besides, who, though of less consequence, served to give the meeting the appearance of numbers. This great council was held about the 26th of August, and it may be supposed they did not amuse themselves much with hunting, though it was the pretence and watchword of their meeting.

Among the noblemen of distinction there appeared in person, or by representation, the Marquis of Huntly, eldest son of the Duke of Gordon; the Marquis of Tulliebardine, eldest son of the Duke of Athole; the Earls of Nithisdale, Marischal, Traquair, Errol, Southesk, Carnwath, Seaforth, and Linlithgow; the Viscounts of Kilsythe, Kenmuir, Kingston, and Stormount; the Lords Rollo, Duffus, Drummond, Strathallan, Ogilvy, and Nairne. Of the chiefs of clans, there attended Glengarry, Campbell of Glendarule, on the part of the powerful Earl of Breadalbane, with others of various degrees of importance in the Highlands.

When this council was assembled, the Earl of Mar addressed them in a species of eloquence which was his principal accomplishment, and which was particularly qualified to succeed with the high-spirited and zealous men by whom he was surrounded. He confessed, with tears in his eyes, that he had himself been but too instrumental in forwarding the Union between England and Scotland, which had given the English the power, as they had the disposition, to enslave the latter kingdom. He urged that the Prince of Hanover was a usurping intruder, governing by means of an encroaching and innovating faction; and that the only mode to escape his tyranny was to rise boldly in defence of their lives and property, and to establish on the throne the lawful heir of these realms. He declared that he himself was determined to set up the standard of James III., and summon around it all those over whom he had influence, and to hazard his fortune and life in the cause. He invited all who heard him to unite in the same generous resolution. He was large in his promises of assistance from France in troops and money, and persisted in the story that two descents were to take place, one in England under the command of Ormond, the other in Scotland under that of the Duke of Berwick. He also strongly assured his hearers of the certainty of a general insurrection in England, but alleged the absolute necessity of showing them an example in the north, for which the present time was most appropriate, as there were few regular troops in Scotland to restrain their operations, and as they might look for assistance to Sweden as well as to France.

It has been said that Mar, on this memorable occasion, showed letters from the Chevalier de St. George, with a commission nominating the Earl his lieutenant-general and commander-in-chief of his armies in Scotland. Other accounts say, more probably, that Mar did not produce any other credentials than a picture of the Chevalier, which he repeatedly kissed, in testimony of zeal for the cause of the original, and that he did not at the time pretend to the supreme command of the enterprise. This is also the account given in the statement of the transaction drawn up by Mar himself, or under his eye, where it is plainly said that it was nearly a month after the standard was set up ere the Earl of Mar could procure a commission.

The number of persons of rank who were assembled, the eloquence with which topics were publicly urged which had been long the secret inmates of every bosom, had their effect on the assembled guests; and every one felt that to oppose the current of the Earl's discourse by remonstrance or objection, would be to expose himself to the charge of cowardice or of disaffection to the common cause. It was agreed that all of them should return home, and raise, under various pretexts, whatever forces they could individually command against a day, fixed for the 3d of September, on which they were to hold a second meeting at Aboyne, in Aberdeenshire, in order to settle how they were to take the field. The Marquis of Huntly alone declined to be bound to any limited time; and, in consequence of his high rank and importance, he was allowed to regulate his own motions at his own pleasure.

Thus ended that celebrated hunting in Braemar which, as the old bard says of that of Chevy Chace, might, from its consequences, be wept by a generation which was yet unborn.[1] There was a circumstance mentioned at the time, which tended to show that all men had not forgotten that the Earl of Mar, on whose warrant this rash enterprise was undertaken, was considered by some as rather too versatile to be fully trusted. As the castle of Braemar was overflowing with guests, it chanced that, as was not unusual on such occasions, many of the

---

[1] "To drive the deer with hound and horn,
        Earl Percy took his way;
    The child may rue that is unborn,
        The hunting of that day."—Ballad of Chevy Chace.

gentlemen of the secondary class could not obtain beds, but were obliged to spend the night around the kitchen fire, which was then accounted no great grievance. An English footman, a domestic of the Earl, was of a very different opinion. Accustomed to the accommodations of the south, he came bustling in among the gentlemen, and complained bitterly of being obliged to sit up all night, notwithstanding he shared the hardship with his betters, saying that rather than again expose himself to such a strait he would return to his own country and turn Whig. However he soon after comforted himself by resolving to trust to his master's dexterity for escaping every great danger. "Let my lord alone," he said; "if he finds it necessary he can turn cat-in-pan with any man in England."

While the Lowland gentlemen were assembling their squadrons, and the Highland chiefs levying their men, an incident took place in the metropolis of Scotland which showed that the spirit of enterprise which animated the Jacobites had extended to the capital itself.

James, Lord Drummond, son of that unfortunate Earl of Perth who, having served James VII. as Chancellor of Scotland, had shared the exile of his still more unfortunate master, and been rewarded with the barren title of Duke of Perth, was at this time in Edinburgh; and by means of one Mr. Arthur, who had been formerly an ensign in the Scots Guards, and quartered in the Castle, had formed a plan of surprising that inaccessible fortress, which resembled an exploit of Thomas Randolph, or the Black Lord James of Douglas, rather than a feat of modern war. This Ensign Arthur found means of seducing, by money and promises, a sergeant named Ainslie, and two privates, who engaged that when it was their duty to watch on the walls which rise from the precipice looking northward, near the Sally-port, they would be prepared to pull up from the bottom certain rope-ladders prepared for the purpose, and furnished with iron grapplings to make them fast to the battlements. By means of these, it was concluded that a select party of Jacobites might easily scale the walls, and make themselves masters of the place. By a beacon placed on a particular part of the Castle, three rounds of artillery, and a succession of fires made from hill to hill through Fife and Angus shires, the signal of success was to be communicated to the Earl of Mar, who was to hasten forward with such forces as he had collected, and take possession of the capital city and chief strength of Scotland.

There was no difficulty in finding agents in this perilous and important enterprise. Fifty Highlanders, picked men, were summoned up from Lord Drummond's estates in Perthshire, and fifty more were selected among the Jacobites of the metropolis. These last were disbanded officers, writers' clerks and apprentices, and other youths of a class considerably above the mere vulgar. Drummond, otherwise called MacGregor, of Balhaldie, a Highland gentleman of great courage, was named to command the enterprise. If successful, this achievement must have given the Earl of Mar and his forces the command of the greater part of Scotland, and afforded them a safe and ready means of communication with the English malcontents, the want of which was afterwards so severely felt. He would also have obtained a large supply of money, arms, and ammunition deposited in the fortress, all of which were most needful for his enterprise. And the apathy of Lieutenant-Colonel Stewart, then deputy-governor of the castle, was so great that, in spite of numerous blunders on the part of the conspirators, and an absolute revelation on the subject made to Government, the surprise had very nearly taken place.

The younger conspirators, who were to go on this forlorn hope, had not discretion in proportion to their courage. Eighteen of them, on the night appointed, were engaged drinking in a tippling house, and were so careless in their communications, that the hostess was able to tell some person who inquired what the meeting was about, that it consisted of young gentlemen who were in the act of having their hair powdered, in order to go to the attack of the castle. At last the full secret was entrusted to a woman. Arthur, their guide, had communicated the plot to his brother, a medical man, and engaged him in the enterprise. But when the time for executing it drew nigh, the doctor's extreme melancholy was observed by his wife, who, like a second Belvidera or Portia, suffered him not to rest, until she extorted the secret from him, which she communicated in an anonymous letter to Sir Adam Cockburn of Ormiston, then Lord Justice-Clerk, who instantly despatched the intelligence to the castle. The news arrived so critically that it was with difficulty the messenger obtained entrance; and even then the deputy-governor, disbelieving the intelligence, or secretly well affected to the cause of the Pretender, contented himself with directing the rounds and patrols to be made with peculiar care, and retired to rest.

In the meantime, the Jacobite storming party had rendezvoused at the churchyard of the West Kirk, and proceeded to post themselves beneath the castle wall. They had a part of their rope-ladders in readiness, but the artificer, one Charles Forbes, a merchant in Edinburgh, who ought to have been there with the remainder, which had been made under his direction, was nowhere to be seen. Nothing could be done during his absence; but, actuated by their impatience the party scrambled up the rock, and stationed themselves beneath the wall, at the point where their accomplice kept sentry. Here they found him ready to perform his stipulated part of the bargain, by pulling up the ladder of ropes which was designed to give them admittance. He exhorted them, however, to be speedy, telling them he was to be relieved by the patrol at twelve o'clock, and if the affair were not completed before that hour, that he could give no further assistance. The time was fast flying, when Balhaldie, the commander of the storming party, persuaded the sentinel to pull up the grapnel, and make it fast to the battlements, that it might appear whether or not they had length of ladder sufficient to make the attempt. But it proved, as indeed they had expected, more than a fathom too short. At half-past eleven o'clock the steps of the patrol, who had been sent their rounds earlier than usual, owing to the message of the Lord Justice-Clerk, were heard approaching, on which the sentinel exclaimed, with an oath, "Here come the rounds I have been telling you of this half hour; you have ruined both yourself and me; I can serve you no longer." With that he threw down the grappling-iron and ladders, and in the hope of covering his own guilt, fired his musket, and cried "Enemy!" Every man was then compelled to shift for himself, the patrol firing on them from the wall. Twelve soldiers of the burgher guard, who had been directed by the Lord Justice-Clerk to make the round of the castle on the outside, took prisoners three youths, who insisted that they were found there by mere accident, and an old man Captain MacLean, an officer of James VII., who was much bruised by a fall from the rocks. The rest of the party escaped alongst the north bank of the North Loch, through the fields called Barefoord's Parks, on which the New Town of Edinburgh now stands. In their retreat they met their tardy engineer, Charles Forbes, loaded with the ladders which were so much wanted a quarter of an hour before. Had it not been for his want of punctuality the information and precautions of the Lord Justice-Clerk would have been insufficient for the safety of the place. It does not appear that any of the conspirators were punished, nor would it have been easy to obtain proof of their guilt. The treacherous sergeant was hanged by sentence of a court-martial, and the deputy-governor (whose name of Stewart might perhaps aggravate the suspicion that attached to him) was deprived of his office, and imprisoned for some time.

It needed not this open attack on the castle of Edinburgh, or the general news of Lord Mar's Highland armament, and the rising of the disaffected gentlemen in arms throughout most of the counties of Scotland, to call the attention of King George's Government to the disturbed state of that part of his dominions. Measures for defence were hastily adopted. The small number of regular troops who were then in Scotland were concentrated, for the purpose of forming a camp at Stirling, in order to prevent the rebels from seizing the bridge over the Forth, and thereby forcing their way into the Low country. But four regiments, on the peace establishment, only mustered two hundred and fifty-seven men each; four regiments of dragoons were considerably under two hundred to a regiment—a total of only fifteen hundred men at the utmost.

To increase these slender forces, two regiments of dragoons, belonging to the Earl of Stair, with two regiments of foot quartered in the north of England, were ordered to join the camp at Stirling with all possible despatch. The foot regiments of Clayton and Wightman, with the dragoons of Evans, were recalled from Ireland. The six thousand auxiliary forces with whom the Dutch had engaged, in case of need, to guarantee the succession of the House of Hanover, were required of States, who accordingly ordered the Scotch regiments in their service to march for the coast, but excused themselves from actually embarking them, in consequence of the French ambassador having disowned, in the strongest manner, any intent on the part of his court to aid the factions in England by sending over the Pretender to Britain, or to assist those who were in arms in his behalf. The Dutch alleged this as a sufficient reason for suspending the shipment of these auxiliaries.

Besides these military measures, the Ministers of George I. were not remiss in taking such others as might check the prime cause of rebellions in Scotland, namely, that feudal influence possessed by the aristocracy over their vassals, tenants, and dependants, by which the great men, when disgraced or disappointed, had the power of calling to arms, at their pleasure, a number of individuals, who, however unwilling they might be to rise against the Government, durst not, and could not, without great loss and risk of oppression, oppose themselves to their superior's pleasure.

On the 30th of August, therefore, an act was passed for the purpose of encouraging loyalty in Scotland, a plant which of late years had
not been found to agree with the climate of that cold and northern
country, or at least, were found to luxuriate, it was of a nature different
from that known by the same name at Westminster.

This statute, commonly called the Clan Act, enacted: 1. That if a
feudal superior went into rebellion, and became liable to the pains of
high treason, all such vassals holding lands under him, as should continue in their allegiance, should in future hold these lands of the
crown. 2. If a tenant should have remained at the King's peace while
his landlord had been engaged in rebellion, and convicted of treason,
the space of two years' gratuitous possession should be added to that
tenant's lease. 3. If the superior should remain loyal and peaceful while
the vassal should engage in rebellion and incur conviction of high treason, then the fief, or lands held by such vassal, shall revert to the superior as if they had never been separated from his estate. 4. Another
clause declared void such settlements of estates and deeds of entail as
might be made on the first day of August 1714, or at any time there-
after, declaring that they should be no bar to the forfeiture of the estates
for high treason, seeing that such settlements had been frequently
resorted to for the sole purpose of evading the punishment of the law.

This remarkable act was the first considerable step towards unloos-
ing the feudal fetters by which the command of the superior became in
some measure the law of the vassal. The clause concerning settlements
and entails was also important, and rendered nugatory the attempts
which had been frequently made to evade the punishment of forfeiture, by settlements made previous to the time when those who
granted the deeds engaged in rebellion. Such deeds as were executed
for onerous causes, that is, for value of some kind received, were justly
excepted from the operation of this law.

There was, moreover, another clause, empowering the crown to
call upon any suspected person or persons in Scotland to appear at
Edinburgh, or where it should be judged expedient, for the purpose of
finding bail, with certification that their failure to appear should subject them to be put to the horn as rebels, and that they should incur
the forfeiture of the liferent escheat. Immediately afterwards, sum-
monses were issued to all the noblemen and gentlemen either actually
in arms or suspected of favouring the Jacobite interest, from the Earl of
Mar and his compeers, down to Rob Roy MacGregor, the celebrated

outlaw. The list amounted to about fifty men of note, of which only two, Sir Patrick Murray and Sir Alexander Erskine, thought proper to surrender themselves.

Besides these general measures, military resistance to the expected rebellion was prepared in a great many places, and particularly in borough towns and seaports. It is here to be remarked that a great change had taken place among the bulk of the people of Scotland from the ill-humour into which they had been put by the conclusion of the Union treaty. At that time, such were the effects of mortified pride, popular apprehension, and national antipathy, that the populace in every town and county would have arisen to place the Pretender on the throne, notwithstanding his professing the Catholic religion, and being the grandson of James VII., of whose persecutions, as well as those in the time of his predecessor Charles II., the Presbyterians of the west nourished such horrible recollections. Accordingly, we have seen that it was only by bribing their chiefs, and deceiving them by means of adroit spies, that the Cameronians, the most zealous of Presbyterians, who disowned the authority of all magistrates who had not taken the Solemn League and Covenant, were prevented from taking arms to dissolve the Union Parliament, and to declare for the cause of James III. But it happened with the Union as with other political measures, against which strong prejudices have been excited during their progress:—the complication of predicted evils were so far from being realised that the opponents of the treaty began to be ashamed of having entertained such apprehensions. None of the violent changes which had been foretold, none of the universal disgrace and desolation which had been anticipated in consequence, had arisen from that great measure. The enforcing of the Malt Tax was the most unpopular, and that impost had been for the time politically suspended. The shopkeepers of Edinburgh, who had supplied the peers of Scotland with luxuries, had found other customers, now that the aristocracy were resident in London, or they had turned their stock into other lines of commerce. The ideal consequence of a legislature of their own holding its sittings in the metropolis of Scotland was forgotten when it became no longer visible, and the abolition of the Scottish Privy Council might, on calm reflection, be considered as a national benefit rather than a privation. In short, the general resentment excited by the treaty of Union, once keen enough to suspend all other motives, was a paroxysm too violent to last—men recovered from it by slow degrees, and though it was still predominant in the minds of some classes, yet the opinions of the lower orders in general had in a great measure returned to their usual channel, and men entertained in the south and west, as well as in many of the boroughs, their usual wholesome horror for the Devil, the Pope, and the Pretender, which, for a certain time, had been overpowered and lost in their apprehensions for the independence of Scotland.

In 1715, also, the merchants and better class of citizens, who began to entertain some distant views of enriching themselves by engaging in the commerce of the plantations, and other lucrative branches of trade, opened up by the Union, were no longer disposed to see anything tempting in the proposal of Mar and his insurgents to destroy the treaty by force; and were, together with the lower classes, much better disposed to listen to the expostulations of the Presbyterian clergy, who, sensible of what they had to expect from a counter-revolution, exerted their influence, generally speaking, with great effect, in support of the present Government of King George. The fruits of this change in the temper and feelings of the middling and lower classes were soon evident in the metropolis and throughout Scotland. In Edinburgh, men of wealth and substance subscribed a bond of association, in order to raise subscriptions for purchasing arms and maintaining troops; and a body of the subscribers themselves formed a regiment, under the name of the Associate Volunteers of Edinburgh. They were four hundred strong. Glasgow, with a prescient consciousness of the commercial eminence which she was to attain by means of the treaty of Union, contributed liberally in money to defend the cause of King George, and raised a good regiment of volunteers. The western counties of Renfrew and Ayrshire offered four thousand men, and the Earl of Glasgow a regiment of a thousand at his own charge. Along the Border, the Whig party were no less active. Dumfries distinguished itself by raising among the inhabitants seven volunteer companies of sixty men each. This was the more necessary, as an attack was apprehended from the many Catholics and disaffected gentlemen who resided in the neighbourhood. The eastern part of Teviotdale supplied the Duke of Roxburgh, Sir William Bennet of Grubet, and Sir John Pringle of Stitchel, with as many men as they could find arms for, being about four companies. The upper part of the county and the neighbouring shire of Selkirk were less willing to take arms. The hatred of the Union still prevailed amongst them more than elsewhere, inflamed, probably, by the very circumstance of their vicinity to England, and the recollection of the long wars betwixt the kingdoms.

The Cameronian preachers, also, had possessed many speculative shepherds with their whimsical and chimerical doubts concerning the right of uncovenanted magistrates to exercise any authority, even in the most urgent case of national emergency. This doctrine was as rational as if the same scrupulous persons had discovered that it was unlawful to use the assistance of firemen during a conflagration, because they had not taken the Solemn League and Covenant. These scruples were not universal, and assumed as many different hues and shades as there were popular preachers to urge them; they tended greatly to retard and embarrass the exertions of Government to prepare for defence in these districts. Even the popularity of the Reverend Thomas Boston, an eminent divine of the period, could not raise a man for the service of Government out of his parish of Ettrick.

Notwithstanding, however, partial exceptions, the common people of Scotland, who were not overawed by Jacobite landlords, remained generally faithful to the Protestant line of succession, and showed readiness to arm in its behalf.

Having thus described the preparations for war on both sides, we will, in the next chapter, relate the commencement of the campaign.

LXVII

The Jacobite Cause

1715

ON the 6th September 1715 the noblemen, chiefs of clans, gentlemen, and others, with such followers as they could immediately get in readiness, assembled at Aboyne; and the Earl of Mar, acting as General on the occasion, displayed the Royal standard[1] at Castletown, in Braemar, and proclaimed, with such solemnity as the time and place admitted, James, King of Scotland, by the title of James VIII., and King of England, Ireland, and their dependencies, by that of James III. The day was stormy, and the gilded ball which was on the top of the standard spear was blown down,—a circumstance which the superstitious Highlanders regarded as ominous of ill fortune; while others called to mind that, by a strange coincidence, something of the same kind happened in the evil hour when King Charles I. set up his standard at Nottingham.[2]

---

[1] The standard was blue, having on one side the Scottish arms wrought in gold, on the other the thistle and ancient motto *Nemo me impune lacesset*, and underneath "No Union." The pendants of white ribbon were inscribed, the one, "for our wronged King and oppressed country," and the other, "for our lives and liberties."

[2] "At Nottingham, on the 25th of August 1642, Charles's standard was erected about six in the evening of a very stormy and tempestuous day, with little other ceremony

After this decisive measure, the leaders of the insurgents separated to proclaim King James in the towns where they had influence, and to raise as many followers as each could possibly command, in order to support the daring defiance which they had given to the established Government.

It was not by the mildest of all possible means that a Highland following, as it is called, was brought into the field at that period. Many vassals were, indeed, prompt and ready for service, for which their education and habits prepared them. But there were others who were brought to their chief's standard by much the same enticing mode of solicitation used in our own day for recruiting the navy, and there were many who conceived it prudent not to stir without such a degree of compulsion as might, in case of need, serve as some sort of apology for having been in arms at all. On this raising of the clans in the year 1715, the fiery cross was sent through the districts or countries, as they are termed, inhabited by the different tribes. This emblem consisted of two branches of wood, in the form of a cross, one end singed with fire, and the other stained with blood. The inhabitants transmitted the signal from house to house with all possible speed, and the symbol implied that those who should not appear at a rendezvous which was named, when the cross was presented, should suffer the extremities of fire and sword.[3] There is an intercepted letter of Mar himself, to John Forbes of Increrau, bailie of his lordship of Kildrummie, which throws considerable light on the nature of a feudal levy:—

"Inverauld, Sept. 9, at Night, 1715.

"Jocke—Ye was in the right not to come with the hundred men you sent up to-night, when I expected four times their numbers. It is a pretty thing my own people should be refractory, when all the Highlands are rising, and all the Lowlands are expecting us to join them. Is not this the thing we are now about which they have been wishing

---

than the sound of drums and trumpets. Melancholy men observed many ill presages. There was not one regiment of foot yet brought thither; so that the trained bands which the Sheriffs had drawn together were all the strength the King had for his person and the guard of the standard. It was blown down the same night it had been set up, by a very strong and unruly wind, and could not be fixed again in a day or two, till the tempest was allayed."—CLARENDON.

[3] See *The Lady of the Lake*, Canto iii.

these 26 years? And now when it is come, and the King and country's cause is at stake, will they for ever sit still and see all perish? I have used gentle means too long, and so I shall be forced to put other orders I have in execution. I send you enclosed an order for the Lordship of Kildrummie, which you will immediately intimate to all my vassals. If they give ready obedience, it will make some amends, and if not, ye may tell them from me, that it will not be in my power to save them (were I willing) from being treated as enemies by those that are soon to join me; and they may depend upon it that I will be the first to propose and order their being so. Particularly, let my own tenants in Kildrummie know, that if they come not forth with their best arms, I will send a party immediately to burn what they shall miss taking from them. And they may believe this only a threat—but by all that's sacred, I'll put it in execution, let my loss be what it will, that it may be an example to others. You are to tell the gentlemen that I expect them in their best accoutrements on horseback, and no excuse to be accepted of. Go about this with all diligence, and come yourself, and let me know your having done so. All this is not only as ye will be answerable to me, but to your King and country."

This remarkable letter is dated three days after the displaying of the standard. The system of social life in the Highlands, when viewed through the vista of years, has much in it that is interesting and poetical; but few modern readers would desire to exchange conditions with a resident within the romantic bounds of Mar's lordship of Kildrummie, where such were liable to a peremptory summons to arms, thus rudely enforced.

Proceeding towards the Lowlands by short marches, Mar paused at the small town of Kirkmichael, and afterwards at Mouline in Perthshire, moving slowly, that his friends might have leisure to assemble for his support. In the meantime, King James was proclaimed at Aberdeen by the Earl Marischal; at Dunkeld by the Marquis of Tullibardine, contrary to the wishes of his father, the Duke of Athole; at Castle Gordon by the Marquis of Huntly; at Brechin by the Earl of Panmure, a rich and powerful nobleman, who had acceded to the cause since the rendezvous at the Braemar hunting. The same ceremony was performed at Montrose by the Earl of Southesk; at Dundee by Graham of Duntroon, of the family of the celebrated Claverhouse, and to whom King James had given that memorable person's title of Viscount of Dundee; and at Inverness by the Laird of Borlum, commonly called Brigadier MacIntosh, from his having held that rank in the service of France. This officer made a considerable figure during the Rebellion in which he had influence to involve his chief and clans, rather contrary to the political sentiments of the former; he judged that Inverness was a station of importance, and therefore left a garrison to secure it from any attack on the part of the Grants, Monroes, or other Whig clans in the vicinity.

The possession of the town of Perth now became a point of great importance, as forming the communication between the Highlands and the Lowlands, and being the natural capital of the fertile countries on the margin of the Tay. The citizens were divided into two parties, but the magistrates, who, at the head of one part of the inhabitants, had declared for King George, took arms and applied to the Duke of Athole, who remained in allegiance to the ruling monarch, for a party to support them. The Duke sent them three or four hundred Athole Highlanders, and the inhabitants conceived themselves secure, especially as the Earl of Rothes, having assembled about four hundred militiamen, was advancing from Fife to their support. The honourable Colonel John Hay, brother to the Earl of Kinnoul took, however, an opportunity to collect together some fifty or a hundred horse from among the gentlemen of Stirling, Perthshire, and Fife, and marched towards the town. The Tory burghers, who were not inferior in numbers, began to assume courage as these succours appeared, and the garrison of Highlanders, knowing that although the Duke of Athole remained attached to the Government, his eldest son was in the Earl of Mar's army, gave way to their own inclinations, which were decidedly Jacobitical, and joined Colonel Hay for the purpose of disarming the Whig burghers, to whose assistance they had been sent. Thus Perth, by a concurrence of accidents, fell into the hands of the insurgent Jacobites, and gave them the command of all the Lowlands in the east part of Scotland. Still, as the town was but slightly fortified, it might have been recovered by a sudden attack, if a detachment had been made for that purpose from the regular camp at Stirling. But General Whetham, who as yet commanded there, was not an officer of activity. He was indeed superseded by the Duke of Argyle, commander-in-chief in Scotland, who came to Stirling on the 14th September; but the opportunity of regaining Perth no longer existed. The town had been speedily reinforced, and secured for the Jacobite interest, by about two hundred men, whom the Earl of Strathmore had raised to join the Earl of Mar, and a body of Fifeshire cavalry who had arrayed themselves for the same service under the Master of Sinclair. Both these noblemen were remarkable characters.

The Earl of Strathmore, doomed to lose his life in this fatal broil, was only about eighteen years old, but at that early age he exhibited every symptom of a brave, generous, and modest disposition, and his premature death disappointed the most flourishing hopes. He engaged in the Rebellion with all the zeal of sincerity, raised a strong regiment of Lowland infantry, and distinguished himself by his attention to the duties of a military life.

The Master of Sinclair, so called as the eldest son of Henry seventh Lord Sinclair, had served in Marlborough's army with good reputation; but he was especially remarkable for having, in the prosecution of an affair of honour, slain two gentlemen of the name of Shaw, brothers to Sir John Shaw of Greenock, and persons of rank and consequence. He was tried by a court-martial and condemned to death, but escaped from prison, not without the connivance of the Duke of Marlborough himself. As the Master of Sinclair's family were Tories, he obtained his pardon on the accession of their party to power in 1712. In 1715 he seems to have taken arms with great reluctance, deeming the cause desperate, and having no confidence in the probity or parts of the Earl of Mar, who assumed the supreme authority. He was a man of a caustic and severe turn of mind, suspicious and satirical, but acute and sensible. He has left Memoirs, curiously illustrative of this ill-fated enterprise, of which he seems totally to have despaired long before its termination.

That part of the Earl of Mar's forces which lay in the eastern and north-eastern parts of Scotland were now assembled at Perth, the most central place under his authority. They amounted to four or five thousand men, and although formidable for courage and numbers, they had few other qualities necessary to constitute an army. They were without a competent general, money, arms, ammunition, regulation, discipline; and, above all, a settled purpose and object of the campaign. On each of these deficiencies, and on the manner and decree in which they were severally supplied, I will say a few words, so as to give you some idea of this tumultuary army, before proceeding to detail what they did and what they left undone.

There can be no doubt that, from the time he embarked in this dangerous enterprise, Mar had secretly determined to put himself at the head of it, and gratify at once his ambition and his revenge. But it does not appear that at first he made any pretensions to the chief command. On the contrary, he seemed willing to defer to any person of higher rank than his own. The Duke of Gordon would have been a natural choice, from his elevated rank and great power. But, besides that he had not come out in person, though it was not doubted that he approved of his son's doing so, the Duke was a Catholic, and it was not considered politic that Papists should hold any considerable rank in the enterprise, as it would have given rise to doubts among their own party, and reproaches from their opponents. Finally, the Duke, being one of the suspected persons summoned by Government to surrender himself, obeyed the call, and was appointed to reside at Edinburgh on his parole. The Duke of Athole had been a leader of the Jacobites during the disputes concerning the Union, and had agreed to rise in 1707 had the French descent then taken place. Upon him, it is said, the Earl of Mar offered to devolve the command of the forces he had levied. But the Duke refused the offer at his hands. He said that if the Chevalier de St. George had chosen to impose such a responsible charge upon him he would have opened a direct communication with him personally; and he complained that Mar, before making this proposal to him, had intrigued in his family; having instigated his two sons the Marquis of Tullibardine and Lord Charles Murray, as well as his uncle, Lord Nairne, to take arms without his consent, and made use of their influence to seduce the Athole men from their allegiance to their rightful lord. He therefore declined the offer which was made to him of commanding the forces now in rebellion, and Mar retained, as if by occupancy, the chief command of the army. As he was brave, high-born, and possessed of very considerable talent, and as his late connection with the chiefs of Highland clans, while distributer of Queen Anne's bounty, rendered him highly acceptable to them, his authority was generally submitted to, especially as it was at first supposed that he acted only as a *locum tenens* for the Duke of Berwick, whose speedy arrival had been announced. Time passed on, however; the Duke came not, and the Earl of Mar continued to act as commander-in-chief, until confirmed in it by an express commission from the Chevalier de St. George. As the Earl was unacquainted with military affairs, he used the experience of Lieutenant-General Hamilton and Clephane of Carslogie, who had served during the late war, to supply his deficiencies in that department. But though these gentlemen had both courage, zeal, and warlike skill, they could not assist their principal in what his own capacity could not attain—the power of forming and acting upon a decided plan of tactics.

Money, also much wanted, was but poorly supplied by such sums as the wealthier adherents of the party could raise among themselves. Some of them had indeed means of their own, but as their funds became exhausted, they were under the necessity of returning home for more; which was with some the apology for absence from their corps much longer and more frequently than was consistent with discipline. But the Highlanders and Lowlanders of inferior rank could not subsist, or be kept within the bounds of discipline, without regular pay of some kind. Lord Southesk gave five hundred pounds, and the Earl of Panmure the same sum, to meet the exigencies of the moment. Aid was also solicited and obtained from various individuals, friendly to the cause, but unequal, from age or infirmity, to take the field in person; and there were many prudent persons, no doubt, who thought it the wisest course to sacrifice a sum of money, which, if the insurrection were successful, would give them the merit of having aided it, while, if it failed, their lives and estates were secured from the reach of the law against treason. Above all, the insurgents took especial care to secure all the public money that was in the hands of collectors of taxes and other public officers, and to levy eight months' cess wherever their presence gave them the authority. At length, considerable supplies were received from France, which in a great measure relieved their wants in that particular. Lord Drummond was appointed to be treasurer to the army.

Arms and ammunition were scarce amongst the insurgents. The Highland clans were, indeed, tolerably armed with their national weapons; but the guns of the Lowlanders were in wretched order, and in a great measure unfit for service. The success of an expedition in some degree remedied this important deficiency.

Among other northern chiefs who remained faithful to George I., amidst the general defection, was the powerful Earl of Sutherland, who, on the news of the insurrection, had immediately proceeded by sea to his castle of Dunrobin, to collect his vassals. In order that they might be supplied with arms, a vessel at Leith was loaded with firelocks, and other weapons, and sailed for the Earl's country. The wind, however, proving contrary, the master of the ship dropped anchor at Burntisland, on the Fife shore of the Firth of Forth, of which he was a native, that he might have an opportunity to see his wife and children before his departure.

The Master of Sinclair, formerly mentioned, whose family estate and interest lay on the shores of the firth, got information of this circumstance, and suggested the seizure of these arms by a scheme which argued talent and activity, and was the first symptom which the insurgents had given of either one or other. This gallant young nobleman, with about fourscore troopers, and carrying with him a number of baggage-horses, left Perth about nightfall, and, to baffle observation, took a circuitous road to Burntisland. His arrival in that little seaport town had all the effect of a complete surprise, and though the bark had hauled out of the harbour into the roadstead, he boarded her by means of boats, and secured possession of all the arms, which amounted to three hundred. Mar, as had been agreed upon, protected the return of the detachment by advancing a body of five hundred Highlanders as far as Auchtertool, half-way between Perth and Burntisland. The Master of Sinclair, who was well acquainted with the usual discipline of war, was greatly annoyed by the disorderly conduct of the volunteer forces under his charge on this expedition. He could not prevail on the gentlemen of his squadron to keep watch with any vigilance, nor prevent them from crowding into alehouses to drink. In returning homeward, several of them broke off without leave, either to visit their own houses which were near the road, or to indulge themselves in the pleasure of teasing such Presbyterian ministers as came in their way. When he arrived at Auchtertool, the disorder was yet greater. The Highland detachment, many of them Mar's own men from Dee-side, had broken their ranks, and were dispersed over the country, pillaging the farmhouses; when Sinclair got a Highland officer to command them to desist and return, they refused to obey, nor was there any means of bringing them off, save by spreading a report that the enemy's dragoons were approaching; then they drew together with wonderful celerity, and submitted to be led back to Perth with the arms that had been seized, which went some length to remedy the scarcity of that most important article in the insurgent army.

A greater deficiency even than that of arms, was the want of a general capable of forming the plan of a campaign, suitable to the emergency and the character of the troops, and carrying it into effect with firmness, celerity, and decision. Generals Hamilton and Gordon, both in Mar's army, were men of some military experience, but unfitted for combined movements on an extended scale; and Mar himself, as already intimated, seems to have been unacquainted even with the mere mechanical part of the profession. He appears to have thought that the principal part of his work was done when the insurrection was set on foot, and that once effected, that it would carry itself on, and the rebels increase in such numbers as to render resistance impossible. The greater part of the Jacobites in East Lothian were, he knew, ready to take horse; so were those of the counties of Dumfries and Lanark; but they were separated from his army by the Firth of Forth, and likely to require assistance from him, in order to secure protection when they assembled. Montrose, or Dundee, with half the men whom Mar had already under him, would have marched without hesitation towards Stirling, and compelled the Duke of Argyle, who had not as yet quite two thousand men, either to fight or retreat, which must have opened the Lowlands and the Borders to the operations of the insurgents. But such was the reputation of the Duke, that Mar resolved not to encounter him until he should have received all the reinforcements from the north and west which he could possibly expect, in the hope, by assembling an overwhelming superiority of force, to counterbalance the acknowledged military skill of his distinguished opponent.

As it was essential, however, to the Earl of Mar's purpose, to spread the flame of insurrection into the Lowlands, he determined not to allow the check which Argyle's forces and position placed on his movements, to prevent his attempting a diversion by passing at all hazards a considerable detachment of his army into Lothian, to support and encourage his Jacobite friends there. His plan was to collect small vessels and boats on the Fife side of the firth, and despatch them across with a division of his army, who were to land on such part of the coast of East Lothian as the wind should permit, and unite themselves with the malcontents wherever they might find them in strength. But ere noticing the fate of this expedition, we must leave Mar and his army, to trace the progress of the insurrection in the south of Scotland and the north of England, where it had already been broken out.

LXVIII

The Fifteen

1715

THE reports of invasion from France—of King James's landing with a foreign force, abundance of arms, ammunition, and treasure, and the full purpose to reward his friends and chastise his enemies—the same exaggerated intelligence from England, concerning general discontent and local insurrection, which had raised the north of Scotland in arms—had their effect also on the gentlemen of Jacobite principles in the south of that country, and in the contiguous frontiers of England, where a number of Catholic families, and others devoted to the exiled family, were still to be found. Ere the hopes inspired by such favourable rumours had passed away, came the more veracious intelligence that the Earl of Mar had set up James's standard in the Highlands, and presently after, that he had taken possession of Perth—that many noblemen of distinguished rank and interest had joined his camp, and that his numbers were still increasing.

These reports gave a natural impulse to the zeal of men, who, having long professed themselves the liege subjects of the Stewart family, were ashamed to sit still when a gallant effort was made to effect their restoration, by what was reported to be, and in very truth was, a very strong party, and an army much larger than those commanded by

Montrose or Dundee, and composed chiefly of the same description of troops at the head of which they had gained their victories. The country, therefore, through most of its districts, was heaving with the convulsive throes which precede civil war, like those which announce an earthquake. Events hurried on to decide the doubtful and embolden the timorous. The active measures resolved on by government, in arresting suspected persons throughout England and the southern parts of Scotland, obliged the professed Jacobites to bring their minds to a resolution, and either expose their persons to the dangers of civil war, or their characters to the shame of being judged wanting in the hour of action, to all the protestations which they had made in those of safety and peace.

These considerations decided men according to their characters, some to submit themselves to imprisonment, for the safety of their lives and fortunes—others to draw the sword, and venture their all in support of their avowed principles. Those gentlemen who embraced the latter course, more honourable, or more imprudent perhaps, began to leave their homes, and drew together in such bodies as might enable them to resist the efforts of the magistrates, or troops sent to arrest them. The civil war began by a very tragical rencounter in a family, with the descendants of which your grandfather has long enjoyed peculiar intimacy, and of which I give the particulars after the account preserved by them, though it is also mentioned in most histories of the times.

Among other families of distinction in East Lothian, that of Mr. Hepburn of Keith was devotedly attached to the interests of the House of Stewart, and he determined to exert himself to the utmost in the approaching conflict. He had several sons, with whom, and his servants, he had determined to join a troop to be raised in East Lothian, under the command of the Earl of Winton. This gentleman being much respected in the county, it was deemed of importance to prevent his showing an example which was likely to be generally followed. For this purpose, Mr. Hepburn of Humbie and Dr. Sinclair of Herdmanston resolved to lay the Laird of Keith under arrest, and proceeded towards his house with a party of the horsemilitia, on the morning of the 8th of October 1715, which happened to be the very morning that Keith had appointed to set forth on his campaign, having made all preparations on the preceding evening. The family had assembled for the last time at the breakfast-table, when it was observed that one of the young ladies looked more sad and disconsolate than even the departure of her father and brothers upon a distant and precarious expedition seemed to warrant at that period, when the fair sex were as enthusiastic in politics as the men.

Miss Hepburn was easily induced to tell the cause of her fears. She had dreamed she saw her youngest brother, a youth of great hopes, and generally esteemed, shot by a man whose features were impressed on her recollection, and stretched dead on the floor of the room in which they were now assembled. The females of the family listened and argued—the men laughed, and turned the visionary into ridicule. The horses were saddled and led out into the courtyard, when a mounted party was discovered advancing along the flat ground, in front of the mansion-house, called the Plain of Keith. The gate was shut; and when Dr. Sinclair, who was most active in the matter, had announced his purpose, and was asked for his warrant, he handed in at a window the commission of the Marquis of Tweeddale, lord-lieutenant of the county. This Keith returned with contempt, and announced that he would stand on his defence. The party within mounted their horses, and sallied out, determined to make their way; and Keith, discharging a pistol in the air, charged the Doctor sword in hand; the militia then fired, and the youngest of the Hepburns was killed on the spot. The sister beheld the catastrophe from the window, and to the end of her life persisted that the homicide had the features of the person whom she saw in her dream. The corpse was carried into the room where they had so lately breakfasted, and Keith, after having paid this heavy tax to the demon of civil war, rode off with the rest of his party to join the insurgents. Dr. Sinclair was censured very generally for letting his party zeal hurry him into a personal encounter with so near a neighbour and familiar friend; he vindicated himself, by asserting that his intentions were to save Keith from the consequences into which his rash zeal for the Stewart family was about to precipitate that gentleman and his family. But Dr. Sinclair ought to have been prepared to expect that a high-spirited man, with arms in his hands, was certain to resist this violent mode of opening his eyes to the rashness of his conduct; and he who attempts to make either religious or political converts by compulsion must be charged with the consequences of such violence as is most likely to ensue.

Mr. Hepburn and his remaining sons joined the Jacobite gentry of the neighbourhood, to the number of fifty or sixty men, and directed their course westward towards the Borders, where a considerable party were in arms for the same cause. The leader of the East Lothian troop was the Earl of Winton, a young nobleman twenty-five years old, said to be afflicted by a vicissitude of spirits approaching to lunacy. His life had been marked by some strange singularities, as that of his living a long time as bellows-blower and assistant to a blacksmith in France, without holding any communication with his country or family. But, if we judge from his conduct in the rebellion, Lord Winton appears to have displayed more sense and prudence than most of those engaged in that unfortunate affair.

This Lothian insurrection soon merged in the two principal southern risings, which took place in Dumfriesshire and Galloway in Scotland, and in Northumberland and Cumberland in England.

On the western frontier of Scotland there were many families not only Jacobites in politics but Roman Catholics in religion, and therefore bound by a double tie to the heir of James II., who, for the sake of that form of faith, may be justly thought to have forfeited his kingdoms. Among the rest, the Earl of Nithsdale, combining in his person the representation of two noble families, those of the Lord Herries and the Lord Maxwell, might be considered as the natural leader of the party. But William, Viscount Kenmure, in Galloway, a Protestant, was preferred as chief of the enterprise, as it was not thought prudent to bring Catholics too much forward in the affair, on account of the scandal to which their promotion might give rise. Many neighbouring gentlemen were willing to throw themselves and their fortunes into the same adventure in which Nithsdale and Kenmure stood committed. The latter was a man of good sense and resolution, well acquainted with civil affairs, but a total stranger to the military art.

In the beginning of October, the plan of insurrection was so far ripened that the gentlemen of Galloway, Nithisdale, and Annandale proposed by a sudden effort to possess themselves of the county town of Dumfries. The town was protected on the one side by the river Nith; on the others it might be considered as open. But the zeal of the inhabitants, and of the Whig gentlemen of the neigbbourhood, baffled the enterprise, which must otherwise have been attended with credit to the arms of the insurgents. The lord-lieutenant and his deputies collected the fencible men of the county, and brought several large parties into Dumfries to support, if necessary, the defence of the place. The provost, Robert Corbett, Esq., mustered the citizens, and putting himself at their head, harangued them in a style peculiarly calculated to inspire confidence. He reminded them that their laws and religion were at stake, and that their cause resembled that of the Israelites, when led by Joshua against the unbelieving inhabitants of the land of Canaan.

"Nevertheless," said the considerate Provost of Dumfries, "as I, who am your unworthy leader, cannot pretend to any divine commission like that of the son of Nun, I do not take upon me to recommend the extermination of your enemies, as the judge of Israel was commanded to do by a special revelation. On the contrary, I earnestly entreat you to use your assured victory with clemency, and remember that the misguided persons opposed to you are still your countrymen and brethren." This oration, which, instead of fixing the minds of his followers on a doubtful contest, instructed them only how to make use of a certain victory, had a great effect in encouraging the bands of the sagacious provost, who, with their auxiliaries from the country, drew out and took a position to cover the town of Dumfries.

Lord Kenmure marched from Moffat with about a hundred and fifty horse, on Wednesday, the 13th of October, with the purpose of occupying Dumfries. But finding the friends of Government in such a state of preparation, he became speedily aware that he could not with a handful of cavalry propose to storm a town, the citizens of which were determined on resistance. The Jacobite gentlemen, therefore, retreated to Moffat, and thence to Langholm and Hawick. From thence they took their departure for the eastward, to join the Northumberland gentlemen who were in arms in the same cause, and towards whom we must now direct our attention.

In England, a very dangerous and extensive purpose of insurrection certainly existed shortly after the Queen's death; but the exertions of Government had been so great in all quarters, that it was everywhere disconcerted or suppressed. The University of Oxford was supposed to be highly dissatisfied at the accession of the House of Hanover; and there, as well as at Bath, and elsewhere in the west, horses, arms, and ammunition were seized in considerable quantities, and most of the Tory gentlemen who were suspected of harbouring dangerous intentions were either arrested or delivered themselves up on the summons of Government. Amongst these was Sir William Wyndham, one of the principal leaders of the High Church party.

In Northumberland and Cumberland, the Tories, at a greater distance from the power of the Government, were easily inclined to action; they were, besides, greatly influenced by the news of the Earl of

Mar's army, which, though large enough to have done more than it ever attempted, was still much magnified by common fame. The unfortunate Earl of Derwentwater, who acted so prominent a part in this short-lived struggle, was by birth connected with the exiled Royal family; his lady also was a bigot in their cause; and the Catholic religion, which he professed, made it almost a crime in this nobleman to remain peaceful on the present occasion. Thomas Forster of Bamborough, member of Parliament for the county of Northumberland, was equally attached to the Jacobite cause; being a Church-of-England man, he was adopted as the commander-in-chief of the insurrection, for the same reason that the Lord Kenmure was preferred to the Earl of Nithsdale in the command of the Scottish levies. Warrants being issued against the Earl of Derwentwater and Mr. Forster, they absconded, and lurked for a few days among their friends in Northumberland, till a general consultation could be held of the principal northern Tories, at the house of Mr. Fenwick of Bywell; when, as they foresaw that if they should be arrested, and separately examined, they could scarce frame such a defence as might save them from the charge of high treason, they resolved to unite in a body, and try the chance that fortune might send them. With this purpose they held a meeting at a place called Greenrig, where Forster arrived with about twenty horse. They went from this to the top of a hill, called the Waterfalls, where they were joined by Lord Derwentwater. This reinforcement made them near sixty horse, with which they proceeded to the small town of Rothbury, and from thence to Warkworth, where they proclaimed King James III. On the 10th of October they marched to Morpeth, where they received further reinforcements, which raised them to three hundred horse, the highest number which they ever attained. Some of these gentlemen remained undecided till the last fatal moment, and amongst these was John Hall of Otterburn. He attended a meeting of the quarter sessions, which was held at Alnwick, for the purpose of taking measures for quelling the rebellion, but left it with such precipitation that he forgot his hat upon the bench, and joined the fatal meeting at the Waterfalls.

The insurgents could levy no foot soldiers, though many men offered to join them; for they had neither arms to equip them nor money to pay them. This want of infantry was the principal cause why they did not make an immediate attack on Newcastle, which had formed part of their original plan. But the town, though not regularly fortified, was surrounded with a high stone wall, with old-fashioned gates. The magistrates, who were zealous on the side of Government, caused the gates to be walled up with masonry, and raised a body of seven hundred volunteers for the defence of the town, to which the keelmen, or bargemen employed in the coal-trade upon the Tyne, made offer of seven hundred more; and, in the course of a day or two, General Carpenter arrived with part of those forces with whom he afterwards attacked the insurgents. After this last reinforcement, the *gentlemen*, as Forster's cavalry were called, lost all hopes of surprising Newcastle. About the same time, however, a beam of success which attended their arms might be said just to glimmer and disappear. This was the exploit of a gentleman named Lancelot Errington, who, by a dexterous stratagem, contrived to surprise the small castle, or fort, upon Holy Island,[1] which might have been useful to the insurgents in maintaining their foreign communication. But before Errington could receive the necessary supplies of men and provisions, the governor of Berwick detached a party of thirty soldiers, and about fifty volunteers, who, crossing the sands at low water, attacked the little fort, and carried it sword in hand. Errington was wounded and taken prisoner, but afterwards made his escape.

This disappointment, with the news that troops were advancing to succour Newcastle, decided Forster and his followers to unite themselves with the Viscount Kenmure and the Scottish gentlemen engaged in the same cause. The English express found Kenmure near Hawick, at a moment when his little band of about two hundred men had almost determined to give up the enterprise. Upon receiving Forster's communication, however, they resolved to join him at Rothbury.

On the 19th of October the two bodies of insurgents met at Rothbury, and inspected each other's military state and equipments with the anxiety of mingled hope and apprehension. The general character of the troops was the same, but the Scots seemed the best prepared for action, being mounted on strong hardy horses, fit for the charge, and, though but poorly disciplined, were well armed with the basket-hilted broadswords then common throughout Scotland. The English

---

[1] "Lindisfarne," about eight miles S.E. of Berwick, "was called Holy Island, from the sanctity of its ancient monastery, and from its having been the Episcopal seat of the See of Durham during the early ages of British Christianity. It is not properly an island, but rather a semi-isle, for, although surrounded by the sea at full tide, the ebb leaves the sands dry between it and the coast of Northumberland, from which it is about three miles distant."—*Note, Marmion.*

gentlemen, on the other hand, were mounted on fleet blood-horses, better adapted for the racecourse and hunting-field than for action. There was among them a great want of war-saddles, curbbridles, and, above all, of swords and pistols; so that the Scots were inclined to doubt whether men so well equipped for flight, and so imperfectly prepared for combat, might not, in case of an encounter, take the safer course, and leave them in the lurch. Their want of swords in particular, at least of cutting swords fit for the cavalry service, is proved by an anecdote: It is said that as they entered the town of Wooler, their commanding officer gave the word—"Gentlemen, you that have got swords, draw them;" to which a fellow among the crowd answered, not irrelevantly—"And what shall they do who have none?" When Forster, by means of one of his captains named Douglas, had opened a direct communication with Mar's army, the messenger stated that the English were willing to have given horses worth £25—then a considerable price—for such swords as are generally worn by Highlanders.

It may also be noticed here, that out of the four troops commanded by Forster, the two raised by Lord Derwentwater and Lord Widrington were, like those of the Scots, composed of gentlemen, and their relations and dependants. But the third and fourth troops differed considerably from the others in their composition. The one was commanded by John Hunter, who united the character of a Border farmer with that of a contraband trader; the other by the same Douglas whom we have just mentioned, who was remarkable for his dexterity and success in searching for arms and horses, a trade which he is said not to have limited to the time of the Rebellion. Into the troops of these last named officers, many persons of slender reputation were introduced, who had either lived by smuggling or by the ancient Border practice of horselifting, as it was called. These light and suspicious characters, however, fought with determined courage at the barricades of Preston.

The motions of Kenmure and Forster were now decided by the news that a detachment from Mar's army had been sent across the Firth of Forth to join them; and this requires us to return to the Northern insurrection, which was now endeavouring to extend and connect itself with that which had broken out on the Border. The Earl of Mar, it must be observed, had from the first moment of his arrival at Perth, or at least as soon as he was joined by a disposable force, designed to send a party over the firth into Lothian, who should encourage the Jacobites in that country to rise; and he proposed to confer this command upon the Master of Sinclair. As, however, this separation of his forces must have considerably weakened his own army, and perhaps exposed him to an unwelcome visit from the Duke of Argyle, Mar postponed his purpose until he should be joined by reinforcements. These were now pouring fast into Perth.

From the north, the Marquis of Huntly, one of the most powerful of the confederacy, joined the army at Perth with foot and horse, Lowlanders and Highlanders to the amount of nearly four thousand men. The Earl Marischal had the day before brought up his own power, consisting of about eighty horse. The arrival of these noblemen brought some seeds of dissension into the camp. Marischal, so unlike the wisdom of his riper years, with the indiscretion of a very young man, gave just offence to Huntly by endeavouring to deprive him of a part of his following.

The occasion was this: The MacPhersons, a very stout, hardy clan, who are called in Gaelic MacVourigh, and headed by Cluny MacPherson, held some possessions of the Gordon family, and therefore naturally placed themselves under the Marquis of Huntly's banner on the present occasion, although it might be truly said that in general they were by no means the most tractable vassals. Marischal endeavoured to prevail on this Clan Vourigh to place themselves under his command instead of that of Huntly, alleging, that as the MacPhersons always piqued themselves on being a distinguished branch of the great confederacy called Clan Chattan, so was he, by his name of Keith, the natural chief of the confederacy aforesaid. Mar is said to have yielded some countenance to the claim, the singularity of which affords a curious picture of the matters with which these insurgents were occupied. The cause of Mar's taking part in such a debate was alleged to be the desire which he had to lower the estimation of Huntly's power and numbers. The MacPhersons, however, considered the broad lands which they held of the Gordon as better reason for rendering him their allegiance than the etymological arguments urged by the Earl Marischal, and refused to desert the banner under which they had come to the field.

Another circumstance early disgusted Huntly with an enterprise in which he could not hope to gain anything, and which placed in peril a princely estate and a ducal title. Besides about three squadrons of gentlemen, chiefly of his own name, well mounted and well armed, be had brought into the field a squadron of some fifty men strong, whom be termed Light Horse, though totally unfit for the service of *petite guerre*, which that name implies. A satirist describes them as consisting of great lubberly fellows, in bonnets, without boots, and mounted on long-tailed little ponies, with snaffle bridles, the riders being much the bigger animals of the two; and instead of pistols, these horsemen were armed with great rusty muskets, tied on their backs with ropes. These uncouth cavaliers excited a degree of mirth and ridicule among the more civilised southern gentry; which is not surprising, any more than that both the men, and Huntly their commander, felt and resented such uncivil treatment—a feeling which was gradually increased into a disinclination to the cause in which they had received the indignity.

Besides these northern forces, Mar also expected many powerful succours from the north-west, which comprehended the tribes termed, during that insurrection, by way of excellence, The Clans. The chiefs of these families had readily agreed to hold the rendezvous which had been settled at the hunting match of Braemar; but none of them, save Glengarry, were very hasty in recollecting their promise. Of this high chief a contemporary says, it would be hard to say whether he had more of the lion, the fox, or the bear in his disposition; for he was at least as crafty and rough as he was courageous and gallant. At any rate, both his faults and virtues were consistent with his character, which attracted more admiration than that of any other engaged in Mar's insurrection. He levied his men, and marched to the braes of Glenorchy, where, after remaining eight days, he was joined by the Captain of Clanranald and Sir John MacLean; who came, the one with the MacDonalds of Moidart and Arisaig, the other with a regiment of his own name from the isle of Mull. A detachment of these clans commenced the war by an attempt to surprise the garrison at Inverlochy. They succeeded in taking some outworks, and made the defenders prisoners, but failed in their attack upon the place, the soldiers being on their guard.

Still, though hostilities were in a manner begun, these western levies were far from complete. Stewart of Appin, and Cameron of Lochiel, would neither of them move; and the Breadalbane men, whose assistance had been promised by the singular Earl of that name, were equally tardy. There was probably little inclination on the part of those clans who were near neighbours to the Duke of Argyle, and some of them Campbells, to displease that powerful and much-respected nobleman. Another mighty limb of the conspiracy, lying also in the north-western extremity of Scotland, was the Earl of Seaforth, chief of the MacKenzies, who could bring into the field from two to three thousand men of his own name, and that of MacRae, and other clans dependant upon him. But he also was prevented from taking the field and joining Mar by the operations of the Earl of Sutherland, who, taking the chief command of some of the northern clans disposed to favour Government—as the Monroes, under their chief Monro of Foulis; the MacKays, under Lord Rae; the numerous and powerful clan of Grant, along with his own following—had assembled a little army with which he made a demonstration towards the bridge of Alness. Thus, at the head of a body of about twelve or fifteen hundred men, Sutherland was so stationed on the verge of Seaforth's country that the latter chief could not collect his men and move southward to join Mar without leaving his estates exposed to ravage. Seaforth prepared to move, however, so soon as circumstances would admit, for while he faced the Earl of Sutherland with about eighteen hundred men, he sent Sir John MacKenzie of Coull to possess himself of Inverness,— Brigadier MacIntosh, by whom it was occupied for James VIII., having moved southward to Perth.

Thus, from one circumstance or another, the raising of the western clans was greatly delayed; and Mar, whose plan it was not to attempt anything till he should have collected the whole force together which he could possibly expect, was, or thought himself, obliged to remain at Perth, long after he had assembled an army sufficient to attack the Duke of Argyle and force his way into the southern part of Scotland, where the news of his success and the Duke's defeat or retreat, together with the hope of plunder, would have decided those tardy western chieftains who were yet hesitating whether they should join him or not. Mar, however, tried to influence them by arguments of a different nature, such as he had the power of offering; and despatched General Gordon to expedite these levies, with particular instructions to seize on the Duke of Argyle's castle at Inverary, and the arms understood to be deposited there. There was afterwards supposed to be some personal spleen in the Earl's thus beginning direct hostilities against his great opponent; but it must be said, to the honour of the rebel general, that he resolved not to set the example of beginning with fire and sword; and therefore directed that though General Gordon might threaten to burn the castle at Inverary, he was on no account to proceed to such extremity without further orders. His object probably was, besides a desire to possess the arms said to be in the place, to effect a complete breach between the Duke of Argyle and the clans in his vicinity, which must have necessarily been attended with great diminution of the Duke's influence. We shall see presently how far this line of policy appears to have succeeded.

During the currency of these events, Mar received information of the partial rising which had taken place in Northumberland, and the disposition to similar movements which showed itself in various parts of Scotland. It might have been thought that these tidings would have induced him at length to burst from the sort of confinement in which the small body commanded by Argyle retained so superior an army. If Mar judged that the troops under his command assembled at Perth were too few to attack a force which they more than doubled, there remained a plan of manoeuvring by which he might encounter Argyle at a yet, greater advantage. He might have commanded General Gordon, when he had collected the western clans, who could not amount to fewer than four thousand men, instead of amusing himself at Inverary to direct their course to the fords of Frew, by which the river Forth may be crossed above Stirling, and near to its source. Such a movement would have menaced the Duke from the westward, while Mar himself might have advanced against him from the north, and endeavoured to possess himself of Stirling Bridge, which was not very strongly guarded. The insurgent cavalry of Lord Kenmure could also have co-operated in such a plan by advancing from Dumfries towards Glasgow, and threatening the west of Scotland. It is plain that the Duke of Argyle saw the danger of being thus cut off from the western counties, where Government had many zealous adherents; for he ordered up five hundred men from Glasgow to join his camp at Stirling; and on the 24th of September commanded all the regiments of fencibles and volunteers in the west of Scotland to repair to Glasgow, as the most advantageous central point from which to protect the country and cover his own encampment; and established garrisons at the village of Drymen, and also in several gentlemen's houses adjacent to the fords of Frew, to prevent or retard any descent of the Highlanders into the Low Country by that pass. But the warlike habits of the Highlanders were greatly superior to those of the raw Lowland levies, whom they would probably have treated with little ceremony.

Nevertheless, the Earl of Mar, far from adopting a plan so decisive, resolved to afford support to Kenmure and Forster by his original plan of marching a detachment to their assistance, instead of moving his whole force towards the Lowlands. This, he conceived, might be sufficient to give them the aid and protection of a strong body of infantry, and enable them to strengthen and increase their numbers, whilst the measure allowed him to remain undisturbed at Perth, to await the final result of his intrigues in the Highlands, and those which he had commenced at the court of the Chevalier de St. George. There were many and obvious dangers in making the proposed movement. A great inlet of the sea was to be crossed; and if the passage was to be attempted about Dunfermline or Inverkeithing, where the Forth was less broad it was to be feared that the bustle of collecting boats and the march of the troops which were to form the detachment might give warning to the Duke of Argyle of what was intended, who was likely to send a body of his dragoons to surprise and cut off the detachment on their arrival at the southern side of the Forth. On the other hand, to attempt the passage over the lower part of the firth, where vessels were more numerous and could be assembled with less observation, was to expose the detachment to the uncertainties of a passage of fifteen or eighteen miles across, which was guarded by men-of-war with their boats and launches, to which the officers of the customs at every seaport had the most strict orders to transmit intelligence of whatever movement might be attempted by the rebels. Upon a choice of difficulties, however, the crossing of the firth from Pittenweem, Crail, and other towns situated to the eastward on the Fife coast was determined on.

The troops destined for the adventure were Mar's own regiment as it was called, consisting of the Farquharsons and others from the banks of the Dee—that of the MacIntoshes—those of Lords Strathmore, Nairne, and Lord Charles Murray; all Highlanders, excepting Lord Strathmore's Lowland regiment. They made up in all about two thousand five hundred men; for in the rebel army the regiments were weak in numbers, Mar having gratified the chiefs by giving each the commission of colonel, and allowing him the satisfaction to form a battalion out of his own followers, however few in number.

The intended expedition was arranged with some address. Considerable parties of horse traversed Fifeshire in various directions, proclaiming James VIII., and levying the cess of the county, though in very different proportions, on those whom they accounted friends or enemies to their cause, their demands upon the latter being both larger and more rigorously enforced. These movements were contrived to distract the attention of the Whigs and that of the Duke of Argyle by various rumours, tending to conceal Mar's real purpose of sending a detachment across the firth. For the same purpose, when their intention could be no longer concealed, the English men-of-war were deceived concerning the place where the attempt was to be made. Mar threw troops into the castle of Burntisland, and seemed busy in collecting vessels in that little port. The armed ships were induced by these appearances to slip their cables, and, standing over to Burntisland, commenced a cannonade, which was returned by the rebels from a battery which they had constructed on the outer port of the harbour, with little damage on either side.

By these feints Mar was enabled to get the troops, designed to form the expedition, moved in secrecy down to Pittenweem, the Elie, Crail, and other small ports so numerous on that coast. They were placed under the command of MacIntosh of Borlum, already mentioned, commonly called Brigadier MacIntosh, a Highland gentleman, who was trained to regular war in the French service. He was a bold, rough soldier; but is stated to have degraded the character by a love of plunder which would have better become a lower rank in the army. But this may have been a false or exaggerated charge.

The English vessels of war received notice of the design, or observed the embarkation from their topmasts, but too late to offer effectual interruption. They weighed anchor, however, at floodtide, and sailed to intercept the flotilla of the insurgents. Nevertheless, they only captured a single boat, with about forty Highlanders. Some of the vessels were, however, forced back to the Fife coast, from which they came; and the boats which bore Lord Strathmore's Lowland regiment, and others filled with Highlanders, were forced into the island of May, in the mouth of the Forth, where they were blockaded by the men-of-war. The gallant young Earl intrenched himself on the island, and harangued his followers on the fidelity which they owed to the cause; and undertook to make his own faith evident by exposing his person wherever the peril should prove greatest, and accounting it an honour to die in the service of the Prince for whom he had taken arms. Blockaded in an almost desert island, this young nobleman had the additional difficulty of subduing quarrels and jealousies betwixt the Highlanders and his own followers from Angus. These dissensions ran so high that the Lowlanders, resolved to embrace an opportunity to escape from the island with their small craft, and leave the Highlanders to their fate. The proposal was rejected by Strathmore with ineffable disdain, nor would he leave his very unpleasant situation till the change of winds and waves afforded him a fair opportunity of leading all who had been sharers in his misfortune in safety back to the coast they sailed from.

Meantime the greater part of the detachment designed for the descent upon Lothian, being about sixteen hundred men, succeeded in their desperate attempt, by landing at North Berwick, Aberlady, Gullane, and other places on the southern shores of the firth, from whence they marched upon Haddington, where they again formed a junction, and refreshed themselves for a night, till they should learn the fate of their friends who had not yet appeared. We have not the means of knowing whether MacIntosh had any precise orders for his conduct when he should find himself in Lothian. The despatches of Mar would lead us to infer that he had instructions, which ought to have directed his march instantly to the Borders, to unite himself with Kenmure and Forster. But he must have had considerable latitude in his orders, since it was almost impossible to frame them in such a manner as to meet, with any degree of precision, the circumstances in which he might be placed, and much must have, of course, been entrusted to his own discretion. The surprise, however, was great, even in the Brigadier's own little army, when, instead of marching southward, as they had expected, they were ordered to face about and advance rapidly on the capital.

This movement Mar afterwards termed a mistake on the Brigadier's part. But it was probably occasioned by the information which MacIntosh received from friends in Edinburgh, that the capital might be occupied by a rapid march, before it could be relieved by the Duke of Argyle, who was lying thirty miles off. The success of such a surprise must necessarily have given great eclât to the arms of the insurgents, with the more solid advantages of obtaining large supplies both of arms and money and of intercepting the communication between the Duke of Argyle and the south. It is also probable that MacIntosh might have some expectation of an insurrection taking place in Edinburgh on the news of his approach. But, whatever were his hopes and motives, he marched with his small force on the metropolis, and the movement excited the most universal alarm.

The Lord Provost, a gentleman named Campbell, was a man of sense and activity. The instant that he heard of the Highlanders having arrived at Haddington he sent information to the Duke of Argyle, and arming the city-guard, trained bands, and volunteers, took such precautions as he could to defend the city, which, though surrounded by a high wall, was far from being tenable even against a coup-de-main. The Duke of Argyle, foreseeing all the advantages which the insurgents would gain even from the temporary possession of the capital, resolved on this, as on other occasions, to make activity supply the want of numbers. He mounted two hundred infantry soldiers on country horses, and uniting them with three hundred chosen dragoons, placed himself at their head, and made a forced march from Stirling to relieve Edinburgh. This he accomplished with such rapidity that he entered the West Port of Edinburgh about ten o'clock at night, just about the same moment that MacIntosh had reached the place where Piershill barracks are now situated, within a mile of the eastern gate of the city. Thus the metropolis, which seemed to be a prey for the first occupant, was saved by the promptitude of the Duke of Argyle. His arrival spread universal joy among the friends of Government, who, from something resembling despair, passed to the opposite extremity of hope and triumph. The town had been reinforced during the day by various parties of horse militia from Berwickshire and Mid-Lothian, and many volunteers, whom the news of the Duke of Argyle's arrival greatly augmented, not so much on account of the number which attended him, as of the general confidence reposed in his talents and character.

The advancing enemy also felt the charm communicated by the Duke's arrival; but to them it conveyed apprehension and dismay, and changed their leader's hopes of success into a desire to provide for the safety of his small detachment, respecting which he was probably the more anxious that the number of the Duke's forces were in all likelihood exaggerated, and, besides, consisted chiefly of cavalry, respecting whom the Highlanders entertained at that time a superstitious terror. Moved by such considerations, and turning off the road to Edinburgh at the place called Jock's Lodge, Brigadier MacIntosh directed his march upon Leith, which he entered without opposition. In the prison of that place he found the forty men belonging to his own detachment who had been taken during the passage, and who were now set at liberty. The Highlanders next took possession of such money and provisions as they found in the Custom House. After these preliminaries they marched across the drawbridge and occupied the remains of a citadel built by Oliver Cromwell during the period of his usurpation. It was a square fort, with five demibastions and a ditch; the gates were indeed demolished, but the ramparts were tolerably entire, and the Brigadier lost no time in barricading all accessible places with beams, planks, carts, and barrels filled with stones, and other similar materials. The vessels in the harbour supplied them with cannon, which they planted on the ramparts, and prepared themselves as well as circumstances admitted for a desperate defence.

Early next morning the Duke of Argyle presented himself before the fortified post of the Highlanders with his three hundred dragoons, two hundred infantry, and about six hundred new-levied men, militia, and volunteers; among the latter class were seen several clergymen, who, in a war of this nature, did not consider their sacred character inconsistent with assuming arms. The Duke summoned the troops who occupied the citadel to surrender, under the penalty of high treason, and declared that if they placed him under the necessity of bringing up cannon, or killed any of his men in attempting a defence, he would give them no quarter. A Highland gentleman, named Kinackin, answered resolutely from the ramparts, "That they laughed at his summons of surrender—that they were ready to abide his assault; as for quarter, they would neither give nor receive it; and if he thought he could force their position he was welcome to try the experiment."

The Duke having received this defiance, carefully reconnoitred the citadel, and found the most important difficulties in the way of the proposed assault. The troops must have advanced two hundred yards before arriving at the defences, and during all that time would have been exposed to a fire from an enemy under cover. Many of those who must have been assailants were unacquainted with discipline, and had never seen action; the Highlanders, though little accustomed to exchange the fire of musketry in the open field, were excellent marksmen from behind walls, and their swords and daggers were likely to be formidable in the defence of a breach or a barricade, where the attack must be in some degree tumultuary. To this was to be added the Duke's total want of cannon and mortars, or artillerymen by whom they could be managed. All these reasons induced Argyle to postpone an attack, of which the result was uncertain, until he should be better provided. The volunteers were very anxious for an attack; but we are merely told, by the reverend historian of the Rebellion, that when they were given to understand that the post of honour, viz. the right of leading the attack, was their just right as volunteers, it made them heartily approve of the Duke's measure in deferring the enterprise. Argyle, therefore retreated to Edinburgh, to make better preparations for an attack with artillery next day.

But as MacIntosh's intention of seizing on the capital had failed, it did not suit his purpose to abide in the vicinity. He left the citadel of Leith at nine o'clock, and conducted his men in the most profound silence along the sands to Seaton House, about ten miles from Edinburgh, a strong castle belonging to the Earl of Winton, surrounded by a high wall. Here they made a show of fortifying themselves, and collecting provisions, as if they intended to abide for some time. The Duke of Argyle, with his wonted celerity, made preparations to attack MacIntosh in his new quarters. He sent to the camp at Stirling for artillerymen, and began to get ready some guns in Edinburgh Castle, with which he proposed to advance to Seaton, and dislodge its now occupants. But his purpose was again interrupted by express upon express, despatched from Stirling by General Whetham, who commanded in the Duke's absence, acquainting his superior with the unpleasing information that Mar, with his whole army, was advancing towards Stirling, trusting to have an opportunity of destroying the few troops who were left there, and which did not exceed a thousand men.

Upon these tidings; the Duke, leaving two hundred and fifty men of his small command under the order of General Wightman, to prosecute the plan of dislodging the Highlanders from their stronghold of Seaton, returned in all haste, with the small remainder of his forces, to Stirling, where his presence was much called for. But before adverting to events which took place in that quarter, we shall conduct MacIntosh and his detachment some days' journey farther on their progress.

On Saturday, the 15th of October, the environs of Seaton House were reconnoitred by a body of dragoons and volunteers. But as the Highlanders boldly marched out to skirmish, the party from Edinburgh thought themselves too weak to hazard an action, and retired towards the city, as did the rebels to their garrison. On Monday, the 17th of October, the demonstration upon Seaton was renewed in a more serious manner, Lord Rothes, Lord Torphichen, and other officers marching against the house with three hundred volunteers and the troops which had been left by the Duke of Argyle, to dislodge MacIntosh. But neither in this third attempt was it found prudent, without artillery, to attack the pertinacious mountaineers, as indeed a repulse, in the neighbourhood of the capital, must necessarily have been attended with consequences not to be rashly risked. The troops of the Government, therefore, returned a third time to Edinburgh, without having further engaged with the enemy than by a few exchanges of shot.

MacIntosh did not consider it prudent to give his opponent an opportunity of attacking him again in his present position. He had sent a letter to General Forster, which, reaching the gentlemen engaged in that unadvised expedition, while they were deliberating whether they should not abandon it, determined then to remain in arms, and unite themselves with those Highlanders who had crossed the firth at such great risk, in order to join them. Forster and Kenmure, therefore, returned an answer to MacIntosh's communication, proposing to meet his forces at Kelso or Coldstream, as should be most convenient for him. Such letters as the Brigadier had received from Mar, since passing the Forth, as well as the tenor of his former and original instructions, directed him to form a junction with the gentlemen engaged on the Borders; and he accepted accordingly of their invitation, and assigned Kelso as the place of meeting. His first march was to the village of Longformachus, which he reached on the evening of the 19th of October. It may be mentioned that, in the course of their march, they passed Herdmanston, the seat of Dr. Sinclair, which MacIntosh, with some of the old vindictive Highland spirit, was extremely desirous to have burned, in revenge of the death of young Hepburn of Keith. He was dissuaded from this extreme course, but the house was plundered by Lord Nairne's Highlanders, who were active agents in this species of punishment. Sir William Bennet of Grubet, who had occupied Kelso for the Government, with some few militia and volunteers, learning that fifteen hundred Highlanders were advancing against him from the eastward, while five or six hundred horse—to which number the united forces of Kenmure and Forster might amount, were marching downwards from the Cheviot mountains, relinquished his purpose of defending Kelso; and, abandoning the barricades, which he had made for that purpose, retired to Edinburgh with his followers, carrying with him the greater part of the arms which he had provided.

The cavalry of Forster and Kenmure, marching from Wooler, arrived at Kelso a few hours before the Highlanders, who set out on the same morning from Dunse. The Scottish part of the horse marched through Kelso without halting, to meet with MacIntosh at Ednam bridge, a compliment which they conceived due to the gallantry with which, through many hazards, the Brigadier and his Highlanders had advanced to their succour. The united forces, when mustered at Kelso, were found to amount to about six hundred horse and fourteen hundred foot, for MacIntosh had lost some men by desertion. They then entered the town in triumph, and possessed themselves of such arms as Sir William Bennet had left behind him. They proclaimed James VIII. in the market-place of this beautiful town, and attended service (the officers at least) in the Old Abbey Church, where a non-juring clergyman preached a sermon on hereditary right, the text being, Deut. xxi. 17, *The right of the first-born is his.* The chiefs, then held a general council on the best mode of following out the purposes of their insurrection. There were two lines of conduct to choose betwixt, one of which was advocated by the Scottish gentlemen, the other by the insurgents from the north of England.

According to the first plan of operations it was proposed that their united forces should move westward along the Border, occupying in their way the towns of Dumfries, Ayr, and Glasgow itself. They expected no resistance on either of these points, which their union with MacIntosh's troops might not enable, them to overcome. Arrived in the west of Scotland, they proposed to open the passes, which were defended chiefly by militia and volunteers, to the very considerable force of the Argyleshire clans, which were already assembled under General Gordon. With the Earl of Mar's far superior army in front, and with the force of MacIntosh, Kenmure, and Forster upon his left flank and in his rear, it was conceived impossible that, with all his abilities, the Duke of Argyle could persevere in maintaining his important post at Stirling; there was every chance of his being driven entirely out of the "ancient kingdom," as Scotland was fondly called.

This plan of the campaign had two recommendations. In the first place, it tended to a concentration of the rebel forces, which, separated as they were, and divided through the kingdom, had hitherto been either checked and neutralised like that of Mar by the Duke of Argyle, or fairly obliged to retreat and shift for safety from the forces of the Government, as had been the fate of Forster and Kenmure. Secondly, the basis on which the scheme rested was fixed and steady. Mar's army, on the one hand, and Gordon with the clans on the other, were bodies of troops existing and in arms, nor was there any party in the field for the Government of strength adequate to prevent their forming the proposed junction.

Notwithstanding these advantages, the English insurgents expressed the strongest wish to follow an opposite course, and carry the war again into England, from which they had been so lately obliged to retreat. Their proposal had at first a bold and spirited appearance, and might, had it been acted upon with heart and unanimity, have had a considerable chance of success. The dragoons and horse which had assembled at Newcastle under General Carpenter were only a thousand strong, and much fatigued with forced marches. Reinforced as the insurgents were with MacIntosh and his infantry, they might have succeeded by a sudden march in attacking Carpenter in his quarters, or fighting him in the field; at all events, their great superiority of numbers would have compelled the English general either to hazard an action at very great disadvantage or to retreat. In either case the Northumbrian gentlemen would have remained masters of their native province, and might have made themselves masters of Newcastle, and interrupted the coal-trade; and, finally, the great possessions and influence of Lord Derwentwater and others would have enabled them to add to their force as many infantry as they might find means of arming, without which the gentry who were in arms could only be considered as a soul without a body, or a hilt without a blade. But Forster and his friends would not agree to a measure which had so much to recommend it, but lost time in empty debates, remaining at Kelso from the 22d to the 27th of October, until it became impossible to put the plan in execution. For they learned that while they were deliberating General Carpenter was acting; and his little army, being reinforced and refreshed, was now advanced to Wooler, to seek them out and give them battle.

Forster and the English officers then insisted on another scheme, which should still make England the scene of the campaign. They proposed that, eluding the battle which General Carpenter seemed willing to offer, they should march westward along the middle and west Borders of Scotland, till they could turn southward into Lancashire, where they assured their Scottish confederates that their friends were ready to rise in numbers, to the amount of twenty thousand men at least, which would be sufficient to enable them to march to London in defiance of all opposition.

Upon this important occasion the insurgents gave a decided proof of that species of credulity which disposes men to receive, upon very slight evidence, such tidings as flatter their hopes and feelings, and which induced Addison to term the Jacobites of that period a race of men who live in a dream, daily nourished by fiction and delusion, and whom he compares to the obstinate old knight in Rabelais, who every morning swallowed a chimera for breakfast.

The Scottish gentlemen, and Lord Winton in particular, were not convinced by the reasoning of their Southern friends, nor do they appear to have been participant of their sanguine hopes of a general rising in Lancashire; accordingly, they strongly opposed the movement in that direction. All, therefore, which the rebels in their divided councils were able to decide upon with certainty, was to move westward along the Border, a course which might advance them equally on their road, whether they should finally determine to take the route to the west of Scotland or to Lancashire. We must refer to a future part of this history for the progress and ultimate fate of this ill-starred expedition.

LXIX

Military Maneuvering

1715

WE must now return to the Earl of Mar's army, which must be considered as the centre and focus of the insurrection. Since his occupation of Perth, Lord Mar had undertaken little which had the appearance of military enterprise. His possession even of Fifeshire and Kinross had been in some degree contested by the supporters of Government. The Earl of Rothes, with a few dragoons and volunteers, had garrisoned his own house of Leslie, near Falkland, and was active in harassing those parties of horse which Mar sent into the country to proclaim James VIII., and levy the cess and public taxes. Upon one of these occasions (28th September) he surprised Sir Thomas Bruce, while in the act of making the proclamation in the town of Kinross, and carried him off a prisoner. The Earl of Rothes retained possession of his garrison till Mar's army became very strong, when he was obliged to withdraw it. But Mar continued to experience occasional checks, even in the military promenades in which he employed the gentlemen who composed his cavalry. It is true, these generally arose from nothing worse than the loose discipline observed by troops of this condition, their carelessness in mounting guards, or in other similar duties, to which their rank and habits of life had not accustomed them.

The only important manœuvre attempted by the Earl of Mar was the expedition across the firth under Brigadier MacIntosh, of which the details are given in the last chapter. Its consequences were such as to force the General himself into measures of immediate activity, by which he had not hitherto seemed much disposed to distinguish himself, but which became now inevitable.

It happened that, on the second day after MacIntosh's departure from Fife, a general review of the troops in Perth was held in the vicinity of that town, and the Earl Marischal's brother, James (afterwards the celebrated Field-Marshal Keith), galloped along the line, disseminating some of those favourable reports which were the growth of the day, and, as one succeeded as fast as another dropped, might be termed the fuel which supplied the fire of the insurrection, or rather, perhaps, the bellows which kept it in excitation. The apocryphal tidings of this day were, that Sir William Wyndham had surprised Bristol for King James III., and that Sir William Blacket had taken both Berwick and Newcastle—intelligence received by the hearers with acclamations, which, if it had been true, were no less than it deserved.

But from these visions the principal persons in the insurrection were soon recalled to sad realities. A meeting of the noblemen, chiefs of clans, and commanders of corps, was summoned, and particular care taken to exclude all intruders of inferior rank. To this sort of council of war Mar announced, with a dejected countenance, that Brigadier MacIntosh, having, contrary to his orders, thrown himself into the citadel of Leith, was invested there by the Duke of Argyle. He laid before them the letter he had received from the Brigadier, which stated that a few hours would determine his fate, but that he was determined to do his duty to the last. The writer expressed his apprehension that cannons and mortars were about to be brought against him. The Earl of Mar said that he gave the detachment up for lost, but suggested it might be possible to operate a diversion in its favour by making a feint towards Stirling. The proposal was seconded by General Hamilton, who said that such a movement might possibly do good, and could produce no harm.

The movement being determined upon, Max marched with a large body of foot to Auchterarder, and pushed two squadrons of horse as far forward as Dunblane, which had the appearance of a meditated attack upon Stirling. It is said to have been the opinion of General Hamilton that the foot should have taken possession of a defile which continues the road from the northern end of Stirling bridge through some low and marshy ground, and is called the Long Causeway. The rebels being in possession of this long and narrow pass, it would have been as difficult for the Duke of Argyle to have got at them as it was for them to reach him. And the necessity of guarding the bridge itself with the small force he possessed must have added to Argyle's difficulties, and afforded General Gordon and the western clans, who were by this time expected to be at Dumbarton, full opportunity to have advanced on Stirling by Drymen and the Loch of Monteith, keeping possession, during their whole march, of high and hilly grounds fit for the operations of Highlanders. In this manner the Duke of Argyle would have been placed between two fires, and must have run the greatest risk of being cut off from the reinforcements which he anxiously expected from Ireland, as well as from the west of Scotland.

Against this very simple and effective plan of the campaign Mar had nothing to object but the want of provisions; in itself a disgrace to a general who had been quartered so long in the neighbourhood of the Carse of Gowrie, and at the end of autumn, when the farmyards are full, without having secured a quantity of meal adequate to the maintenance of his army for a few days. General Hamilton combated this objection, and even demonstrated that provisions were to be had; and Mar apparently acquiesced in his reasoning. But having come with the infantry of his army as far as Ardoch, the Earl stopped short and refused to permit the movement on the Long Causeway to be made, alleging that Marischal and Linlithgow had decided against the design. It seems probable that, as the affair drew to a crisis, Mar, the more that military science was wanted, felt his own ignorance the more deeply, and, afraid to attempt any course by which he might have controlled circumstances, adopted every mode of postponing a decision, in the hope they might, of themselves, become favourable in the long run.

In the meantime the news of Mar's march to Auchterarder and Dunblane had, as we have elsewhere noticed, recalled the Duke of Argyle to his camp at Stirling, leaving a few of his cavalry, with the militia and volunteers, to deal with MacIntosh and his nimble Highlanders, who escaped out of their hands, first by their defence of Seaton and then by their march to Kelso. Argyle instantly took additional defensive measures against Mar, by barricading the bridge of Stirling and breaking down that which crosses the Teith at the village of Doune. But his presence so near his antagonist was sufficient to induce the Earl of Mar to retreat with his whole force to his former quarters at Perth and wait the progress of events.

These were now approaching to a crisis. With MacIntosh's detachment Mar had now no concern; they were to pursue their good or evil destiny apart. The Earl of Mar had also received a disagreeable hint that the excursions by which he used to supply himself with funds, as well as to keep up the terror of his arms, were not without inconvenience. A detachment of about fourscore horse and three hundred Highland foot, chiefly followers of the Marquis of Huntly, was sent to Dunfermline to raise the cess. The direct road from Perth to Dunfermline is considerably shorter, but the troops had orders to take the route by Castle-Campbell, which prolonged the journey considerably, for no apparent purpose save to insult the Duke of Argyle's garrison there, by marching in their view. When the detachment arrived at Dunfermline, Gordon of Glenbucket, who commanded the Highlanders, conducted them into the old abbey, which is strongly situated, and there placed a sentinel. He took up his own quarters in the town, and placed a sentinel there also. The commander of the horse, Major Graham, took the ineffectual precaution of doing the same at the bridge, but used no further means to avoid surprise. The gentlemen of the squadron sought each his personal accommodation, with their usual neglect of discipline, neither knowing with accuracy where they were to find their horses, nor fixing on any alarm-post where they were to rendezvous. Their officers sat down to a bottle of wine. During all this scene of confusion the Honourable Colonel (afterwards Lord) Cathcart was lying without the town with a strong party of cavalry, and obtaining regular information from his spies within it.

About five in the morning of the 24th of October he entered the town with two parties of his dragoons, one mounted and the other on foot. The surprisal was complete, and the Jacobite cavaliers suffered in proportion; several were killed and wounded, and about twenty made prisoners, whose loss was the more felt as they were all gentlemen, and some of them considerable proprietors. The assailants lost no time in their enterprise, and retreated as speedily as they entered. The neighbourhood of the Highland infantry in the Abbey was a strong reason for despatch. This slight affair seemed considerable in a war which had been as yet so little marked by military incident. The appearance of the prisoners at Stirling, and the list of their names, gave eclât to the Duke of Argyle's tactics, and threw disparagement on those of Mar. On the other side stories were circulated at Perth of the loss which Cathcart had sustained in the action, with rumours of men buried in the night, and horses returned to Stirling without their riders. This account, however fabulous, was received with credit even by those who were engaged at Dunfermline; for the confusion having been general, no one knew what was the fate of his comrade. But in very deed the whole return of casualties on Colonel Cathcart's side amounted to a dragoon hurt in the cheek and a horse wounded. This little affair was made the subject of songs and pasquils in the army at Perth, which increased the Marquis of Huntly's disgust at the enterprise.

By this time three regiments of infantry and Evans's dragoons had joined the Duke of Argyle, who now felt himself strong enough to make detachments without the fear of weakening his own position. A battalion of foot was sent to Kilsythe, along with a detachment of dragoons, who were to watch the motions of the troops of Forster and Kenmure, in case the whole, or any part of them, should resolve to penetrate into the west of Scotland.

The Earl of Mar was also on the point of being joined by the last reinforcements which he could expect, the non-arrival of which had hitherto been the cause, or at least the apology, for his inactivity. The various causes of delay had been at length removed in the following manner: Seaforth, it must be remembered, was confronted by Lord Sutherland with his own following, and the Whig clans of Grant, Munro, Ross, and others. But about the same time the Earl of Seaforth was joined by Sir Donald MacDonald of Skye, with seven hundred of his own clan, and as many MacKinnons, Chisholms, and others as raised the total number to about four thousand men. The Earl of Sutherland, finding this force so much stronger than what he was able to bring against it, retreated to the Bonar, a strait of the sea dividing Ross-shire from Sutherland, and there passed to his own side of the ferry. Seaforth, now unopposed, advanced to Inverness, and, after leaving a garrison there, marched to Perth to join the Earl of Mar, to whose insurrectionary army his troops made a formidable addition.

The clans of the West were the only reinforcements which Mar had now to expect; these were not only considerable from their numbers, but claimed a peculiar fame in arms even over the other Highlanders, both from their zeal for the Jacobite cause and their distinguished bravery. But Mar had clogged General Gordon, who was to bring up this part of his forces, with a commission which would detain him some time in Argyleshire. His instructions directed him especially to take and garrison the castle of Inverary, the principal seat of the Duke of Argyle. The clans, particularly those of Stewart of Appin and Cameron of Lochiel, though opposed to the Duke in political principles, respected his talents, and had a high regard for his person as an individual, and therefore felt reluctance at entering upon a personal quarrel with him by attacking his castle. These chiefs hung back accordingly, and delayed joining. When Glengarry and Clanranald had raised their clans, they had fewer scruples. During this time Campbell of Finab was entrusted with the difficult task of keeping the assailants in play until the Duke of Argyle should receive his expected reinforcements from Ireland. He was soon joined by the Earl of Islay, the Duke's younger brother. By the assistance of Sir James Campbell of Auchinbreck, about a thousand men were assembled to defend Inverary, when four or five thousand appeared in arms before it. A sort of treaty was entered into by which the insurgent clans agreed to withdraw from the country of Argyle; with which purpose, descending Strathfillan, they marched towards Castle-Drummond, which is in the vicinity of Perth, and within an easy march of Mar's headquarters.

One important member of the insurrection must also be mentioned. This was the Earl of Breadalbane, the same unrelenting statesman who was the author of the Massacre of Glencoe. He had been employed by King William in 1689 to achieve, by dint of money, the settlement and pacification of the Highlands; and now, in his old age, he imagined his interest lay in contributing to disturb them. When cited to appear at Edinburgh as a suspected person, he procured a pathetic attestation, under the hand of a physician and clergyman, in which the Earl was described as an infirm man, overwhelmed with all the evils that wait on old age. None of his infirmities, however, prevented him from attending the Earl of Mar's summons on the very day after the certificate is dated. Breadalbane is supposed to have received considerable sums of money from the Earl of Mar, who knew the only terms on which he could hope for his favour. But for a long time the wily Earl did nothing decisive, and it was believed that he entertained a purpose of going to Stirling and reconciling himself with the Duke of Argyle, the head of the elder branch of his house. This, however, Breadalbane did not do, but, on the contrary, appeared in the town of Perth, where the singular garb and peculiar manners of this extraordinary old chief attracted general attention. He possessed powers of satirical observation in no common degree, and seemed to laugh internally at whatever he saw which he considered as ridiculous, but without suffering his countenance to betray his sentiments, except to very close observers. Amidst the various difficulties of the insurgents, his only advice to them was, to procure a printing press and lose no time in issuing gazettes.

Mar took the hint, whether given in jest or earnest. He sent to Aberdeen for a printing press, in order to lose no time in diffusing intelligence more widely by that comprehensive organ of information. It was placed under the management of Robert Freebairn, one of the printers to the late Queen Anne, whose principles had led him to join the insurgent army. He was chiefly employed in extending by his art the delusions through means of which the insurrection had been originally excited, and was in a great measure kept afloat. It is a strong example of this, that while Mar actually knew nothing of the fate of Forster and Kenmure, with the auxiliary party of Highlanders under MacIntosh, yet it was boldly published that they were masters of Newcastle, and carried all before them; and that the Jacobites around London had taken arms in such numbers that King George had found it necessary to retire from the metropolis.

It does not appear that the Earl of Breadalbane was so frank in affording the rebels his military support, which was very extensive and powerful, as in imparting his advice how to make an impression on the public mind by means of the press. His own age excused him from taking the field; and it is probable his experience and sagacious observation discovered little in their counsels which promised a favourable result to their enterprise, though supported certainly by a very considerable force in arms. A body of his clan, about four or five hundred strong, commanded by the Earl's kinsman, Campbell of Glendarule, joined the force under General Gordon, but about four hundred, who had apparently engaged in the enterprise against Inverary, and were embodied for that purpose, dispersed, and returned to their own homes without joining Mar.

The whole force being now collected on both sides, it seemed inevitable that the clouds of civil war which had been so long lowering on the horizon, should now burst in storm and tempest on the devoted realm of Scotland.

LXX

The Cause of Mar

1715

I HAVE delayed till this point in the Scottish history some attempt to investigate the causes and conduct of the Rebellion, and to explain, if possible, the supineness of the insurgent general and chiefs, who, having engaged in an attempt so desperate, and raised forces so considerable, should yet, after the lapse of two months, have advanced little farther in their enterprise than they had done in the first week after its commencement.

If we review the Earl of Mar's conduct from beginning to end, we are led to the conclusion that the insurrection of 1715 was as hastily as rashly undertaken. It does not appear that Mar was in communication on the subject with the court of the Chevalier de St. George previous to Queen Anne's death. That event found him at liberty to recommend himself to the favour of King George, and show his influence with the Highland chiefs, by procuring an address of adhesion from them, of a tenor as loyal as his own. These offers of service being rejected, as we have already said, in a harsh and an affronting manner, made the fallen Minister conclude that his ruin was determined on; and his private resentment, which, in other circumstances, would have fallen to the ground ineffectual and harmless, lighted unhappily amongst those combustibles which the general adherence to the exiled family had prepared in Scotland.

When Mar arrived in Fifeshire from London, it was reported that he was possessed of £100,000 in money,—instructions from the Pretender, under his own hand, and a commission appointing him lieutenant-general, and commander-in-chief of his forces in Scotland. But though these rumours were scattered in the public ear, better accounts allege that in the commencement of the undertaking Mar did not pretend to assume any authority over the other noblemen of his own rank, or produce any other token from the Chevalier de St. George than his portrait. A good deal of pains were taken to parade a strong-box, said to enclose a considerable sum of money, belonging to the Earl of Mar; but it was not believed to contain treasure to the amount of more than £3000, if, indeed, it held so much. As to the important point of a general to command in chief, the scheme, when originally contemplated at the Court of St. Germains, turned upon the Duke of Ormond's landing in England, and the Duke of Berwick in Scotland, whose well-known talents were to direct the whole affair. After commencing his insurrection, there can be little doubt that Max did the utmost, by his agents in Lorraine, to engage the favourable opinion of the Chevalier; and the unexpected success of his enterprise, so far as it had gone, and the great power he had been able to assemble, were well calculated to recommend him to confidence. In the meantime, it was necessary there should be a general to execute the duties of the office *ad interim*. Mar offered, as I have told you, the command to the Duke of Athole, who refused to be connected with the affair. Huntly, from his power and rank in possession and expectation, might have claimed the supreme authority, but his religion was an obstacle. Seaforth lay distant, and was late in coming up. The claims of these great nobles being set aside, there was nothing so natural as that Mar himself should assume the command of an insurrection which would never have existed without his instigation. He was acceptable to the Highlanders, as having been the channel through which the bounty of the late Queen Anne had been transmitted to them; and had also partisans, from his liberality to certain of the Lowland nobles who had joined him, whose estates and revenues were not adequate to their rank, a circumstance which might be no small cause for their rushing into so ruinous an undertaking. Thus Mar assumed the general's truncheon which chance offered to his hand, because there was no other who could pretend to it.

Like most persons in his situation, he was not inclined to distrust his own capacity for using to advantage the power which he had almost fortuitously become possessed of; or, if he nourished any doubt upon this subject, he might consider his military charge to be but temporary, since, from the whole tenor of his conduct, it appears he expected from France some person whose trade had been war, and to whom he might with honour resign his office. Such an expectation may account for the care with which the Jacobite commander abstained from offensive operations, and for his anxious desire to augment his army to the highest point, rather than to adventure it upon the most promising enterprise.

It is probable Mar was encouraged to persevere in his military authority, in which he must have met with some embarrassment, when he found himself confirmed in it by Ogilvie of Boyne, an especial messenger from the Chevalier de St. George, who, greatly flattered by the favourable state of affairs in Scotland, conferred upon the Earl of Mar in form, that command which he had so long exercised in point of fact, and it was said, brought a patent, raising him to the dignity of Duke of Mar. Of the last honour little was known, but the commission of Mar as general was read at the head of every corps engaged in the insurrection.

It might be matter of wonder that the vessel which brought over Mr. Ogilvie, the bearer of this commission, had not been freighted with men, money, or provisions. The reason appears to have been that the Chevalier de St. George had previously expended all the funds he could himself command, or which he could borrow from foreign courts favourable to his title, in equipping a considerable number of vessels designed to sail from Havre-de-Grace and Dieppe, with large quantities of arms and ammunition. But the Earl of Stair, having speedily discovered the destination of these supplies, remonstrated with the Court of France upon proceedings so inconsistent with the treaty of Utrecht; and Sir George Byng, with a squadron of men-of-war, blockaded the ports of France, with the purpose of attacking the vessels if they should put to sea. The Regent Duke of Orleans immediately gave orders to the inspectors of naval affairs to prevent the arming and sailing of the vessels intended for the service of the Chevalier de St. George. Thus the supplies designed for the insurgents were intercepted, and the whole expense which had been laid out upon the projected expedition was entirely lost. This affords a satisfactory reason why the exiled Prince could send little to his partisans in Scotland, unless in the shape of fair words and commissions.

In the meantime the Earl of Mar, and the nobles and gentlemen embarked in his enterprise, although disappointed in these sanguine expectations under which it had been undertaken, and in finding that the death of Louis XIV., and the prudence of his successor in power, would deprive them of all hopes of foreign assistance, were yet desirous to receive that species of encouragement which might be derived from seeing the Chevalier de St. George himself at the head of the army, which they had drawn together in his name and quarrel. An address, therefore, was made to King James VIII., as he was termed, praying him to repair to Scotland, and to encourage, by his personal presence, the flame of loyalty, which was represented as breaking out in every part of that kingdom, pledging the lives and honour of the subscribers for his personal security, and insisting on the favourable effect likely to be produced upon their undertaking by his placing himself at its head. Another address was drawn up to the Regent Duke of Orleans, praying him, if he was not pleased to aid the heir of the House of Stewart at this crisis of his fate, that he would at least permit him to return to his own country, to share the fate of his trusty adherents, who were in arms in his behalf. This paper had rather an extraordinary turn, sounding as if the Chevalier de St. George had been in prison, and the Regent of France the keeper of the key. The addresses, however, were subscribed by all the men of quality at Perth, though great was the resentment of these proud hidalgos to find that the King's printer, Mr. Robert Freebairn, was permitted to sign along with them. The papers were, after having been signed, entrusted to the care of the Honourable Major Hay, having as his secretary the historian Dr. Abercromby,[1] with charge to wait upon the Chevalier at the court of Lorraine, or where he might happen to be, and urge the desire of the subscribers. The choice of the ambassador, and the secrecy which was observed on the subject of his commission, were regarded as deserving censure by those in the army who conceived that, the general welfare being concerned in the measures to be adopted, they had some right to be acquainted with the mode in which the negotiation was to proceed. Mar afterwards despatched two additional envoys on the same errand; the first was Sir Alexander Erskine of Alva, who was

---

[1] Author of *The Martial Achievements of the Scots Nation.*

wrecked on his return; the second, an agent of considerable acuteness, named Charles Forbes.

The Earl of Mar had not ascended to the pitch of power which he now enjoyed without experiencing the usual share of ill-will and unfavourable construction. The Master of Sinclair, a man of a temper equally shrewd and severe, had from the beginning shown himself dissatisfied with the management of the insurrection, and appears, like many men of the same disposition, to have been much more ready to remark and censure errors than to assist in retrieving them. The Earl of Huntly seems also to have been disobliged by Mar, and to have looked on him with dislike or suspicion; nor were the Highlanders entirely disposed to trust him as their general. When Glengarry, one of their ablest chiefs, joined the army at Perth, he was anxious that the western clans should keep separate from those first assembled at Perth, and act in conjunction with the forces of the Earl of Huntly; and it was proposed to Sinclair to join in this sort of association, by which the army would in fact have been effectually separated into two parts. Glengarry, however, was dissuaded from this secession; and although it is intimated, that in order to induce him to abandon his design the arguments arising from good cheer and good fellowship were freely resorted to, it is not the less true that his returning to the duty of a soldier was an act of sober reason.

The Earl of Mar, amidst his other duties, having a wish to prepare a place of arms for the residence of the Chevalier de St. George on his expected arrival, made an attempt to cover Perth by fortifications, so as to place it out of danger from a coup-de-main. General Hamilton attended to this duty for a short time; but afterwards it was almost entirely given up to the direction of a Frenchman, who had been a dancing and fencing master, and whose lines of defence furnished much amusement to the English engineers, who afterwards became possessed of them.

Before resuming the narrative, I may tell you that in this same eventful month of October, when there were so many military movements in Scotland, the Duke of Ormond was despatched by the Chevalier de St. George, with arms and ammunition, and directions to land on the coast of England. Three cannon were fired as a signal to the Jacobites, who were expected to flock in numbers to the shore, the name of Ormond being then most popular among them. But the signals not being answered, the vessel bore off, and returned to France.

Had the Duke landed, the Jacobite party would have been in the singular predicament of having a general in England without an army, and an army in Scotland without an effective general.

We now approach the catastrophe of these intestine commotions; for the Earl of Mar had by the beginning of November received all the reinforcements which he had to expect, though it may be doubted whether he had rendered his task of forcing or turning the Duke of Argyle's position more easy, or his own army much stronger, by the time he had spent in inactivity. His numbers were indeed augmented, but so were those of the Duke, so that the armies bore the some proportion to each other as before. This was a disadvantage to the Highlanders; for where a contest is to take place betwixt undisciplined energy and the steadiness of regular troops, the latter must always attain superiority in proportion as their numbers in the field increase, and render the day likely to be decided by manœuvres. Besides this, the army of Mar sustained a very great loss by desertion during the time he lay at Perth. The Highlanders, with the impatience and indolence of a half-civilised people, grew weary alike of remaining idle and of being employed in the labour of fortification, or the dull details of ordinary parade exercise. Many also went home for the purpose of placing in safety their accumulation of pay, and what booty they had been able to find in the Lowlands. Such desertions were deemed by the clans to be perfectly in rule, and even the authority of the chiefs was inadequate to prevent them.

Neither do the plans of the Earl of Mar seem to have been more distinctly settled, when he finally determined on the important step of making a movement in advance. It seems to have been given out that he was to make three feigned attacks upon the Duke's army at one and the same time—namely, one upon the Long Causeway and Stirling bridge; another at the Abbey ford, a mile below Stirling; and a third at the Drip-coble, a ford a mile and a half above that town. By appearing on so many points at once, Mar might hope to occupy the Duke's attention so effectually, as to cross the river with his main body at the fords of Forth. But, as the Duke of Argyle did not give his opponent time to make these movements, it cannot be known whether Mar actually contemplated them.

It is, however, certain that the Earl of Mar entertained the general purpose of reaching, if possible, the fords of Forth, where that river issues out of Lochard, and thus passing over to the southern side. To reach this part of the river required a march of two days through a hilly and barren country. Nor were Mar and his advisers well acquainted with the road, and they had no other guide but the celebrated free-booter, Rob Roy MacGregor, who they themselves said was not to be trusted, and who, in point of fact, was in constant communication with his patron, the Duke of Argyle, to whom he sent intelligence of Mar's motions.[1] It was said, too, that this outlaw only knew the fords from having passed them with Highland cattle—a different thing certainly, from being acquainted with them in a military point of view. It was probably, however, with a view to the information which Rob Roy could give on this point, that Mar, in a letter of the 4th of November, complains of that celebrated outlaw for not having come to Perth, where he wished much to have a meeting with him.

But if Mar and his military council had known the fords of Forth accurately, still it was doubtful in what situation they might find the passes when they arrived there. They might have been fortified and defended by the Duke of Argyle, or a detachment of his army; or they might be impassable at this advanced season of the year, for they are at all times of a deep and impracticable character. Last of all, before they could reach the heads of the Forth, Mar and his army must have found the means of crossing the Teith, a river almost as large and deep as the Forth itself, on which Argyle had destroyed the bridge of Doune, which afforded the usual means of passage.

Such were the difficulties in the way of the insurgents; and they are of a kind which argues a great want of intelligence in a camp which must have contained many persons from Menteith and Lennox, well acquainted with the country through which the Highland army were to pass, and who might have reconnoitred it effectually, notwithstand-ing the small garrisons of west country militia and volunteers, which the Duke had placed in Gartartan, and other houses of strength in the neighbourhood of Aberfoyle. But it was not the will of Heaven that the insurgents should ever march far enough on their expedition to experi-ence inconveniences from the difficulties we have pointed out; for the

---

[1] "The period of the Rebellion approached soon after Rob Roy had attained celebrity. His Jacobite partialities were now placed in opposition to his sense of the obligations which he owed to the indirect protection of the Duke of Argyle. But the desire of 'drowning his sounding steps amid the din of general war' induced him to join the forces of the Earl of Mar, although his patron, the Duke of Argyle, was at the head of the army opposed to the Highland insurgents."—*Introduction to Rob Roy*.

Duke of Argyle, though far inferior in force, adopted the soldier-like resolution of drawing out such strength as he had, and interrupting the march of the insurgents by fighting them, before they should have an opportunity of descending upon the Forth. For this purpose, he called in all his garrisons and outposts, and having mustered a main body of not quite four thousand men, he marched from Stirling towards Dunblane on the morning of Saturday the 12th of November.

On the 10th of November the Earl of Mar had broken up from his quarters at Perth, and advanced to Auchterarder, where the infantry were quartered, while the cavalry found accommodation in the vicinity.

But, during that night, the Highland army suffered in its nominal strength by two considerable desertions. The one was that of the whole clan of Fraser, amounting to four hundred men. They had joined Mar's army very recently, under Fraser of Fraserdale, who had married the heiress of their late chieftain. Just at this crisis, however, the heir-male of the family, the celebrated Fraser of Lovat, arrived in the north, and recalled by his mandate the clan of Fraser from the standards of King James VIII. to transfer them to those of George I. The Frasers, deeming their duty to their chief paramount to that which they owed to either monarch, and recognising the right of the male-heir to command them in preference to that of the husband of the heir-female, unanimously obeyed the summons of the former, and left the camp, army, and cause in which they were engaged. There will be occasion to mention more of the Frasers hereafter.

The other desertion was that of two hundred of the Earl of Huntly's Highland followers, who complained of having been unjustly overburdened with what is called fatigue-duty. Thus diminished, the army, after having been reviewed by their general, marched off their ground in the following order: The Master of Sinclair with the Fifeshire squadron, and two squadrons of Huntly's cavalry, formed the advance of the whole. The western clans followed, being, first, the MacDonalds, under their different chiefs of Clan Ranald, Glengarry, Sir Donald MacDonald, Keppoch, and Glencoe. The next were Breadalbane's men, with five regiments, consisting of the following clans—the MacLeans, under Sir John MacLean, their chief; the Camerons, under Lochiel; the Stewarts, commanded by Appin; and those who remained of Huntly's followers from Strathdon and Glenlivet, under Gordon of Glenbucket. This chosen body of Highlanders were in high spirits, and so confident of success that they boasted that their division of Mar's army only would be more than enough to deal with the Duke of Argyle and all the force be commanded. General Gordon was commander of the whole Highland vanguard.

The rest of the army, commanded by Mar in person, with the assistance of General Hamilton, followed the advanced division; and it was settled that the rearguard should march only as far as Ardoch, while the vanguard should push forward as far as the town of Dunblane, where they had quartered on their former march from Perth, eight miles to the west of Ardoch where the rear was to halt.

The horse, at the head of the first column, were advancing according to their orders, when a lame boy, running as fast as his infirmity would permit him, stated to the Master of Sinclair, who commanded the advance, that he was sent by the wife of the Laird of Kippendavie, whose husband was in the Jacobite army, to tell the Earl of Mar that the Duke of Argyle was in the act of marching through Dunblane. The news, though the appearance of the messenger excited some doubt, was entitled to be treated with respect. A reconnoitring party was sent forward, an express was despatched to Mar, who was six or seven miles in the rear, and General Gordon anxiously looked around him to find some strong ground on which to post the men. The river Allan lay in their front, and the Master of Sinclair proposed pushing across, and taking possession of some farmhouses, visible on the opposite side, where the gentlemen might find refreshment and the horses forage. But General Gordon justly thought that the passing a river at nightfall was a bad preparation for a body of infantry, who were to lie out till morning in the open air, in a hard frost, in the middle of November. At length the dispute was terminated on two farmhouses being discovered on the left side of the river, where the horse obtained some accommodation, though in a situation in which they might have been destroyed by a sudden attack, before they could have got out of the enclosures, among which they were penned up like cattle rather than quartered like soldiers. To guard against such a catastrophe, General Gordon posted advanced guards and videttes, and sent out patrols with the usual military precautions. Soon after they had taken their quarters for the night, Lord Southesk and the Angusshire cavalry came up, with the intelligence that Mar and the whole main body were following, and the Earl accordingly appeared at the bivouac of the vanguard about nine o'clock at night.

Fresh intelligence came to them from Lady Kippendavie, who seems to have been as correct in her intelligence and accurate in communicating with the insurgent army as she was singular in her choice of messengers, this last being an old woman, who confirmed the tidings of the enemy's approach. The reconnoitring parties sent forward by Sinclair came in with news to the same purpose.

The whole of Mar's army being now collected together within a very narrow circumference, slept on their arms, and wrapped in their plaids, feeling less inconvenience from the weather, which was a severe frost, than would probably have been experienced by any other forces in Europe.

By daybreak, on Sunday, 13th November, the insurgent army drew up in two lines of battle, on the plain above the place where they had spent the night. They had not long assumed this posture when they perceived a strong squadron of horse upon an eminence to the south of their lines. This was the Duke of Argyle, who, with some general officers, had taken this post in advance, for the purpose of reconnoitring the enemy's position and proceedings. In this he succeeded but imperfectly, on account of the swells and hollows which lay between him and Mar's army.

In the meantime, Mar, after satisfying himself that he was in presence of the enemy, called a council of his nobles, general officers, chiefs of clans, and commanders of corps. He is allowed on this occasion to have made them a most animating speech. It sunk, in part, upon unwilling ears, for there were already several persons of consequence, among whom Huntly and Sinclair seem to have been the leaders, who, despairing of the cause in which they were engaged, were desirous to open a communication with the Duke of Argyle, in order to learn whether he had power to receive their submission and admit them to pardon on their former footing of living quietly under Government. This, however, was only whispered among themselves; for even those who entertained such opinions were at the same time conscious that the crisis was come, in which they must fight for peace sword-in-hand, and that, by gaining a victory, they might dictate honourable terms; while, if they attempted a retreat, they would be no longer able to keep their Highland levies together, or to open a negotiation with the air of strength absolutely necessary to command a tolerable capitulation.

When, therefore, the Earl of Mar reminded his military auditors of the injustice done to the Royal family, and the oppression of Scotland under the English yoke, and conjured them not to let slip the opportunity which they had so long languished for, but instantly attack the enemy with that spirit which their cause and their wrongs were calculated to inspire, his words awakened a corresponding energy in the bearers. The Earl of Huntly only asked, whether a battle won would, in their present circumstances, place their rights and those of their country within their reach? or whether there was any hope of foreign aid to enable them to withstand the arms of England and her allies? "All this," he said, "my Lord of Mar could doubtless inform them of, since he had lately received a letter from Lord Bolingbroke, which he desired might be laid before the council."

The critical circumstances of the moment, and the enthusiasm which had been excited in the assembly, enabled Mar to dispense with attending to questions which he might have found it difficult to answer. Gliding over the interruption given by Huntly, he stated to the council the question, in the words, "Fight or not?" The chiefs, nobles, and officers, answered with a universal shout of "Fight;" and their resolution reaching the two lines, as they stood drawn up in order of battle, was welcomed with loud huzzas, tossing up of hats and bonnets, and a cheerfulness, which seemed even to those who had been before uncertain and doubtful of the issue a sure presage of speedy victory.

In this state of excited feeling the army of Mar advanced towards the enemy. The two lines in which they stood upon the moor were broken up each into two columns, so that it was in four columns that they pursued the order of their march, descending the hill which they had first occupied, crossing a morass, which the hard frost of the night before had rendered passable for cavalry as well as infantry, and ascending the opposite height, from which the Duke of Argyle was observing their movements. The Duke, on his part, as soon as he saw the extremity of Mar's wing wheel to the right, in order to make the movement we have described, immediately comprehended that their purpose was to avail themselves of their superiority of numbers, and attack his small force at once on the left flank and in front. He rode hastily down the eminence, at the foot of which his force was drawn up, in order at once to get them into such a disposition as might disappoint the object of the enemy, and to lead his troops up the hill. He drew up his little army of about four thousand men, extending his disposition considerably to the right, placing three squadrons of horse on that wing, and as many on the left of his front line; the centre being

composed of six battalions of foot. Each wing of horse was supported
by a squadron of dragoons. The second line was composed of two battalions in the centre, with a squadron of dragoons on either wing. In
this order, and having his right considerably advanced against the
enemy's left, so as to admit of his withdrawing his own left wing from a
flank attack, the Duke ascended the hill, seeing nothing of the enemy,
who had left the high grounds and were advancing to meet him on the
other side of the same height which he was in the act of mounting. The
Highlanders, as has been already stated, advanced in four columns,
marching by their right.

Each column of infantry, four in number, was closed by a body of
cavalry, which, when the column should deploy into line, were to take
up their ground on the flank. The Highlanders marched, or rather ran,
with such eagerness towards the enemy, that the horse were kept at the
gallop in the rear. Both armies were thus ascending the hill in column,
and met, as it were unexpectedly upon the top, being in some points
within pistol-shot before they were aware of each other's presence.
Both, therefore, endeavoured at the same time to form line-of-battle,
and some confusion occurred on either side. In particular, two
squadrons of the insurgent cavalry were placed in the centre of the
right wing, instead of being stationed on the flank, as had been
intended, and as the rules of war required. This discovery, however,
was of much less consequence to the Highlanders, whose terrors consisted in the headlong fury of the onset, whilst the strength of the regulars depended on the steadiness of their discipline.

It was at this moment that an old chief, impatient for the command to charge, and seeing the English soldiers getting into order,
became enraged at seeing the favourable minute pass away, and made
the memorable exclamation, "Oh, for one hour of Dundee!"

The Duke's left wing was commanded by General Whitham, who
does not appear to have been distinguished either for courage or conduct. The right of Mar's line was hastily formed, consisting of the
western clans, MacDonalds, MacLeans, and the followers of Breadalbane, when old Captain Livingstone rode up, a veteran soldier, who
had served in King James's army before the Revolution, and with several oaths called to General Gordon, who commanded the right wing,
instantly to attack. The General hesitated, but the chiefs and clans
caught the enthusiasm of the moment. A gentleman, named
MacLean, who lived to a great age, thus described the attack of his

own tribe, and there can be no doubt that the general onset was made under similar circumstances: When his clan was drawn up in deep order, the best born, bravest, and best armed of the warriors in front,[1] Sir John MacLean placed himself at their head, and said, with a loud voice, "Gentlemen, this is a day we have long wished to see. Yonder stands MacCallanmore for King George—Here stands MacLean for King James—God bless MacLean and King James!— Charge, gentlemen!"

The clan then muttered a very brief prayer, fixed the bonnet firm on the head, stripped off their plaids, which then comprehended the philabeg also,[2] and rushed on the enemy, firing their fusees irregularly, then dropping them, and drawing their swords, and uniting in one wild yell, when they mingled among the bayonets. The regular troops on the left received this fierce onset of the mountaineers with a heavy fire, which did considerable execution. Among others who dropped was the gallant young chief of Clan Ranald, mortally wounded. His fall checked for an instant the impetuosity of his followers, when Glengarry, so often mentioned, started from the ranks, waved his bonnet around his head, exclaiming, "Revenge, revenge! to-day for revenge, and to-morrow for mourning!" The Highlanders, resuming the fury of their attack, mingled with the regulars, forced their line in every direction, broke through them and dispersed them, making great slaughter among men less active than themselves, and loaded with an unwieldy musket, which in individual or irregular strife has scarce ever been found a match for the broadsword. The extreme left of Argyle's army was thus routed with considerable slaughter, for the Highlanders gave no quarter; but the troops of the centre, under General Wightman, remained unbroken; and it would seem to have been the business of the rebel cavalry to have charged them in the flank or rear, exposed as they must have been by the flight of Whitham and the left wing. Of their cavalry, however, two squadrons, commanded

---

[1] The very existence of this regiment was an instance of the tenacity of clan attachment. The lands on which they lived in the isle of Mull were become the property of the Duke of Argyle, and their chief resided for the most part in France, on an allowance which Queen Anne had assigned him; yet he found no difficulty in raising seven or eight hundred men in opposition to their actual landlord; so inferior was the feudal claim to the patriarchal.

[2] The Highlanders wore long shirts, which were disposed in a particular manner on such occasions.

by Drummond and Marischal, went off in pursuit of those whom the Highlanders had scattered; while Lord Huntlys and that of Fife, under the Master of Sinclair, remained inactive on the field of battle, without engaging at all. It would seem that they were kept in check by the dragoons of Argyle's second line, who did not fly like the first, but made an orderly retreat in the face of the enemy.

On the right wing and centre, the event of the battle was very different. The attack of the Highlanders was as furious as on their right. But their opponents, though a little staggered, stood their ground with admirable resolution, and the Duke of Argyle detached Colonel Cathcart, with a body of horse, to cross a morass, which the frost had rendered passable, and attack the Highlanders on the flank as they advanced to the charge. In this manner their rapid assault was checked and baffled; and although the Camerons, Stewarts, and other clans of high reputation, formed the left wing of Mar's army, yet that, and his whole second line, were put to flight by the masterly movement of the Duke of Argyle, and the steadiness of the troops he commanded. But his situation was very perilous; for, as the fugitives consisted of five thousand men, there was every prospect of their rallying and destroying the Duke's small body, consisting only of five squadrons of horse, supported by Wightman, with three battalions of infantry, who had lately composed the centre of the army. Argyle took the bold determination to press on the fugitives with his utmost vigour, and succeeded in driving them back to the river Allan, where they had quartered the night before. The fugitives made frequent halts, and were as often again attacked and broken. This was particularly remarked of the body of horse who carried James's standard, and was called the Restoration squadron. The gentlemen composing it made repeated and vigorous attacks, in which they were only broken and borne down by the superior weight of the English cavalry. It was in one of these reiterated charges that the gallant young Earl of Strathmore lost his life, while in vain attempting to rally his Angusshire regiment. He was slain by a private dragoon, after having had quarter given to him. The Earl of Panmure was also wounded and made prisoner by the Royalists, but was rescued by his brother, Mr. Henry Maule.

The field of battle now presented a singular appearance, for the left of both armies were broken and flying, the right of both victorious and in pursuit. But the events of war are of less consequence than the use which is made of them. It does not appear that any attempt was made on the part of Mar to avail himself of his success on the right. General Whitham had indeed resigned the field of battle to his opponents, and from thence fled almost to Stirling bridge. The victorious Highlanders did not take the trouble to pursue them, but having marched across the scene of action, drew up on an eminence, called the Stony Hill of Kippendavie, where they stood in groups with their drawn swords in their hands. One cause of their inactivity at this critical moment may be attributed to their having dropped their firearms, according to their fashion when about to charge; another, certainly, was the want of active aides-de-camp to transmit orders; and a third, the character of the Highlanders, who are not always disposed to obedience. This much is certain, that had their victorious right wing pursued in the Duke of Argyle's rear when he advanced towards the river Allan, they must have placed him in the greatest danger, since his utmost exertion was scarce equal to keep the multitude before him in full retreat. It is also stated that some of the Highlanders showed an unwillingness to fight. This is alleged to have been particularly the case with the celebrated Rob Roy, a dependant, it will be observed, of the Duke of Argyle's, and in the habit, during the whole insurrection, of furnishing him with intelligence from the enemy's camp. A strong party of MacGregors and MacPhersons were under the command of this outlaw, who, when ordered to charge, answered coolly, "If they cannot do it without me, they cannot do it with me." It is said that a bold man of the Clan Vourigh, called Alister MacPherson, who followed Rob Roy's original profession of a drover, impatient at the inactivity in which they were detained, threw off his plaid, drew his sword, and called on the MacPhersons to follow. "Hold, Sandie," said Rob Roy; "were the question about a drove of sheep you might know something; but as it concerns the leading of men, it is for me to decide."—"Were the question about a drove of Glen-Angus wethers," retorted the MacPherson, "the question with you, Rob, would not be who should be last but who should be first." This had almost produced a battle betwixt the two champions: but in the meantime the opportunity of advancing was lost.[1]

The Duke of Argyle having returned back from his pursuit of the enemy's left wing, came in contact with their right, which, victorious as

---

[1] "Rob did not, however, neglect his own private interest on the occasion. In the confusion of an undecided field of battle he enriched his followers by plundering the baggage

we have intimated, was drawn up on the hill of Kippendavie. Mutual menaces of attack took place, but the combat was renewed on neither side. Both armies showed a disposition to retreat, and Mar, abandoning a part of his artillery, drew back to Auchterarder, and from thence retired to Perth. Both generals claimed the victory, but as Mar abandoned from that day all thoughts of a movement to the westward, his object must be considered as having been completely defeated; while Argyle attained the fruits of victory in retaining the position by which he defended the Lowlands, and barred against the insurgents every avenue by which they could enter them.

The numbers slain in the battle of Sheriffmuir were considerable. Seven or eight hundred were killed on the side of the rebels, and the Royalists must have lost five or six hundred. Much noble and gentle blood was mixed with that of the vulgar. A troop of volunteers, about sixty in number, comprehending the Dukes of Douglas and Roxburgh, the Earls of Haddington, Lauderdale, Loudon, Belhaven, and Rothes, fought bravely, though the policy of risking such a *troupe dorée* might be questionable. At all events, it marked a great change of times, when the Duke of Douglas, whose ancestors could have raised an army as numerous as those of both sides in the field of Sheriffmuir, fought as a private trooper, assisted only by two or three servants. This body of volunteers behaved in a manner becoming their rank. Many of them were wounded, and the Earl of Forfar was slain.

The loss of the Earl of Strathmore and of the young Clan Ranald was a severe blow to the Insurrection. The last was a complete soldier, trained in the French Guards, and full of zeal for the cause of James. "My family," he replied to Mar's summons to join him, "have been on such occasions ever wont to be the first on the field and the last to leave it." When he fell out of the ranks, mortally wounded, Mar met him, and, ignorant of what had happened, demanded why he was not in the front. "I have had my share," said the dying chief and fell dead

---

and the dead on both sides. The fine old satirical ballad on the battle of Sheriffmuir does not forget to stigmatise our hero's conduct on this memorable occasion.

"'Rob Roy he stood watch
On a hill for to catch
The booty, for aught that I saw, man;
For he ne'er advanc'd
From the place he was stanc'd
Till nae mair was to do there at a', man.'"

Introduction to Rob Roy.

before his commander. Many of his men retired from the army in consequence of his death.

Thus began and thus ended a confused affray, of which a contemporary ballad-maker truly says, "there is nothing certain, except that there was actually a battle, which he witnessed."[1]

---

[1] "There's some say that we wan,
　Some say that they wan,
　Some say that nane wan at a', man;
　But ae thing I'm sure,
　That at Sheriffmuir,
　A battle there was which I saw, man;
　And we ran, and they ran."

LXXI

The Demise of the Jacobites

1715-1716

THE confused battle of Sheriffmuir being ended by the approach of night, both parties had time to count what they had lost and won in the course of the day. That of the insurgents was easily summed up. The Highlanders, on their right, had behaved with their usual courage, and maintained the reputation which they had acquired of old times under Montrose, and more lately when commanded by Dundee. But in every other particular the events of the battle were unfavourable to the insurgents. A great many of their best men had retired without leave, as was their invariable practice, to see their families, or to secure their small stock of booty, which some of them had augmented by plundering the baggage of their own army. This desertion thinned the ranks even of those clans who had been victorious, and the Highlanders of the vanquished division of the army had much better reasons for following the example thus set. Their numbers that morning had been from eight to ten thousand men; and at the close of the day about four thousand of them were missing. Some leaders, too, of high rank and quality, had graced the retreat by their example; and it was said of Huntly and Seaforth in particular, that they were the first fugitives of any rank or condition who reached Perth, and discouraged their numerous followers by their retreat from the field of action. It was therefore in vain for the insurgents, under this state of diminution and discouragement, to abide a second battle, or endeavour to renew the attempt to pass the Forth, which they had not been able to accomplish with double their now reduced numbers.

> And they ran, and we ran,
>   and we ran, and they ran away, man.
>   * * * * * *
> So there such a race was,
>   As ne'er in that place was,
> And as little chase was at a', man;
>   Frae ither they ran
> Without touk o' drum,
>   They did not make use o' a paw, man."

But besides the effects of desertion, the insurgent army had other difficulties to contend with. The improvidence of their leaders had been so unpardonably great, that they had set out from one of the most fertile to a comparatively barren district of Scotland, with provisions for two or three days only, and their ammunition was proportionally scanty. It was therefore evident that they were in no condition to renew the attempt in which they had that morning miscarried; nor had Mar any alternative, save that of leading back his army to their old quarters at Perth, to wait until some unexpected event should give them spirits for a fresh effort. Accordingly, as already mentioned, having passed the night after the action among the enclosures of Auchterarder, he returned towards Perth the next morning. The Duke of Argyle, on the other hand, having fallen back on Dunblane, with the troops he himself commanded, and, rejoined by such of the fugitives of the left wing as could be collected, he lay on his arms all night, expecting to renew the action on the succeeding day.

On approaching the field of battle on Monday, the 14th of November, at break of day, Argyle found it abandoned by the enemy, who had left their dead and wounded at his disposal, together with the honours of the field, amongst which the principal trophies were fourteen colours or standards, and six pieces, of field cannon, which Mar had brought to the field in a useless bravado, since he had neither ammunition nor men to serve them, and which he had found himself unable to remove. Amongst the gentlemen who fell on this occasion were several on both sides alike eminent for birth and character. The body of the gallant young Earl of Strathmore was found on the field, watched by a faithful old domestic, who, being asked the name of the person whose body he waited upon with so much care, made this striking reply, "He was a man yesterday."[1]

The Earl of Mar had endeavoured to pave the way for a triumphant return to Perth, by a species of Gazette, in which he claimed the victory on the right and centre, and affirmed that had the left wing and the second line behaved as his right and the rest of the first line did, the victory had been complete. But he could not again excite the enthusiasm of his followers, many of whom began now in earnest to despair of their situation, the large odds of numbers which they possessed in the field of Sheriffmuir having been unable to secure them a decided victory.

Many rumours were in the meantime spread among the insurgents, concerning successes which were reported to have been obtained by Forster and his troops over General Carpenter in England, and bonfires and rejoicings were made for these supposed victories, at a time when, in fact, Forster and Kenmure were totally defeated, their soldiers dispersed, and themselves prisoners.

You must not forget that the force of General Forster consisted of the troops of horse levied on the Northumberland frontier by the Earl of Derwentwater and others, joined with the gentlemen of Galloway and Dumfriesshire under Lord Kenmure, and the Lothian Jacobites under the Earl of Winton, composing altogether a body of five or six hundred horse, to whom must be added about fourteen hundred Highlanders, being those sent across the firth by the Earl of Mar, under command of MacIntosh of Borlum. You must also recollect that in this little army there were great differences of opinion as to the route which they were to pursue. The English gentlemen persisted in the delusion that they had only to show themselves in the west of England in order to draw the whole country to their standard, while the Scots, both the

---

[1] Compare the finding the body of Sir John Swinton, in the dramatic sketch of Halidon Hill.

"*Edward.*—Where is he?

Chandos.—Here lies the giant! Say his name, young Knight?

Gordon.—Let it suffice, he was a man this morning."

Act II. Scene III.

Lowland gentlemen and Highlanders, desired to march upon Dumfries, and, after taking possession of that town, proceed to the west of Scotland, and force open a communication betwixt their force and the main army under Mar, by which they reasonably hoped to dislodge Argyle from his post at Stirling.

Unfixed which course to pursue, and threatened by General Carpenter, who moved against them from Newcastle towards Kelso, at the head of a thousand horse, the insurgents left the latter town, where they had been joined by the Brigadier MacIntosh, and marched to Jedburgh, not without one or two false alarms. They had, however, the advantage of outstripping General Carpenter, and the English gentlemen became still more impatient to return into their own country and raise the Jacobites of the west. The Highlanders, learning that such a plan was at last adopted, separated themselves from the horse as soon as the march began, and drawing up on a moor above the town of Hawick, declared that if the insurgents proposed to march against the enemy they would fight it out to the last, but that they would not go into England to be kidnapped and made slaves of, as their ancestors were in Cromwell's time. And when the horse drew up, as if for the purpose of attack, the Highlanders cocked their pieces and prepared for action, saying, that if they must needs be made a sacrifice, they would prefer their own country as the scene of their death. The discontented mountaineers would listen to no one save the Earl of Winton, who joined them in desiring to march westward to the assistance of the Earl of Mar; to whom, indeed, by preventing Argyle from concentrating his forces, they might have done excellent service, for the Duke could never have recalled a regiment of horse which he had at Kilsyth, had the southern insurgents threatened that post. The Highlanders were at length put in motion, under a declaration that they would abide with the army while they remained in Scotland, but should they enter England they would return back.

In the meantime the citizens of the town of Dumfries saw themselves again threatened by the rebel forces, and assuming an attitude of resistance, marched out to occupy a position in front of the place, on which they threw up some hasty fortifications. At the same time they received intelligence from General Carpenter, who had now reached Jedburgh, that if they could but defend themselves for six hours he would within that time attack the rear of the enemy.

The news that the Dumfries citizens intended to defend their town, which lay in front, while Carpenter was prepared to operate in the rear of the rebels, induced Mr. Forster and his friends to renew with great urgency their proposal of entering England, affirming to their northern associates that they were possessed of letters of advice assuring them of a general insurrection. The Scots, worn out with the perseverance of their English associates, and unable to believe that men would have deceived themselves or others by illusory hopes, when engaged in such a momentous undertaking, at length yielded to their remonstrances. Accordingly, having reached Ecclefechan on their way to Dumfries, the English counsels prevailed, and the insurgents halted at the former village, turned south, and directed their march on Langholm, with the design of making for the west of England.

The Earl of Winton dissented so widely from the general resolution, that he left the army with a considerable part of his troop, and it seemed for a time as if he had renounced the undertaking entirely. Ashamed, however, to break off abruptly from a cause which he had embraced from motives of duty and conscience, he changed his purpose, and again joined the main body. But though this unfortunate young nobleman returned to the fatal standard, it was remarked that from this time he ceased to take any interest in the debates or deliberations of his party, but seized with a kind of reckless levity upon such idle opportunities of amusement as chance threw in his way, in a manner scarce resembling one engaged in an important and perilous enterprise.[1]

The Highlanders were again divided from their confederates in their opinion respecting the alteration of the line of march, and the object of their expedition. Many agreed to march into England. Others, to the number of four hundred, broke away entirely from their companions, with the purpose of returning to their mountains through the western districts and by the heads of the Forth. They might have accomplished this but for the difficulty of finding provisions, which obliged them to separate into small parties, several of which were made prisoners by the peasantry, who in that country were chiefly Cameronians, and accustomed to the use of arms.

---

[1] 'He was never again invited to their council of war, and was otherwise treated with marked disrespect. These slights gave the Earl but little trouble; he continued to amuse himself with such company as chance threw in his way, and entertained them with stories of his travels and adventures in low life.'

The rest of the army, diminished by this desertion, proceeded to Brampton, near Carlisle, where Mr. Forster, producing his commission to that effect, was recognised as General of King James's forces in England. It is possible that the desire to obtain the supreme command of the army might have made this gentleman the more anxious for having the march directed on his native country; and his first exploit in his new capacity seemed to give a lustre to his undertaking, although the success was more owing to the fears of the opposite party than to any particular display of courage on the part of the Jacobite general and his little army.

It must be observed that the horse-militia of Westmoreland, and of the northern parts of Lancashire, had been drawn out to oppose the rebels; and now the *posse comitatus* of Cumberland, amounting to twelve thousand men, were assembled along with them at Penrith, by summons from Lord Lonsdale, sheriff of the county. But being a mere undisciplined mob, ill-armed, and worse arrayed, they did not wait for an attack either from the cavalry or the Highlanders, but dispersed in every direction, leaving to the victors the field of battle, covered with arms, and a considerable number of horses. Lonsdale, deserted by every one save about twenty of his own servants, was obliged to make his escape, and found shelter in the old castle of Appleby.

In marching through Cumberland and Westmoreland, there was little seen of that enthusiasm in the Jacobite cause which the English officers had taught their associates to expect. Manchester was on this, as upon a later occasion, the first town where the inhabitants seemed disposed to embark in the insurrection, and form a company for that purpose. Intimation of their friendly disposition reached the insurgents at Lancaster, and encouraged them to advance. It was, indeed, time that their friends should join them, for they had daily news of troops marching to oppose and surround them. On their side they resolved to extend themselves, the more easily to gather fresh forces; and having moved from Lancaster to Preston, they resolved to possess themselves of Warrington bridge, with a view to securing Liverpool.

While they were scheming an attack on this celebrated seaport, which its citizens were preparing to defend with much vigour, the Government forces, which had assembled around them, were advancing upon them on several quarters.

It seems strange, that while possessing a strong party of friends in the country, being a very large proportion of the landed gentry, with a

considerable proportion of the populace, the insurgents should nevertheless have suffered themselves to be so completely surprised. But the
spirit of delusion which possessed the whole party, and pervaded all
their proceedings, was as remarkable here as on other occasions. While
Forster and his companions were thinking of extending the fire of
insurrection to Manchester and Liverpool, General Willis, who commanded in Cheshire for King George, had taken measures for extinguishing it entirely. This active general issued orders to several
regiments, chiefly of horse and dragoons, quartered in the neighbouring counties, appointing them to rendezvous at Warrington bridge on
the 10th of November, on which day he proposed to place himself at
their head and dispute with the rebels their approach to Manchester.
At the same time, Willis entered into communication with General
Carpenter, whose unwearied exertions had dogged the insurgents from
Northumberland, and who was now advancing upon them.

These tidings came like a thunderbolt on Forster's army. Forster
had but a choice of difficulties, namely, either to march out and dispute
with Major-General Willis the passage of the river Ribble, by which
Preston is covered, or abide within an open town, and defend it by
such assistance from fortifications, barricades, and batteries, as could
be erected within a few hours.

The first of these courses had its advantages. The bridge across the
Ribble was long, narrow, and might have been easily defended, especially as there was a party of one hundred chosen Highlanders stationed
there, under the command of John Farquharson of Invercauld, a chief
of great character for courage and judgment; and who, though General
Willis was approaching very near to the bridge, might have been relied
on as secure of maintaining his ground till succours were despatched
from the town. Beyond the bridge there extended a long and deep lane,
bordered with hedges, well situated for defence, especially against cavalry. All this was in favour of the defence of the bridge; but, on the other
hand, if Forster had drawn his squadrons of gentlemen out of Preston,
he must have exposed them to the rough shock of ordinary troopers,
which they were neither mounted nor armed so as to sustain. It was
probably this which determined the Jacobite leader to maintain his
defence in the town of Preston itself, rather than in front of it. The insurgents took judicious measures for this purpose, and pursued them with
zeal and spirit. Four barricades were hastily erected. The Earl of Derwentwater, stripping to the waistcoat, encouraged the men to labour as

well by his own example as his liberality, and the works were speedily completed.

One of these barriers was situated a little below the church and was supported by the gentlemen volunteers, who mustered in the churchyard. The defence was commanded by Brigadier MacIntosh. The second was formed at the end of a lane, which was defended by Lord Charles Murray; the third was called the Windmill barricade—it was held out by the Laird of MacIntosh, chief of the name; the fourth barricade was drawn across the street leading towards Liverpool, and was stoutly manned by Hunter, the Northumbrian freebooter, and his moss-troopers. Each barricade was protected by two pieces of cannon; and the houses on both sides of the street were occupied by defenders, so as to pour a destructive flanking fire on any assailant. General Willis, having accurately surveyed the defences, resolved upon attacking them.

On Saturday, the 12th of November, being the day previous to that on which the battle of Sheriffmuir was fought, General Willis commenced his operations upon the town of Preston by a double attack. The barricade on the street below the church was assaulted with great fury; but so insupportable a fire was opened from the defences and the houses adjacent that the assailants were beat off with considerable loss. It would seem, that to aid him in the defence of his post, Brigadier MacIntosh had called in some soldiers who had been posted in the street leading to Wigan. Preston's regiment (well known as the Old Cameronian, and forming part of Willis's attacking force) were therefore enabled to penetrate through that avenue, and seizing two houses which overlooked the town, did the defendants more injury than they sustained from any other attack. The barricade commanded by Lord Charles Murray was in like manner stoutly attacked and fiercely defended, but the Jacobite officer receiving a reinforcement of fifty volunteers, his resistance was ultimately successful. Captains Hunter and Douglas likewise made a desperate defence at the barrier entrusted to them, and the assault upon the post defended by the Chief of MacIntosh was equally fatal to the assailants.

When the soldiers of Willis retired from their various points of attack, they set fire, according to their orders, to the houses betwixt them and the barricades. By the light afforded by this conflagration, the skirmish was carried on during the night; and had not the weather been uncommonly still, Preston, which was the scene of contest, must have been burned to the ground.

Although the insurgents had preserved the advantage in every attack, it was evident, that, cut off from all assistance, and cooped up in the streets of a burning town, where they had but few men to maintain an extended circle of defence, nothing short of a miracle could relieve them. General Willis, whilst directing the attack on the barricades, had, at the same time, guarded every pass the devoted band could escape. Of those who desperately attempted to sally, several were cut to pieces; and it was but very few who escaped by hewing their way through the enemy.

On the morning of the 13th, being the day after the attack, the situation of Forster and his army became yet more desperate. General Carpenter, so long their pursuer, now came up with so many additional forces, chiefly cavalry, completed the blockade of the place, and left the besieged no hope of escape or relief. Willis, as inferior in rank, offered to resign, of course, the charge of siege to his superior officer; but General Carpenter generously refused to take the command, observing, that Willis deserved the honour of finishing the affair which he had begun so auspiciously. The dispositions of the latter general were therefore so actively followed up, that the blockade of the town was effectually completed, and the fate of the rebels became inevitable.

The scene of unavoidable destruction had different effects upon the different characters of the unfortunate insurgents in Preston, in like manner as the approach of imminent peril has upon domesticated and savage animals when they are brought to extremity,—the former are cowed into submission, while the latter, brought to bay, become more desperately ferocious in their resistance. The English gentlemen began to think upon the possibility of saving their lives, and entertained the hope of returning once more to the domestic enjoyments of their homes and their estates; while the Highlanders, and most of the Scottish insurgents, even of the higher classes, declared for sallying out and dying like men of honour, with sword in hand, rather than holding their lives on the base tenure of submission.

Such being their different views of the measures to be adopted, the English determined to accomplish a capitulation at all events; and Oxburgh, an Irish Catholic, who had been Forster's tutor in military matters, went out to propose a surrender to the English generals. The mission was coldly received, and he was distinctly given to understand, that no terms would be granted excepting those of unconditional surrender, with the sole provision that they should be secured from immediate execution. He returned to the town, and the errand on which he had visited the enemy's position being understood, General Forster was nearly pistolled by a Scottish gentleman, named Murray, and his life only saved by a friendly hand, which struck the weapon upwards in the act of its being discharged.

Captain Dalzell, brother of the Earl of Carnwath, then went out in the name of the Scots, but could obtain no more favourable terms. Some time, however, was gained, in which the principal leaders had time to consider that Government might be satisfied with a few examples, while the greater part of the insurgents, in which every one's confidence in his individual good luck led him to hope he would be included, would escape at least the extremity of punishment. After the Scots, and especially the Highlanders, had persisted for some time in their determination of resistance, they at length found themselves obliged to surrender on no better terms than the English, which amounted only to this, that they should not be instantly put to the sword. Their leaders were surrendered as hostages; and at length, after manifesting the greatest unwillingness to give up their arms, they accepted the capitulation, if such it could be called. It certainly appears, that by surrendering at discretion, the greater part of them expected at least to save their lives.

On laying down their arms, the unhappy garrison were enclosed in one of the churches, and treated with considerable rigour, being stripped and ill-used by the soldiery.[1] About fourteen hundred men, of all sorts, were included in the surrender; amongst whom there were about two hundred domestic servants, followers of the gentlemen who

---

[1] The laced clothes of the gentlemen was the temptation to this outrage. The prisoners were obliged to strip the pews of their baize linings, in order to apply the cloth to the purpose of decent covering. A family tradition runs thus: A gentleman, who fought as a trooper in one of the Scottish squadrons, was shot through the body at the barricade. He was conceived to be mortally wounded, and lay stretched in a pew in the church, an affectionate comrade supporting his head, and expecting every moment to receive his last sigh. After much sickness, the wounded man's stomach is said to have relieved itself by discharging a piece of his scarlet waistcoat, which the ball had carried into his body. The assistant, much amazed at such a phenomenon, being also one of that class of men who cannot forbear a jest, even in the most melancholy circumstances, observed, "Hegh, Walter, I am fain to see you have a stock of braid cloth in your bowels; and since it is sae, I wish you would exert yourself again, and bring up as much as would make a pair of brecks, for I am in mickle need o' them." The wounded man afterwards recovered.

had assumed arms, about three hundred gentlemen volunteers, the rest consisting of Brigadier MacIntosh's command of Highlanders. Six of the prisoners were condemned to be shot by martial law, as holding commissions under the government against which they had borne arms. Lord Charles Murray obtained a reprieve with difficulty, through the interest of his friends. Little mercy was shown to the misguided private men, whose sole offence was having complied with what was in their eyes a paramount duty, the obedience to their chiefs. Very many underwent the fate which made them so unwilling to enter England, namely, that of banishment to the plantations in America.

The prisoners of most note were sent up to London, into which they were introduced in a kind of procession, which did less dishonour to the sufferers than to the mean minds who planned and enjoyed such an ignoble triumph. By way of balancing the influence of the Tory mob, whose violences in burning chapels, &c., had been of a formidable and highly criminal character, plans had been adopted by government to excite and maintain a rival spirit of tumult among such of the vulgar as were called, or called themselves, the Low Church party. Party factions often turn upon the most frivolous badges of distinction. As the Tories had affected a particular passion for ale, as a national and truly English potation, their parliamentary associations taking the title of the October and the March Clubs; so, in the spirit of opposition, the Whigs of the lower rank patronised beer, (distinguished, according to Dr. Johnson, from ale, by being either older or smaller,) and mughouses were established, held by landlords of orthodox Whig principles, where this protestant and revolutionary liquor was distributed in liberal quantities, and they speedily were thronged by a set of customers, whose fists and sticks were as prompt to assault the admirers of High Church and Ormond, as the Tories were ready to defend them. It was for the gratification of the frequenters of these mug-houses, as they were called, that the entrance of the Preston prisoners into London was graced with the mock honours of a triumphal procession.

The prisoners, most of them men of birth and education, were, on approaching the capital, all pinioned with cords like the vilest criminals. This ceremony they underwent at Barnet. At Highgate they were met by a large detachment of horse grenadiers and foot guards, preceded by a body of citizens decently dressed, who shouted to give example to the mob. Halters were put upon the horses ridden by the prisoners, and each man's horse was led by a private soldier. Forster, a man of high family, and still Member of Parliament for Northumberland, was exposed in the same manner as the rest. A large mob of the patrons of the mug-houses attended on the occasion, beating upon warming-pans, (in allusion to the vulgar account of the birth of the Chevalier de St. George,) and the prisoners, with all sort of scurrilous abuse and insult, were led through the streets of the city in this species of unworthy triumph, and deposited in the jails of Newgate, the Marshalsea, and other prisons in the metropolis.

In consequence of this sudden increase of tenants, a most extraordinary change took place in the discipline of these melancholy abodes. When the High Church party in London began to recover the astonishment with which they had witnessed the suppression of the insurrection, they could not look back with much satisfaction on their own passive behaviour during the contest, if it could be called one, and now endeavoured to make up for it by liberally supplying the prisoners, whom they regarded as martyrs in their cause, with money and provisions, in which wine was not forgotten. The fair sex are always disposed to be compassionate, and certainly were not least so in this case, where the objects of pity were many of them gallant young cavaliers, sufferers in a cause which they had been taught to consider as sacred. The consequence was, that the prisons overflowed with wine and good cheer, and the younger and more thoughtless part of the inmates turned to revelling and drowning in liquor all more serious thoughts of their situation; so that even Lord Derwentwater himself said of his followers, that they were fitter inhabitants for Bridewell than a state prison. Money, it is said, circulated so plentifully among them, that when it was difficult to obtain silver for a guinea in the streets, nothing was so easy as to find change, whether of gold or silver, in the jail. A handsome, high-spirited young Highland gentleman, whom the pamphlets of the day call Bottair, (one of the family of Butter in Athole,) made such an impression on the fair visitors who came to minister to the wants of the Jacobite captives, that some reputations were put in peril by the excess of their attentions to this favourite object of compassion.

When such a golden shower descends on a prison, the jailor generally secures to himself the largest share of it; and those prisoners who desired separate beds, or the slightest accommodation in point of lodging, had to purchase them at a rate which would have paid for many years the rent of the best houses in St. James's Square or Piccadilly.

Dungeons, the names of which indicate their gloomy character, as the Lion's Den, the Middle Dark, and the like, were rented at the same extravagant prices, and were not only filled with prisoners, but abounded with good cheer.

These riotous scenes went on the more gaily that almost all had nursed a hope, that their having surrendered at discretion would be admitted as a protection for their lives. But when numerous bills of high treason were found against them, escape from prison began to be thought of, which the command of money, and the countenance of friends without doors, as well as the general structure of the jails, rendered more easy than could have been expected, Thus, on the 10th of April, 1716, Thomas Forster escaped from Newgate, by means of false keys, and, having all things prepared, got safely to France. On the 10th of May, Brigadier MacIntosh, whom we have so often mentioned, with fourteen other gentlemen, chiefly Scottish, took an opportunity to escape in the following manner. The Brigadier having found means to rid himself of his irons, and coming down stairs about eleven at night, he placed himself close by the door of the jail; and as it was opened to admit a servant at that time of night, (no favourable example of prison discipline,) he knocked down the jailor, and made his escape with his companions, some of whom were retaken in the streets, from not knowing whither to fly.

Among the fugitives who broke prison with MacIntosh, was Robert Hepburn of Keith, the same person in whose family befell the lamentable occurrence mentioned at page 46.

This gentleman had pinioned the arms of the turnkey by an effort of strength, and effected his escape into the open street without pursuit. But he was at a loss whither to fly, or where to find a friendly place of refuge. His wife and family were, he knew, in London; but how, in that great city, was he to discover them, especially as they most probably were residing there under feigned names? While he was agitated by this uncertainty, and fearful of making the least enquiry, even had he known in what words to express it, he saw at a window in the street an ancient piece of plate, called the Keith Tankard, which had long belonged to his family. He immediately conceived that his wife and children must be inhabitants of the lodgings, and entering, without asking questions, was received in their arms. They knew of his purpose of escape, and took lodgings as near the jail as they could, that they might afford him immediate refuge; but dared not give him any hint where they were, otherwise than by setting the well-known flagon where it might by good fortune catch his eye. He escaped to France.

The noblemen who had placed themselves at the head of the rebellion were now called to answer for their guilt; and articles of impeachment of high treason were exhibited by the House of Commons against the Earl of Derwentwater, and the Lord Widrington, in England; and the Earls of Nithisdale, Winton, and Carnwath, Lord Viscount Kenmure, and Lord Nairne, in Scotland. They severally pleaded Guilty to the articles, excepting the Earl of Winton, who pleaded Not Guilty.

Lord Derwentwater and Lord Kenmure suffered death on the 24th February, 1715–16. The Earl of Derwentwater, who was an amiable private character, hospitable and generous, brave and humane, revoked on the scaffold his plea of Guilty, and died firmly avowing the political creed for which he suffered. Lord Kenmure, a quiet, modest gentleman, shared Derwentwater's fate; and he showed the same firmness. There is a tradition that the body of Lord Derwentwater was carried down to Westmoreland in great pomp, the procession, however, moving only by night, and resting by day in chapels dedicated to the exercise of the Catholic religion, where the funeral services of that church were performed over the body during the day, until the approach of night permitted them to resume their progress northward; and that the remains of this unfortunate nobleman were finally deposited in his ancestors' burial place at Dilstone Hall. His large estates were confiscated to the crown, and now form the valuable property of Greenwich Hospital.

Charles Ratcliff, brother to the Earl of Derwentwater, and doomed to share his fate, after a long interval of years saved himself for the time by breaking prison.

But what chiefly attracted the attention of the public, was the escape of the Earl of Nithisdale, who was destined to have shared the fate of Derwentwater and Kenmure.

The utmost intercession had been made, in every possible shape, to save the lives of these unfortunate noblemen, and their companions in misfortune, but it had been found unavailing. Lady Nithisdale, the bold and affectionate wife of the condemned Earl, having in vain thrown herself at the feet of the monarch to implore mercy for her husband, devised a plan for his escape of the same kind with that since practised by Madame Lavalette. She was admitted to see her husband in the Tower upon the last day which, according to his sentence, he had to live. She had with her two female confidants. One brought on her person a double suit of female clothes. This individual was instantly dismissed, when relieved of her second dress. The other person gave her own clothes to the Earl, attiring herself in those which had been provided. Muffled in a riding-hood and cloak, the Earl, in the character of lady's maid, holding a handkerchief to his eyes, as one overwhelmed with deep affliction, passed the sentinels, and being safely conveyed out of the Tower, made his escape to France. We are startled to find, that, according to the rigour of the law, the life of the heroic Countess was considered as responsible for that of the husband whom she had saved; but she contrived to conceal herself.

Lord Winton received sentence of death after trial, but also made his escape from the Tower. As Charles Ratcliff had already broke prison about the same time, we may conclude either that the jailors and marshals did not exhibit much vigilance on this occasion, or that the prisoners found means of lulling it to sleep. The Earl of Carnwath, Lords Widdrington and Nairne, were, after a long imprisonment, pardoned as far as their lives were concerned, in consequence of a general bill of indemnity.

Of inferior persons, about twenty of the most resolute of the Preston prisoners were executed at that place and at Manchester, and four or five suffered at Tyburn. Amongst these the execution of William Paul, a clergyman, a true friend, as he boasted himself, of the anti-revolutionary church of England, made a strong impression on those of his party.

Thus closed the Rebellion and its consequences, so far as England was concerned. We must now take a view of its last scenes as exhibited in Scotland.

LXXII

The Highlanders Retreat

1716

WE left the insurgents when the melancholy news of the termination of the campaign of Forster, with his Highland auxiliaries, at the barricades of Preston, had not yet reached them; the moment it did, all hopes of a general insurrection in England, or any advantage being obtained there, were for ever ended.

The regular troops which had been detained in England to suppress the northern insurgents, were now set at liberty, and Mar could no longer rely upon Argyle's remaining inactive for want of men. Besides, the Estates of the United Provinces had now, upon the remonstrance of General Cadogan, despatched for Britain the auxiliary forces which they were bound by treaty to furnish in case of invasion, and three thousand of them had landed at Deptford. The other three thousand Dutch troops, designed for ports in the north, had been dispersed by a storm, and driven into Harwich, Yarmouth, and elsewhere, which induced the government to order those at Deptford, as the most disposable part of this auxiliary force, to move instantly down to Scotland.

Events equally unfavourable to the rebels were taking place in the North of Scotland; and, in order to ascertain the progress of these, it is necessary to trace some passages of the life of Simon Fraser, one of the most remarkable characters of his time.

He was by birth the nearest male heir to the estate of Lovat, and to the dignity of Chief of the Frasers—no empty honour, since the clan contained a following of from seven hundred to a thousand men. The chief last deceased, however, had left a daughter, and Simon was desirous, by marriage with this young lady, to unite her pretensions to the chieftainship and estate with his own. As his character was bad, and his circumstances accounted desperate, the widowed, mother of the young heiress, a lady of the house of Athole, was averse to this match, and her powerful family countenanced her repugnance. Being a man of a daring character, deep powers of dissimulation, and master of the tempers of the lower class of Highlanders, Simon found it no difficult matter to obtain the assistance of a strong party of Frasers, chiefly desperate men, to assist in a scheme of seizing on the person of the young heiress. She escaped his grasp, but her mother, the widow of the late Lord Lovat, fell into his power. Equally shortsighted as unprincipled, Fraser imagined that by marrying this lady instead of her daughter, he would secure, through her large jointure, some legal interest in the estate. With this view he accomplished a forced marriage betwixt the Dowager Lady Lovat and himself, and enforced his rights, as her pretended husband, with the most brutal violence. For this abominable and atrocious outrage against a matron, widow of his own near connexion, and a sister of the powerful Marquis of Athole, letters of fire and sword were granted against Fraser and his adherents, and, being outlawed by the High Court of Justiciary, he was forced to fly to France. Here he endeavoured to recommend himself at the court of St. Germains, by affecting much zeal for the Jacobite cause, and pretending to great interest with the Highland chiefs, and the power of rendering effectual service amongst them. The Chevalier de St. George and the French King were aware of the infamy of the man's character and distrusted the proposal which he laid before them, for raising an insurrection in the Highlands. Mary of Este, more credulous, was disposed to trust him; and he was detached on a Jacobite mission, which he instantly betrayed to the Duke of Queensberry, and which created much disturbance in the year 1703, as we have noticed in its place. His double treachery being discovered, Simon Fraser was, on his return to France, thrown into the Bastile, where he remained for a considerable time. Dismissed from this imprisonment, he waited for an opportunity where he might serve his own interest, and advance his claims upon the chieftainship of the clan Fraser and the estate of Lovat, by adopting the political side betwixt the contending parties which should bid fairest to serve his purpose.

The time seemed now arrived, when, by the insurrection of Mar, open war was declared betwixt the parties. His cousin, the heiress of Lovat, had been married to MacKenzie of Fraserdale, who, acting as chief of his wife's clan, had summoned the Frasers to arms, and led a body of five hundred clansmen to join the standard of the Chevalier de St. George. They marched to Perth accordingly. In the meantime, Simon Fraser arrived in Scotland, and made his appearance, like one of those portentous sea monsters whose gambols announce the storm. He was first seen at Dumfries, where he offered his personal services to join the citizens, who were in arms to repel an attack from Kenmure, Nithisdale, and their followers. The Dumfriesians, however, trusted him not, nay, were disposed to detain him a prisoner; and only permitted him to pass northward, on the assurance of the Marquis of Annandale, that his presence there would be favourable to King George and his cause. It proved so accordingly.

Simon Fraser arrived in Inverness-shire, and hastened to form an intimate alliance with Duncan Forbes, brother of John Forbes of Culloden, and a determined friend to government, Forbes was an excellent lawyer, and a just and religious man. At another time, he would probably have despised associating himself with a desperate outlaw to his country, black with the charges of rape, murder, and double treachery. But the case was an extreme one, in which no assistance that promised to be available was to be rejected. Simon Fraser obtained pardon and favour, and the influence of the patriarchal system was never more remarkably illustrated than in his person. His character was, as we have seen, completely infamous, and his state and condition that of an adventurer of the very worst description. But by far the greater number of the clan were disposed to think, that the chiefship descended to the male heir, and therefore preferred Simon's title to that of Fraserdale, who only commanded them as husband of the heiress. The mandates of Fraser, now terming himself Lovat, reached the clan in the town of Perth. They were respected as those of the rightful chief; and the Frasers did not hesitate to withdraw from the cause of the Chevalier de St. George, and march northwards, to place themselves under the command of their restored patriarch by male descent, who had embraced the other side. This change of sides was the more remarkable, as most of the Frasers were in personal opinion Jacobites, We have already noticed, that the desertion of the Frasers took place the very morning when Mar broke up to march on Dublane; and, as a bold and warlike clan, their absence, on the 12th November, was of no small disadvantage to the party from whom they had retired.

Shortly after this, the operations of this clan, under their new leader, became directly hostile to the Jacobite cause. Sir John MacKenzie of Coul had, at the period of the Earl of Seaforth's march to Perth, been left with four hundred MacKenzies, to garrison Inverness, which may be termed the capital of the North Highlands. Hitherto his task had been an easy one, but it was now likely to become more difficult. Acting upon a plan concerted betwixt him and Duncan Forbes, Lovat assembled his clan, and with those of the Monros, Rosses, and Grants, who had always maintained the Whig interest, attacked Inverness, with such success, that they made themselves masters of the place, which Sir John MacKenzie found himself compelled to evacuate without serious resistance. The Earl of Sutherland also, who was still in arms, now advanced across the Murray Frith, and a considerable force was collecting in the rear of the rebels, and in a position which threatened the territories of Huntly, Seaforth, and several other chief leaders in Mar's army.

These various events tended more and more to depress the spirits of the noblemen and heads of clans who were in the Jacobite army. The indefinite, or rather unfavourable, issue of the affair of Sheriffmuir, had discouraged those who expected, by a decisive victory, if not to carry their principal and original purpose, at least to render themselves a foe to whom the Government might think it worth while to grant honourable terms of accommodation.

Most men of reflection, therefore, now foresaw the inevitable ruin of the undertaking; but the General, Mar, having formally invited the Chevalier de St. George to come over and put himself at the head of the insurrectionary army, was under the necessity, for his own honour, and to secure the chance which such an impulse might have given to his affairs, of keeping his troops together to protect the person of the Prince, in case of his accepting this perilous invitation, which, given before the battle of Sheriffmuir, was likely to be complied with. In this dilemma he became desirous, by every species of engagement, to bind those who had enrolled themselves under the fatal standard, not to quit it.

For this purpose, a military oath was proposed, in name of King James VIII.; an engagement, which, however solemn, has been seldom found stronger than the severe compulsion of necessity operating against it. Many of the gentlemen engaged, not willing, to preclude themselves from endeavouring to procure terms, in case of need, refused to come under this additional obligation. The expedient of an association was next resorted to, and Mar summoned a general council of the principal persons in the army. This was the fourth time such a meeting had been convoked since the commencement of the affair; the first had taken place when MacIntosh's detachment was in peril; the second for the purpose of subscribing an invitation to the Chevalier de St. George to join them, and the third on the field of battle at Sheriffmuir.

The Marquis of Huntly, who had already well-nigh determined on taking separate measures, refused to attend the meeting but sent a draught of an association to which he was willing to subscribe, and seemed to admit that the insurgents might make their peace separately. Mar flung it scornfully aside, and said it might be a very proper form, providing it had either sense or grammar. He then recommended his own draught, by which the subscribers agreed to continue in arms, and accept no conditions unless under the royal authority, and by the consent of the majority of the gentlemen then in arms. The proposed measure was opposed by the Master of Sinclair and many of the Lowland gentlemen. They complained, that by using the phrase "Royal authority," they might be considered as throwing the free power of deciding for themselves into the hands of Mar, as the royal General, with whose management hitherto they had little reason to be satisfied. The Master of Sinclair demanded to know what persons were to vote, as constituting the majority of gentlemen in arms, and whether voices must be allowed to all who went by that general name, or whether the decision was to be remitted to those whom the General might select. Sir John MacLean haughtily answered, that unless some such power of selection were lodged in the commander in chief, all his regiment of eight hundred men must be admitted to vote, since every MacLean was a gentlemen. Mar endeavoured to soothe the disaffected. He admitted the king's affairs were not in such a state as he could have desired; but contended that they were far from desperate, intimated that he still entertained hopes, and in the same breath deprecated answering the questions put to him on the nature of his expectations. He was, however, borne down with queries; and being reminded that he could not propose remaining at Perth, when the Duke of Argyle, reinforced by six thousand Dutch, should move against him on one side, and Sutherland, with all the northern clans in the government interest, should advance on the other, it was demanded, where he proposed to make a stand. Inverness was named; and the shire of Murray was pointed out as sufficient to find subsistence for a considerable army. But Inverness, if not already fallen, was in imminent danger; Murray, though a fertile country, was a narrow district, which would be soon exhausted; and it seemed to be the general opinion, that if pressed by the Government forces, there would be no resource save falling back into the barren regions of the Highlands. The Master of Sinclair asked, at what season of the year forage and other necessaries for cavalry were to be found in the hills? Glengarry made a bizarre but very intelligible reply, "that such accommodations were to be found in the Highlands at every season—by those who were provident enough to bring them with them."

The main argument of Mar was, to press upon the dissentients the dishonour of deserting the King, when he was on the point of throwing himself on their loyalty. They replied, he alone knew the King's motions; of which they had no such assurances as could induce them to refuse any opportunity of saving themselves, their families, and estates from perdition, merely to preserve some punctilious scruples of loyalty, by which the King could gain no real advantage. They complained that they had been lured into the field, by promises of troops, arms, ammunition, treasure, and a general of military talent—all to be sent by France; and that, these reports proving totally false, they did not incline to be detained there upon rumours of the King's motions, which might be equally fallacious, as they came from the same quarter. In a word, the council of war broke up without coming to a resolution; and there was, from that time, established in the army a party who were opposed to Mar's conduct of affairs, who declared for opening a negotiation with the Duke of Argyle, and were distinguished at headquarters as grumblers and mutineers.

These gentlemen held a meeting at the Master of Sinclair's quarters, and opened a communication with Mar, in which they urged the total inadequacy of resistance which they could now offer—the exhaustion of their supplies of ammunition, provision, and money—the impossibility of their making a stand until they reached the Highland mountains—and the equal impossibility of subsisting their cavalry if they plunged into these wildernesses. They declared, that they did not desire to separate themselves from the army; all they wished to know was, whether an honourable capitulation could be obtained for all who were engaged; and if dishonourable terms were offered, they expressed themselves determined to fight to the death rather than accept them.

While such were the sentiments of the Low-country gentlemen, dejected at their total want of success, and the prospect of misery and ruin which they saw fast approaching, the Highland chiefs and clans were totally disinclined to any terms of accommodation. Their warlike disposition made the campaign an enjoyment to them; the pay, which Mar dispensed liberally, was, while it lasted, an object with people so poor; and, finally, they entertained the general opinion, founded upon the convention made with their ancestors after the war of 1688–9, that they might at worst retreat into their hills, where, rather than incur the loss of men and charges necessary for suppressing them, the Government would be glad to grant them peace upon their own terms, and, perhaps, not averse to pay them for accepting it. Another class of men having influence in such a singular camp, were the nobility, or men of quality, who had joined the cause. Most of these were men of high titles but broken fortunes, whose patrimony was overburdened with debt. They had been early treated by Mar with distinction and preference, for their rank gave credit to the cause which their personal influence could not greatly have advanced. They enjoyed posts of nominal rank in the insurrectionary army; and the pay conforming to these was not less acceptable to them than to the Highlanders. It may be also supposed, that they were more particularly acquainted than others with the reasons Mar had for actually expecting the King: and might, with spirit worthy of their birth, be willing to incur the worst extremities of war, rather than desert their monarch at the moment when, by their own invitation, he came to throw himself on their fidelity. These noblemen, therefore, supported the measures and authority of the commander, and discountenanced any proposals to treat.

Notwithstanding the aid of the nobles and the Highland chiefs, Mar found himself compelled so far to listen to the representations of the discontented party, as to consent that application should be made to the Duke of Argyle to learn whether any capitulation could be allowed. There was so little faith betwixt the officers and their general, that the former insisted on naming one of the delegates who were to be sent to Stirling about the proposed negotiation. The offer of submission upon terms was finally intrusted to Lieutenant-Colonel Lawrence, the officer of highest rank who had been made prisoner at Sheriffmuir. The colonel, agreeably to a previous engagement, returned with an answer to the proposal of submission, that the Duke of Argyle had no commission from court to treat with the insurgents as a body, but only with such individuals as might submit themselves; but his Grace promised that he would send the Duke of Roxburghe to court, for the purpose of soliciting such powers for a general pacification. A more private negotiation, instituted by the Countess of Murray, whose second son, Francis Stewart, was engaged in the rebellion, received the same answer, with this addition, that the Duke of Argyle would not hear her pronounce the name of Mar, in whose favour she had attempted to make some intercession.

Upon this unfavourable reception of the proposal of submission, it was not difficult to excite the resentment of those who had declared for war, against that smaller party which advocated peace. The High-landers, whose fierce temper was easily awakened to fury, were encouraged to insult and misuse several of the Low-country gentry, particularly the followers of Huntly, tearing the cockades out of their hats, and upbraiding them as cowards and traitors. The Master of Sinclair threatened by Farquharson of Inverey, a Highland vassal of the Earl of Mar; but his well-known ferocity of temper, with his habit of going continually armed, seemed to have protected him.

About this time, there were others among Mar's principal associates who became desirous of leaving his camp at Perth. Huntly, much disgusted with the insults offered to his vassals, and the desperate state of things at Perth, was now preparing to withdraw to his own country, alleging that his presence was necessary to defend it against the Earl of Sutherland, whose march southward must be destructive to the estates of his family. The movements of the same Earl with the clans of Rosses, MacKays, Frasers, Grants, and others, alarmed Seaforth also for the security of his dominions in Kintail; and he left Perth, to march northward, for the defence of his property, and the wives, families, and houses of his vassals in arms. Thus were two great limbs lopped off, Mar's army, at the time when it was about to be assailed by government with collected strength. Individuals also became dispirited, and deserted the enterprise. There was at least one man of consideration

who went home from the field of battle at Sheriffmuir—sat down by
his own hearth, and trusting to the clemency of the government,
renounced the trade of King-making. Others, in parties or separately,
had already adopted the same course; and those who, better known, or
more active, dared not remain at home, were seeking passages to foreign parts from the eastern ports of Scotland. The Master of Sinclair,
after exchanging mutual threats and defiances with Mar and his
friends, left the camp at Perth, went north and visited the Marquis of
Huntly. He afterwards escaped abroad from the Orkney islands.

Amidst this gradual but increasing defection, Mar, by the course of
his policy, saw himself at all rates obliged to keep his ground at Perth,
since he knew, what others refused to take upon his authority, that the
Chevalier de St. George was very shortly to be expected in his camp.

This Prince, unfortunate from his very infancy, found himself, at the
time of this struggle in his behalf, altogether unable to assist his partisans. He had been expelled from France by the Regent Duke of Orleans,
and even the provision of arms and ammunition, which he was able to
collect from his own slender funds, and those of his followers, or by the
munificence of his allies, was intercepted in the ports of France. Having,
therefore, no more effectual mode of rendering them assistance, he generously, or desperately, resolved to put his own person in the hazard, and
live and die along with them. As a soldier, the Chevalier de St. George
had shown courage upon several occasions; that is, he had approached
the verge of battle as near as persons of his importance are usually suffered to do. He was handsome in person, and courteous and pleasing in
his manners; but his talents were not otherwise conspicuous, nor did he
differ from the ordinary class of great persons, whose wishes, hopes, and
feelings are uniformly under the influence and management of some
favourite minister, who relieves his master of the inconvenient trouble of
thinking for himself upon subjects of importance. The arrival of a chief
graced with such showy qualities as James possessed, might have given
general enthusiasm to the insurrection at its commencement, but could
not redeem it when it was gone to ruin; any more than the unexpected
presence of the captain on board a half-wrecked vessel can, of itself,
restore the torn rigging which cannot resist the storm, or mend the shat-
tered planks which are yawning to admit the waves.

The Chevalier thus performed his romantic adventure: Having traversed Normandy, disguised in a mariner's habit, he embarked at
Dunkirk aboard a small vessel, formerly a privateer, as well armed and

manned as time would admit, and laden with a cargo of brandy. On the 22d December 1715 he landed at Peterhead, having with him a retinue of only six gentlemen; the rest of his train and equipage being to follow him in two other small vessels. Of these, one reached Scotland, but the other was shipwrecked. The Earl of Mar, with the Earl Marischal, and a chosen train of persons of quality, to the number of thirty, went from Perth to kiss the hands of the Prince for whose cause they were in arms. They found him at Fetteresso, discomposed with the ague,—a bad disorder to bring to a field of battle. The deputation was received with the courtesy and marks of favour which could not be refused, although their news scarce deserved a welcome. While the Episcopal clergy of the diocese of Aberdeen congratulated themselves and James on the arrival of a Prince trained, like Moses, Joseph, and David, in the school of adversity, his general had to apprise his sovereign of the cold tidings that his education in that severe academy had not yet ended. The Chevalier de St. George now for the first time received the melancholy intelligence that for a month before his arrival it had been determined to abandon Perth, which had hitherto been their headquarters, and that, as soon as the enemy began to advance, they would be under the necessity of retreating into the wild Highlands.

This was a reception very different from what the Prince anticipated. Some hopes were still entertained that the news of the Chevalier's actual arrival might put new life into their sinking cause, bring back the friends who had left their standard, and encourage new ones to repair thither, and the experiment was judged worth trying. For giving the greater effect to his presence, he appeared in royal state as he passed through Brechin and Dundee and entered Perth itself with an affectation of majesty.

James proceeded to name a privy council, to whom he made a speech, which had little in it that was encouraging to his followers. In spite of a forced air of hope and confidence, it was too obvious that the language of the Prince was rather that of despair. There was no rational expectation of assistance in men, money, or arms, from abroad, nor did his speech hold out any such. He was come to Scotland, he said, merely that those who did not choose to discharge their own duty might not have it in their power to make his absence an apology; and the ominous words escaped him, "that for him it was no new thing to be unfortunate, since his whole life, from his cradle, had been a constant series of misfortune, and he was prepared, if it pleased God, to suffer the extent of the threats which his enemies threw out against

him." These were not encouraging words, but they were the real sentiments of a spirit broken with disappointment. The Grand Council, to
whom this royal speech was addressed, answered it by a declaration of
their purpose of fighting the Duke of Argyle; and it is incredible how
popular this determination was in the army, though reduced to one-
fourth of their original numbers. The intelligence of the arrival of the
Chevalier de St. George was communicated to Seaforth, Lord Huntly,
and other persons of consequence who had formerly joined his standard, but they took no notice of his summons to return thither. He
continued, notwithstanding, to act the sovereign. Six proclamations
were issued in the name of James the Eighth of Scotland and Third of
England: The first appointed a general thanksgiving for his safe arrival
in the British kingdoms—a second, commanded prayers to be offered
up for him in all churches—a third, enjoined the currency of foreign
coins,—a fourth, directed the summoning together the Scottish Convention of Estates—a fifth, commanded all the fencible men to join his
standard—and a sixth, appointed the 23d of January for the ceremony
of his coronation. A letter from the Earl of Mar was also published
respecting the King, as he is called, in which, with no happy selection
of phrase, he is termed the *finest* gentleman in person and manners,
with the *finest* parts and capacity for business, and the *finest* writer
whom Lord Mar ever saw; in a word, every way fitted to make the
Scots a happy people, were his subjects worthy of him.

But with these flattering annunciations came forth one of a different
character. The village of Auchterarder, and other hamlets lying between
Stirling and Perth, with the houses, corn, and forage, were ordered by
James's edict to be destroyed, lest they should afford quarters to the
enemy in their advance. In consequence of this, the town above named
and several villages were burned to the ground, while their inhabitants,
with old men and women, children and infirm persons, were driven
from their houses in the extremity of one of the hardest winters which
had for a long time been experienced even in these cold regions. There
is every reason to believe that the alarm attending, this violent measure
greatly overbalanced any hopes of better times excited by the flourishing proclamations of the newly arrived candidate for royalty.

While the insurgents at Perth were trying the effect of adulatory
proclamations, active measures of a very different kind were in
progress. The Duke of Argyle had been in Stirling since the battle of
12th November, collecting gradually the means of totally extinguising

the rebellion. His secret wish probably was, that it might be ended without further bloodshed of his misguided countrymen, by dissolving of itself. But the want of a battering train, and the extreme severity of the weather, served as excuses for refraining from active operations. The Duke, however, seems to have been suspected by Government of being tardy in his operations; and perhaps of having entertained some idea of extending his own power and interest in Scotland by treating the rebels, with clemency, and allowing them time for submission. This was the rather believed, as Argyle had been the ardent opponent of Marlborough, now Captain-General, and could not hope that his measures would be favourably judged by a political and personal enemy. The intercession of a part of the English ministry, who declared against the impeachment of the rebel lords, had procured them punishment in the loss of their places; and, notwithstanding the services he had performed, in arresting with three thousand men the progress of four times that number, Argyle's slow and temporising measures subjected him to a shade of malevolent suspicion, which his message to Government, through the Duke of Roxburghe, recommending an amnesty, perhaps tended to increase.

Yet he had not neglected any opportunity to narrow the occupation of the country by the rebels, or to prepare for their final suppression. The English ships of war in the firth, acting under the Duke's orders, had driven Mar's forces from the castle of Burntisland, and the royal troops had established themselves throughout a great part of Fifeshire, formerly held exclusively by the rebel army.

The Dutch auxiliaries now, however, began to join the camp at Stirling; and as the artillery designed for the siege of Perth lay windbound in the Thames, a field-train was sent from Berwick to Stirling, that no further time might be lost. General Cadogan also, the intimate friend of Marlborough, was despatched from London to press the most active operations; and Argyle, if he had hitherto used any delay, in pity to the insurgents, was now forced on the most energetic measures.

On the 24th of January the advance from Stirling and the march on Perth were commenced, though the late hard frost, followed by a great fall of snow, rendered the operations of the army slow and difficult. On the last day of January the troops of Argyle crossed the Earn without opposition, and advanced to Tullibardine, within eight miles of Perth.

On the other hand, all was confusion at the headquarters of the rebels. The Chevalier de St. George had expressed the greatest desire to see the little kings, as he called the Highland chiefs, and their clans; but, though professing to admire their singular dress and martial appearance, he was astonished to perceive their number so greatly inferior to what he had been led to expect and expressed an apprehension that, he been deceived and betrayed. Nor did the appearance of this Prince excite much enthusiasm on the part of his followers. His person was tall and thin; his look and eye dejected by his late bodily illness; and his whole bearing lacking the animation and fire which ought to characterise the leader of an adventurous, or rather desperate cause. He was slow of speech and difficult of access, and seemed little interested in reviews of his men, or martial displays of any kind. The Highlanders, struck with his resemblance to an automaton, asked if he could speak; and there was a general disappointment, arising rather, perhaps, from the state of anxiety and depression in which they saw him, than from any natural want of courage in the unhappy Prince himself. His extreme attachment to the Catholic religion also reminded such of his adherents as acknowledged the reformed church of the family bigotry on account of which his father had lost his kingdom; and they were much disappointed at his refusal to join in their prayers and acts of worship, and at the formal precision with which he adhered to his Popish devotions.

Yet the Highlanders, though few in numbers, still looked forward with the utmost spirit, and something approaching to delight, to the desperate conflict which they conceived to be just approaching; and when, on the 28th January, they learned that Argyle was actually on his march towards Perth, it seemed rather to announce a jubilee than a battle with fearful odds. The chiefs embraced, drank to each other, and to the good day which was drawing near; the pipes played, and the men prepared for action with that air of alacrity which a warlike people express at the approach of battle.

When, however, a rumour, first slowly whispered, then rapidly spreading among the clans, informed them that notwithstanding all the preparations in which they had been engaged, it was the general's purpose to retire before the enemy without fighting, the grief and indignation of these men, taught to think so highly of their ancestors' prowess, and feeling no inferiority in themselves, rose to a formidable pitch of fury, and they assailed their principal officers in the streets with every species of reproach. "What can we do?" was the helpless answer of one of these gentlemen, a confident of Mar. "Do?" answered an indignant

Highlander; "Let us do that which we were called to arms for, which certainly was not to run away. Why did the King come hither?—was it to see his subjects butchered like dogs, without striking a blow for their lives and honour?" When the safety of the King's person was urged as a reason for retreat, they answered—"Trust his safety to us; and if he is willing to die like a prince, he shall see there are ten thousand men in Scotland willing to die with him."

Such were the general exclamations without doors, and those in the councils of the Chevalier were equally violent. Many military men of skill gave it as their opinion that though Perth was an open town, yet it was so far a safe post that an army could not, by a coup-de-main, take it out of the hands of a garrison determined on its defence. The severity of the snow-storm and of the frost precluded the opening of trenches; the country around Perth was laid desolate; the Duke of Argyle's army consisted in a great measure of Englishmen and foreigners, unaccustomed to the severe climate of Scotland; and vague hopes were expressed that, if the general of Government should press an attack upon the town, he might receive such a check as would restore the balance between the parties. To this it was replied, that not only the superiority of numbers, and the advantage of discipline, were on the side of the royal army, but that the garrison at Perth was destitute of the necessary provisions and ammunition; and that the Duke of Argyle had men enough at once to form the blockade of that town, and take possession of Dundee, Aberdeen, and all the counties to the northward of the Tay, which they lately occupied; while the Chevalier, cooped up in Perth, might be permitted for some time to see all the surrounding country in his enemy's possession, until it would finally become impossible for him to escape. In the end it was resolved in the councils of the Chevalier de St. George that to attempt the defence of Perth would be an act of desperate chivalry. To reconcile the body of the army to the retreat reports were spread that they were to make a halt at Aberdeen, there to be joined by a considerable body of troops which were expected to arrive from abroad, and advance again southwards under better auspices. But it was secretly understood that the purpose was to desert the enterprise, to which the contrivers might apply the lines of the poet—

> "In an ill hour did we these arms commence,
> Fondly brought her; and foolishly sent hence."

LXXIII

The Jacobite Exile

1716-1719

WHATEVER reports were spread among the soldiers, the principal leaders had determined to commence a retreat, at the head of a discontented army, degraded in their own opinion, distrustful of their officers, and capable, should these suspicions ripen into a fit of fury, of carrying off both King and general into the Highlands, and there waging an irregular war after their own manner.

On the 28th of January an alarm was given in Perth of the Duke of Argyle's approach; and it is remarkable, that, although in the confusion the general officers had issued no orders what measures were to be taken in case of this probable event, yet the clans themselves, with intuitive sagacity, took the strongest posts for checking any attack; and, notwithstanding a momentary disorder, were heard to cheer each other with the expression, "they should do well enough." The unhappy Prince himself was far from displaying the spirit of his partisans. He was observed to look dejected, and to shed tears, and heard to say, that instead of bringing him to a crown they had led him to his grave. "Weeping," said Prince Eugene, when he heard this incident, "is not the way to conquer kingdoms."

The retreat commenced under all these various feelings. On the 30th of January the anniversary of Charles the First's decapitation, and ominous therefore to his grandson, the Highland army filed off upon the ice which then covered the Tay. The town was shortly after taken possession of by a body of the Duke of Argyle's dragoons; but the weather was so severe, and the march of the rebels so regular, that it was impossible to push forward any vanguard of strength sufficient to annoy their retreat.

On the arrival of the rebels at the seaport of Montrose, a rumour arose among the Highlanders that the King, as he was termed, the Earl of Mar, and some of their other principal leaders were about to abandon them, and take flight by sea. To pacify the troops, orders were given to continue the route towards Aberdeen; the equipage and horses of the Chevalier de St. George were brought out before the gate of his lodgings, and his guards were mounted as if to proceed on the journey. But before the hour appointed for the march James left his apartments privately for those of the Earl of Mar, and both took a by-road to the water's edge, where a boat waited to carry them in safety on board a small vessel prepared for their reception. The safety of these two personages being assured, boats were sent to bring off Lord Drummond, and a few other gentlemen, most of them belonging to the Chevalier's household; and thus the son of James II. once more retreated from the shores of his native country, which, on this last occasion, he seemed to have visited for no other purpose than to bring away his general in safety.

General Gordon performed the melancholy and irksome duty of leading to Aberdeen the disheartened remains of the Highland army, in which the Lord Marischal lent him assistance, and brought up the rear. It is probable that the rage of the men, on finding themselves deserted, might have shown itself in some acts of violence and insubordination; but the approach of the Duke of Argyle's forces, which menaced them in different columns, prevented this catastrophe. A sealed letter, to be opened at Aberdeen, contained the secret orders of the Chevalier for General Gordon and his army, When opened, it was found to contain thanks for their faithful services; an intimation that disappointments had obliged him to retire abroad; and a full permission to his adherents either to remain in a body and treat with the enemy, or disperse, as should best appear to suit the exigency of the time. The soldiers were at the same time apprised that they would cease to receive pay.

A general burst of grief and indignation attended these communications. Many of the insurgents threw down their arms in despair, exclaiming, that they had been deserted and betrayed, and were now left without either king or general. The clans broke up into different bodies, and marched to the mountains, where they dispersed, each to its own hereditary glen. The gentlemen and Lowlanders who had been engaged either skulked among the mountains or gained the more northerly shires of the country, where vessels, sent from France to receive them, carried a great part of them to the Continent.

Thus ended the Rebellion of 1715, without even the usual sad eclât of a defeat. It proved fatal to many ancient and illustrious families in Scotland, and appears to have been an undertaking too weighty for the talents of the person whom chance, or his own presumption, placed at the head of it. It would be unjust to the memory of the unfortunate Mar not to acquit him of cowardice or treachery, but his genius lay for the intrigues of a court, not the labours of a campaign. He seems to have fully shared the chimerical hopes which he inspired amongst his followers, and to have relied upon the foreign assistance which the Regent Duke of Orleans wanted both power and inclination to afford. He believed, also, the kingdom was so ripe for rebellion that nothing was necessary save to kindle a spark in order to produce a general conflagration. In a word, his trust was reposed in what is called the chapter of accidents. Before the battle of Sheriffmuir his inactivity seems to have been unpardonable, since he suffered the Duke of Argyle, by assuming a firm attitude, to neutralise and control a force of four times his numbers; but after that event, to continue the enterprise was insanity, since each moment he lingered brought him nearer the edge of the precipice. Yet even the Chevalier was invited over to share the dangers and disgrace of an inevitable retreat. In short, the whole history of the insurrection shows that no combination can be more unfortunate than that of a bold undertaking with an irresolute leader.

The Earl of Mar for several years afterwards managed the state affairs of the Chevalier de St. George, the mock minister of a mock cabinet, until the beginning of the year 1731, when he became deprived of his master's confidence. He spent the rest of his life abroad, and in retirement. This unfortunate Earl was a man of fine taste, and in devising modes of improving Edinburgh, the capital of Scotland, was more fortunate than he had been in schemes for the alteration of her government. He gave the first hints for several of the modern improvements of the city.

The Duke of Argyle having taken the most active measures for extinguishing the embers of the Rebellion, by dispersing the bodies of men who were still in arms, directed movable columns to traverse the Highlands in every direction, for receiving the submission of such as were humbled, or exercising force on those who might resist. He arrived at Edinburgh on the 27th of February, when the magistrates, who had not forgot his bold march to rescue the city when menaced by Brigadier MacIntosh, entertained him with magnificence. From thence he proceeded to London, where he was received with distinction by George I.

And now you are doubtless desirous of knowing with what new honours, augmented power, or increased wealth, the King of England rewarded the man whose genius had supplied the place of fourfold numbers, and who had secured to his Majesty the crown of one at least of his kingdoms at a moment when it was tottering on his head. I will answer you in a word. In a very short while after the conclusion of the war *the Duke of Argyle was deprived of all his employments.* The cause of this extraordinary act of court ingratitude must be sought in the personal hatred of the Duke of Marlborough, in the high spirit of the Duke of Argyle, which rendered him a troublesome and unmanageable member of a ministerial cabinet, and probably in some apprehension of this great man's increasing personal influence in his native country of Scotland, where he was universally respected and beloved by many even of the party which he had opposed in the field.

It is imagined, moreover, that the Duke's disgrace at court was, in some degree, connected with a legislative enactment of a very doubtful tendency, which was used for the trial of the rebel prisoners. We have already mentioned the criminal proceedings under which the Preston prisoners suffered. Those who had been taken in arms at Sheriffmuir and elsewhere in Scotland ought, according to the laws both of Scotland and England, to have been tried in the country where the treason was committed. But the English lawyers had in recollection the proceedings in the year 1707, when it was impossible to obtain from Grand Juries in Scotland the verdict of a true bill, on which the prisoners could be sent to trial. The close connection, by friendship and alliance, even of those families which were most opposed as Whigs and Tories, made the victorious party in Scotland unwilling to be the means of distressing the vanquished, and disposed them to afford a loophole for escape even at the expense of strict justice. To obviate the difficulties of conviction, which might have been an encouragement to future acts of high treason, it was resolved, that the Scottish offenders against the treason-laws should be tried in England, though the offence had been committed in their own country. This was no doubt extremely convenient for the prosecution, but it remains a question where such innovations are to stop, when a government takes on itself to alter the formal proceedings of law in order to render the conviction of criminals more easy. The Court of Oyer and Terminer sat, notwithstanding, at Carlisle, and might have been held by the same parity of reason at the Land's End in Cornwall, or in the isles of Scilly. But there was a studied moderation towards the accused, which seemed to intimate that if the prisoners abstained from challenging the irregularity of the court, they would be favourably dealt with. Many were set at liberty, and though twenty-four were tried and condemned, not one was ever brought to execution. It is asserted that the Duke of Argyle, as a Scottish man, and one of the framers of the Union, had in his Majesty's councils declared against an innovation which seemed to infringe upon that measure, and that the offence thus given contributed to the fall of his power at court.

Free pardons were liberally distributed to all who had seceded from the Rebellion before its final close. The Highland chiefs and clans were in general forgiven, upon submission, and a surrender of the arms of their people. This was with the disaffected chiefs a simulated transaction, no arms being given up but such as were of no value, while all that were serviceable were concealed and carefully preserved. The loyal clans, on the other hand, made an absolute surrender, and were afterwards found unarmed when the Government desired their assistance.

Meantime the principles of Jacobitism continued to ferment in the interior of the country, and were inflamed by the numerous exiles, men of rank and influence, who were fugitives from Britain in consequence of attainder. To check these, and to intimidate others, the estates of the attainted persons were declared forfeited to the crown, and vested in trustees, to be sold for the benefit of the public. The revenue of the whole, though comprising that of about forty families of rank and consideration, did not amount to £30,000 yearly. These forfeited estates were afterwards purchased from Government by a great mercantile company in London, originally instituted for supplying the city with water by raising it from the Thames, but which, having fallen under the management of speculative persons, its funds, and the facilities vested in it by charter, had been applied to very different purposes. Among others, that of purchasing the forfeited estates was one of the boldest, and, could the company have maintained their credit, would have been one of the most lucrative transactions ever entered into. But the immediate return arising from this immense extent of wood and wilderness, inhabited by tenants who were disposed to acknowledge no landlords but the heirs of the ancient families, and lying in remote districts where law was trammelled by feudal privileges, and affording little protection to the intruders, was quite unequal to meet the interest of the debt which that company had incurred. The purchasers were, therefore, obliged to let the land in many cases to friends and connections of the forfeited proprietors, through whom the exiled owners usually derived the means of subsisting in the foreign land to which their errors and misfortunes had driven them. The affairs of the York Buildings Company, who had in this singular manner become Scottish proprietors to an immense extent, afterwards became totally deranged, owing to the infidelity and extravagance of their managers. Attempts were, from time to time, made to sell their Scottish estates, but very inefficiently, and at great disadvantage. Men of capital showed an unwillingness to purchase the forfeited property; and in two or three instances the dispossessed families were able to repurchase them at low rates. But after the middle of the eighteenth century, when the value of this species of property began to be better understood, rival purchasers came forward, without being deterred by the scruples, which, in earlier days, prevented men from bidding against the heirs of the original possessor. Every new property as exposed to sale brought a higher price, sometimes in a tenfold proportion, than those which had been at first disposed of, and after more than a century of insolvency, the debts of the bankrupt company were completely discharged.

Before proceeding to less interesting matter, I must here notice two plans originating abroad, which were founded upon an expectation of again reviving in Scotland the intestine war of 1715. Two years after that busy period Baron Gorz, minister of Charles XII. of Sweden, a man whose politics were as chimerical as his master's schemes of conquest, devised a confederacy for dethroning George I. and replacing on the

throne the heir of the House of Stewart. His fiery master was burning
with indignation at George for having possessed himself of the towns
of Bremen and Verden. Charles's ancient enemy, the Czar Peter, was
also disposed to countenance the scheme, and Cardinal Alberoni, then
the all-powerful minister of the King of Spain, afforded it his warm
support. The plan was, that a descent of ten thousand troops should be
effected in Scotland, under the command of Charles XII. himself, to
whose redoubted character for courage and determination the success
of the enterprise was to be entrusted. It might be amusing to consider
the probable consequences which might have arisen from the iron-
headed Swede placing himself at the head of an army of Highland
enthusiasts, with courage as romantic as his own. In following the
speculation, it might be doubted whether this leader and his troops
would be more endeared to each other by a congenial audacity of
mind, or alienated by Charles's habit of despotic authority, which the
mountaineers would probably have found themselves unable to
endure. But such a speculation would lead us far from our proper path.
The conspiracy was discovered by the spies of the French Government,
then in strict alliance with England, and all possibility of the proposed
scheme being put into execution was destroyed by the death of Charles
XII. before Frederickshall in 1718.

But although this undertaking was abandoned, the enterprising
Alberoni continued to nourish hopes of being able to effect a counter-
revolution in Great Britain by the aid of the Spanish forces. The Chevalier de St. George was, in 1719, invited to Madrid, and received there
with the honours due to the King of England. Six thousand troops,
with twelve thousand stand of arms, were put on board of ten ships of
war, and the whole armada was placed under the command of the
Duke of Ormond. But all efforts to assist the unlucky House of Stewart
were frowned on by fortune and the elements. The fleet was encountered by a severe tempest off Cape Finisterre, which lasted two days,
drove them back to Spain, and disconcerted their whole enterprise. An
inconsiderable part of the expedition, being two frigates from
St. Sebastian, arrived with three hundred men, some arms, ammunition, and money at their place of destination in the island of Lewis. The
exiled leaders on board were the Marquis of Tullibardine, the Earl
Marischal, and the Earl of Seaforth.

We have not had occasion to mention Seaforth since he separated
from the army of Mar at the same time with the Marquis of Huntly, in

order to oppose the Earl of Sutherland, whom the success of Lovat at Inverness had again brought into the field on the part of the Government. When the two Jacobite leaders reached their own territories, they found the Earl of Sutherland so strong, and the prospects of their own party had assumed so desperate an aspect, that they were induced to enter into an engagement with Sutherland to submit themselves to Government. Huntly kept his promise, and never again joined the rebels, for which submission he received a free pardon. But the Earl of Seaforth again assumed arms in his island of Lewis about the end of February 1715–16. A detachment of regular troops was sent against the refractory chief, commanded by Colonel Cholmondely, who reduced those who were in arms. Seaforth had escaped to France, and from thence to Spain, where he had resided for some time, and was now, in 1719, despatched to his native country, with a view to the assistance so powerful a chief could give to the projected invasion.

On his arrival at his own island of Lewis, Seaforth speedily raised a few hundred Highlanders, and crossed over to Kintail, with the purpose of giving a new impulse to the insurrection. Here he made some additions to his clan levies; but, ere he could gather any considerable force, General Wightman marched against him with a body of regular troops from Inverness, aided by the Monroes, Rosses, and other loyal or Whig clans of the northern Highlands.

They found Seaforth in possession of a pass called Strachells, near the great valley of Glenshiel. A desultory combat took place, in which there was much skirmishing and sharp-shooting, the Spaniards and Seaforth's men keeping the pass. George Munro, younger of Culcairn, engaged on the side of Government, received during this action a severe wound by which he was disabled for the time. As the enemy continued to fire on him, the wounded chief commanded his servant, who had waited by him, to retire, and, leaving him to his fate, to acquaint his father and friends that he had died honourably. The poor fellow burst into tears, and, asking his master how he could suppose he would forsake him in that condition, he spread himself over his body, so as to intercept the balls of the enemy, and actually received several wounds designed for his master. They were both rescued from the most imminent peril by a sergeant of Culcairn's company, who had sworn an oath on his dirk that he would accomplish his chief's deliverance.

The battle was but slightly contested; but the advantage was on the side of the MacKenzies, who lost only one man, while the Government troops had several killed and wounded. They were compelled to retreat without dislodging the enemy, and to leave their own wounded on the field, many of whom the victors are said to have despatched with their dirks. But though the MacKenzies obtained a partial success, it was not such as to encourage perseverance in the undertaking, especially as their chief, Lord Seaforth, being badly wounded, could no longer direct their enterprise. They determined, therefore, to disperse as soon as night fell, the rather that several of their allies were not disposed to renew the contest. One clan, for example, had been lent to Seaforth for the service of the day, under the special paction on the part of the chief, that however the battle went, they should return before next morning—this occasional assistance being only regarded in the light of a neighbourly accommodation to Lord Seaforth.

The wounded Earl, with Tullibardine and Marischal, escaped to the Continent. The three hundred Spaniards next day laid down their arms, and surrendered themselves prisoners. The affair of Glenshiel might be called the last faint sparkle of the Great Rebellion of 1715, which was fortunately extinguished for want of fuel. A vague rumour of Earl Marischal's having re-landed, had, however, well-nigh excited a number of the most zealous Jacobites once more to take the field, but it was contradicted before they adopted so rash a step.

LXXIV

Pacification of the Highlands

1719-1736

IT might well have been expected, after the foundations of the throne
had been so shaken by the storm in 1715, that the Government would
have looked earnestly into the causes which rendered the Highland
clans so dangerous to the public tranquillity, and that some measures
would have been taken for preventing their ready valour being abused
into the means of ruining both themselves and others. Accordingly, the
English ministers lost no time in resorting to the more forcible and obvious means of military subjugation, which necessarily are, and must be,
the most immediate remedy in such a case, though far from being the
most effectual in the long run. The law for disarming the Highlanders,
although in many cases evaded, had yet been so generally enforced as to
occasion general complaints of robbery by bands of armed men, which
the country had no means of resisting. Those complaints were not without foundation; but they were greatly exaggerated by Simon Fraser, now
called Lord Lovat, and others, who were desirous to obtain arms for
their vassals, that they might serve purposes of their own.

Accordingly, in 1724 a warrant, under the sign manual, was granted
to Field-Marshal Wade, an officer of skill and experience, with instructions narrowly to inspect and report upon the state of the Highlands;

the best measures for enforcing the laws and protecting the defenceless; the modes of communication which might be opened through the country; and whatever other remedies might conduce to the quiet of a district so long distracted. In 1725 a new sign manual was issued to the same officer for the same purpose. In consequence of the Marshal's report, various important measures were taken. The clan of the MacKenzies had for years refused to account for the rents on Seaforth's forfeited estate to the collector nominated by Government, and had paid them to a factor appointed amongst themselves, who conveyed them openly to the exiled Earl. This state of things was now stopped, and the clan compelled to submit and give up their arms, the Government liberally granting them an indulgence and remission for such arrears as they had transmitted to Seaforth in their obstinate fidelity to him. Other clans submitted, and made at least an ostensible surrender of their arms, although many of the most serviceable were retained by the clans which were hostile to Government. An armed vessel was stationed on Lochness to command the shores of that extensive lake. Barracks were rebuilt in some places, founded anew in others, and filled with regular soldiers.

Another measure of very dubious utility, which had been resorted to by King William and disused by George I., was now again had recourse to. This was the establishment of independent companies to secure the peace of the Highlands, and suppress the gangs of thieves who carried on so bold a trade of depredation. These companies, consisting of Highlanders dressed and armed in their own peculiar manner, were placed under the command of men well affected to Government, or supposed to be so, and having a great interest in the Highlands. It was truly said that such a militia, knowing the language and manners of the country, could do more than ten times the number of regular troops to put a stop to robbery. But, on the other hand, it had been found by experience that the privates in such corps often, from clanship or other motives, connived at the thefts, or compounded for them with the delinquents. Their officers were accused of imposing upon Government by false musters; and above all, the doubtful faith even of those chiefs who made the strongest show of affection to Government, rendered the re-establishment of Black soldiers, as they were called, to distinguish them from the regular troops, who wore the red national uniform, a measure of precarious policy. It was resorted to, however, and six companies were raised on this principle.

Marshal Wade had also the power of receiving submission and granting protections to outlaws or others exposed to punishment for the late rebellion, and received many of them into the King's peace accordingly. He granted, besides, licenses to drovers, foresters, dealers in cattle, and others engaged in such traffic, empowering them to carry arms for the defence of their persons and property. In all his proceedings towards the Highlanders, there may be distinguished a general air of humanity and good sense which rendered him a popular character even while engaged in executing orders which they looked upon with the utmost degree of jealousy and suspicion.

The Jacobite partisans in the meanwhile, partly by letters from abroad, partly by agents of ability who traversed the country on purpose, did all in their power to thwart and interrupt the measures which were taken to reduce the Highlands to a state of peaceful cultivation. The act for disarming the body of the people they represented in the most odious colours, though, indeed, it is hardly possible to aggravate the feelings of shame and dishonour in which a free people must always indulge at being deprived of the means of self-defence. And the practical doctrine was not new to them, that if the parties concerned could evade this attempt to deprive them of their natural right and lawful property, either by an elusory surrender, or by such professions as might induce the Government to leave them in possession of their weapons, whether under license or as members of the independent companies, it would be no dishonour in oppressed men meeting force by craft, and eluding the unjust and unreasonable demands which they wanted means openly to resist. Much of the quiet obtained by Marshal Wade's measures was apparent only; and while he boasts that the Highlanders, instead of going armed with guns, swords, dirks, and pistols, now travelled to churches, markets, and fairs with only a staff in their hands, the veteran General was ignorant how many thousand weapons, landed from the Spanish frigates in 1719, or otherwise introduced into the country, lay in caverns and other places of concealment, ready for use when occasion should offer.

But the gigantic part of Marshal Wade's task, and that which he executed with the most complete success, was the establishment of military roads through the rugged and desolate regions of the north, ensuring the free passage of regular troops in a country of which it might have been said, while in its natural state, that every mountain was a natural fortress, every valley a defensible pass. The roads, as they were termed, through the Highlands, had been hitherto mere tracks, made by the feet of men and the cattle which they drove before them, interrupted by rocks, morasses, torrents, and all the features of an inaccessible country, where a stranger, even unopposed, might have despaired of making his solitary way, but where the passage of a regular body of troops, with cavalry, artillery, and baggage, was altogether impossible. These rugged paths by the labours of the soldiers employed under Field-Marshal Wade, were, by an extraordinary exertion of skill and labour, converted into excellent roads of great breadth and sound formation, which have ever since his time afforded a free and open communication through all parts of the Scottish Highlands.

Two of these highways enter among the hills from the low country, the one at Crieff, twenty miles north of Stirling, the other at Dunkeld, fifteen miles north of Perth. Penetrating around the mountains from different quarters, these two branches unite at Dalnacardoch. From thence a single line leads to Dalwhinnie, where it again divides into two. One road runs north-west through Garviemore, and over the tremendous pass of Corryarrack, to a new fort raised by Marshal Wade, called Fort Augustus. The second line extends from Dalnacardoch north to the barracks of Ruthven, in Lochaber, and thence to Inverness. From that town it proceeds almost due westward across the island, connecting Fort Augustus, above mentioned, with Inverness, and so proceeding to Fort William, in Lochaber, traversing the country inhabited by the Camerons, the MacDonalds of Glengarry, and other clans judged to be the worst affected to the reigning family.

It is not to be supposed that the Highlanders of that period saw with indifference the defensive character of their country destroyed, and the dusky wildernesses, which had defied the approach of the Romans, rendered accessible in almost every direction to the regular troops of the Government. We can suppose that it affected them as the dismantling of some impregnable citadel might do the inhabitants of the country which it protected, and that the pang which they experienced at seeing their glens exposed to a hostile, or at least a stranger force, was similar to that which they felt at the resignation of the weapons of their fathers. But those feelings and circumstances have passed away, and the Highland military roads will continue an inestimable advantage to the districts which they traverse, although no longer required to check apprehended insurrection, and will long exhibit a public monument of skill and patience, not unworthy of the ancient Romans. Upon the Roman principle, also, the regular soldiers were employed in this laborious work, and reconciled to the task by some trifling addition of pay; an experiment which succeeded so well as to excite some surprise that public works have not been more frequently executed by similar means.

Other measures of the most laudable character were resorted to by the Government and their friends, for the improvement of the Highlands; but as they were of a description not qualified to produce ameliorating effects, save after a length of time, they were but carelessly urged. They related to the education of this wild population, and the care necessary to train the rising generation in moral and religious principles; but the Act of Parliament framed for this end proved in a great measure ineffectual. Those exertions, which ought to have been national, were in some degree supplied by the Society for the Propagation of Christian Knowledge in the Highlands and Isles, who, by founding chapels and schools in different places, did more for enlightening the people of that country than had been achieved by any prince who had yet reigned in or over Scotland.

While Marshal Wade was employed in pacifying the Highlands, and rendering them accessible to military forces, a subject of discontent broke out in the Lowlands which threatened serious consequences. The Government had now become desirous to make the income of Scotland a source of revenue to the general exchequer, as hitherto it had been found scarcely adequate to maintain the public institutions of the kingdom, and to pay and support the troops which it was necessary to quarter there for the general tranquillity. Now a surplus of revenue was desirable, and the Jacobites invidiously reported that the immediate object was chiefly to find funds in Scotland for defraying an expense of about ten guineas weekly, allowed to every North British Member of Parliament for supporting the charge of his residence in London. This expense had been hitherto imposed on the general revenue, but now, said the Jacobites, the Scottish members were made aware by Sir Robert Walpole that they were to find, or acquiesce in, some mode of making up this sum out of the Scottish revenue; or, according to a significant phrase, that they must in future lay their account with tying up their stockings with their own garters,

With this view of rendering the Scottish revenue more efficient, it was resolved to impose a tax of sixpence per barrel on all ale, brewed in Scotland. Upon the appearance of a desperate resistance to this proposal, the tax was lowered to three-pence per barrel, or one-half of what was originally proposed. In this modified proposal the Scottish members acquiesced. Yet it did not become more popular in Scotland; for it went to enchance the rate of a commodity in daily request, and excited by the inflammatory language of those whose interest it was to incense the populace, the principal towns in Scotland prepared to resist the imposition at all hazards.

Glasgow, so eminent for its loyalty in 1715, was now at the head of this opposition; and on the 23d June 1725, when the duty was to be laid on, the general voice of the people of that city declared that they would not submit to its payment, and piles of stones were raised against the doors of the breweries and malt-houses, with a warning to all excise officers to keep their distance. On the appearance of these alarming symptoms, two companies of foot, under Captain Bushell, were marched from Edinburgh to Glasgow to prevent further disturbances. When the soldiers arrived, they found that the mob had taken possession of the guard house, and refused them admittance. The provost of the city, a timid or treacherous man, prevailed on Captain Bushell to send his men into their quarters without occupying the guard-house, or any other place proper to serve for an alarm-post or rendezvous. Presently after the rabble, becoming more and more violent, directed their fury against Daniel Campbell of Shawfield, member for the city, and the set of boroughs in which it is included. His mansion, then the most elegant in Glasgow, was totally destroyed; and the mob, breaking into his cellars, found fresh incitement to their fury in the liquors there contained. All this was done without opposition, although Captain Bushell offered the assistance of his soldiers to keep the peace.

Next day the provost ventured to break open the guard-room door, and the soldiers were directed to repair thither. One or two rioters were also apprehended. Upon these symptoms of reviving authority an alarm was beat by the mob, who assembled in a more numerous and formidable body than ever, and surrounding Bushell's two companies, loaded them with abuse, maltreated them with stones, and compelled them at last to fire, when nine men were killed and many wounded. The rioters, undismayed, rung the alarm bell, broke into the town magazine of arms, seized all the muskets they could find, and continued the attack on the soldiers. Captain Bushell, by the command, and at the entreaty of the provost, now commenced a retreat to Dumbarton Castle, insulted and pursued by the mob a third part of the way.

In the natural resentment excited by this formidable insurrection, the Lord Advocate for the time (the celebrated Duncan Forbes) advanced to Glasgow at the head of a considerable army of horse, foot, and artillery. Many threats were thrown out against the rioters, and the magistrates were severely censured for a gross breach of duty. But the cool sagacity of the Lord Advocate anticipated the difficulty which, in the inflamed state of the public mind, he was likely to experience in procuring a verdict against such offenders as he might bring to trial. So that the affair passed away with less noise than might have been expected, it having been ascertained that the riot had no political tendency; and though inflamed by the leading Jacobites, was begun and carried on by the people of Glasgow solely on the principle of a resolution to drink their twopenny ale untaxed.

The metropolis of Scotland took this excise tax more coolly than the inhabitants of Glasgow, for though greatly averse to the exaction, they only opposed it by a sort of *vis inertiæ*, the principal brewers threatening to resign their trade, and, if the impost was continued, to brew no more ale for the supply of the public. The Lords of the Court of Session declared by an Act of Sederunt, that the brewers had no right to withdraw themselves from their occupation; and when the brewers, in reply, attempted to show that they could not be legally compelled to follow their trade, after it had been rendered a losing one, the court appointed their petition to be burnt by the hands of the common hangman, assuring them they would be allowed no alternative between the exercise of their trade or imprisonment. Finally, four of the recusants were actually thrown into jail, which greatly shook the firmness of these refractory fermentators; and at length, reflecting that the ultimate loss must fall not on them but on the public, they returned to the ordinary exercise of their trade, and quietly paid the duties imposed on their liquor.

The Union having now begun in some degree to produce beneficial effects, the Jacobite party were gradually losing much of the influence over the public mind which had arisen out of the general prejudices against that measure, and the natural disgust at the manner in which it was carried on and concluded. Accordingly, the next narrative of a historical character which occurs as proper to tell you is unmingled with politics of Whig and Tory, and must be simply regarded as a strong and powerful display of the cool, stern, and resolved manner in which the Scottish, even of the lower classes, can concert and execute a vindictive purpose.

The coast of Fife, full of little boroughs and petty seaports, was, of course, much frequented by smugglers, men constantly engaged in disputes with the excise officers, which were sometimes attended with violence. Wilson and Robertson, two persons of inferior rank, but rather distinguished in the contraband trade, had sustained great loss by a seizure of smuggled goods. The step from illicit trading to positive robbery is not a long one. The two men robbed the collector, to indemnify themselves from the effects of the seizure.[1] They were tried before the Court of Justiciary, and condemned to death.

While the two criminals were lying under sentence in the tolbooth of Edinburgh, two horse-stealers, named Ratcliffe and Stewart, were confined in the room immediately above where they lay. These last having opened a communication with their unfortunate companions by boring a large hole in the floor of their apartment, about two o'clock in the morning hauled them up; this done, they commenced by means of spring saws and other instruments, with which they had provided themselves, to cut through the thick iron bars that secured a window on the inside, and afterwards the cross-gratings on the out. One party sung psalms, to drown the noise, while the others were sawing. Having opened what they supposed a sufficient aperture, one of the horse-stealers was let down in safety, and the others might have escaped but for the obstinacy of Wilson. This man, of a bulky person, insisted on making the next essay of the breach which had been accomplished, and having stuck fast between the bars, was unable either to get through or to return back. Discovery was the consequence, and precautions were taken against any repetition of such attempts to escape. Wilson reflected bitterly on himself for not having

---

[1] "Wilson, with two of his associates, entered the collector's apartment, while Robertson, the fourth, kept watch at the door, with a drawn cutlass in his hand. The officer of the Customs, conceiving his life in danger, escaped out of his bedroom window, and fled in his shirt, so that the plunderers, with much ease, possessed themselves of about two hundred pounds of public money. This robbery was committed in a very audacious manner, for several persons were passing in the street at the time. But Robertson, representing the noise they heard as a dispute or fray betwixt the collector and the people of the house, the worthy citizens of Pittenweem felt themselves no way called on to interfere in behalf of the obnoxious revenue officer; so, satisfying themselves with this very superficial account of the matter, like the Levite in the parable they passed on the opposite side of the way. An alarm was at length given, military were called in, the depredators were pursued, the booty recovered, and Wilson and Robertson tried and condemned to death, chiefly on the evidence of an accomplice."—*Heart of Mid-Lothian.*

permitted his comrade to make the first trial, to whom, as being light and slender, the bars would have been no obstacle. He resolved, with a spirit worthy of a better man, to atone to his companion, at all risks, for the injury he had done him.

At this time it was the custom in Edinburgh for criminals under sentence of death to be carried, under a suitable guard, to hear divine service, on the Sabbath before the execution, in a church adjacent to the prison. Wilson and Robertson were brought thither accordingly, under the custody of four soldiers of the city-guard. Wilson, who was a very strong man, suddenly seized a soldier with each hand, and calling to his comrade to fly for his life, detained a third by grappling his collar with his teeth. Robertson shook himself clear of the fourth, and making his escape over the pews of the church, was no more heard of in Edinburgh. The common people, to whose comprehension the original crime for which the men were condemned had nothing very abhorrent in it, were struck with the generosity and self-devotion that this last action evinced, and took such an interest in Wilson's fate that it was generally rumoured there would be an attempt to rescue him at the place of execution. To prevent, as was their duty, any riotous plan of this kind, the magistrates ordered a party of the guard of the city, a sort of *maréchaussé* or *gensdarmes*, armed and trained as soldiers, to protect the execution.

The captain of the party was the celebrated John Porteous, whose name will long be remembered in Scotland. This man whose father was a burgess and citizen of Edinburgh had himself been bred in the regular army, which recommended him to the magistrates, when in the year 1715 they were desirous to give their civic guard something of a more military character. As an active police officer Porteous was necessarily often in collision with the rabble of the city, and being strict, and even severe in the manner in which he repressed and chastised petty riots and delinquencies, he was, as is usual with persons of his calling, extremely unpopular and odious to the rabble. They also accused him of abusing the authority reposed in him to protect the extravagancies of the rich and powerful, while he was inexorable in punishing the license of the poor. Porteous had, besides, a good deal of the pride of his profession, and seems to have been determined to show that the corps he commanded was adequate, without assistance, to dispel any commotion in the city of Edinburgh. For this reason, he considered it rather as an affront that the magistrates, on occasion of

Wilson's execution, had ordered Moyle's regiment to be drawn up in the suburbs to enforce order, should the city-guard be unable to maintain it. It is probable from what followed that the men commanded by Porteous shared their leader's jealousy of the regular troops, and his dislike to the populace, with whom in the execution of their duty they were often engaged in hostilities.

The execution of Wilson, on the 14th of April 1736, took place in the usual manner without any actual or menaced interruption. The criminal, according to his sentence, was hanged to the death, and it was not till the corpse was cut down that the mob, according to their common practice, began to insult and abuse the executioner, pelting him with stones, many of which were also thrown at the soldiers. At former executions it had been the custom for the city-guard to endure such insults with laudable patience, but on this occasion they were in such a state of irritation that they forgot their usual moderation, and repaid the pelting of the mob by pouring amongst them a fire of musketry, killing and wounding many persons. In their retreat also to the guard-house, as the rabble pressed on them with furious execrations, some soldiers in the rear of the march again faced round and renewed the fire. In consequence of this unauthorised and unnecessary violence, and to satisfy the community of Edinburgh for the blood which had been rashly shed, the magistrates were inclined to have taken Porteous to trial under the Lord Provost's authority as High Sheriff within the city. Being advised, however, by the lawyers whom they consulted, that such proceeding would be subject to challenge, Porteous was brought to trial for murder before the High Court of Justiciary. He denied that he ever gave command to fire, and it was proved that the fusee which he himself carried had never been discharged. On the other hand, in the perplexed and contradictory evidence which was obtained, where so many persons witnessed the same events from different positions, and perhaps with different feelings, there were witnesses who said that they saw Porteous take a musket from one of his men and fire it directly at the crowd. A jury of incensed citizens took the worst view of the case, and found the prisoner guilty of murder. At this time King George II. was on the Continent, and the regency was chiefly in the hands of Queen Caroline, a woman of very considerable talent, and naturally disposed to be tenacious of the crown's rights. It appeared to her Majesty and her advisers that though the action of Porteous and his soldiers was certainly rash and unwarranted, yet that, considering the purpose by which it was dictated, it must fall considerably short of the guilt of murder. Captain Porteous, in the discharge of a duty imposed on him by legal authority, had unquestionably been assaulted without provocation on his part, and had therefore a right to defend himself; and if there were excess in the means he had recourse to, yet a line of conduct originating in self-defence cannot be extended into murder, though it might amount to homicide. Moved by these considerations, the Regency granted a reprieve of Porteous's sentence, preliminary to his obtaining a pardon, which might perhaps have been clogged with some conditions.

When the news of the reprieve reached Edinburgh, they were received with gloomy and general indignation. The lives which had been taken in the affray were not those of persons of the meanest rank, for the soldiers, of whom many, with natural humanity, desired to fire over the heads of the rioters, had, by so doing, occasioned additional misfortune, several of the balls taking effect in windows which were crowded with spectators, and killing some persons of good condition. A great number, therefore, of all ranks were desirous that Porteous should atone with his own life for the blood which had been so rashly spilt by those under his command. A general feeling seemed to arise, unfavourable to the unhappy criminal, and public threats were cast out, though the precise source could not be traced, that the reprieve itself should not save Porteous from the vengeance of the citizens of Edinburgh.

The 7th day of September, the day previous to that appointed for his execution, had now arrived, and Porteous, confident of his speedy deliverance from jail, had given an entertainment to a party of friends, whom he feasted within the tolbooth, when the festivity was strangely interrupted. Edinburgh was then surrounded by a wall on the east and south sides; on the west it was defended by the castle, on the north by a lake called the North Loch. The gates were regularly closed in the evening and guarded. It was about the hour of shutting the ports, as they were called, when a disorderly assemblage began to take place in the suburb called Portsburgh, a quarter which has been always the residence of labourers and persons generally of inferior rank. The rabble continued to gather to a head, and, to augment their numbers, beat a drum which they had taken from the man who exercised the function of drummer to the suburb. Finding themselves strong enough to commence their operations, they seized on the West Port, nailed and barricaded it. Then going along the Cowgate and gaining the High Street by the numerous lanes which run between these two principal streets of the Old Town, they secured the Cowgate Port and that of the Netherbow, and thus, except on the side of the castle, entirely separated the city from such military forces as were quartered in the suburbs. The next object of the mob was to attack the city-guard, a few of whom were upon duty as usual. These the rioters stripped of their arms, and dismissed from their rendezvous, but without otherwise maltreating them, though the agents of the injury of which they complained. The various halberds, Lochaber axes,[1] muskets, and other weapons, which they found in the guard-house, served to arm the rioters, a large body of whom now bent their way to the door of the jail, while another body, with considerable regularity, drew up across the front of the Luckenbooths. The magistrates, with such force as they could collect, made an effort to disperse the multitude. They were strenuously repulsed, but with no more violence than was necessary to show that, while the populace were firm in their purpose, they meant to accomplish it with as little injury as possible to any one, excepting their destined victim. There might have been some interruption of their undertaking had the soldiers of Moyle's regiment made their way into the town from the Canongate, where they were quartered, or had the garrison descended from the castle. But neither Colonel Moyle nor the governor of the castle chose to interfere on their own responsibility, and no one dared to carry a written warrant to them on the part of the magistrates.[2]

In the meantime the multitude demanded that Porteous should be delivered up to them; and as they were refused admittance to the jail

---

[1] "A long pole, namely, with an axe at the extremity, and a hook at the back of the hatchet. The hook was to enable the bearer of the Lochaber axe to scale a gateway by grappling the top of the door, and swinging himself up by the staff of his weapon."— *Note, Heart of Mid-Lothian.*

[2] "Mr. Lindsay, member of Parliament for the city, volunteered the perilous task of carrying a verbal message from the Lord Provost to Colonel Moyle, the commander of the regiment lying in the Canongate, requesting him to force the Netherbow port, and enter the city to put down the tumult. But Mr. Lindsay declined to charge himself with any written order, which, if found on his person by an enraged mob, might have cost him his life; and the issue of the application was, that Colonel Moyle, having no written requisition from the civil authorities, and having the fate of Porteous before his eyes as an example of the severe construction put by a jury on the proceedings of military men acting on their own responsibility, declined to encounter the risk to which the Provost's verbal communication invited him."—*Heart of Mid-Lothian.*

they prepared to burst open the doors. The outer gate, as was necessary to serve the purpose, was of such uncommon strength as to resist the united efforts of the rioters, though they employed sledge hammers and iron crows to force it open. Fire was at length called for, and a large bonfire, maintained with tar-barrels and such ready combustibles, soon burnt a hole in the door, through which the jailer flung the keys. This gave the rioters free entrance. Without troubling themselves about the fate of the other criminals, who naturally took the opportunity of escaping, the rioters or their leaders went in search of Porteous. They found him concealed in the chimney of his apartment, which he was prevented from ascending by a grating that ran across the vent, as is usual in such edifices. The rioters dragged their victim out of his concealment, and commanded him to prepare to undergo the death he had deserved; nor did they pay the least attention either to his prayers for mercy or to the offers by which he endeavoured to purchase his life. Yet, amid all their obduracy of vengeance, there was little tumult, and no more violence than was inseparable from the action which they meditated. Porteous was permitted to entrust what money or papers he had with him to a friend, for the behoof of his family. One of the rioters, a grave and respectable-looking man, undertook, in the capacity of a clergyman, to give him ghostly consolation suited to his circumstances, as one who had not many minutes to live. He was conducted from the tolbooth to the Grassmarket, which, both as being the usual place of execution and the scene where their victim had fired, or caused his soldiers to fire, on the citizens, was selected as the place of punishment. They marched in a sort of procession, guarded by a band of the rioters, miscellaneously armed with muskets, battle-axes, etc., which were taken from the guard-house, while others carried links or flambeaux. Porteous was in the midst of them, and as he refused to walk, he was carried by two of the rioters on what is in Scotland called the King's cushion, by which two persons alternately grasping each others wrists, form a kind of seat on the backs of their hands, upon which a third may be placed. They were so cool as to halt when one of the slippers dropped from his foot, till it was picked up, and replaced.[1]

The citizens of the better class looked from their windows on this extraordinary scene, but terrified beyond the power of interference, if

---

[1] "This little incident, characteristic of the extreme composure of this extraordinary mob, was witnessed by a lady who, disturbed like others from her slumbers, had gone to the window. It was told to the author by the lady's daughter."—*Note, Heart of Mid-Lothian.*

they had possessed the will. In descending the West Bow, which leads to the place of execution, the rioters, or conspirators—a term, perhaps, more suited to men of their character—provided themselves with a coil of ropes, by breaking into the booth of a dealer in such articles, and left at the same time a guinea to pay for it; a precaution which would hardly have occurred to men of the lowest class, of which in external appearance the mob seemed to consist. A cry was next raised for the gallows, in order that Porteous might die according to all the ceremony of the law. But as this instrument of punishment was kept in a distant part of the town, so that time must be lost in procuring it, they proceeded to hang the unfortunate man over a dyer's pole, as near to the place of execution as possible. The poor man's efforts to save himself only added to his tortures; for as he tried to keep hold of the beam to which he was suspended, they struck his hands with guns and Lochaber axes, to make him quit his hold, so that he suffered more than usual in the struggle which dismissed him from life.

When Porteous was dead the rioters dispersed, withdrawing without noise or disturbance all the outposts which they had occupied for preventing interruption, and leaving the city so quiet, that had it not been for the relics of the fire which had been applied to the jail door; the arms which lay scattered in disorder on the street, as the rioters had flung them down; and the dead body of Porteous, which remained suspended in the place where he died; there was no visible symptom of so violent an explosion of popular fury having taken place.

The Government, highly offended at such a daring contempt of authority, imposed on the crown counsel the task of prosecuting the discovery of the rioters with the utmost care. The report of Mr. Charles Erskine, then solicitor-general, is now before me,[1] and bears witness to his exertions in tracing the reports, which were numerous, in assigning to various persons particular shares in this nocturnal outrage. All of them, however, when examined, proved totally groundless, and it was evident that they had been either wilful falsehoods, sent abroad to deceive and mislead the investigators, or at least idle and unauthenticated rumours which arise out of such commotions, like bubbles on broken and distracted waters. A reward of two hundred pounds was offered by Government for the discovery of any person concerned in the riot, but without success.

---

[1] Given in Note D. to the *Heart of Mid-Lothian*.

Only a single person was proved to have been present at the mob, and the circumstances in which he stood placed him out of the reach of punishment. He was footman to a lady of rank, and a creature of weak intellects. Being sent into Edinburgh on a message by his mistress, he had drunk so much liquor as to deprive him of all capacity whatever, and in this state mixed with the mob, some of whom put a halberd in his hand. But the witnesses who proved this apparent accession to the mob, proved also that the accused could not stand without the support of the rioters, and was totally incapable of knowing for what purpose they were assembled, and consequently of approving of or aiding their guilt. He was acquitted accordingly, to the still further dissatisfaction of the Ministry, and of Queen Caroline, who considered the commotion, and the impunity with which it was followed, as an insult to her personal authority.[1]

A bill was prepared and brought into Parliament for the punishment of the city of Edinburgh, in a very vindictive spirit, proposing to abolish the city charter, demolish the city walls, take away the town-guard,[1] and declare the Provost incapable of holding any office of public trust. A long investigation took place on the occasion, in which many persons were examined at the bar of the House of Lords, without throwing the least light on the subject of the Porteous Mob, or the character of the persons by whom it was conducted. The penal conclusions of the bill were strenuously combated by the Duke of Argyle, Duncan Forbes, and others, who represented the injustice of punishing with dishonour the capital of Scotland for the insolence of a lawless mob, which, taking advantage of a moment of security, had committed a great breach of the peace, attended with a cruel murder. As men's minds cooled, the obnoxious clauses were dropped out of the bill, and at length its penal consequences were restricted to a fine of £2000 sterling on the city, to be paid for the use of Captain Porteous's widow. This person, having received other favours from the town, accepted of £1500 in full of the fine; and so ended the affair, so far as the city of Edinburgh was concerned.

---

[1] "It is still recorded in popular tradition that her Majesty, in the height of her displeasure, told the celebrated John, Duke of Argyle, that sooner than submit to such an insult (the execution of Porteous), she would make Scotland a hunting-field.—'In that case, Madam,' answered that high-spirited nobleman, with a profound bow, 'I will take leave of your Majesty, and go down to my own country to get my hounds ready.' The import of the reply had more than met the ear."—*The Heart of Mid-Lothian.*

[2] This ancient corps was disbanded in 1817.

But, as if some fatality had attended the subject, a clause was thrown in, compelling the ministers of the Scottish Church to read a proclamation from the pulpit, once every month during the space of a whole year, calling on the congregation to do all in their power for discovering and bringing to justice the murderers of Captain Porteous, or any of them, and noticing the reward which Government had promised to such as should bring the malefactors to conviction. Many of the Scottish clergy resented this imposition, as indecorously rendering the pulpit a vehicle for a hue and cry, and still more as an attempt, on the part of the state, to interfere with the spiritual authorities of the kirk, which amounted, in their opinion, to an Erastian heresy. Neither was it held to be matter of indifference that, in reading the proclamation of the Legislature, the clergymen were compelled to describe the bishops as the "Lords Spiritual in Parliament assembled;" an epithet seemingly acknowledging the legality and the rank of an order disavowed by all true Calvinists. The dispute was the more violent as it was immediately subsequent to a schism in the church, on the fruitful subject of patronage, which had divided from the communion of the Established Church of Scotland that large class of dissenters generally called Seceders. Much ill blood was excited, and great dissensions took place betwixt those clergymen who did, and those who did not, read the proclamation. This controversy, like others, had its hour, during which little else was spoken of, until in due time the subject was worn threadbare and forgotten.

The origin of the Porteous Mob continued long to exercise the curiosity of those by whom the event was remembered, and from the extraordinary mixture of prudence and audacity with which the purpose of the multitude had been conceived and executed, as well as the impenetrable secrecy with which the enterprise was carried through, the public were much inclined to suspect that there had been among its actors men of rank and character, far superior to that belonging to the multitude who were the ostensible agents. Broken and imperfect stories were told of men in the disguise of women and of common artisans, whose manner betrayed a sex and manners different from what their garb announced. Others laughed at these as unauthorised exaggerations, and contended that no class were so likely to frame or execute the plan for the murder of the police officer as the populace to whom his official proceedings had rendered him obnoxious, and that the secrecy so wonderfully preserved on the occasion arose out of the constancy and fidelity which the Scottish people observe towards each other when engaged in a common cause. Nothing is, or probably ever will be, known with certainty on the subject; but it is understood that several young men left Scotland in apprehension of the strict scrutiny which was made into that night's proceedings; and in your grandfather's younger days the voice of fame pointed out individuals, who, long absent from their country, had returned from the East and West Indies in improved circumstances, as persons who had fled abroad on account of the Porteous Mob. One story of the origin of the conspiracy was stated to me with so much authority, and seemed in itself so simple and satisfactory, that although the degree of proof, upon investigation, fell far short of what was necessary as full evidence, I cannot help considering it as the most probable account of the mysterious affair. A man, who long bore an excellent character, and filled a place of some trust as forester and carpenter to a gentleman of fortune in Fife, was affirmed to have made a confession on his death-bed that he had been not only one of the actors in the hanging of Porteous, but one of the secret few by whom the deed was schemed and set on foot. Twelve persons of the village of Path-head—so this man's narrative was said to proceed—resolved that Porteous should die, to atone for the life of Wilson, with whom many of them had been connected by the ties of friendship and joint adventure in illicit trade, and for the death of those shot at the execution. This vengeful band crossed the Forth by different ferries, and met together at a solitary place near the city, where they distributed the party which were to act in the business which they had in hand; and giving a beginning to the enterprise, soon saw it undertaken by the populace of the city, whose minds were precisely in that state of irritability which disposed them to follow the example of a few desperate men. According to this account, most of the original devisers of the scheme fled to foreign parts, the surprise of the usual authorities having occasioned some days to pass over ere the investigations of the affair were commenced. On making inquiry of the surviving family of this old man, they were found disposed to treat the rumoured confession as a fiction, and to allege that although he was of an age which seemed to support the story, and had gone abroad shortly after the Porteous Mob, yet he had never acknowledged any accession to it, but, on the contrary, maintained his innocence when taxed, as he sometimes was, with having a concern in the affair. The report, however, though probably untrue in many of its circumstances, yet seems to give a very probable account of the origin of the riot in the vindictive purpose of a few resolute men, whose example was quickly followed by the multitude, already in a state of mind to catch fire from the slightest spark.

This extraordinary and mysterious outrage seems to be the only circumstance which can be interesting to you, as exclusively belonging to the history of Scotland, betwixt the years immediately succeeding the civil war of 1715 and those preceding the last explosion of Jacobitism in that country in 1745–46.

LXXV

Bonnie Prince Charlie

1736-1745

AFTER the temporary subjection of the Highlands in 1720, and the years immediately succeeding, had been in appearance completed by the establishment of garrisons, the formation of military roads, and the general submission of the Highland clans who were most opposed to Government, Scotland enjoyed a certain degree of internal repose, if not of prosperity. To estimate the nature of this calm, we must look at the state of the country in two points of view, as it concerned the Highlands and the Lowlands.

In the Lowlands a superior degree of improvement began to take place, by the general influence of civilisation rather than by the effect of any specific legislative enactment. The ancient laws, which vested the administration of justice in the aristocracy, continued to be a cause of poverty amongst the tenantry of the country. Every gentleman of considerable estate possessed the power of a baron, or lord of regality, and by means of a deputy, who was usually his factor or land-steward, exercised the power of dispensing justice, both civil and criminal, to those in his neighbourhood. In the most ordinary class of lawsuits one party was thus constituted the judge in his own cause; for in all cases betwixt landlord and tenant, the questions were decided in the court of the baron, where the landlord, by means of an obsequious deputy, in fact possessed the judicial power. The nature of the engagements between the proprietor and the cultivator of the ground rendered the situation of the latter one of great hardship. The tenants usually held their farms from year to year, and, from the general poverty of the country, could pay but little rent in money. The landlords, who were usually struggling to educate their children and set them out in the world, were also necessitous, and pursued indirect expedients for subjecting the tenants in services of a nature which had a marked connection with the old slavish feudal tenures. Thus the tenant was bound to grind his meal at the baron's mill, and to pay certain heavy duties for the operation, though he could have had it ground more conveniently and cheaply elsewhere. In some instances he was also obliged to frequent the brewery of his landlord. In almost every case he was compelled to discharge certain services, of driving coals, casting peats,[1] or similar domestic labour, for the proprietor. In this manner the tenant was often called upon to perform the field work of the laird when that of his own farm was in arrear, and deprived of that freedom of employing his powers of labour to the best possible account which is the very soul of agriculture.

Nevertheless, though the Scottish lairds had the means of oppression in their hands, a judicious perception of their own interest prevented many, and doubtless a sense of justice warned others, from abusing those rights to the injury of their people. The custom, too, of giving farms in lease to younger sons or other near relatives tended to maintain the farmers above the rank of mere peasantry, into which they must have otherwise sunk; and as the Scottish landholders of those days lived economically and upon terms of kindness with their tenants there were fewer instances of oppression or ill-usage than might have been expected from a system which was radically bad, and which, if the proprietors had been more rapacious and the estates committed to the management of a mere factor or middle-man who was to make the most of them, must have led to a degree of distress which never appears to have taken place in Scotland. Both parties were in general poor, but they united their efforts to bear their indigence with patience.

The younger sons of gentlemen usually went abroad in some line of life in which they might speedily obtain wealth, or at least the means of subsistence. The colonies afforded opportunities of advancement to

---

[1] Digging peats for fuel.

many; others sought fortune in England, where the calmer and more provident character of the nation, joined with the ready assistance which each Scotsman who attained prosperity extended to those who were struggling for it, very often led to success. The elder sons of the Scottish landholders were generally, like those of France, devoted to the law or to the sword, so that in one way or other they might add some means of increase to the family estates. Commerce was advancing by gradual steps. The colonial trade had opened slow but increasing sources of exertion to Glasgow, which is so conveniently situated for the trade with North America, of which that enterprising town early acquired a respectable portion.

The Church of Scotland still afforded a respectable asylum for such as were disposed to turn their thoughts towards it. It could, indeed, in no shape afford wealth, but it gave sufficiency for the moderate wants of a useful clergyman, and a degree of influence over the minds of men which, to a generous spirit, is more valuable than opulence. The respectability of the situation and its importance in society reconciled the clergyman to its poverty, an evil little felt where few could be termed rich.

Learning was not so accurately cultivated as in the sister country. But although it was rare to find a Scottish gentleman, even when a divine or lawyer, thoroughly grounded in classical lore, it was still more uncommon to find men in the higher ranks who did not possess a general tincture of letters, or, thanks to their system of parochial education, individuals even in the lowest classes without the knowledge of reading, writing, and arithmetic. A certain degree of pedantry, indeed, was considered as a characteristic of the nation, and the limited scholarship which it argued proved eminently useful to Scotsmen, who, going abroad, or to England, which they considered as a foreign country, mixed in the struggle for success with the advantage of superior information over those of the same class elsewhere. Thomson, Mallet, and others engaged in the pursuits of literature, were content to receive their reward from the sister country; and if we except the Poems of Allan Ramsay, praised by his countrymen, but neither relished nor understood by South Britons, the Scots made little figure in composition compared to the period of Gawin Douglas and Dunbar. Upon the whole, the situation of Scotland during the early part of the eighteenth century was like that of a newly transplanted forest-tree, strong enough to maintain itself in its new situation, but too much influenced by the recent violence of the change of position to develop with freedom its principles of growth or increase.

The principal cause, which rendered Scotland stationary in its advance towards improvement was the malevolent influence of political party. No efforts seem to have been made to heal the rankling wounds which the civil war of 1715 had left behind it. The party in favour failed not, as is always the case, to represent those who were excluded from it as the most dangerous enemies of the King on the throne and the constitution by which he reigned; and those who were branded as Jacobites were confirmed in their opinions by finding themselves shut out from all prospect of countenance and official employment. Almost all beneficial situations were barred against those who were suspected of harbouring such sentiments by the necessity imposed on them not only of taking oaths to the established government, but also such as expressly denounced and condemned the political opinions of those who differed from it. Men of high spirit and honourable feelings were averse to take oaths by which they were required openly to stigmatise and disown the opinions of their fathers and nearest relatives, although perhaps they themselves saw the fallacy of the proscribed tenets, and were disposed tacitly to abandon them. Those of the higher class, once falling under suspicion, were thus excluded from the bar and the army, which we have said were the professions embraced by the elder sons of gentlemen. The necessary consequence was that the sons of Jacobite families went into foreign service and drew closer those connections with the exiled family which they might have otherwise been induced to drop, and became confirmed in their party opinions even from the measures employed to suppress them. In the rank immediately lower many young men of decent families were induced to renounce the privileges of their birth and undertake mechanical employments in which their conduct could not be obstructed by the imposition of the obnoxious oaths.

It was fortunate for the peace of the kingdom that, though many of the landed gentry were still much imbued with the principles of Jacobitism, they did not retain the influence which so long rendered them the active disturbers of the Government; for although the feudal rights still subsisted in form, it was now a more difficult matter for a great lord to draw into the field the vassals who held of him by military tenure. The various confiscations which had taken place operated as serious warnings to such great families as those of Gordon, Athole,

Seaforth, or others, how they rashly hoisted the standard of rebellion, while the provisions of the Clan Act and other statutes enabled the vassal so summoned to dispense with attendance upon it without hazarding, as in former times, the forfeiture of his fief. Nor was the influence of the gentry and landed proprietors over the farmers and cultivators of the soil less abridged than that of the great nobles. When the proprietors, as was now generally the case throughout the Lowlands, became determined to get the highest rent they could obtain for their land, the farmer did not feel his situation either so easy or so secure that he should, in addition, be called on to follow his landlord to battle. It must also be remembered that though many gentlemen, on the north of the Tay especially, were of the Episcopal persuasion, which was almost synonymous with being Jacobites, a great proportion of the lower classes were Presbyterian in their form of worship and Whigs in political principle, and every way adverse to the counter-revolution which it was the object of their landlords to establish. In the south and west the influence of the established religion was general amongst both gentry and peasantry.

The fierce feelings occasioned throughout Scotland generally by the recollections of the Union had died away with the generation which experienced them, and the benefits of the treaty began to be visibly, though slowly, influential on their descendants. The Lowlands, therefore, being by far the wealthiest and most important part of Scotland, were much disposed to peace, the rather that those who might have taken some interest in creating fresh disturbances had their power of doing so greatly diminished.

It is also to be considered that the Lowlanders of this later period were generally deprived of arms and unaccustomed to use them. The Act of Security, in the beginning of the eighteenth century, had been made the excuse for introducing quantities of arms into Scotland and disciplining the population to the use of them; but the consequences of this general arming and training act had long ceased to operate, and, excepting the militia, which were officered and received a sort of discipline, the use of arms was totally neglected in the Lowlands of Scotland.

The Highlands were in a very different state, and from the tenacity with which the inhabitants retained the dress, language, manners, and customs of their fathers, more nearly resembled their predecessors of centuries long since past than any other nation in Europe. It is true they were no longer the ignorant and irreclaimable barbarians, in which light they were to be regarded so late perhaps as the sixteenth century. Civilisation had approached their mountains. Their manners were influenced by the presence of armed strangers, whose fortresses were a check to the fire of their restless courage. They were obliged to yield subjection to the law, and in appearance, at least, to pay respect to those by whom it was administered. But the patriarchial system still continued, with all the good and bad which attached to its influence. The chief was still the leader in war, the judge and protector in peace The whole income of the tribe, consisting of numerous but petty articles of rude produce, was paid into the purse of the chief, and served to support the rude hospitality of his household, which was extended to the poorest of the clan. It was still the object of each leader by all possible means to augment the number capable of bearing arms; and, of course, they did not hesitate to harbour on their estates an excess of population, idle, haughty, and warlike, whose only labour was battle and the chase, and whose only law was the command of their chieftain.

It is true that in the eighteenth century we no longer hear of the chiefs taking arms in their own behalf, or fighting pitched battles with each other, nor did they, as formerly, put themselves at the head of the parties which ravaged the estates of rival clans or the Lowlands. The creaghs or inroads took place in a less open and avowed manner than formerly, and were interrupted frequently both by the regular soldiers from the garrisons, and by the soldiers of the independent companies, called the Black Watch. Still, however, it was well understood that on the estates, or *countries*, as they are called, of the great chiefs, there was suffered to exist, under some bond of understood but unavowed conditions of allegiance on the one side, and protection on the other, amongst, pathless woods and gloomy valleys, gangs of banditti ready to execute the will of the chief by whom they were sheltered, and upon a hint darkly given and easily caught up, willingly disposed to avenge his real or supposed wrongs. Thus the celebrated Rob Roy, at the commencement of the eighteenth century, was able, though an outlawed and desperate man, to maintain himself against every effort of the Montrose family, by the connivance which he received from that of Argyle, who allowed him, as the phrase then went, "wood and water," that is to say, the protection of their lakes and forests.

This primitive state of things must, in the gradual course of events, have suffered great innovations. The young Highlanders of fortune received their education in English or Lowland schools, and, gradually adopting the ideas of those with whom they were brought up, must have learned to value themselves less on their solitary and patriarchal power than on the articles of personal expenditure and display which gave distinction to those around them. This new passion would have been found in time inconsistent with the performance of the duties which the tribe expected and exacted from their chief, and the bonds which connected them, though so singularly intimate, must have in time given way. The Reverend Peter Rae, historian of the Rebellion in 1715, states that, even in his own time, causes of the nature we have hinted at were beginning to operate, and that some chiefs, with the *spaghlin*, or assumption of consequence not uncommon to the Celtic race, had addicted themselves to expenses and luxuries to which their incomes were not equal, and which began already to undermine their patriarchal power and authority over their clans.

But the operation of such causes, naturally slow, was rendered almost imperceptible, if not altogether neutralised, by the strong and counteracting stimulus afforded by the feelings of Jacobitism common to the western chiefs. These persons and their relations had many of them been educated or served as soldiers abroad, and were in close intercourse with the exiled family, who omitted no means by which they could ensure the attachment of men so able to serve them. The communication of the Stewart family with the Highlands was constant and unceasing, and was, no doubt, most effectual in maintaining the patriarchal system in its integrity. Each chief looked upon himself as destined to be raised to greatness by the share he might be able to take in the eventful and impending struggle which was one day to restore the House of Stewart to the throne, and that share must be greater or less according to the number of men at whose head he might take the field. This prospect, which to their sanguine eyes appeared a near one, was a motive which influenced the lives, and regulated the conduct, of the Highland chiefs, and which had its natural effect in directing their emulous attention to cement the bonds of clanship, that might otherwise have been gradually relaxed.

But though almost all the chiefs were endeavouring to preserve their people in a state to take the field, and to assist the cause of the heir of the Stewart family when the moment of enterprise should arrive, yet the individual character of each modified the manner in which he endeavoured to provide for this common object; and I cannot propose to you a stronger contrast than the manner in which the patriarchal power was exercised by Donald Cameron of Lochiel, and the notorious Fraser of Lovat.

The former was one of the most honourable and well-intentioned persons in whom the patriarchal power was ever lodged. He was grandson of that Sir Evan Dhu, or Black Sir Evan, who made so great a figure in Cromwell's time, and of whom I have already told you many stories in the former volume of this work.[1] Far from encouraging the rapine which had been, for a long time, objected to the men of Lochaber, he made the most anxious exertions to put a stop to it by severe punishment; and while he protected his own people and his allies, would not permit them to inflict any injury upon others. He encouraged among them such kinds of industry as they could be made to apply themselves to; and in general united the high spirit of a Highland chief with the sense and intelligence of a well-educated English gentleman of fortune. Although possessed of an estate, of which the income hardly amounted to seven hundred a year, this celebrated chief brought fourteen hundred men into the Rebellion, and he was honourably distinguished by his endeavours on all occasions to mitigate the severities of war, and deter the insurgents from acts of vindictive violence.

A different picture must be presented of Lord Lovat, whose irregular ambition induced him to play the Highland chief to the very utmost, while he cared for nothing save the means of applying the power implied in the character to the advancement of his own interest.

---

[1] I there said that Sir Evan Dhu lived to extreme old age, and that he sunk at length into a sort of second childhood, and was rocked to sleep like an infant; but I have since had reason to think that the last part of the tradition was an exaggeration. The ancient chieftain used a contrivance such as is sometimes applied to sick-beds in the present day, for enabling the patient to turn himself in bed; and it was undoubtedly some misconception of the purpose of this machine which produced the report of his being rocked in a cradle. He was in perfect possession of his faculties during the year 1715, and expressed great regret that his clan, the Camerons, being in the Earl of Mar's left wing, had been compelled to fly on that occasion. "The Camerons," he said, "were more numerous than they were in his day, but they were become much less warlike." This was a reproach which the clan speedily wiped away. From the evidence preserved in the family, it appears Sir Evan had preserved to the extremity of human life the daring expression of command which dignified his features, the tenacious power of his gripe, and his acute resentment of injuries. An English officer, who came from Fort-William on a visit, having made use of some words which the old chief took amiss, he looked on him sternly and said, "Had you used that expression but a few months since, you had never lived to repeat it."

His hospitality was exuberant, yet was regulated by means which savoured much of a paltry economy. His table was filled with Frasers, all of whom he called his cousins, but took care that the fare with which they were regaled was adapted, not to the supposed equality, but to the actual importance of his guests. Thus the claret did not pass below a particular mark on the table; those who sat beneath that limit had some cheaper liquor, which had also its bounds of circulation; and the clansmen at the extremity of the board were served with single ale. Still it was drunk at the table of their chief, and that made amends for all. Lovat had a Lowland estate, where he fleeced his tenants without mercy, for the sake of maintaining his Highland military retainers. He was a master of the Highland character, and knew how to avail himself of its peculiarities. He knew every one whom it was convenient for him to caress; had been acquainted with his father; remembered the feats of his ancestors, and was profuse in his complimentary expressions of praise and fondness. If a man of substance offended Lovat, or, which was the same thing, if he possessed a troublesome claim against him, and was determined to enforce it, one would have thought that all the plagues of Egypt had been denounced against the obnoxious individual. His house was burnt, his flocks driven off, his cattle houghed; and if the perpetrators of such outrages were secured, the jail of Inverness was never strong enough to detain them till punishment. They always broke prison. With persons of low rank, less ceremony was used; and it was not uncommon for witnesses to appear against them for some imaginary crime, for which Lord Lovat's victims suffered the punishment of transportation.

We cannot wonder that a man of Lovat's disposition should also play the domestic tyrant; but it would be difficult to conceive the excess to which he carried enormities in this character. After his return to Scotland in 1715 he was twice married; first in 1717, to a daughter of the Laird of Grant, by whom he had two sons and two daughters; his second, or rather his third wife, was a Campbell, a relation of the Argyle family. It is supposed he married her with a view to secure the friendship of that great family. Finding himself disappointed in this expectation, he vented his resentment on the poor lady, whom he shut up in a turret of his castle, neither affording her food, clothes, or other necessaries in a manner suitable to her education, nor permitting her to go abroad, or to receive any friend within doors. Dark rumours went forth of the treatment of the wife of this daring chief, who had thus vanished from society. She had a friend, whose fearless interest in her fate induced her to surmount all sense of personal danger, and to visit Castle Downie with the purpose of ascertaining the situation of Lady Lovat. She contrived to announce her arrival so unexpectedly, as to leave Lovat no apology by which he could escape her intrusive visit. He took his resolution, went to the prison-chamber of his unfortunate wife, and announced to her the arrival of her friend. "As it is my pleasure, madam," he said, "that you receive your visitor in the character of a contented and affectionate wife, you will please to dress yourself" (laying proper apparel before her), "and come down with the easy and free air of the mistress of the mansion, happy in her husband's affection and unlimited trust. It will become you to be aware how you give the least hint of any discord between you and me; for secret eyes will be upon you, and you know what reason you have to dread disobeying my commands." In this manner the poor lady met her friend, with her tongue padlocked concerning all that she would willingly have disclosed, Lovat contriving all the while to maintain so constant a watch on his wife and her visitor, that they could not obtain the least opportunity of speaking apart. The visitor, however, in the very silence and constraint of her friend, had seen enough to satisfy her that all was not well; and when she left Castle Downie, became importunate with Lady Lovat's family to be active in her behalf. She in consequence obtained a separation from her cruel husband, whom she long survived.

Such acts of tyranny were the dismal fruits of the patriarchal power, when lodged in the hands of a man of fraud and violence. But Lovat's conduct was so exaggerated, as inclines us to believe there must have been a certain mixture of deranged intellect with his wickedness; a compound perfectly reconcilable to the profound craft which displayed itself in other points of his character. I must not forget to notice that Lord Lovat, having obtained the command of one of the Highland independent companies, in consequence of his services in the year 1715, took advantage of the opportunity it gave him to make all the men of his clan familiar with the use of arms; for though he could not legally have more than a certain number of men under arms at once, yet nothing was more easy than to exchange the individuals from time to time, till the whole younger Frasers had passed a few months at least in the corps. He became incautious, however, and appeared too publicly in some suspicious purchases of arms and ammunition from abroad. Government became alarmed about his intentions, and withdrew his commission in the Black Watch. This happened in 1737, and it was, as we shall hereafter see, the indignation arising from being deprived of this independent company that finally determined him on rushing into the rebellion.

Few of the Highland chiefs could claim the spotless character due to Lochiel; and none, so far as is known to us, descended to such nefarious practices as Lovat. The conduct of most of them hovered between the wild and lawless expedients of their predecessors in power, and the new ideas of honour and respect to the rights of others which recent times had introduced; and they did good or committed evil as opportunity and temptation were presented to them. In general, a spirit of honour and generosity was found to unite easily and gracefully with their patriarchal pretensions; and those who had to deal with them gained more by an appeal to their feelings than by arguments addressed to their understandings.

Having thus taken a view of the situation of Scotland both in the Highlands and Lowlands, we must next take some notice of the political condition of the two contending families, by whom the crown of Great Britain was at the time disputed.

George, the first of his family who had ascended the British throne, had transmitted the important acquisition to his son, George II. Both sovereigns were men of honour, courage, and good sense; but, being born and educated foreigners, they were strangers to the peculiar character, no less than to the very complicated form of government, of the country over which they were called by Providence to reign. They were successively under the necessity of placing the administration in the hands of a man of distinguished talent, the celebrated Sir Robert Walpole. Unfortunately, this great statesman was a man of a coarse mind, who, altogether disbelieving in the very existence of patriotism, held the opinion that every man had his price, and might be bought if his services were worth the value at which he rated them. His creed was as unfavourable to the probity of public men as that of a leader who should disbelieve in the existence of military honour would be degrading to the character of a soldier. The venality of Sir Robert Walpole's administration became a shame and reproach to the British nation, which was also burdened with the means of supplying the wages of the national corruption.

The kings also, George I. and II., under whom Sir Robert Walpole conducted public affairs, were themselves unpopular from a very natural reason. They loved with fond partiality their paternal dominions of Hanover, and the manners and customs of the country in which they had been born and bred. Their intimacy and confidence were chiefly imparted to those of their own nation; and so far, though the preference might be disagreeable to their British subjects, the error flowed from a laudable motive. But both the royal father and son suffered themselves to be hurried further than this. Regard for their German territories was the principle which regulated their political movements, and both alliances and hostilities were engaged in for interests and disputes which were of a nature exclusively German, and with which the British nation had nothing to do. Out of this undue partiality for their native dominions arose a great clamour against the two first kings of the House of Guelph, that, called to the government of so fair and ample a kingdom as Britain, they neglected or sacrificed its interests for those of the petty and subaltern concerns of their electorate of Hanover.

Besides other causes of unpopularity, the length of Sir Robert Walpole's administration was alone sufficient to render it odious to a people so fickle as the English, who soon become weary of one class of measures, and still sooner of the administration of any one minister. For these various reasons, the government of Sir Robert Walpole, especially towards its close, was highly unpopular in England, and the Opposition attacked it with a degree of fury which made those who watched the strife from a distance imagine that language so outrageous was that of men in the act of revolt. The foreign nations, whose ideas of our constitution were as imperfect formerly as they are at this moment, listened like men who hear what they conceive to be the bursting of a steam-engine, when the noise only announces the action of the safety-valves.

While the family of Hanover maintained an uneasy seat on an unpopular throne, the fortunes of the House of Stewart seemed much on the decline. Obliged to leave France, Spain, and Avignon, and not permitted to settle in Germany, the Chevalier de St. George was obliged, shortly after his Scottish enterprise of 1715, to retire to Italy, where the sufferings of his father for the Roman Catholic religion gave him the fairest right to expect hospitality. He was then in the thirtieth year of his age, the last male of his unfortunate family, when, by the advice of his counsellors, he fixed his choice of a wife on the Princess Clementina Sobieski, daughter to Prince James Sobieski of Poland, and grand-daughter to that King John Sobieski who defeated the Turks before Vienna. This young lady was accounted one of the greatest fortunes in Europe. The dazzling pretensions to the British crown set forth by the negotiator of the marriage on the part of James, propitiated the parents of the princess, and it was agreed that she should be conducted privately to Bologna, with a view to her union with the Chevalier de St. George. Some extra preparation on the part of the princess and her mother, in the way of dress and equipage, brought the intrigue to the knowledge of the British court, who exerted all their influence with that of Austria for the interruption of the match. The Emperor, obliged to keep measures with Britain on account of his pretensions to Sicily, which were supported by the English fleet, arrested the bride as she passed through Innsbruck, in the Tyrol, and detained her, along with her mother, prisoners in a cloister of that town. The Emperor also deprived Prince James Sobieski, the lady's father, of his government of Augsburg, and caused him to be imprisoned.

A bold attempt for the release of the princess was contrived and executed by Charles Wogan, who had been one of the prisoners at Preston, and was a devoted partisan of the cause in which he had nearly lost his life. He obtained a passport from the Austrian ambassador, in the name of Count Cernes and family, stated to be returning from Loretto to the Low Countries. A Major Misset and his wife personated the supposed count and countess; Wogan was to pass for the brother of the count; the Princess Clementina, when she should be liberated, was to represent the count's sister, which character was in the meantime enacted by a smart girl, a domestic of Mrs. Misset. They represented to the wench that she was only to remain one or two days in confinement, in the room of a lady whom Captain Toole, one of the party, was to carry off, and whose escape it might be necessary to conceal for some time. Captain Toole, with two other steady partisans, attended on the party of the supposed Count Cernes, in the dress and character of domestics.

They arrived at Innsbruck on the evening of the 27th of April 1719, and took a lodging near the convent. It appears that a trusty domestic of the princess had secured permission of the porter to bring a female with him into the cloister, and conduct her out at whatever hour he pleased. This was a great step in favour of their success, as it permitted the agents of the Chevalier de St. George to introduce the young female, and to carry out Clementina Sobieski in her stead. But while they were in consultation upon the means of executing their plan, Jenny, the servant girl, heard them name the word princess, and afraid of being involved in a matter where persons of such rank were concerned, declared she would have nothing more to do with the plot. Many fair words, a few pieces of gold, and the promise of a fine suit of damask belonging to her mistress, overcame her scruples, and, taking advantage of a storm of snow and hail, Jenny was safely introduced into the cloister, and the princess, changing clothes with her, came out at the hour by which the stranger was to return, Through bad roads and worse weather they pushed on till they quitted the Austrian territories, and entered those of Venice. On the 2d of May, after a journey of great fatigue and some danger they arrived at Bologna, where the princess thought it unnecessary to remain longer incognita.

In the meantime, while his destined bride made her escape from the Tyrol, the Chevalier had been suddenly called on to undertake a private expedition to Spain. The lady was espoused in his absence by a trusty adherent, who had the Chevalier's proxy to that effect, and the bridegroom's visit to Spain having terminated in nothing satisfactory, he soon after returned to complete the marriage.

The Jacobites drew many happy omens from the success with which the romantic union of the Chevalier de St. George was achieved, although, after all, it may be doubted whether the Austrian Emperor, though obliged in appearance to comply with the remonstrances of the British Court, was either seriously anxious to prevent the princess's escape or extremely desirous that she should be retaken.

By this union the Chevalier de St. George transmitted his hereditary claims, and with them his evil luck, to two sons. The first, Charles Edward, born the 31st of December 1720, was remarkable for the figure he made during the civil war of 1745–46; the second, Henry Benedict, born the 6th of March 1725, for being the last male heir, in the direct line, of the unfortunate House of Stewart. He bore the title of Duke of York, and entering the Church of Rome was promoted to the rank of Cardinal.

The various schemes and projects which were agitated, one after another, in the councils of the Chevalier de St. George, and which for a time served successively to nourish and keep afloat the hopes of his partisans in England and Scotland, were so numerous, so indifferently concocted, and so ineffectual in their consequences, that, to borrow an expression from the poet, the voyage of his life might be said to be spent in shallows.

With whatever court Britain happened to have a quarrel, thither came the unfortunate heir of the House of Stewart, to show his miseries and to boast his pretensions. But though treated with decency, and sometimes fed with hopes which proved altogether fallacious, the Chevalier found his eloquence too feeble to persuade any Government to embarrass themselves by making common cause with him after the miscarriage of the Spanish invasion of 1719, which only gave rise to the petty skirmish of Glenshiel. In the intervals of these ineffectual negotiations, the Chevalier's domestic establishment was divided by petty intrigues among his advisers, in which his wife occasionally took such keen interest, as to proclaim, in a public and scandalous degree, their domestic disunion. From all these circumstances, from his advance in years, and the disappointments which he brooded over, the warmest adherents of the House of Stewart ceased to expect anything from the personal exertions of him whom they called their King, and reposed the hopes of their party in the spirit and talents of his eldest son, Charles Edward, whose external appearance, and personal accomplishments, seemed at first sight to justify his high pretensions, and to fit him well for the leader of any bold and gallant enterprise by which they might be enforced.

In attempting to describe to you this remarkable young man, I am desirous of qualifying the exaggerated praise heaped upon him by his enthusiastic adherents, and no less so to avoid repeating the disparaging language of public and political opponents, and of discontented and disobliged followers, who have written rather under the influence of their resentments than in defence of truth.

Prince Charles Edward, styling himself Prince of Wales, was a youth of tall stature and fair complexion. His features were of a noble and elevated cast, but tinged with an expression of melancholy. His manners were courteous, his temper apparently good, his courage of a nature fit for the most desperate undertakings, his strength of constitution admirable, and his knowledge of manly exercises and accomplishments perfect. These were all qualities highly in favour of one who prepared to act the restorer of an ancient dynasty. On the other hand, his education had been strangely neglected in certain points of the last consequence to his success. Instead of being made acquainted with the rights and constitution of the English nation by those who superintended his education, they had taken care to train him up exclusively in those absurd, perverse, exaggerated, and antiquated doctrines of divine hereditary right and passive obedience, out of which had arisen the errors and misfortunes of the reign of his ancestor, James the Second of England. He had been also strictly brought up in the Roman Catholic faith, which had proved so fatal to his grandfather; and thus he was presented to the British nation without any alteration or modification of those false tenets in church and state so obnoxious to those whom he called his subjects, and which had cost his ancestor a throne. It was a natural consequence of the high ideas of regal prerogative in which he was trained, though it might also be in some respects owing to a temper naturally haughty and cold, that the young Prince was apt to consider the most important services rendered him, and the greatest dangers encountered in his cause, as sufficiently to reward the actors by the internal consciousness of having discharged their duties as loyal subjects; nor did he regard them as obligations laying him under a debt which required acknowledgment or recompense. This degree of indifference to the lives or safety of his followers (the effect of a very bad education) led to an indulgence in rash and sanguine hopes, which could only be indulged at an extravagant risk to all concerned. It was the duty of every subject to sacrifice everything for his Prince, and if this duty was discharged, what results could be imagined too difficult for their efforts? Such were the principles instilled into the mind of the descendant of the ill-starred House of Stewart.

It is easy to be imagined that these latter attributes were carefully veiled over in the accounts of the character of the young Chevalier, as spread abroad by his adherents within Scotland and England; and that he was held up to hope and admiration as a shoot of the stem of Robert Bruce, and as one who, by every perfection of mind and body, was ordained to play anew the part of that great restorer of the Scottish monarchy.

The state of the Jacobite party, both in the Highlands and Lowlands of Scotland, has been already noticed. In England it was far inferior to its strength in 1715; the fatal affair of Preston was remembered with dread. But many great families attached to the High Church principles continued to look with a longing eye towards him whom they regarded as the heir of the crown, by indefeasible right; and some, at considerable risk to their persons and estates, maintained an intercourse with the agents of the old Chevalier de St. George, who thus received intelligence of their hopes and plans. The principal of these were the Wynnes of Wynnstay, in Wales, with the great family of Windham. Other houses, either Catholics or High Churchmen, in the west, were united in the same interest. A great part of the Church of England clergy retained their ancient prejudices, and the Universities, Oxford in particular, still boasted a powerful party, at the head of which was Dr. William King, Principal of St. Mary's Hall, who entered into the same sentiments.

Such being the state of affairs when war was declared betwixt Britain and Spain in 1740, seven daring Scottish Jacobites signed an association, engaging themselves to risk their lives and fortunes for the restoration of the Stewart family, provided that France would send a considerable body of troops to their assistance. The titular Duke of Perth, the Earl of Traquair, Lochiel, and Lovat, were of the number who signed this association.[1]

The agent employed to advocate the cause of the Jacobites at Paris was Drummond, *alias* MacGregor of Bohaldie, with whom was joined a person whom they called Lord Semple; these agents were supposed to have ready access to the French ministers. Bohaldie was closely related to several chieftains of the Scottish clans, and in particular to Cameron of Lochiel, on whose judgment and prudence the others were in a great degree disposed to rely. But after a protracted negotiation, nothing could be resolved upon with any certainty; for the French ministers, on the one hand, were afraid that the Jacobites in their political zeal might dupe both themselves and France by inducing them to hazard the forces of the latter kingdom upon a distant and dangerous expedition; while, on the other hand, the Jacobites, who were to risk their all in the enterprise, were alike apprehensive that France, if she could by their means excite a civil war in England, and oblige its Government to recall her troops from Germany, would not, after that point was gained, greatly concern herself about their success or failure.

At length, however, when France beheld the interest which Britain began to take in the German war, assisting the Empress Queen both with troops and money, her administration seems suddenly to have taken into serious consideration the proposed descent upon Scotland. With a view to the arrangement of an enterprise, Cardinal de Tencin,

---

[1] The others were Sir James Campbell of Auchinbreck, John Stuart, brother to Lord Traquair, and Lord John Drummond, uncle to the Duke of Perth.

who had succeeded Cardinal Fleury in the administration of France, invited Charles Edward, the eldest son of the old Chevalier de St. George, to repair from Italy to Paris. The young Prince, on receiving a message so flattering to his hopes, left Rome as if on a hunting expedition, but instantly took the road to Genoa, and, embarking on board a small vessel, ran through the English fleet at great risk of being captured, and arriving safe at Antilles, proceeded to Paris. He there took part in counsels of a nature highly dangerous to Great Britain. It had been settled by the French court that a French army of fifteen thousand men should be landed in England under the celebrated Field-Marshal Saxe, who was to act under the commission of the Chevalier de St. George as commander-in-chief. Having intimated this determination to the Earl Marischal and Lord Elcho, eldest son of the Earl of Wemyss, who were then in the French capital, Charles left Paris to superintend the destined embarkation, and took up his residence at Gravelines, in the beginning of February 1744. Here he resided in the most strict privacy, under the name of the Chevalier Douglas. Bohaldie waited upon him as his secretary.

The French fleet was got in readiness, and the troops designed for the invasion embarked; but the alertness of the British navy disconcerted this as it had done former expeditions. The French army no sooner appeared off Torbay than they were confronted by a fleet of twenty-one sail of the line, under Admiral Sir John Norris. The elements also took part in the strife, and, as usually happened on former occasions, decided against the House of Stewart. A heavy tempest arose, obliging both the English and French to scud before the wind. The latter fleet were dispersed, and suffered damage. The plan of invasion was once more given up, and the French troops were withdrawn from the coast.

It is in vain to inquire upon what principles the French Ministry preferred this attempt upon England, at great expense, and with a large army, to an invasion of Scotland, where they were sure to be joined by a large body of Jacobites, and where one-third part of the troops would have made a serious, perhaps a fatal impression. History is full of attempts to assist malcontents in an enemy's country, which have miscarried from being ill-concerted in point of place or time. That the present did not arise out of any very accurate combinations is certain, for so little had the French Ministers thought on the means of propitiating the English Jacobites, that they did not at first design that the

Duke of Ormond should embark with the expedition, though the most popular of the Chevalier's adherents in South Britain. The Duke was at length hastily summoned from Avignon to join the armament when it was on the eve of sailing, but receiving information while he was on the road that the design was given up he returned to his residence. It is probable that the French were determined to make England the object of attack, merely because they could more easily either reinforce or bring off their expedition than if it was sent against Scotland.

Lord Marischal had repaired to the Prince at Gravelines, but was not much consulted on the objects of the expedition. When he asked concerning the embarkation for Scotland, he was informed that it would take place after that to England was despatched. But after the miscarriage of the enterprise and disembarkation of the troops Charles Edward invited the Earl to visit him at Gravelines, when he seriously proposed to hire a boat and go with him to Scotland, where, he said, he was sure he had many friends who would join him. This idea, from which he was diverted with difficulty, seems to have been the slight sketch which was afterwards the groundwork of the rash expedition of 1745–46. In the end of summer Prince Charles left Gravelines and went to Paris, where he resided for the winter, little noticed by French families of fashion, but much resorted to by the Irish and Scots who were in that capital.

In the month of August 1744 John Murray of Broughton, who had been for three or four years an agent of the old Chevalier, and much trusted by him and his adherents, returned to Paris from Scotland, carrying with him the joint opinion of the Jacobites in that country upon the subject of an invasion. Mr. Murray was a gentleman of honourable birth and competent fortune, being the son of Sir David Murray by his second wife, a daughter of Sir John Scott of Ancrum. His early travels to Rome gave him an opportunity of offering his services to the old Chevalier, and he had ever since retained his confidence. The opinion which he now delivered to Charles, as the united sentiments of his friends in Scotland, was, that if he could persuade the French Government to allow him six thousand auxiliary troops, ten thousand stand of arms, and thirty thousand louis-d'or, he might assuredly reckon on the support of all his Scottish friends. But Murray had been charged at the same time to say, that if the Prince could not obtain succours to the amount specified, they could do nothing in his behalf. The answer which the Prince returned by Murray to his Scottish adherents was, that he was weary and disgusted with waiting upon the timid, uncertain, and faithless politics of the court of France; and that, whether with or without their assistance or concurrence, he was determined to appear in Scotland in person and try his fortune. Mr. Murray has left a positive declaration that he endeavoured as much as possible to divert the Prince from an attempt which rather announced desperation than courage; but as there were other reasons for imputing blame to the agent, many of those who suffered by the expedition represent him as having secretly encouraged the Prince in his romantic undertaking, instead of dissuading him from so rash a course. Whether encouraged by Murray or otherwise, Charles Edward continued fixed in his determination to try what effect could be produced by his arrival in Scotland, with such slender supplies of money and arms as his private fortune might afford.

With a view to this experiment, the Prince sent Murray back to Scotland, with commissions to those whom he regarded as the most faithful friends of his family, given in his own name, as Prince of Wales and Regent for James VIII., for which last title he possessed an ample warrant from his father. The arrival of these documents in Scotland excited the utmost surprise and anxiety; and at a full meeting of the principal Jacobites held at Edinburgh, it was agreed to despatch Mr. Murray to the Highlands, to meet, if possible, the young adventurer on his first coming upon the coast, and communicating their general disapprobation of an attempt so desperate, to entreat him to reserve himself and the Scottish friends of his family for some period in which fortune might better favour their exertions. The titular Duke of Perth alone dissented from the opinion of the meeting, and declared, in a spirit of high-strained loyalty, that he would join the Prince if he arrived without a single man. The others were unanimous in a different judgment, and Murray, empowered by them, remained on the watch on the Highland coast during the whole month of June, when, the Chevalier not appearing, he returned to his own seat in the south of Scotland, supposing naturally that the young man had renounced an attempt which had in it so much of the headlong rashness of youth, and which he might be fairly believed to have laid aside on mature consideration.

But the Chevalier had resolved on his expedition. He was distrustful of the motives, doubtful of the real purposes of France, and was determined to try his fate upon his own resources, however inadequate to the purpose he meant to effect. It is said that Cardinal Tencin was the only member of the French Government to whom his resolution was made known, to which the minister yielded his acquiescence rather than his countenance; and at length, as England and France were now engaged in open war, he generously consented that Charles should pursue his desperate enterprise upon his own risk and his own means, without further assistance than a very indirect degree of encouragement from France. The fatal defeat at Fontenoy happened about the same period, and as the British forces in Flanders were much weakened, the Adventurer was encouraged to hope that no troops could be spared from thence to oppose his enterprise.

In consequence of the understanding betwixt Charles and Tencin, a man-of-war of sixty guns, named the *Elizabeth*, was placed at the disposal of the adventurous Prince, to which Charles Edward added a frigate or sloop of war, called the *Doutelle*, which had been fitted out by two merchants of Dunkirk, named Rutledge and Walsh, to cruise against the British trade. In this latter vessel he embarked, with a very few attendants, and with the whole or greater part of the money and arms which he had provided.

The expedition was detained by contrary winds till the 8th of July, when the vessels set sail upon this romantic adventure. But the chances of the sea seem to have been invariably unpropitious to the line of Stewart. The next day after they left port, the *Lion*, an English ship of war, fell in with them, and engaged the *Elizabeth*. The battle was desperately maintained on both sides, and the vessels separated after much mutual injury. The *Elizabeth*, in particular, lost her first and second captains, and was compelled to bear away for Brest to refit.

The *Doutelle*, on board of which was Charles Edward and his suite, had kept at a distance during the action, and seeing its termination, stood away for the north-west of Scotland, so as to reach the Hebrides. Avoiding another large vessel, understood to have been an English man-of-war, which they met in their course, the sloop that carried the young Prince and his fortunes at length moored near the island of South Uist, one of the isles belonging to MacDonald of Clanranald and his kinsfolk. Clanranald was himself on the mainland; but his uncle, MacDonald of Boisdale, by whose superior talents and sagacity the young chief was much guided, was at that time on South Uist, where his own property lay. On being summoned by the Prince, he came on board the *Doutelle*.

Charles Edward immediately proposed to Boisdale to take arms, and to engage his powerful neighbours, Sir Alexander MacDonald and the Chief of the MacLeods, in his cause. These two chiefs could each bring to the field from 1200 to 1500 men. Boisdale replied, with a bluntness to which the Adventurer had not been accustomed, that the enterprise was rash to the verge of insanity; that he could assure him that Sir Alexander MacDonald and the Laird of MacLeod were positively determined not to join him unless on his bringing the forces stipulated by the unanimous determination of the friends of his family; and that, by his advice, his nephew Clanranald would also adopt the resolution of remaining quiet. The young Chevalier argued the point for some time, still steering towards the mainland; until, finding Boisdale inexorable, he at length dismissed him, and suffered him to take his boat and return to South Uist. It is said that this interview with Boisdale had such an influence on the mind of Charles that he called a council of the principal followers who accompanied him in the *Doutelle*, when all voices, save one, were unanimous for returning, and Charles himself seemed for a moment disposed to relinquish the expedition. Sir Thomas Sheridan alone, an Irish gentleman, who had been his tutor, was inclined to prosecute the adventure further, and encouraged his pupil to stand his ground and consult some more of his Scottish partisans before renouncing a plan on which he had ventured so far, that to relinquish it without further trial would be an act of cowardice, implying a renunciation of the birthright he came to seek. His opinion determined his pupil, who was on all occasions much guided by it, to make another appeal to the spirit of the Highland leaders.

Advancing still towards the mainland, Charles with his sloop of war entered the bay of Lochnanuagh, between Moidart and Arisaig, and sent a messenger ashore to apprise Clanranald of his arrival. That chieftain immediately came on board, with his relation MacDonald of Kinloch-Moidart, and one or two others. Charles applied to them the same arguments which he had in vain exhausted upon Boisdale, their relation, and received the same reply, that an attempt at the present time, and with such slender means, could end in nothing but ruin. A young Highlander, a brother of Kinloch-Moidart, began now to understand before whom he stood, and, grasping his sword, showed visible signs of impatience at the reluctance manifested by his chief and his brother to join their Prince. Charles marked his agitation, and availed himself of it.

He turned suddenly towards the young Highlander, and said, "You at least will not forsake me?"

"I will follow you to death," said Ranald, "were there no other to draw a sword in your cause."

The Chief, and relative of the warm-hearted young man, caught his enthusiasm, and declared that, since the Prince was determined, they would no longer dispute his pleasure. He landed accordingly, and was conducted to the house of Borodale, as a temporary place of residence. Seven persons came ashore as his suite. These were the Marquis of Tullibardine, outlawed for his share in the insurrection of 1715, elder brother of James, the actual Duke of Athole; Sir Thomas Sheridan, the Prince's tutor; Sir John MacDonald, an officer in the Spanish service; Francis Strictland, an English gentleman; Kelly, who had been implicated in what was called the Bishop of Rochester's Plot; Æneas MacDonald, a banker in Paris, a brother of Kinloch-Moidart; and Buchanan, who had been entrusted with the service of summoning the Chevalier from Rome to Paris. One of his attendants, or who immediately afterwards joined him, has been since made generally known by the military renown of his son, Marshal MacDonald, distinguished by his integrity, courage, and capacity, during so many arduous scenes of the great revolutionary war.[1]

This memorable landing in Moidart took place on the 25th of July 1745. The place where Charles was lodged was remarkably well situated for concealment, and for communication with friendly clans, both in the islands and on the mainland, without whose countenance and concurrence it was impossible that his enterprise could succeed.

Cameron of Lochiel had an early summons from the Prince, and waited on him as soon as he received it. He came fully convinced of the utter madness of the undertaking and determined, as he thought, to counsel the Adventurer to return to France, and wait a more favourable opportunity.

"If such is your purpose, Donald," said Cameron of Fassiefern to his brother of Lochiel, "write to the Prince your opinion; but do not

---

[1] His father was one of a tribe of MacDonalds residing in South Uist, named MacEachen, or sons of Hector, descended from the house of Clanranald by birth, and united with them by intermarriage. Young MacDonald, or MacEachen, had been bred at Saint Omers, with a view to taking priest's orders; he, therefore, understood the Latin as well as the English, French, and Gaelic languages, and his services were important to Charles as an interpreter, or private secretary.

trust yourself within the fascination of his presence. I know you better than you know yourself, and you will be unable to refuse compliance."

Fassiefern prophesied truly. While the Prince confined himself to argument Lochiel remained firm, and answered all his reasoning. At length Charles, finding it impossible to subdue the chief's judgment, made a powerful appeal to his feelings.

"I have come hither," he said, "with my mind unalterably made up to reclaim my rights or to perish. Be the issue what will, I am determined to display my standard, and take the field with such as may join it. Lochiel, whom my father esteemed the best friend of our family, may remain at home, and learn his Prince's fate from the newspapers."

"Not so," replied the chief, much affected, "if you are resolved on this rash undertaking, I will go with you, and so shall every one over whom I have influence."

Thus was Lochiel's sagacity overpowered by his sense of what he esteemed honour and loyalty, which induced him to front the prospect of ruin with a disinterested devotion, not unworthy the best days of chivalry. His decision was the signal for the commencement of the Rebellion; for it was generally understood at the time that there was not a chief in the Highlands who would have risen if Lochiel had maintained his pacific purpose.

He had no sooner embraced the Chevalier's proposal, than messengers were despatched in every direction to summon such clans as were judged friendly, announcing that the royal standard was to be erected at Glenfinnan on the 19th of August, and requiring them to attend on it with their followers in arms.

Sir Alexander MacDonald of Sleat, and MacLeod of MacLeod, were, as already mentioned, men of the greatest note in the Hebrides, and their joint forces were computed at more than three thousand men. They had declared themselves friendly to the Prince's cause, and Clanranald was despatched to them to hasten their junction. The envoy found them both at Sir Alexander MacDonald's, and said all he could to decide them to raise their following; but that chieftain alleged that he had never come under any explicit engagement to join Charles, nor could he be persuaded to do so in such a desperate undertaking. MacLeod's engagements are said to have been more peremptory; but he appears to have been as reluctant as Sir Alexander MacDonald to comply with Charles Edward's summons, alleging that his agreement depended on the Prince bringing certain auxiliaries and supplies, which were not forthcoming. He, moreover, pleaded to Clanranald that a number of his men resided in the distant islands, as an additional excuse for not joining the standard immediately. Clanranald's mission was therefore unsuccessful, and the defection of these two powerful chiefs was indifferently supplied by the zeal displayed by others of less power.

Charles, however, displayed great skill in managing the tempers, and gaining the affections of such Highlanders as were introduced to him during his abode at Borodale.[1] The Prince's Lowland friends were also acquainted with his arrival, and prepared for his designs.

Government was, at the same time, rendered vigilant by the visible stir which seemed to take place among the Jacobites, and proceeded to

---

[1] The Memoirs of an officer named MacDonald, engaged in Charles's army, give an interesting account of his person and behaviour. He appears to have been one of the seven gentlemen of the clan MacDonald who, being the earliest to join Charles Edward, were long distinguished by the name of the Seven Men of Moidart. Their curiosity had been excited by the appearance of the *Doutelle* when it arrived on the coast, and they hastened to the shore to learn the news.

"We called for the ship's boat, and were immediately carried on board, and our hearts were overjoyed to find ourselves so near our long-wished-for Prince. We found a large tent erected with poles on the ship's deck, covered and well furnished with variety of wines and spirits. As we enter'd this pavilion, we were most chearfully welcom'd by the Duke of Athole, to whom some of us had been known in the year 1715. While the Duke was talking with us, Clanranald was amissing, and had, as we understood, been called into the Prince's cabin; nor did we look for the honour of seeing H.R.H. at least for that night. After being 3 hours with the P., Clanranald returned to us; and, in about half ane hour after, there entered the tent a tall youth, of a most agreeable aspect, in a plain black coat, with a plain shirt, not very clean, and a cambric stock, fixed with a plain silver buckle, a fair round wig out of the buckle, a plain hatt, with a canvas string, haveing one end fixed to one of his coat buttons; he had black stockins, and brass buckles in his shoes. At his first appearance, I found my heart swell to my very throat. We were immediately told by one Obrian, a churchman, that this youth was also an English clergyman, who had long been possess'd with a desire to see and converse with Highlanders.

"When this youth entered, Obrian forbid any of those who were sitting to rise; he saluted none of us, and we only made a low bow at a distance. I chanced to be one of those who were standing when he came in, and he took his seat near me, but immediately started up again, and caused me sitt down by him upon a chest. I at this time, taking him to be only a passenger, or some clergyman, presumed to speak to him with too much familiarity, yet still retained some suspicion he might be one of more note than he was said to be. He asked me if I was not cold in that habite? (viz. the Highland garb). I answered, I was so habituated to it that I should rather be so if I was to change my dress for any other. At this he laughed heartily, and next inquired how I the arrest of suspicious persons. Among these, one of the principal was the titular Duke of Perth, upon whose ancestor the court of St. Germains had conferred that rank. He was son of Lord John Drummond who flourished in 1715, and grandson of the unfortunate Earl of Perth, Lord Chancellor to James VII. before the Revolution. The present descendant of that honourable house was a man respected for his high rank, popular manners, dauntless bravery, and sweetness of disposition, but not possessed of any extraordinary degree of talent. This nobleman was residing at Castle Drummond when Captain Campbell of Inverawe, who commanded an independent Highland company lying at Muthil in the neighbourhood, received orders to lay him under arrest. Campbell, by the mediation of a friend, procured himself an

---

lay with it at night, which I explained to him. He said, that by wrapping myself so closs in my plaid, I would be unprepared for any sudden defence in the case of a surprise. I answered, that in such times of danger or during a war, we had a different method of using the plaid, so that with one spring, I could start to my feet with drawn sword and cocked pistol in my hand, without being in the least encumbered with my bed-cloaths. Several such questions he put to me; then rising quickly from his seat, he calls for a dram, when the same person whispered me a second time, to pledge the stranger, but not to drink to him, by which seasonable hint I was confirmed in my suspicion who he was. Having taken a glass of wine in his hand, he drank to us all round, and soon after left us."

The writer then mentions the difficulties under which the Adventurer struggled, and adds—

"So all may judge, how hazardous ane enterprise we (i.e. Clanranald's people) were now engaged in, being for some time quite alone, who, notwithstanding, resolved to follow our P. most chearfully, and risque our fate with him. We there did our best to give him a most hearty welcome to our country, the P. and all his company, with a guard of about 100 men, being all entertained in the house, &c., of Angus M'Donald of Borradel, in Arisaig, in as hospitable a manner as the place could afford. H.R.H. being seated in a proper place, had a full view of all our company, the whole neighbourhood, without distinction of age or sex, crouding in upon us to see the P. After we had all eaten plentifully and drank chearfully, H.R.H. drunk the grace drink in English, which most of us understood; when it came to my turn, I presumed to distinguish myself by saying audibly in Erse (or Highland language), *Deoch slaint an Reogh*; H.R.H. understanding that I had drunk the King's health, made me speak the words again in Erse, and said, he could drink the King's health likewise in that language, repeating my words; and the company mentioning my skill in the Highland language, H.R.H. said I should be his master for that language, and so I was made to ask the healths of the Prince and Duke."

The original journal of this simple-minded and high-spirited young Highlander, who seems to have wooed danger as a bride, will be found in the *Lockhart Papers*, vol. ii. p. 479.

invitation to dine at Drummond Castle, and caused his men to
approach the place as near as they could without causing suspicion.
When dinner was over, and the ladies had retired, Inverawe put the
arrest into execution and told the Duke he was his prisoner, stating at
the same time his orders in apology. The Duke seemed to treat the
thing with indifference, and said, since it was so there was no help for
it. But, in leaving the apartment, he made the captain pass before him
as if by a natural motion of politeness, and turning short on his heel,
instead of following him, left the room, and by a private door fled from
the house into the wood. There was an instant pursuit, and the Duke
would probably have been retaken had he not found a pony and leapt
upon its back, with only a halter on its head and without a saddle. By
the advantage thus afforded him he was enabled to escape to the neighbouring Highlands, where he lay safe from pursuit, and soon after
obtained knowledge of the young Chevalier's having landed, and made
preparation to join him.

John Murray of Broughton, in the meanwhile, had discharged the
perilous task of having the manifestoes printed which were to be dispersed when the invasion should become public, as well as that of
warning several persons who had agreed to give supplies of money
and arms. He now left his house where he had lived for the last three
weeks in constant danger and fear of arrest, and set out to join the
Prince. His active genius meditated some other exploits. By the assistance of a Jacobite friend, of a fearless and enterprising disposition,
he laid a scheme for surprising the Duke of Argyle (brother and successor to the famous Duke John) and making him prisoner at his own
castle of Inverary. Another project was to cause Government to
receive information which, though false in the main, was yet
coloured with so many circumstances of truth as to make it seem
plausible, and which came to them through a channel which they did
not mistrust. The reports thus conveyed to them bore that the Jacobite chiefs were to hold a great consultation in the wilds of Rannoch,
and that Murray had left his house in the south to be present at the
meeting. It was proposed to those managing on the part of Government to seize the opportunity of despatching parties from Fort
William and Fort Augustus to secure the conspirators at their rendezvous. The object of the scheme was, that the Highlanders might
have an opportunity of surprising the forts, when the garrison should
be diminished by the proposed detachments. Mr. Murray having thus

planned two exploits which, had they succeeded, must have been most advantageous to the Prince's cause, proceeded to join Charles Edward whom he found at the house of MacDonald of Kinloch-Moidart, who had advanced to that place from Borodale. Many Highland gentlemen had joined him, and his enterprise seemed to be generally favoured by the chiefs on the mainland. Clanranald had also joined with three hundred and upwards of his clan. Regular guards were mounted on the person of the Prince; his arms and treasure were disembarked from the *Doutelle*, and distributed amongst those who seemed most able to serve him. Yet he remained straitened for want of provisions, which might have disconcerted his expedition had not the *Doutelle* fallen in with and captured two vessels laden with oatmeal, a supply which enabled him to keep his followers, together, and to look with confidence to the moment which had been fixed for displaying his standard.

Mr. Murray, to whose management so much of the private politics of Prince Charles had been confided, was recognised as his Secretary of State, and trusted with all the internal management of the momentous undertaking.

LXXVI

The Rising

1745

IN the meanwhile, and even before the day appointed by Charles Edward for erecting his standard, the civil war commenced. This was not by the capture of the Duke of Argyle, or the projected attack upon the forts, neither of which took place. But the hostile movements of the Highlanders had not escaped the attention of the governor of Fort Augustus, who, apprehensive for the safety of Fort William,[1] which lay nearest to the disaffected clans, sent a detachment of two companies under Captain John Scott, afterwards General Scott. He marched early in the morning of the 16th of August, with the purpose of reaching Fort William before nightfall. His march ran along the military road which passes by the side of the chain of lakes now connected by the Caledonian Canal. Captain Scott and his detachment had passed the lakes, and were within eight miles of Fort William, when they approached a pass called High Bridge, where the river Spean is crossed by a steep and narrow bridge, surrounded by rocks and woods. Here he was alarmed

---

[1] "Fort William, Fort Augustus, and Fort George, called also the Castle of Inverness, formed the chain of forts which had reached from the east to the west sea. The country between Fort William and Inverness is one of the wildest parts of the Highlands, and was then inhabited altogether by the disaffected clans."—HOME.

by the sound of a bagpipe, and the appearance of Highlanders in arms. This was a party of men belonging to MacDonald of Keppoch, and commanded by his kinsman, MacDonald of Tiendreich. They did not amount to more than twelve or fifteen men, but showing themselves in different points, it was impossible for Captain Scott to ascertain their number. He detached a steady sergeant in advance, accompanied by a private soldier, to learn the meaning of this opposition; but they were instantly made prisoners by the mountaineers.

Scott, who was a man of unquestionable courage, was desirous of pursuing his route and fighting his way. But his officers were of a different opinion, considering that they were to storm a strong pass in the face of an enemy of unknown strength, and the privates, who were newly raised men, showed symptoms of fear. In this predicament Captain Scott was induced to attempt a retreat by the same road along which he had advanced. But the firing had alarmed the country; and the Highlanders assembling with characteristic promptitude, their numbers increased at every moment. Their activity enabled them to line the mountains, rocks, and thickets overhanging the road, and by which it was commanded, and the regulars were overwhelmed with a destructive fire, to which they could only make a random return upon an invisible enemy. Meanwhile the hills, the rocks, and dingles, resounded with the irregular firing, the fierce shrieks of the Highlanders, and the yellings of the pibroch. The soldiers continued to retreat, or rather to run, till about five or six miles eastward from High Bridge, when Keppoch came up with about twenty more men, hastily assembled since the skirmish began. Others, the followers of Glengarry, had also joined, making the number about fifty. The Highlanders pressed their advantage, and showed themselves more boldly in front, flank, and rear, while the ammunition of the soldiers was exhausted without having even wounded one of their assailants. They were now closely surrounded, or supposed themselves to be so; their spirits were entirely sunk, and on Keppoch coming in front, and summoning them to surrender, on pain of being cut to pieces, they immediately laid down their arms. Captain Scott was wounded, as were five or six of his men. About the same number were slain. This disaster, which seems to have arisen from the commanding officer's neglecting to keep an advanced guard, gave great spirits to the Highlanders, and placed in a flattering light their peculiar excellence as light troops. The prisoners were treated with humanity, and carried to Lochiel's house of Auchnacarrie, where the wounded were carefully attended to. As the governor of

Fort Augustus would not permit a surgeon from that garrison to attend Captain Scott, Lochiel, with his wonted generosity, sent him on parole to the Fort, that he might have medical assistance.

The war being thus openly commenced, Charles moved from the House of Glenaladale, which had been his last residence, to be present at the raising of his standard at the place of rendezvous in Glenfinnan. He arrived early on the 19th of August in that savage and sequestered vale, attended only by a company or two of the MacDonalds, whose chief, Clanranald, was absent, raising his men in every quarter where he had influence. Two hours elapsed, and the mountain ridges still looked as lonely as ever, while Charles waited as one uncertain of his fate, until at length Lochiel and the Camerons appeared. This body amounted to seven or eight hundred. They advanced in two lines, having betwixt them the two companies who had been taken on the 16th, disarmed and marching as prisoners. Keppoch arrived shortly afterwards with three hundred men, and some chieftains of less importance brought in each a few followers.

The standard was then unfurled; it was displayed by the Marquis of Tullibardine, exiled, as we have already said, on account of his accession to the rebellion in 1715, and now returned to Scotland with Charles in the *Doutelle*. He was supported by a man on each side as he performed the ceremony.[1] The manifesto of the old Chevalier, and the commission of regency granted to his son Charles Edward, were then read, and the Adventurer made a short speech, asserting his title to the throne, and alleging that he came for the happiness of his people, and had chosen this part of the kingdom for the commencement of his enterprise, because he knew he should find a population of brave gentlemen, zealous as their noble predecessors for their own honour and the rights of their sovereign, and as willing to live and die with him as he was willing at their head to shed the last drop of his blood.[2]

---

[1] "The Standard erected at Glenfinnan was made of white, blue, and red silk; and when displayed was about twice the size of an ordinary pair of colours."—HOME.

[2] "Glenfinnan is a narrow vale, in which the river Finnan runs between high and craggy mountains not to be surmounted but by travellers on foot. At each end of the glen is a lake (Loch Eil and Loch Shiel) about twelve miles in length; and behind the mountain on one side of the glen is also a lake, behind the other, an arm of the sea."—HOME. At the head of Loch Shiel there now stands a monument bearing, on three of its sides, a Latin inscription composed by the late Dr. Gregory of Edinburgh, and translations of it in Gaelic and English: "On the spot where Prince Charles Edward first raised his standard

A leader of the clan of MacLeod appeared at this rendezvous, and renounced on the occasion his dependence upon his chief, whom indeed he did not acknowledge as such, and promised to join with his own following. Lochiel and some others of the chiefs present took this opportunity of writing to MacLeod and Sir Alexander MacDonald, to engage them to join, as the writers alleged their honour obliged them. This letter gave great offence to both the chiefs, and to Sir Alexander in particular, who alleged the insinuation it contained as a reason for the part he afterwards took in this affair.

Tidings were soon heard that the Government troops were in motion to put down the insurrection.

The Prince had resolved to avoid the great mistake of Mar in the year 1715, and to avail himself to the uttermost of the fierce and ardent activity of the troops whom he commanded, and it was with pleasure that he heard of the enemy's approach. He remained for a few days at Auchnacarrie, the house of Lochiel, and finding the unwillingness which the Highlanders evinced to carry baggage, the impossibility of finding horses, and the execrable character of the roads, he left a quantity of swivel-guns and pioneer's tools behind, as tending only to encumber his march. In the meantime, be was joined by the following clans:—MacDonald of Glencoe brought with him 150 men; the Stuarts of Appin, under Ardshiel, amounting to 250; Keppoch brought 300 MacDonalds;[3] Glengarry, the younger, joined the army as it marched eastward with about 300—making a total of nearly 2000 men.

There was an association drawn up and signed at Auchnacarrie by the chiefs who had taken the field, in which the subscribers bound themselves never to abandon the Prince while he remained in the

---

on the 19th day of August 1745, when he made the daring and romantic attempt to recover a throne lost by the imprudence of his ancestors, this column was erected by Alexander Macdonald, Esq. of Glenaladale, to commemorate the generous zeal, the undaunted bravery, and the inviolable fidelity of his forefathers, and the rest of those who fought and bled in that arduous and unfortunate enterprise."

[3] Keppoch, it is said, would have brought more men to the field, but there existed a dispute betwixt him and his clan,—a rare circumstance in itself, and still more uncommon as it arose from a point of religion. Keppoch was a Protestant, his clan were Catholics, a difference which would have bred no discord between them if Keppoch would have permitted the priest to accompany his hearers on the march. But the chief would not; the clansmen took offence, and came in smaller numbers than otherwise would have followed him, for he was much and deservedly beloved by them.

realm, or to lay down their arms, or make peace with Government, without his express consent.

While the insurrection was thus gathering strength and consistency, the heads of the official bodies at Edinburgh became apprised of its existence, which, however rash on the part of the Adventurer, was yet very hazardous to the state, on account of the particular time when it broke out. George II. was absent in Hanover, and the Government was in the hands of a Council of Regency, called Lords Justices, whose councils seemed neither to have evinced sagacity nor vigour.

Early in summer they had received intelligence that the young Chevalier had a design to sail from Nantes with a single vessel; and, latterly, they had heard a rumour that he had actually landed in the Highlands. This intelligence was sent by the Marquis of Tweeddale to the commander-in-chief; to Lord Milton, a Scottish judge, who was much consulted in state affairs; to the Lord Advocate, the President of the Court of Session, and the Lord Justice-Clerk. These principal officers or advisers of Government formed a sort of council for the direction of state affairs.

The report of Charles's landing at length reached Edinburgh with such marks of authenticity as no longer to admit of doubt. The alarm was very considerable, for the regular forces of Britain were chiefly engaged on the Continent. There were not in all Scotland quite three thousand troops, exclusive of garrisons. Of three battalions and a half of infantry, only one battalion was an old corps; the rest were newly raised. Two regiments of dragoons, Hamilton's and Gardiner's, were the youngest in the service. There were independent companies levied for the purpose of completing the regiments which were in Flanders; and there were several companies of a Highland regiment, which Lord Loudon commanded, but who, being Highlanders, were not to be much trusted in the present quarrel. Out of this small force, two of the newly raised companies had been made prisoners at High Bridge. Yet, reduced as his strength was, Sir John Cope, the commander-in-chief, deemed it equal to the occasion, and resolved to set out northward at the head of such troops as he could most hastily assemble, to seek out the Adventurer, give him battle, and put an end to the rebellion. The Lords Justices approved of this as a soldier-like resolution, and gave orders to the general to proceed to put his plan in execution.

Sir John took the field accordingly on the 19th of August, and marched to Stirling, where he left the two regiments of dragoons, as they could have been of little use in the hills, and it would have been difficult to obtain forage for them. His infantry consisted of between fourteen and fifteen hundred men; and, together with a train of artillery and a superfluity of baggage, he had with him a thousand stand of spare muskets, to arm such loyal clans as he expected to join him. None such appearing, he sent back 700 of the firelocks from Crieff to Stirling. His march was directed upon Fort Augustus, from which, as a central point, he designed to operate against the insurgents, wherever he might find them. As this route was the same with that by which the Highland army were drawing towards the Lowlands, Sir John Cope had no sooner arrived at Dalnacardoch, than he learned, from undoubted intelligence, that the Highlanders were advancing, with the purpose of meeting and fighting him at the pass of Corryarrack. How this intelligence affected the motions of the English general I will presently tell you, but must, in the first place, return to the operations of the young Chevalier and his insurrectionary army.

Amongst other persons of consequence with whom the Prince had held correspondence since his landing was the celebrated Lord Lovat, who, highly discontented with Government for depriving him of his independent company, had long professed his resolution to return to his original allegiance to the Stewart dynasty, and was one of those seven men of consequence who subscribed the invitation to the Chevalier in the year 1740. As no one, however, suspected Lovat of attachment either to King or political party further than his own interest was concerned, and as the Chevalier had come without the troops, money, and arms, which had been stipulated in that offer of service, there was great reason to suspect that the old wily chief might turn against the Adventurer, and refuse him his support. It chanced, however, that Lovat had attached considerable importance to the idea of becoming Duke of Fraser, and Lord-Lieutenant of Invernesshire; and the desire of obtaining these objects, though but of ideal value, induced him, notwithstanding his natural selfish sagacity, to endeavour to secure them, at the same moment while he was meditating how to escape from fulfilling the promises of which these titular honours and offices were to be the guerdon.

While the Chevalier lay at Invergarry, Fraser of Gortuleg, an especial confident of Lovat, waited upon the Prince in the capacity of his chief's envoy, and made an humble request for the patent of the dukedom and the lieutenancy, which King James VIII. had promised to him.

At the same time the emissary brought a specious but evasive protesta-
tion of Lovat's respect for the Stewart family, and his deep regret that
his age and infirmities, with other obstacles, would not permit him
instantly to get his clan to take up arms.

Such a message was easily seen to evince a desire to seize the
bait, without, if possible, swallowing the hook it covered. But Lovat
was a man of great importance at the time. Besides his own clan,
which he retained in high military order, he had also great influence
over the Laird of Cluny, his son-in-law, and chief of the MacPhersons,—over the MacIntoshes, the Farquharsons, and other clans
residing in the neighbourhood of Inverness who were likely to follow
his example in rising or remaining quiet. Sir Alexander MacDonald of
Sleat, and the Laird of MacLeod, were also much in the habit of
taking his advice, and following his example. He was not, therefore,
to be disobliged; and as the original patents, subscribed by James
himself, had been left behind with the heavy baggage, the Chevalier
caused new deeds of the same tenor to be written out, and delivered
to Gortuleg for Lovat's satisfaction.

The crafty old man, by the same messenger, made another request,
which had a relish of blood in it. I have told you that Lovat's most intimate friend had been Duncan Forbes, now Lord President of the Court
of Session, to whose assistance he owed his establishment in the country and estate of his ancestors, in the year 1715. They had continued
since that period on the most intimate terms, Lord Lovat applying,
according to his nature, every expression of devotion and flattery
which could serve to secure the President's good opinion. As Duncan
Forbes, however, was a man of perfect knowledge of the world, he
speedily traced Lovat's growing dislike to the established government;
and being, by his office, as well as his disposition, a decided friend to
the ruling dynasty, he easily fathomed Lovat's designs, and laboured to
render them abortive. Their correspondence, though still full of profession and adulation, on Lovat's side, assumed a tone of mutual suspicion and alarm, which made the latter to grow weary of the President's
active, vigilant, and frequent remonstrances. Gortuleg, therefore, stated
Lovat's extreme sense of the power which the President had to hurt the
cause of the Stewart family, and demanded a warrant from the Prince,
authorising him to secure his friend the President, dead or alive. The
Prince declined granting it in the terms required, but signed a warrant
for seizing the President's person, and detaining him in close custody.

With these documents Fraser of Gortuleg returned to his wily and double-dealing old master.

In the meantime, Lovat's conduct exhibited strange marks of indecision. He became apprised by the Lord President that Sir Alexander MacDonald and MacLeod had declined to join the Chevalier,—a resolution, indeed, to which the prudential advice of Forbes had strongly contributed,—and he expressed his own determination to adhere to the established government.

While these intrigues were in progress, the Chevalier obtained accurate accounts of Sir John Cope's movements, from deserters who frequently left Lord Loudon's companies, which consisted chiefly of Highlanders, these men having a strong temptation to join the ranks of the Chevalier, in whose service their relations and chief were engaged.

The Prince was so much animated at the prospect of battle that be summoned together his clans, now augmented by the Grants of Glenmorriston, in number one hundred men—burned and destroyed all that could impede his march, and sacrificed his own baggage, that the men might not complain of hardship. By a forced march he assembled his adherents at Invergarry, where he gave them some hours' repose, in order that they might be the better fitted for the fatigues of the impending battle.

On the morning of the 26th August, the Chevalier marched to Aberchallader, within three miles of Fort Augustus, and rested for the evening. On the dawning of the next morning, he resumed his march, to dispute with Sir John Cope, whom all reports announced to be advancing the passage of the rugged pass of Corryarrack. This mountain is ascended by a part of Marshal Wade's military road, which attains the summit by a succession (seventeen) of zig-zags, or traverses, gaining slowly and gradually on the steep and rugged elevation on the south side, by which General Cope was supposed to be advancing. The succession of so many steep and oblique windings on the side of the hill, the other parts of which are in the highest degree impracticable, bears the appropriate name of the Devil's Staircase. The side of the mountain, save where intersected by this uncouth line of approach, is almost inaccessible, and the traverses are themselves intersected by deep mountain ravines and torrents, crossed by bridges which might be in a very short time broken down, and, being flanked with rocks and thickets, afford innumerable points of safe ambush to sharpshooters or enfilading parties. The Chevalier hastened to ascend the northern side, and possess himself of the top of the hill, which has all the effect of a natural fortress, every traverse serving for a trench. He displayed exulting hope and spirits, and while putting on a new pair of Highland brogues, said with high glee, "Before I throw these off I shall fight with General Cope." He expected to meet the English general about one o'clock.

MacDonald of Lochgarry, with the Secretary Murray, were ordered to ascend the hill on the north side, and reconnoitre the position of the supposed enemy. But to their astonishment, when they reached the summit, instead of seeing the precipitous path filled with the numerous files of Cope's army in the act of ascent, they looked on silence and solitude. Not a man appeared on the numerous windings of the road, until at length they observed some people in the Highland garb, whom they at first took for Lord Loudon's Highlanders, who, as familiar with the roads and the country, it was natural to think might form the advanced guard of the English army. On a nearer approach, these men were discovered to be deserters from Cope's army, who brought the intelligence that that general had entirely altered his line of march, and, avoiding the expected contest, was in full march to Inverness.

The truth proved to be that General Cope, when he approached within a day's march of the Chevalier and his little army, saw objections to his plan of seeking out the Adventurer and fighting him, which had not occurred to him while there was a greater distance between them. It could have required no great powers of anticipation to suppose that the Highlanders would rally round their Prince in considerable numbers, impressed by the romantic character of his expedition; or to conjecture that, in so very rugged a country, an irregular army would take post in a defile. But General Cope had not imagined such a rapid assembling of the mountaineers as had taken place, or a pass so formidable as the Devil's Staircase on Corry-arrack. This unlucky general, whose name became a sort of laughing-stock in Scotland, was not by any means a poltroon, as has been supposed; but he was one of those second-rate men, who are afraid of responsibility, and form their plan of a campaign more with reference to the vindication of their own character than the success of their enterprise. He laid his embarrassments before a council of war, the usual refuge of generals who find themselves unable to decide, of their own judgment, upon arduous points of difficulty. He had received exact information concerning the numbers and disposition of the enemy from Captain Sweetenham, an

English officer, who was taken prisoner by the insurgents while on his route to take the command of three companies lying at Fort William, and, having been present at the setting up of the standard, described the general huzzas and clouds of bonnets which were flung up on the occasion. The prisoner had been treated with much courtesy, and dismissed to carry the report that the rebels intended to give General Cope battle. Sir John Cope laid the intelligence before the council. He stated the unexpected numbers of the Highland insurgents, the strength of their position, the disappointment which he had met with in not being joined, as he expected, by any of the well-affected inhabitants of the country, and he asked the advice of his officers.

It was now too late to inquire whether the march into the Highlands was at all a prudent measure, unless the English general has possessed such a predominant force as to be certain of crushing the rebellion at once; or whether the forming a camp at Stirling, and preventing the Chevalier from crossing the Forth, while, at the same time, troops were sent by sea to raise the northern clans who were friendly to Government, in the rear of the Adventurer's little army, might not have been a preferable scheme. The time for option was ended. General Cope had proposed, and the Government had sanctioned, the advance into the north, and the plan had been acted upon. Still it does not appear to have been necessary that Cope should have relinquished his purpose so meanly as was implied in the march, or rather flight, to Inverness, which so much dispirited his troops and gave such enthusiastic courage to the insurgents. Indeed, no general in his senses would have attacked the defile of Corryarrack; but had Cope chosen to have encamped on the plain, about two miles to the south of Dalwhinnie, he could not have been forced to fight but on his own terms, with the full advantage of his artillery and his superior discipline, and Charles must have either given battle at a disadvantage or suffered extremely by the want of money and provisions. Sir John, in the meantime, might have drawn his supplies from Athole, and would have overawed that highly disaffected district, the inhabitants of which, relieved from his presence by his march to Inverness, immediately joined the rebels. The superiority of the Highland army in numbers was but trifling, and such as the discipline of regular troops had always been esteemed sufficient to compensate, although there is reason to think that it was greatly exaggerated to the English general. None of this reasoning seemed to influence the council of war; they gave it as their opinion that the troops should be drawn off to Inverness, instead of making a stand, or retiring to Stirling although the option involved the certain risk of exposing the low country to the insurgents.

Sir John Cope, having his motions thus sanctioned by the opinion of the council of war, advanced for a mile or two, on the morning of the 27th of August, in his original direction, till he reached the point where the road to Inverness leaves that which leads to Fort Augustus, when the march was suddenly altered, and the route to Inverness adopted.

The exultation which filled the Highlanders on learning Cope's retreat was of a most exuberant description; but it was mingled with disappointment, like that of hunters whose prey has escaped them. There was a unanimous call to follow the retreating general with all despatch and compel him to fight. Cope had, indeed, some hours the start; but, in a council of chiefs, it was proposed to march five hundred picked men across the country, to throw themselves by rapid marches between Inverness and the English general's forces, and detain the regulars until the rest of the army came up in their rear. The advantages to be gained by an unopposed march into the Lowlands were, however, superior to what could be obtained by the pursuit, or even the defeat of Sir John Cope, and the latter plan was given up accordingly.

An attempt was made on the part of the Highlanders to surprise or burn the barracks of Ruthven; but they were bravely defended by the little garrison, and the attempt proved unsuccessful. They therefore directed their march southward upon Garviemore.

In the meantime, the intrigues of Lord Lovat continued to agitate the north, while the Lord President Forbes endeavoured, by soliciting Government for arms, by distributing commissions for independent companies, of which twenty were entrusted to his disposal, and by supplying money from his private purse to animate the clans who remained attached to Government, and to confirm those which were doubtful.

The old chief of the clan Fraser, apparently seconding all his measures, was, in fact, counteracting them as far as he could, and endeavouring, if not to turn the scale in favour of the young Adventurer, at least to preserve the parties in such a state of equality that he himself might have a chance of determining the balance when he could see on which side there was most to be gained. He feared, however, the shrewd sense, steady loyalty, and upright character of the President, and regarded him with a singular mixture of internal fear and hatred, and external affected respect and observance.

The line of conduct to be adopted by MacPherson of Cluny, whose numerous and hardy clan is situated chiefly in the district of Badenoch, was at this time a matter of great importance. This chief was a man of a bold and intrepid disposition, who had shown more respect for the laws of property, and more attention to prevent depredations, than any other chief in the Highlands, Lochiel perhaps excepted. He entered into extensive contracts with the Duke of Gordon, and many of the principal proprietors in countries exposed to the Highland caterans, agreeing for a moderate sum of yearly black-mail to secure them against theft. This species of engagement was often undertaken by persons like Rob Roy, who prosecuted the trade of a freebooter, and was in the habit of stealing at least as many cattle as he was the means of recovering. But Cluny MacPherson pursued the plain and honourable system expressed in the letter of his contract, and by actually securing and bringing to justice the malefactors who committed the depredations, he broke up the greater part of the numerous gangs of robbers in the shires of Inverness and Aberdeen. So much was this the case, that when a clergyman began a sermon on the heinous nature of the crime of theft, an old Highlander of the audience replied that he might forbear treating of the subject, since Cluny, with his broadsword, had done more to check it than all the ministers in the Highlands could do by their sermons.

MacPherson had been named captain of an independent company, and therefore remained, in appearance, a friend of Government; but, in fact, he only watched an opportunity to return to the allegiance of James VIII., whom he accounted his lawful sovereign. In compliance with his father-in-law Lovat's mysterious politics, Cluny waited on Sir John Cope on the 27th of August, and received that general's orders to embody his clan. But on the next morning the chief of the MacPhersons was made prisoner in his own house, and carried off to the rebel camp. Whether he was entertained there as a captive, or as a secret friend, we have not now the means of knowing. He was conveyed along with the Highland army to Perth, seemingly by constraint.

On 28th August the Prince bivouacked at Dalwhinnie, himself and his principal officers lying on the moor, with no other shelter than their plaids. On the 29th he reached Dalnacardoch being thus enabled by the retreat of the English army to possess himself of the passes of the mountains between Badenoch and Athole, and to descend upon the latter country. On the 30th Charles arrived at Blair in Athole, a castle belonging to the Duke of Athole, whose family, with his Grace's elder brother, Lord Tullibardine, and his uncle, Lord Nairne, were well disposed to the cause of the Prince, though his Grace, who enjoyed the title, was favourable to Government. The families and clans of Stewarts of Athole, Robertsons, and others of less importance, were all inclined to support the insurgents, having never forgotten the fame which their ancestors had obtained in a like cause during the wars of Montrose. The name and authority of the Marquis of Tullibardine was well calculated to call these ready warriors to arms. He was, as we have said, the elder brother of the Duke who enjoyed the title, and had been forfeited for his share in the rebellion of 1715,—a merit in the eyes of most of the vassals of his family.

The Prince remained two days at Blair, where he was joined by Viscount Strathallan and his son; by Mr. Oliphant of Gask and his son; and the Honourable Mr. Murray, brother to the Earl of Dunmore. John Roy Stewart, a most excellent partisan officer, also joined the Prince (to whom he had devoted his service) at this place. He had just arrived from the Continent, and brought several letters with him from persons of distinction abroad. They contained fair and flourishing promises of good wishes and services to be rendered, none of which civilities ever ripened into effectual assistance.

On the 3d of September, in the evening, the Highland army reached Perth, where it was joined by two persons of first-rate consequence; namely, the Duke of Perth, with two hundred men, whom he had collected while in hiding, in consequence of the warrant which was out for the purpose of arresting him, and the celebrated Lord George Murray, fifth brother of the Marquis of Tullibardine, already mentioned. Both these noblemen were created lieutenant-generals in the Prince's service.

It was at this time, and upon this occasion, that a sort of jealousy took place between these two great men which had a sinister effect upon the future affairs of Charles Edward.

We have already given the character of the Duke of Perth, as he was called, a gentleman in the highest degree courtly, pleasing, and amiable, particularly calculated to be agreeable to a person educated abroad, like the Prince, and not likely to run the risk of displeasing him by rough admonition and blunt contradiction. All his habits and opinions had been formed in France, where he had spent the first twenty years of his life. He even spoke English with some marks of a foreigner, which he concealed under the use of the broad Scottish dialect. He was a man of the most undoubted courage, but had no peculiar military talent.

Lord George Murray was a man of original and powerful character. He had been engaged with his brother, the Marquis of Tullibardine, in the affair of 1715, was also present at the battle of Glenshiel, in 1719, and had served for some time in the Sardinian army, then no bad school of war. He had at a later period been reconciled to the reigning family by the interest of his brother, the actual Duke of Atholle. It is said he had even solicited a commission in the English army. It was, however, refused; and in 1745 he reassumed his original sentiments, and joined Prince Charles Edward. Lord George Murray was in many respects an important acquisition. He was tall, hardy, and robust; and had that intuitive acquaintance with the art of war which no course of tactics can teach. Being little instructed by early military education, he was unfettered by its formal rules; and perhaps in leading an army of Highlanders, themselves undisciplined, except from a sort of tact which seemed natural to them, he knew far better how to employ and trust their native energies than a tactician accustomed to regular troops would have ventured to attempt. He was, moreover, undauntedly brave, and in the habit of fighting sword-in-hand in the front of the battle; he slept little, meditated much, and was the only person in the Highland army who seemed to study the movements of the campaign. The chiefs only led their men to the attack in the field, and the French and Irish officers had been so indifferently selected, that their military knowledge did not exceed the skill necessary to relieve a guard; and only one or two had served in a rank above that of captain. Over such men Lord George Murray had great superiority. He had, however, his failings, and they were chiefly those of temper and manners. He was proud of his superior talents, impatient of contradiction, and haughty and blunt in expressing his opinions.

It happened also, not unfrequently, that the Prince himself and his tutor Sir Thomas Sheridan, both extremely ignorant of the British constitution and habits of thinking, suffered sentiments of arbitrary power to escape them, as impolitic as they were ungracious. In checking and repelling such opinions, Lord George Murray did a most valuable service to his master; but the manner in which he performed a task necessarily unpleasing was often rude and assuming, and with the best intentions he gave offence, which was not the less sensibly felt by the Prince that his situation obliged him to suppress all outward indication of his displeasure.

From this peculiarity of Lord George Murray's temper there was early formed in the Prince's council a party who set up the Duke of Perth in opposition to him; although the gentle, honourable, and candid temper of the Duke mitigated the animosity of the internal faction. John Murray, the secretary, who having been the early agent of Prince Charles's party, possessed a great share of his master's confidence, was supposed to have been chiefly desirous of setting the claims of the Duke of Perth in opposition to those of Lord George Murray, as he considered the former a person over whom his own ambitious and active disposition might preserve an influence, which he could not hope to gain over the haughty and confident temper of the latter nobleman. Mr. Murray is supposed chiefly to have insisted upon Lord George's having taken the oaths to Government, and having been willing to serve the House of Hanover. By these insinuations he impressed on the Prince a shade of suspicion towards the general who was the most capable of directing the movements of his army, which was never entirely eradicated from his mind, even while he most felt the value of Lord George Murray's services. Charles's high idea of the devotion due to his rights by his subjects rendered him jealous of the fidelity of a follower who had not at all times been a pure royalist, or who had shown any inclination, however transitory, to make his own peace by a compromise with the reigning family. The disunion arising from these intrigues had an existence even at Perth, in the very commencement of their enterprise, and continued till the very end of the affair to vex and perplex the councils of the insurgents.

On his arrival at Perth also, the Chevalier first found the want of money, which has been well called the sinews of war. When he entered that town he showed one of his followers that his purse contained only a single guinea of the four hundred pounds which he had brought with him in the *Doutelle*. But Dundee, Montrose, and all the Lowland towns north of the Tay, as far as Inverness, were now at his command. He proceeded to levy the cess and public revenue in name of his father; and as such of his adherents who were too old or timid to join the standard sent in contributions of money according to their ability, his military chest was by these resources tolerably supplied. Parties were sent for this purpose to Dundee, Aberbrothwick, Montrose, and other towns. They proclaimed King James VIII., but committed little violence except opening the prisons; and it is remarkable, that even in my own time, a chieftain of high rank had to pay a large sum of money on account of his ancestors having set at liberty a prisoner who was detained for a considerable amount of debt.

It was no less necessary to brigade the men assembled under this adventurous standard. This was, however, easily done, for the Highlanders were familiar with a species of manœuvring exactly suited to their own irregular tactics. They marched in a column of three abreast, and could wheel up with prompt regularity, in order to form the line, or rather succession of clan columns, in which it was their fashion to charge. They were accustomed also to carry their arms with habitual ease, and handle them with ready promptitude; to fire with a precise aim, and to charge with vigour, trusting to their national weapons, the broadsword and target, with which the first rank of every clan, being generally gentlemen, was completely armed. They were, therefore, as well prepared for the day of battle as could be expected from them; and as there was no time to instruct them in more refined manœuvres, Lord George Murray judiciously recommended to the Prince to trust to those which seemed naturally their own. Some modelling and discipline was however resorted to, so far as the short interval would permit.

The time which Charles Edward could allot to supply his finances, arrange the campaign, and discipline his army, was only from the 4th to the 11th of September; for he had already adopted the daring resolution to give eclât to his arms by taking possession of the Scottish capital, and was eager to advance upon it ere Sir John Cope could, with his forces, return from the north for its defence.

LXXVII

Entrance into Edinburgh

1745

EDINBURGH had long been a peaceful capital; little accustomed to the din of arms, but considerably divided by factions, as was the case of other towns in Scotland. The rumours from the Highlands had sounded like distant thunder during a serene day, for no one seemed disposed to give credit to the danger as seriously approaching. The unexpected intelligence that General Cope had marched to Inverness, and left the metropolis in a great measure to its own resources, excited a very different and more deep sensation, which actuated the inhabitants variously, according to their political sentiments. The Jacobites, who were in considerable numbers, hid their swelling hopes under the cover of ridicule and irony, with which they laboured to interrupt every plan which was adopted for the defence of the town. In truth, in a military point of view, no town, not absolutely defenceless, was worse protected than Edinburgh. The spacious squares and streets of the New Town had then, and for a long time after, no existence, the city being strictly limited to its original boundaries, established as early as the fourteenth or fifteenth century. It had defences, but they were of a singularly antique and insufficient character. A high and solid wall enclosed the city from the West Port to the Potterrow Port. It was embattled, but the parapet was too narrow for mounting cannon, and, except upon one or two points, the wall neither exhibited redoubt, turret, or re-entering angle, from which the curtain or defensive line might be flanked or defended. It was merely an ordinary park-wall of uncommon height and strength, of which you may satisfy yourself by looking at such of its ruins as still remain. The wall ran eastward to what is called the South Back of the Canongate, and then, turning northward, ascended the ridge on which the town is built, forming the one side of a suburb called Saint Mary's Wynd, where it was covered by houses built upon it from time to time, besides being within a few feet of the other side of the wynd, which is narrow, and immediately in its front. In this imperfect state the defence reached the Netherbow Port, which divided the city from the Canongate. From this point the wall ran down Leith Wynd, and terminated at the hospital called Paul's Work, connecting itself on that point with the North, or Nor' Loch, so called because it was on the northern side of the city, and its sole defence or that quarter.

The nature of the defensive protections must, from this sketch, be judged extremely imperfect; and the quality of the troops by which resistance must have been made good, if it should be seriously thought upon, was scarce better suited to the task. The town's people, indeed, such as were able to bear arms, were embodied under the name of Trained Bands, and had firelocks belonging to them, which were kept in the town's magazines. They amounted nominally to sixteen companies, of various strength, running between eighty and a hundred men each. This would have been a formidable force had their discipline and good-will corresponded to their numbers. But, for many years, the officers of the Trained Bands had practised no other martial discipline than was implied in a particular mode of flourishing their wine-glasses on festive occasions; and it was well understood that, if these militia were called on, a number of them were likely enough to declare for Prince Charles, and a much larger proportion would be unwilling to put their persons and property in danger for either the one or the other side of the cause. The only part of the civic defenders of Edinburgh who could at all be trusted was the small body of foot called the city-guard, whom we have already seen make some figure in the affair of Porteous. The two regiments of dragoons, which General Cope had left behind him for the protection of the Lowlands, were the only regular troops.

Yet, though thus poorly provided for defence, there was a natural reluctance on the, part of the citizens of Edinburgh, who were in general friendly to Government, to yield up their ancient metropolis to a few hundred wild insurgents from the Highlands without even an effort at defence. So early as the 27th of August, when it was known in the capital that the regular troops had marched to Inverness, and that the Highlanders were directing their march on the Lowlands, a meeting of the friends of Government was held, at which it was resolved that the city should be put in a state of defence, its fortifications repaired or improved as well as time would permit, and a regiment of a thousand men raised by general subscription among the inhabitants. This spirit of resistance was considerably increased by the arrival of Captain Rogers, aide-de-camp to General Cope, who came from Inverness by sea, with directions that a number of transports, lying then at Leith, should be despatched, without loss of time, for Aberdeen. He announced that General Cope was to march his troops from Inverness to Aberdeen, and embark them at the latter seaport, by the means which he was now providing for that purpose. The General, he stated, would with his army thus return to Lothian by sea, in time, as he hoped, for the safety of the city.

These tidings highly excited the zeal of those who had thus voted for defending the capital. As the regiment which had been voted could not be levied without the express warrant of Government, several citizens, to the number of an hundred, petitioned to be permitted to enroll themselves as volunteers for the defence of the city. Their numbers soon increased. At length, on the 11th September, six companies were appointed, and officers named to them. In the meantime, fortifications were added to the walls, under the scientific direction of the celebrated M'Laurin, professor of mathematics in the University of Edinburgh. The volunteers were taught with all possible speed the most necessary parts of military discipline; cannon were also mounted on the walls, chiefly obtained from the shipping at Leith. The whole city rung with the din of preparation; and much seemed to depend on the event of a struggle for time. The party which was uppermost for the moment expressed their eager wishes and hopes for General Cope's arrival from Aberdeen; while those who hoped soon to change positions with them, whispered to each other in secret their hopes that the English general would be anticipated by the arrival of the Highland army.

In the meantime Charles Edward, having stopped at Perth only long enough to collect some money, refresh and regulate his army, and receive a few supplies of men, proceeded on his venturous march on the 11th September. His manifestoes, in his father's name and his own, had already announced his purpose of remedying all the grievances of which the nation could complain. Among these the dissolution of the Union was proposed as a principal object of reformation. It certainly continued to be felt as a grievance by many of the country gentlemen in Scotland, whose importance it had greatly diminished; but the commercial part of the nation had begun to be sensible of its advantages, and were not greatly captivated by the proposed dissolution of the national treaty, which had so much enlarged their sources of foreign traffic. Another proclamation was issued, in answer to one which had set the price of 130,000 upon the Adventurer's head. He should reply to this, he said, by a similar announcement, but in confidence that no adherent of his would ever think of doing anything to merit such a reward. Accordingly, he published a reward for the Elector of Hanover's person. Charles's original idea was to limit the sum offered to £30, but it was ultimately extended to the same amount which had been placed upon his own.

On the evening of the 11th, the Chevalier reached Dunblane with the vanguard of his army, or rather detachments of the best men of every clan. It was found very difficult to remove the others from the good quarters and provisions of Perth, which were superior to what they had to expect on a march. The fords of Frew, situated on the Forth, about eight miles above Stirling, which the Earl of Mar, with a much more numerous army of Highlanders had in vain attempted to cross, formed no obstacle to the advance of their present more adventurous leader. The great drought which prevailed that year, and which in Scotland is generally most severe towards the end of autumn, made it easy to cross the river. Gardiner's regiment of dragoons, which had been left at Stirling, offered no opposition to the enemy, but retreated to Linlithgow, to interpose betwixt the Highlanders and Edinburgh,—a retrograde movement which had a visible effect on the spirits of the soldiers.

In the meantime, the confusion in the capital was greatly increased by the near approach of the insurgent army. The volunteers had at no time amounted to more than about four hundred men, a small proportion of the population of the city, sufficiently indicating that the far greater majority of the inhabitants were lukewarm, and probably a great many positively disaffected to the cause of Government. Of those also who had taken arms, many had done so merely to show a zeal for the cause which they never expected would be brought to a serious test; others had wives and families, houses and occupations, which they were, when it came to the push, loath to put in hazard for any political consideration. The citizens also entertained a high idea of the desperate courage of the Highlanders and a dreadful presentiment of the outrages which a people so wild were likely to commit, if they should succeed, which appeared likely, in forcing their way into the town. Still, however, there were many young students and others at that period of life when honour is more esteemed than life, who were willing and even eager to prosecute their intentions of resistance and defence.

The corps of volunteers, being summoned together, were informed that Gardiner's dragoons, having continued to retreat before the enemy, were now at Corstorphine, a village within three miles of the city; and that the van of the rebels had reached Kirkliston, a little town about four or five miles farther to the west. In these critical circumstances, General Guest, lieutenant-governor of the castle of Edinburgh, submitted to the corps of volunteers, that instead of waiting to be attacked, within a town, which their numbers were inadequate to defend, they should second an offensive movement which he designed to make in front of the city, in order to protect it by an instant battle. For this purpose he proposed that the second regiment of dragoons, called Hamilton's, should march from Leith, where they were encamped, and form a junction with Gardiner's at Corstorphine; and that they should be supported by the volunteer corps of four hundred men. The Provost, having agreed to this proposal, offered, after some hesitation, that ninety of the city-guard, whom he reckoned the best troops his disposal, should march out with the armed citizens. Mr. Drummond, an active officer of the volunteers, and who displayed more than usual zeal, harangued the armed association. The most spirited shouted with sincere applause, and by far the greater part followed their example. Out of the whole volunteers about two hundred and fifty were understood to pledge themselves to the execution of the proposed movement in advance of the city. The sound of the fire-bell was appointed as the signal for the volunteers to muster in the Lawnmarket. In the meantime, orders were sent to Hamilton's dragoons to march through the city on their way to Corstorphine. The parade and display of these disciplined troops would, it was thought, add spirit to the raw soldiers.

The following day was Sunday, the 15th of September. The fire-bell, an ominous and ill-chosen signal, tolled for assembling the volunteers, and so alarming a sound, during the time of divine service, dispersed those assembled for worship, and brought out a large crowd of the inhabitants to the street. The dragoon regiment appeared, equipped for battle. They huzzaed and clashed their swords at sight of the volunteers, their companions in peril, of which neither party were destined that day to see much. But other sounds expelled these war-like greetings from the ears of the civic soldiers. The relatives of the volunteers crowded around them, weeping, protesting, and conjuring them not to expose lives so invaluable to their families to the broadswords of the savage Highlanders.[1] There is nothing of which men, in general, are more easily persuaded than of the extreme value of their own lives; nor are they apt to estimate them more lightly when they see they are highly prized by others. A sudden change of opinion took place among the body. In some companies, the men said that their officers would not lead them on; in others, the officers said that the privates would not follow them. An attempt to march the corps towards the West Port, which was their destined route for the field of battle, failed. The regiment moved, indeed, but the files grew gradu-ally thinner and thinner as they marched down the Bow[2] and through the Grassmarket, and not above forty-five reached the West Port. A hundred more were collected with some difficulty, but it seems to have been under a tacit condition that the march to Corstorphine should be abandoned, for out of the city not one of them issued.[3] The volunteers were led back to their alarm-post, and dismissed for the evening, when a few of the most zealous left the town, the defence of which began no longer to be expected, and sought other fields in which to exercise their valour.

In the meantime, their less warlike comrades were doomed to hear of the near approach of the Highland clans. On the morning of Monday, a person named Alves, who pretended to have approached the rebel army by accident, but who was, perhaps, in reality, a favourer

---

[1] Many of the Edinburgh corps were moreover *Oneyers* and *Moneyers*, as Falstaff says, men whose words upon 'Change would go much farther than their blows in battle. Most had shops to be plundered, houses to be burned, children to be brained with Lochaber axes, and wives, daughters, and favourite handmaidens to be treated accord-ing to the rules of war.

[2] The descent of the *Bow* presented localities and facilities equally convenient for desertion; and a pamphleteer of that period assures us that a friend of his, who had made a poetical description of the march of the volunteers from the Lawnmarket to the West Port, when they went out, or, more properly, seemed to be about to go out, to meet the ruthless rebels, had invented a very magnificent simile to illustrate his

of their cause, brought word that he had seen the Duke of Perth, to whom he was personally known, and had received a message to the citizens of Ediuburgh informing them that if they opened their gates the town should be favourably treated, but if they attempted resistance, they might lay their account with military execution; "and he concluded," said Alves, "by addressing a young man by the title of Royal Highness, and desiring to know if such was not his pleasure." This message, which was publicly delivered, struck additional terror into the inhabitants, who petitioned the Provost to call a general meeting of the citizens, the only purpose of which must have increased the confusion in their councils. Provost Stewart refused to convoke such a meeting. The town was still covered by two regiments of dragoons. Colonel Gardiner, celebrated for his private worth, his bravery, and his devotional character, was now in command of Hamilton's regiment as well as his own, when he was suddenly superseded by General Fowkes, who had been sent from London by sea, and arrived on the night of the 15th of September.

Early the next morning the new general drew up the dragoons near the north end of the Colt Bridge which crosses the Water of Leith, about two miles from Corstorphine, from which last village the Highlanders were now advancing. On their van coming in sight of the regulars, a few of the mounted gentlemen who had joined the insurgents were despatched to reconnoitre. As this party rode up, and fired their pistols at the dragoons, after the usual manner of skirmishers, a humiliating spectacle ensued. The soldiers, without returning a shot, fell into such disorder that their officers were compelled to move them from the ground, with the purpose of restoring their ranks. But no

---

subject. He compared it to the course of the Rhine, which rolling pompously its waves through fertile fields, instead of augmenting in its course is continually drawn off by a thousand canals, and at last becomes a small rivulet, which loses itself in the sands before it reaches the ocean.

[3] We remember an instance of a stout Whig and a very worthy man, a writing-master by occupation, who had ensconced his bosom beneath a professional cuirass, consisting of two quires of long foolscap writing paper; and doubtful that even this defence might be unable to protect his valiant heart from the claymores, amongst which its impulses might carry him, had written on the outside, in his best flourish, "This is the body of J—— M——; pray give it Christian burial." Even this hero, prepared as one practised how to die, could not find it in his heart to accompany the devoted battalion farther than the door of his own house, which stood conveniently open about the head of the *Lawnmarket*.

sooner did the two regiments find themselves in retreat, than it became impossible to halt or form them. Their panic increased their speed from a trot to a gallop, and the farther they got even from the very appearance of danger, the more excessive seemed to be their terror. Galloping in the greatest confusion round the base of the castle, by what were called the Lang Dykes, they pursued their disorderly course along the fields where the New Town is now built, in full view of the city and its inhabitants, whose fears were reasonably enough raised to extremity at seeing the shameful flight of the regular soldiers, whose business it was to fight—a poor example to those who were only to take up the deadly trade as amateurs. Even at Leith, to which, as they had last encamped there, they returned by a kind of instinct, those recreant horsemen could only be halted for a few minutes. Ere their minds had recovered from their perturbation, some one raised a cry that the Highlanders were at hand; and the retreat was renewed. They halted a second time near Prestonpans; but, receiving a third alarm from one of their own men falling into a waste coal-pit, the race was again resumed in the darkness of the night, and the dragoons only stopped at Dunbar, North Berwick, and other towns on the coast; none of them, at the same time, able to render a reason why they fled, or to tell by whom they were pursued.

In Edinburgh the citizens were driven to a kind of desperation of terror. Crowds gathered on the streets and surrounded the Provost, entreating him to give up all thoughts of defending the town, which would have been indeed an impossibility after the scandalous retreat of the dragoons. Whatever the Provost might think of the condition of the city he maintained a good countenance; and convoking a meeting of the magistracy, sent for the Justice-Clerk, the Lord Advocate, and Solicitor-General, to come and partake their councils. But these functionaries had wisely left the city when the danger of its falling into the hands of the rebels became so very imminent. In the meantime, other citizens, uninvited, intruded themselves into the place where the council was held, which speedily assumed the appearance of a disorderly crowd, most part of whom were clamorous for surrender. Many of the loudest were Jacobites, who took that mode of serving the Prince's cause.

While the council was in this state of confusion, a letter, subscribed Charles Stewart, P. R., was handed into the meeting, but the Provost would not permit it to be read, which gave rise to a furious debate. The volunteers, in the meantime, were drawn up on the street, amid the same clamour and consternation which filled the council. They received no orders from the Provost, nor from any one else. At this juncture a man, who has never since been discovered, mounted on a gray horse, rode along the front of their line, calling out, to the great augmentation of the general alarm, that the Highlanders, were just at hand, and were sixteen thousand strong! The unlucky volunteers, disheartened, and in a great measure deserted resolved at length to disembody themselves, and to return their arms to the King's magazine in the castle. The muskets were received there accordingly, and the volunteers might be considered as disbanded as well as disarmed. If some wept at parting with their arms, we believe the greater part were glad to be fairly rid of the encumbrance.

In the interim the letter with the alarming signature was at length read in the council, and was found to contain a summons to surrender the city, under a promise of safety to the immunities of the corporation, and the property of individuals. The conclusion declared, that the Prince would not be responsible for the consequences if he were reduced to enter the city by force, and that such of the inhabitants as he found in arms against him must not expect to be treated as prisoners of war.

The perusal of this letter increased the cry against resistance, which, indeed, the flight of the dragoons, and dispersion of the volunteers, rendered altogether impossible, the armed force being reduced to the city-guard, and a few recruits of the newly raised Edinburgh regiment. It was at length agreed on, by general consent, to send a deputation of the council to wait on the young Prince at Gray's Mill, within two miles of the city; they were instructed to require a suspension of hostilities until they should have time to deliberate on the letter which had been forwarded to them.

The deputation had not long set forth on its destination, when one of those turns of fortune which so unexpectedly threaten to derange the most profound calculations of human prudence, induced many of the citizens to wish that the step of communicating with the rebels had been delayed. Intelligence arrived, acquainting the magistrates and council that Sir John Cope's army had arrived in the transports from Aberdeen, and that the fleet was seen off Dunbar, where the General intended to land his troops, and move instantly to the relief of Edinburgh. A messenger was sent to recall the deputation, but he proved unable to overtake them. General Guest was resorted to with various proposals. He was asked to recall the dragoons; but replied, he considered it better for the service that they should join General Cope. The more zealous citizens then requested a new issue of arms to the volunteers; but General Guest seems to have been unwilling to place them again in irresolute hands; he said the magistrates might arm those whom they could trust from the city's magazine. Still, as it appeared that a day's time gained might save the city, there were proposals to resume the purpose of defence, at least for the time which Cope's march from Dunbar was likely to occupy. It was therefore proposed to beat to arms, ring the fire-bell, and reassemble the volunteers, schemes which were abandoned as soon as moved, for it was remembered that the deputation of the magistrates and counsellors were in the power of the Highlandmen, who, on the sound, of an alarm in the town, were likely enough to hang them without ceremony.

About ten o'clock at night the deputation returned, with an answer to the same purpose with the previous summons, demanding, at the same time, a positive reply before two in the morning. The deliberations of the magistrates were further embroiled by this peremptory demand of instant surrender, which made them aware that the insurgents were as sensible as they could be of the value of hours and minutes in a discussion so critical. They could think of nothing better than to send out a second deputation to Gray's Mill, with instructions entreat for further time. It is important to state that this party went to the Highland headquarters in a hackney-coach. The Prince refused to see them, and dismissed them without an answer.

In the meantime the Chevalier and his counsellors agitated several plans for carrying the city by a sudden surprise. There was more than one point which gave facilities for such a coup-de-main. A house belonging to a gentleman of the name of Nicolson stood on the outside of the town-wall, only a few feet distant from it, and very near the Potterrow Port. It was proposed to take possession of this house, and, after clearing the wall by a fire of musketry from the upper windows, either to attempt an escalade or to run a mine under the fortification. At the same time, the position of the hospital called Paul's Work was favourably situated to cover an attack on the main sluice of the North Loch. The College Church gave ready means of gaining the hospital; and an alarm on the northern termination of the wall would have afforded a point of diversion, while the main attack might be made by means of the row of houses in St. Mary's Wynd, composing the western side of that lane, and actually built upon, and forming part of the wall, which in that place was merely a range of buildings. Such were the points of assault which might be stormed simultaneously, and with the greater prospect of success that their defenders were deficient both in numbers and courage.

With these and similar views, the Chevalier ordered Lochiel to get his men under arms, so as to be ready, if the magistrates did not surrender at the appointed hour of two in the morning, to make an attack on either of the points we have mentioned, or take any other opportunity that might occur of entering the city; Mr. Murray of Broughton, who was familiar with all the localities of Edinburgh, acting as a guide to the Camerons. The party amounted to about nine hundred men. The strictest caution was recommended to them in marching, and they were enjoined to rigid abstinence from spirituous liquors. At the same time, each man was promised a reward of two shillings if the enterprise was successful. Colonel O'Sullivan was with the party as quartermaster. The detachment marched round by Merchiston and Hope's Park, without being observed from the castle, though they could hear the watches call the rounds within that fortress. Approaching, the Netherbow Port, Lochiel and Murray reconnoitred the city-wall more closely, and found it planted with cannon, but without sentinels. They could therefore have forced an entrance by any of the houses in St. Mary's Wynd; but having strict orders to observe the utmost caution, Lochiel hesitated to resort to actual violence till they should have final commands to do so. In the meantime, Lochiel sent forward one of his people, disguised in a riding coat and hunting cap, with orders to request admission by the Netherbow Port. This man was to personate the servant of an English officer of dragoons, and in that character to call for admittance. An advanced guard of twenty Camerons were ordered to place themselves on each side of the gate; a support of sixty men were stationed in deep silence in St. Mary's Wynd; and the rest of the detachment remained at some distance, near the foot of the lane. It was Lochiel's purpose that the gate, if opened, should have been instantly secured by the forlorn hope of his party. The watch, however (for there were sentinels at the gate, though none on the city-wall), refused to open the gate, threatened to fire on the man who desired admittance, and thus compelled him to withdraw.

It was now proposed by Murray, that as the morning was beginning to break, the detachment should retire to the craggy ground called
Saint Leonard's Hill, where they would be secure from the cannon of
the castle, and there wait for further orders. Just when the detachment
was about to retreat, an accident happened which gratified them with
an unexpected opportunity of entrance.

I have told you of a second deputation sent out by the magistrates
to entreat from the Chevalier additional time to deliberate upon his
summons, which he refused to grant, declining even to see the messengers. These deputies returned into the city long after midnight, in the
hackney-coach which had carried them to the rebel camp. They
entered at the West Port, and left the coach after they had ascended the
Bow and reached the High Street. The hackney-coachman, who had
his own residence and his stables in the Canongate, was desirous to
return to that suburb through the Netherbow Port, which then closed
the head of the Canongate. The man was known to the waiters, or
porters, as having been that night engaged in the service of the magistrates and, as a matter of course, they opened the gate to let him go
home. The leaves of the gate had no sooner unfolded themselves, than
the Camerons rushed in, and secured and disarmed the few watchmen.
With the same ease they seized on the city guard-house, disarming
such soldiers as they found there.

Colonel O'Sullivan despatched parties to the other military posts
and gates about the city, two of which were occupied with the same
ease, and without a drop of blood being spilt. The Camerons, in the
dawn of morning, were marched up to the Cross, when the castle, now
alarmed with the news of what had happened, fired a shot or two
expressive of defiance. These warlike sounds waked such of the citizens of Edinburgh as the tumult of the Highlanders' entrance had not
yet roused, and many with deep anxiety, and others with internal exultation, found that the capital was in the hands of the insurgents.

Much noisy wonder was expressed at the tame surrender of the
metropolis of Scotland to the rebels; and, as if it had been necessary to
find a scape-goat to bear the disgrace and blame of the transaction, a
great proportion of both was imputed to the Lord Provost Stewart,
who, after a long and severe imprisonment was brought to trial for
high treason and although he was honourably acquitted, his name
was often afterwards mentioned in a manner as if his judicial acquittal
had not been sanctioned by the public voice. There is no room to

inquire of what cast were Provost Stewart's general politics, or how far, even from the mere circumstance of namesake, he was to be accounted a Jacobite. Neither is the chief magistrate of a corporation to be condemned, to death as a traitor because he does not possess those attributes of heroism by means of which some gifted individuals have raised means of defence when hope seemed altogether lost, and, by their own energies and example, have saved communities and states which were, in the estimation of all others, doomed to despair. The question is, whether Provost Stewart, as an upright and honourable man, sought the best advice in an exigency so singular, and exerted himself assiduously to carry it into execution when received? The flight of the dragoons, the disbanding of the volunteers, the discontinuance of the defence, received no encouragement from him; even the opening a communication with the enemy was none of his fault, since he was one of the last who either despaired of preserving the city or used discouraging language to the citizens. But he could not inspire panic-struck soldiers with courage, or selfish burghers with patriotic devotion and, like a man who fights with a broken weapon, was unequal to maintain the cause which to all appearance he seems to have, been sincere in defending.

The Highlanders, amid circumstances so new, and stimulating to them as attended the capture of Edinburgh, behaved themselves with the utmost order and propriety. The inhabitants, desirous to conciliate their new masters, brought them provisions, and even whisky but having been enjoined by Lochiel not to taste the latter spirits, they unanimously rejected a temptation which besets them strongly. They remained where they were posted, in the Parliament Square, from five in the morning till eleven in the forenoon, without a man leaving his post, though in a city taken, it may be said, by storm, and surrounded with a hundred objects to excite their curiosity or awaken their cupidity. They were then quartered in the Outer Parliament House.

About noon on this important day (the 17th of September) Charles Edward prepared to take possession of the palace and capital of his ancestors.

It was at that time, when, winding his march round by the village of Duddingston, to avoid the fire of the castle, he halted in the hollow between Arthur's Seat and Salisbury Crags. As Charles approached the palace by the eastern access, called the Duke's Walk, he called for his horse, as if to show himself to the populace, who assembled in great numbers, and with loud acclamations. The young Adventurer had begun his march on foot, but the immense crowd with which he was surrounded, many of whom pressed to touch his clothes, or kiss his hand, almost threw him down. He again mounted his charger as he approached the palace, having on his right the Duke of Perth, on his left Lord Elcho, the eldest son of the Earl of Wemyss, who had joined him a few days before, and followed by a concourse of chiefs and gentlemen. The personal appearance of the Chevalier was as prepossessing, as the daring character and romantic circumstances of his enterprise were calculated to excite the imagination. His noble mien, graceful manners, and ready courtesy, seemed to mark him no unworthy competitor for a crown. His dress was national. A short tartan coat, a blue bonnet with a white rose, and the order and emblem of the thistle, seemed all chosen to identify himself with the ancient nation he summoned to arms; and, upon the whole, so far as acclamations and signs of joy could express it, he was so favourably received, that none of his followers doubted that he might levy a thousand men in the streets of Edinburgh in half an hour, if he could but find arms to equip them.

But they who were able to look beyond the mere show and clamour, discerned symptoms of inward weakness in the means by which the Chevalier was to execute his weighty undertaking. The duinhéwassals, or gentlemen of the clans, were, indeed, martially attired in the full Highland dress, with the various arms which appertain to that garb, which, in full equipment, comprehends a firelock, a broadsword, dirk, and target, a pair of pistols, and a short knife, used occasionally as a poniard. But such complete appointments fell to the lot of but few of the followers of the Prince. Most were glad to be satisfied with a single weapon, a sword, dirk, or pistol. Nay, in spite of all evasions of the Disarming Act, it had been so far effectual that several Highlanders were only armed with scythe blades, set straight on the handle, and some with only clubs or cudgels. As arms were scarce among the Highlanders, so the scanty and ill-clothed appearance of the poorer amongst them gave them an appearance at once terrible and wretched. Indeed many were of the opinion of an old friend of your Grandfather's, who, as he looked on a set of haggard and fierce-looking men, some wanting coats, some lacking hose and shoes, some having their hair tied back with a leathern strap, without bonnet or covering of any kind, could not help observing that they were a proper set of ragamuffins with which to propose to overturn an established government.[1] On the whole, they wanted that regularity and uniformity of appearance which, in our eye, distinguishes regular soldiers from banditti; and their variety of weapons, fierceness of aspect, and sinewy limbs, combined with a martial look and air proper to a people whose occupation was arms, gave them a peculiarly wild and barbarous appearance.

The Prince had been joined by many persons of consequence since he reached Lothian. Lord Elcho has already been mentioned. He was a man of high spirit and sound sense, but no Jacobite in the bigoted sense of the word; that is, no devoted slave to the doctrines of hereditary right or passive obedience. He brought with him five hundred pounds on the part of his father, Lord Wemyss, who was too old to take the field in person. This was an acceptable gift in the state of the Prince's finances. Sir Robert Thriepland had also joined him as he approached Edinburgh; and by the private information which he brought from his friends in that city had determined him to persevere in the attack which proved so successful.

The Earl of Kelly, Lord Balmerino, Lockhart, the younger of Carnwath, Graham, younger of Airth, Rollo, younger of Powburn, Hamilton of Bangour, a poet of considerable merit, Sir David Murray, and other gentlemen of distinction, had also joined the standard.

Amongst these James Hepburn of Keith, son of that Robert Hepburn respecting whose family a remarkable anecdote is mentioned at page 46 of this volume, and whose escape from Newgate is narrated at page 102 of the same, distinguished himself by the manner in which he devoted himself to the cause of Charles Edward. As the Prince entered the door of the palace of Holyrood, this gentleman stepped from the crowd, bent his knee before him in testimony of homage, and, rising up, drew his sword, and, walking before him, marshalled him the way into the palace of his ancestors. Hepburn bore the highest character as the model of a true Scottish gentleman. He, like Lord Elcho, disclaimed the slavish principles of the violent Jacobites, but conceiving his country wronged, and the gentry of Scotland degraded by the Union, he, in this romantic manner, dedicated his sword to the service of the Prince who offered to restore him to his rights. Mr. John

---

[1] My friend, who was the Jonathan Oldbuck of the *Antiquary*, made his observation rather at an ill-chosen place and time, in consequence of which he was nearly brought to trouble.

Home, whose heart sympathised with acts of generous devotion, from whatever source they flowed, feelingly observes, that "the best Whigs regretted that this accomplished gentleman—the model of ancient simplicity, manliness, and honour—should sacrifice himself to a visionary idea of the independence of Scotland."[1] I am enabled to add that, after having impaired his fortune and endangered his life repeatedly in this ill-fated cause, Mr. Hepburn became convinced that, in the words of Scripture, he had laboured a vain thing. He repeatedly said in his family circle that had he known, as the after progress of the expedition showed him, that a very great majority of the nation were satisfied with the existing Government, he would never have drawn sword against his fellow subjects, or aided to raise a civil war merely to replace the Stewart dynasty.[2]

---

[1] "John Home's profession as a Presbyterian clergyman, his political opinions, and those of his family, decided the cause which he was to espouse, and he became one of the most active and eager members of a corps of volunteers, formed for the purpose of defending Edinburgh against the expected assault of the Highlanders. Under less strong influence of education and profession, which was indeed irresistible, it is possible he might have made a less happy option; for the feeling, the adventure, the romance, the poetry, all that was likely to interest the imagination of a youthful poet—all, in short, save the common sense, prudence, and sound reason of the national dispute—must be allowed to have lain on the side of the Jacobites. Indeed, although mortally engaged against them, Mr. Home could not, in the latter part of his life, refrain from tears when mentioning the gallantry and misfortunes of some of the unfortunate leaders in the Highland army; and we have ourselves seen his feelings and principles divide him strangely when he came to speak upon such topics."—*Review of Home's Life.*

[2] A hereditary intimacy with the late Lieutenant-Colonel Hepburn (son of Mr. Hepburn of Keith), and the friendship of the members of his surviving family, enable me to make this assertion. No doubt there were many of the more liberal and intelligent Jacobites who entertained similar sentiments, and conceived that, in furthering the cause of the Prince, they were asserting the rights of the country.

LXXVIII

The Cross and Prestonpans

1745

THE possession of Edinburgh threw a gleam of splendour upon Charles Edward's fortunes, but can scarcely be said to have produced very important consequences.

King James VIII. was proclaimed at the Cross. At this ceremony the heralds and pursuivants were obliged to assist in their official dresses, and the magistrates in their robes. A great multitude attended on this occasion, and made the city ring with their acclamations. The gunners of the castle were disposed to give a different turn to this mirth by throwing a bomb, so calculated as to alight near the Cross, and interrupt the ceremonial. Fortunately this act of violence, which might have endangered the lives of many of King George's good subjects, whom mere curiosity had drawn to the spot, was prohibited by General Guest.

At night there was a splendid ball at Holyrood, where might be seen a great display both of rank and beauty, the relatives of the gentlemen who were in arms. But it was a remarkable and ominous circumstance that of the common people who by thousands crowded round the Prince's person when he went abroad, pressing, to kiss his hands and touch his clothes, with every display of affection, scarcely one could be induced to enlist in his service. The reflection that a battle must take place betwixt Prince Charles and General Cope in the course of a very few days was to the populace of a large city a sufficient check upon their party zeal.

One of the most solid advantages which the Prince obtained by his possession of the city, besides the encouragement which his adherents received from such a signal proof of success, was the acquisition of about a thousand muskets, in indifferent condition, being the arms of the Trained Bands, which were lodged in the city magazine. These served to arm many of his followers, but still some remained unprovided with weapons. Charles also laid upon the city a military requisition for a thousand tents, two thousand targets, six thousand pairs of shoes, and six thousand canteens. The magistrates had no alternative but to acquiesce, and employ workmen to get ready the articles demanded.

Upon the 18th of September, the day after the occupation of Edinburgh, Lord Nairne came up from the north and joined the Highland camp with a thousand men, consisting of Highlanders from Athole, together with the chief of MacLauchlan and his followers. The Prince visited his camp, and passed in review, at the same time with the rest of his forces, these new associates of his enterprise.

While these things were passing in Edinburgh, General Cope landed his troops at Dunbar, anxious to repair the false step which he had committed in leaving the Lowlands open to the young Adventurer, and desirous to rescue the capital of Scotland, since he had not been able to protect it. He began the disembarkation of his troops on the 17th, but it was not completed till the next day. The two regiments of cavalry which had made such extraordinary speed to join him were also united to his army, though their nerves had not yet recovered the rapid and disorderly retreat from Colt Bridge to East Lothian. The number of infantry was about 2000, that of the two regiments of dragoons about 600; Sir John Cope was also joined by volunteers, among whom the Earl of Home was the most conspicuous, making his army up to near 3000 men in all. They had six pieces of artillery, but what seems strange, no gunners or artillerymen to work them. In other respects they formed a small but very well-appointed force, and made an impressive appearance in a country so long disused to war as had been the case with Scotland. At the head of this respectable body of men Sir John departed from Dunbar, and marched as far as Haddington or its vicinity on his proposed advance on Edinburgh.

In the meantime Charles Edward had taken a resolution corresponding with the character of his enterprise. It was that of moving eastward, to meet Sir John Cope upon his route, and give him battle. All his counsellors agreed in this courageous sentiment. The Prince then asked the Chiefs what was to be expected from their followers. They answered by the mouth of Keppoch, who had served in the French army, that the gentlemen of every clan would lead the attack with determined gallantry, in which case there was no doubt that the clansmen, who were much attached to their chiefs and superiors, would follow them with fidelity and courage. The Prince declared he would himself lead the van, and set them an example how to conquer or die. The Chiefs unanimously remonstrated against his exposing a life on which the whole success of the expedition must depend, and declared that, if he persisted in that resolution, they would break up the army and return home. There can be little doubt that Charles was sincere in his resolution, and no doubt at all that he was very wise in withdrawing from it on the remonstrance of his faithful followers.

Orders were given to prepare next morning for the evacuation of Edinburgh, in order that the whole Highland army might be collected for the battle, which was expected to ensue. For this purpose, the troops employed in mounting the several guards of the city, in number 1000 men, were withdrawn to the camp at Duddingston. It might have been expected that a sally from the castle would have taken place in consequence of their retreat, if not for any ulterior purpose, at least to seize on the different articles which had been got ready at the requisition of the Prince, and put a stop to their completion. The presence of mind of a common Highlander prevented this. The man being intoxicated when his countrymen were withdrawn, found himself, when he recovered his senses, the only one of his party left in the town. Being a ready-witted fellow, to those who inquired of him why he had lingered behind his countrymen, he answered, "That he was neither alone, nor alarmed for his safety; five hundred Highlanders," he said, "had been left in cellars and secret places about town, for the purpose of cutting off any detachment that might sally from the castle." These false tidings being transmitted to General Guest, were for the time received as genuine; nor was there time to discover the deceit before the victory of Prestonpans enabled Charles Edward to return in triumph to the capital. The man's presence of mind secured also his own safety.

The men had lain on their arms the night of the 19th, their Chiefs and the Chevalier occupying such houses as were in the neighbourhood. On the morning of the 20th they were all on the march, in high spirits, determined for action, and eager to meet the enemy. They formed in one narrow column, keeping the high ground from Duddingston towards Musselburgh, where they crossed the Esk by the old bridge, and then advanced to the eminence of which Carberry Hill is the termination to the south-west, near which, about Musselburgh or Inveresk, they expected to meet the enemy. On putting himself at the head of his army, the Prince drew his sword and said to his followers, "Gentlemen, I have flung away the scabbard," which was answered by shouts of acclamation. Their movements were the simplest imaginable. On their march they formed a column of three men in front. When about to halt, each individual faced to the right or left as directed, and the column became a line of three men deep, which, by filing off from either flank, might again become a column at the word of command. Their handful of cavalry, scarcely amounting to fifty men, were occupied on the march in reconnoitring. They obtained a tolerably accurate account of the Strength of Cope's army, excepting as to the number of his guns, which one report augmented to twenty field-pieces, and none rated under twelve, though, as I have already said, there were only six in all.

When the Highlanders had advanced as far as Falside Hill, near Carberry, their scouts brought in notice that they had seen parties of dragoons abort Tranent, and it was reported that Sir John Cope was in that quarter with his whole army. The Chevalier's army, which had hitherto marched in one column, now divided into two, being their intended line of battle, and keeping towards the right, so as to preserve the upper ground, which was a great point in Highland tactics, marched onwards with steadiness and celerity.

When they arrived where the hill immediately above Tranent slopes suddenly down upon a large cultivated plain, then in stubble, the harvest having been unusually early, the Highlanders beheld the enemy near the western extremity of this plain, with their front towards the ridge of high ground which they themselves occupied.

It appears that Sir John Cope had directed his march under the idea that because a road passing from Seaton House to Preston was the usual highway from Haddington, therefore the Highlanders would make use of that, and no other, for their advance. He either did not know, or forgot, that an irregular army of mountaineers, unencumbered with baggage and inured to marching, would not hesitate to prefer the rougher and less level road if it possessed any advantages.[1]

Two mounted volunteers, Francis Garden, afterwards Lord Gardenstone, and a Mr. Cunninghame, had been detached by the English general to collect intelligence; but unhappily, as they halted to refresh themselves beyond Musselburgh, they fell into the hands of John Roy Stewart, a more skilful partisan than themselves, by whom they were made prisoners, and led captive to the Chevalier's headquarters.[2] Sir John Cope, deprived of the information he expected from his scouts, seems to have continued to expect the approach of the rebels from the west, until he suddenly saw them appear from the southward, on the ridge of the acclivity upon his left. He immediately changed his front, and drew up his troops with military precisions in order of battle. His foot was placed in the centre, with a regiment of dragoons and three pieces of artillery upon each flank. The wall of Colonel Gardiner's park (for his mansion was in the vicinity of the plain which was destined to prove fatal to him), as well as that of Mr. Erskine of Grange, covered the right flank of the regulars; Cope's baggage was stationed at Cockenzie, on the rear of his left, and a small reserve was stationed in front of the village of Prestonpas, which lay on the rear of the general's right.

In front of both armies, and separating the higher ground on which the Highland army was drawn up from the firm and level plain on which the regulars were posted, lay a piece of steep and swampy ground, intersected with ditches and enclosures, and traversed near the bottom by a thick strong hedge running along a broad wet ditch, and covering the front of the royal army. It was the object of the Chevalier to indulge the impatience of his troops by pressing forward to instant battle. For this purpose he employed an officer of experience, Mr. Ker of Graden, who,

---

[1] "On the present occasion he was, as sportsmen say, at fault. He well knew that the high-road from Edinburgh to the south lies along the coast, and it seems never to have occurred to him that it was possible the Highlanders might choose, even by preference, to cross the country and occupy the heights, at the bottom of which the public road takes its course, and thus have him and his army in so far at their mercy, that they might avoid, or bring on battle at their sole pleasure. On the contrary, Sir John trusted that their Highland courtesy would induce them, if they moved from Edinburgh, to come by the very road on which he was advancing towards that city, and thus meet him on equal terms."—*Review of Home's Life.*

[2] See *Ibid.*

mounted on a gray pony, coolly reconnoitred the seemingly impracticable ground which divided the armies, crossed it in several directions,
deliberately alighted, pulled down gaps in one or two walls of dry stone,
and led his horse through them, many balls being fired at him while performing this duty. This intrepid gentleman returned to the Chevalier to
inform him that the morass could not be passed, so as to attack the front
of General Cope's army, without sustaining a heavy and destructive fire
of some continuance. A waggon-way for the conveyance of coal worked
in the vicinity of Tranent, for the use of the saltworks at Cockenzie, did
indeed cross the morass, but it would have been ruinous to have
engaged troops in such a narrow road, which was exposed to be swept in
every direction both by artillery and musketry.

The position of general Cope might therefore be considered as
unassailable; and that general, with a moderation which marked his
mediocrity of talent, was happy in having found, as he thought, safety,
when he ought to have looked for victory.

Lieutenant-Colonel Gardiner, and other officers, pressed on the
commander the necessity of a bolder line of tactics. They were of opinion that the regular soldiers should be led against the rebels while the
former showed spirit for the encounter, and that remaining merely on
the defensive was likely to sink the courage of the troops, as delay gave
the infantry time to recollect that they had avoided an encounter with
these Highlanders at Corryarrack, and the cavalry leisure to remember
their recent and ignominious flight from the vicinity of Edinburgh
before this new description of enemy. The lieutenant-colonel pressed
his advice with earnestness, dropped some expressions of the result
which was to be apprehended, and, finding his suggestions rejected,
made the preparations of a good and brave man for doing his duty,
and, if necessary, for dying in the discharge of it.

Some movements now took place. The regular troops huzzaed to
show their willingness to come to action; the Highlanders replied, in
their manner, by wild shouts. A party of Highlanders were stationed in
Tranent churchyard, as an advantageous post; but Sir John Cope
advancing two light field-pieces, made that position too hot for them.
Still the insurgents continued anxiously bent on battle, and expressed
the most earnest desire to attack the enemy, who, they supposed,
intended to escape from them, as at Corryarrack. They offered to make
the attack through the morass, without regard to the difficulties of the
ground, and to carry fascines with them, for the purpose of rendering

the ditch passable. They were exhorted to patience by their Chiefs; and, to allay their fears of the escape of the enemy, the Chevalier detached Lord Nairne with five hundred men to the westward, that he might be in a situation to intercept Sir John Cope in case he should attempt to move off towards Edinburgh without fighting.

Satisfied with this precaution, the Highlanders lay down to rest in a field of pease, which was made up in ricks upon the ground.[1] The minds of the Chiefs were still occupied with the means of discovering a path by which they might get clear of the morass, gain the open and firm ground, and rush down on Cope and his army, whom they regarded as their assured prey, if they could but meet them in a fair field.

There was in the Chevalier's army a gentleman named Anderson of Whitburgh, in East Lothian, to whom the ground in the vicinity was perfectly known, and who bethought him of a path leading from the height on which their army lay, sweeping through the morass, and round the left wing of General Cope's army, as it was now disposed, and which might conduct them to the level and extensive flat, since called the field of battle. Mr. Anderson communicated this important fact to Mr. Hepburn of Keith. By Mr. Hepburn he was conducted to Lord George Murray, who, highly pleased with the intelligence, introduced him to Prince Charles Edward.

The candidate for a diadem was lying with a bunch of pease-straw beneath his head, and was awakened with news which assured him of battle, and promised him victory. He received the tidings with much cheerfulness, and immediately, for the night was well spent, prepared to put the scheme into execution.

---

[1] "The roll of the drum and shrill accompaniment of the pipes swelled up the hill—died away—resumed its thunder—and was at length hushed. The trumpets and kettle-drums of the cavalry were next heard to perform the beautiful and wild point of war appropriated as a signal for that piece of nocturnal duty, and then finally sunk upon the wind with a shrill and mournful cadence. The western sky twinkled with stars, but a frost-mist, rising from the ocean, covered the eastern horizon, and rolled in white wreaths along the plain where the adverse army lay couched upon their arms. Their advanced posts were pushed as far as the side of the great ditch at the bottom of the descent, and had kindled large fires at different intervals, gleaming with obscure and hazy lustre through the heavy fog which encircled them with a doubtful halo. The Highlanders, 'thick as leaves in Vallambrosa,' lay stretched upon the ridge of the hill, buried (excepting their sentinels) in the most profound repose. How many of these brave fellows will sleep more soundly before to-morrow night!"—*Waverley*.

An aide-de-camp was instantly despatched to recall Lord Nairne from his demonstration to the westward, and cause him with his detachment to rejoin the army as speedily as possible. In the meantime, the whole of the Highland arm got under arms, and moved forward with incredible silence and celerity, by the path proposed. A point of precedence was now to be settled, characteristic of the Highlanders. The tribe of MacDonalds, though divided into various families, and serving under various chiefs, still reckoned on their common descent from the great Lords of the Isles, in virtue of which they claimed, as the post of honour, the right of the whole Highland army in the day of action. This was disputed by some of the other clans, and it was agreed that they should cast lots about this point of precedence. Fortune gave it to the Camerons and Stewarts, which was murmured at by the numerous Clan-Colla, the generic name for the MacDonalds. The sagacity of Lochiel induced the other chiefs to resign for the day a point on which they were likely to be tenacious. The precedence was yielded to the MacDonalds accordingly, and the first line of the Highlanders moved off their ground by the left flank, in order that the favoured tribe might take the post of honour. They marched, as usual, in two columns of three men in front. The first of these was led by young Clanranald with about sixty men, under the guidance of Anderson of Whitburgh. The first line consisted of the following clan regiments:— Clanranald, 250 strong; Glengarry, 350; Keppoch and Glencoe, 450; Perth, with some MacGregors, 200; Appin, 250; and Lochiel, 500. The second line consisted of three regiments,—Lord George Murray's Athole men, 350; Lord Nairne's regiment, 350; and Menzies of Shian's, 300. Lord Strathallan, with his handful of cavalry, was appointed to keep the height above the morass, that they might do what their numbers permitted, to improve the victory, in case it should be gained. This troop consisted of about thirty-six horsemen. From these details, it appears that the Highland army was about 3000 in number, being very nearly the same with Sir John Cope's.

Anderson guided the first line. He found the pathway silent and deserted; it winded to the north-east, down a sort of hollow, which at length brought them to the eastern extremity of the plain, at the west end of which the King's army was stationed, with its left flank to the assailants. No guns had been placed to enfilade this important pass, though there was a deserted embrasure which showed that the measure had been in contemplation; neither was there a sentinel or patrol to observe the motions of the Highlanders in that direction. On reaching the firm ground, the column advanced due northward across the plain, in order to take ground for wheeling up and forming line of battle. The Prince marched at the head of the second column, and close in the rear of the first. The morass was now rendered difficult by the passage of so many men. Some of the Highlanders sunk knee-deep, and the Prince himself stumbled, and fell upon one knee. The morning was now dawning, but a thick frosty mist still hid the motions of the Highlanders. The sound of their march could, however, no longer be concealed, and an alarm-gun was fired as a signal for Cope's army to get under arms.

Aware that the Highlanders had completely turned his left flank, and were now advancing from the eastward along a level and open plain, without interruption of any kind, Sir John Cope hastened to dispose his troops to receive them. Though probably somewhat surprised, the English general altered the disposition which he had made along the morass, and formed anew, having the walls of Preston Park, and that of Bankton, the seat of Colonel Gardiner, close in the rear of his army; his left flank extended towards the sea, his right rested upon the morass which had lately been in his front. His order of battle was now extended from north to south, having the east in front. In other respects the disposition was the same as already mentioned, his infantry forming his centre and on each wing a regiment of horse. By some crowding in of the piquets, room enough was not left for Gardiner's corps to make a hill front upon the right wing so that one squadron was drawn up in the rear of the other. The artillery was also placed before this regiment a disposition which the colonel is said to have remonstrated against, having too much reason to doubt the steadiness of the horses, as well as of the men who composed the corps. There was no attention paid to his remonstrances, nor was there time to change the disposition.

The Highlanders had no sooner advanced so far to the northward as to extricate the rear of the column from the passage across the morass, and place the whole on open ground, than they wheeled to the left, and formed a line of three men deep. This thin long line they quickly broke up into a number of small masses or phalanxes, each, according to their peculiar tactics, containing an individual clan, which disposed themselves for battle in the manner following: The best-born men of the tribe, who were also the best armed, and had almost all targets, threw themselves in front of the regiment. The followers closed on the rear, and forced the front forward by their weight. After a brief prayer, which was never omitted, the bonnets were pulled over the brows, the pipers blew the signal, and the line of clans rushed forward, each forming a separate wedge.

These preparations were made with such despatch on both wings, that the respective aides-de-camp of the Duke of Perth and Lord George Murray met in the centre, each bringing news that his general was ready to charge. The whole front line accordingly moved forward, and, as they did so, the sun broke out, and the mist rose from the ground like the curtain of a theatre. It showed to the Highlanders the hue of regular troops drawn up in glittering array like a complete hedge of steel and at the same time displayed to Cope's soldiers the furious torrent, which, subdivided into such a number of columns, or rather small masses, advanced with a cry which gradually swelled into a hideous yell, and became intermingled with an irregular but well-directed fire, the mountaineers presenting their pieces as they ran, dropping them when discharged, and rushing on to close conflict sword in hand. The events of the preceding night had created among the regulars an apprehension of their opponents, not usual to English soldiers. General Cope's tactics displayed a fear of the enemy rather than a desire to engage him; and now this dreaded foe, having selected his own point of advantage, was coming down on them in all his terrors, with a mode of attack unusually furious, and unknown to modern war.

There was but an instant to think of these things, for this was almost the moment of battle. But such thoughts were of a nature which produce their effect in an instant, and they added to the ferocity of the Highlanders, while they struck dismay into their opponents. The old seamen and gunners, who had been employed to serve the artillery on the light wing showed the first symptoms of panic, and fled from the gulls they had undertaken to work, carrying with them the priming flasks. Colonel Whitefoord, who had joined Cope's army as a volunteer, fired five of the guns on the advancing Highlanders, and, keeping his ground while all fled around him, was with difficulty saved from the fury of the Camerons and Stewarts, who, running straight on the muzzles of the cannon, actually stormed the battery. The regiment of dragoons being drawn up, as has been said, in two lines, the foremost squadron, under Lieutenant-Colonel Whitney, having received orders to advance, were, like the gunners, seized with a panic, dispersed under the fire of the Highlanders, and went off without even an attempt to charge, riding down the artillery guard in their flight. The rearmost squadron, commanded by Gardiner, might, if steady, have yet altered the fate of the day, by charging the Highlanders when disordered with attacking the guns. Gardiner, accordingly, commanded them to advance, and charge, encouraging them by his voice and example to rush upon the confused masses before them. But those to whom he spoke were themselves disordered at the rapid advance of the enemy, and disturbed by the waving of plaids, the brandishing and gleaming of broadswords and battle-axes, the rattle of the dropping fire, and the ferocious cry of the combatants. They made a feint to advance, in obedience to the word of command, but almost instantly halted, when first the rear rank went off by four or five files at a time, and then the front dispersed in like manner; none maintaining their ground, except about a score of determined men, who were resolved to stand or fall with their commander.

On Cope's left the cause of King George was not more prosperous. Hamilton's dragoons receiving a heavy rolling fire from the MacDonalds as they advanced broke up in the same manner, almost at the same moment, with Gardiner's, and scattering in every direction, left the field of blood, galloping some from the enemy, some, in the recklessness of their terror, past the enemy, and some almost through them. The dispersion was complete and the disorder irretrievable. They fled west, east, and south, and it was only the broad sea which prevented them from flying to the north also, and making every point of the compass witness to their rout.

Meantime, the infantry, though both their flanks were uncovered by the flight of the dragoons received the centre of the Highland line with a steady and regular fire, which cost the insurgents several men,—among others, James MacGregor, a son of the famous Rob Roy, fell, having received five wounds, two of them from balls that pierced through his body. He commanded a company of the Duke of Perth's regiment, armed chiefly with the straightened scythes already mentioned, a weapon not unlike the old English bill. He was so little daunted by his wounds as to raise himself on his elbow, calling to his men to advance bravely, and swearing he would see if any should misbehave.

In fact, the first line of the Highlanders were not an instant checked by the fire of the musketry; for, charging with all the energy of victory, they parried the bayonets of the soldiers with their targets, and

the deep clumps, or masses, into which the clans were formed, penetrated and broke, in several points, the extended and thin lines of the
regulars. At the same moment Lochiel attacking the infantry on the left,
and Clanranald on the right flank, both exposed by the flight of the
dragoons, they were unavoidably and irretrievably routed. It was now
perceived that Sir John Cope had committed an important error in
drawing up his forces in front of a high parkwall, which barred their
escape from their light-heeled enemies. Fortunately there had been
breaches made in the wall, which permitted some few soldiers to
escape; but most of them had the melancholy choice of death or submission. A few fought, and fell bravely. Colonel Gardiner was in the act
of encouraging a small platoon of infantry, which continued firing,
when he was cut down by a Highlander, with one of those scythes
which have been repeatedly mentioned. The greater part of the foot
soldiers then laid down their arms, after a few minutes' resistance. The
second line, led by Prince Charles himself, had, during the whole
action, kept so near the first, that to most of Sir John Cope's army they
appeared but as one body; and as this unfortunate Prince's courage has
been impeached, it is necessary to say that he was only fifty paces
behind the vanguard in the very commencement of the battle,—which
was, in fact, a departure from his implicit paction with the Chiefs that
he should not put his person in imminent danger.

Had there been any possibility of rallying the fugitives, the day
might have been in some degree avenged, if not retrieved, for the first
line of the Highlanders dispersed themselves almost wholly, in quest
of spoil and prisoners. They were merciful to the vanquished after the
first fury of the onset, but gave no quarter to the dragoon horses,
which, they considered as taught to bear a personal share in the battle.

The second line were with difficulty restrained from disbanding in
like manner, until a report was spread that the dragoons had rallied,
and were returning to the field. Lochiel caused the pipes to play, which
recalled many of his men. But the dragoons looked near them no more.
It is true, that Sir John Cope himself, the Earl of Home, General Whitney, and other officers, had, with pistols at the men's heads, turned a
number of the fugitives off the high-road to Edinburgh, into a field
close to Preston on the west, where they endeavoured to form a
squadron. But the sound of a pistol, discharged by the accident,
renewed their panic; the main body followed Sir John Cope in his
retreat, while a few stragglers went off at full gallop to Edinburgh,

entered by the Watergate, and rode up the High Street in the most disorderly manner.

An old friend, whom I have already quoted, gave me a picturesque account of the flight of such fugitives as took this direction, which he had himself witnessed. Although the city was evacuated by the Highlanders, an old Jacobite of distinction was, nevertheless, left there with the title of Governor. This dignitary was quietly seated in a well-known tavern (afterwards Walker's, in Writers' Court), when a tremendous clatter on the street announced the arrival of the dragoons, or a part of them, in this disorderly condition. The stout old commander presented himself before them, with a pistol in his hand, and summoned them to surrender to his Royal Highness's mercy. The dragoons seeing but one or two men, received the proposal with a volley of curses and pistol-balls, and having compelled the Jacobite commandant to retreat within the Thermopylae of Writers' Court, they continued their race up to the Castle-hill, thinking that fortress the most secure place of refuge. Old General Preston, who had now thrown himself into the castle, of which he was governor, and superseded General Guest in his office, had no idea of admitting these recreant cavaliers, into a fortress which was probably on the eve of a siege. He therefore sent them word to begone from the Castle-hill, or he would open his guns on them, as cowards, who had deserted their officers and colours. Alarmed at this new dancer, the runaways retreated, and scrambling down the steep declivity called the Castle Wynd, rode out at the West Port, and continued their flight to Stirling and the west country.

The greater part of the dragoons were collected by Sir John Cope, with the assistance of the earls of Home and Loudon, and conducted in a very disreputable condition by Lauder to Coldstream, and from thence to Berwick. At the latter place, Lord Mark Ker, of the family of Lothian, a house which has long had hereditary fame for wit as well as courage, received the unfortunate general with the well-known sarcasm, "That he believed he was the first general in Europe which had brought the first tidings of his own defeat."

But the presence of the general in person on the field, since there was not even the semblance of an army, could not have remedied the disaster. There was never a victory more complete. Of the infantry, two thousand five hundred men, or thereabout, scarce two hundred escaped; the rest were either slain or made prisoners. It has been generally computed that the slain amounted to four hundred, for the

Highlanders gave little quarter in the first moments of excitation, though those did not last long. Five officers were killed, and eighty made prisoners. The number of prisoners amounted to upwards of two thousand. Many of them exhibited a frightful spectacle, being hideously cut with the broadsword. The field-artillery, with colours, standards, and other trophies, remained in the hands of the victors. The military chest of the army was placed during the action in the house of Cockenzie, the baggage in a large field adjoining, originally in the rear of Cope's line of battle, but at the moment of action upon the left. It was guarded by a few Highlanders of the regiment which the Earl of Loudon was raising for Government, and which was much reduced by desertion, many of the privates joining their clans so soon as the Rebellion broke out. The baggage-guard surrendered themselves prisoners on seeing the event of the battle, and the baggage and military chest, with £2500 in specie, became the booty of the conquerors. The Highlanders looked with surprise and amazement upon the luxuries of a civilised army. They could not understand the use of chocolate; and watches, wigs, and other ordinary appurtenances of the toilette were equally the subject of wonder and curiosity.

On the part of the victors, the battle, though brief, had not been bloodless. Four officers, and thirty privates of their army, were killed; six officers and seventy men wounded.

Such were the results of the celebrated battle of Prestonpans, in which the pride of military discipline received an indelible disgrace at the hands of a wild militia. Sir John Cope, whom it would be easy to vindicate so far as personal courage goes, was nevertheless overwhelmed with a ridicule due to poltroonery, as well as to want of conduct, and was doomed to remain

> "Sacred to ridicule his whole life long,
> And the sad burden of a merry song."

LXXIX

The Court at Holyrood

1745

THE night after the battle of Prestonpans the Chevalier slept at Pinkie House, near Musselburgh; the next morning he returned to Duddingston, and entered the capital, was received with the acclamations of the populace[1] and all the honours which the official authorities could render. Several proclamations were issued upon his arrival, all of them adapted to influence the popular mind.

He prohibited all rejoicings for the victory, assigning for his reason the loss which had been sustained by his father's misguided subjects. The clergy of Edinburgh were, by another edict, exhorted to resume the exercise of their religious functions, and assured of the Prince's protection. This venerable body sent a deputation to know whether they would be permitted, in the course of divine service, to offer up their prayers for King George. It was answered, on the part of the Chevalier,

---

[1] "The Highlanders by whom the Prince was surrounded, in the license and extravagance of this joyful moment, fired their pieces repeatedly, and one of these having been accidentally loaded with ball, the bullet grazed a young lady's temple, as she waved her handkerchief from a balcony—Miss Nairne, a lady with whom the author had the pleasure of being acquainted. 'Thank God,' said she, the instant she recovered, 'that the accident happened to me, whose principles are known. Had it befallen a Whig, they would have said it was done on purpose.'"—*Waverley*.

that to grant the request would be in so far to give the lie to those family pretensions for the assertion of which he was in arms; but that, notwithstanding, he would give them his royal assurance that they should not be called to account for any imprudent language which they might use in the pulpit. The ministers of Edinburgh seem to have doubted the guarantee, as the only one who resumed his charge was the Rev. Mr. MacVicar, minister of the West Church, who regularly officiated under the protection of the guns of the castle. A number of the Highland officers, as well as the citizens, attended on Mr. MacVicar's ministry, in the course of which he not only prayed for King George, but stoutly asserted his right to the throne. This was represented to Charles Edward by some of his followers, as a piece of unjustifiable insolence, deserving of punishment; but the Prince wisely replied that the man was an honest fool, and that he would not have him disturbed. I do not know if it was out of gratitude for this immunity, but Mr. MacVicar on the following Sunday added to his prayers in behalf of King George, a petition in favour of the Chevalier, which was worded thus:—"As to this young person who has come among us seeking an earthly crown, do thou, in thy merciful favour, give him a heavenly one."

A good deal of inconvenience had arisen in consequence of the banking companies having retreated into the castle, carrying with them the specie which supplied the currency of the country. A third proclamation was issued, inviting these establishments to return to the town and resume the ordinary course of their business; but, like the clergy, the bankers refused to listen to the invitation. They, as well as the clergy, did not probably place much confidence in the security offered.

It is now time to take a more general view of the effects which the battle of Prestonpans, or of Gladsmuir,[1] as the Jacobites preferred calling it, had produced upon the affairs of the young Adventurer.

---

[1] They affected this name to reconcile the victory to some ancient metrical prophecies which happen to fix on Gladsmuir as a field of battle in which the Scottish should be victorious:—

"On Gladsmuir sall the battle be,"

saith the *Book of Prophecies*.—Printed by Andro Hart, Edinburgh, 1615.

Gladsmuir is a long mile from the actual place of conflict in 1745. Indeed, the old soothsayer seems to have had a better judgment for selecting a field of battle than Sir John Cope. Gladsmuir is a large bold open heath, on which his cavalry would have had full room to act, and he himself a commanding situation. It must be always subject of wonder that he did not halt to receive the Highlanders there, instead of cooping himself up in a pinfold at Preston, and waiting for their attack.

Until that engagement the Chevalier could not be said to possess a spot of Scotland, save the ground which was occupied by his Highland army. The victory had reversed this; and there was no place within the ancient kingdom of his ancestors, except the castles of Edinburgh and Stirling, and the four small garrisons on the Highland chain, which dared disavow his authority and abide by the consequences. It was therefore a question of high import to decide in what manner this splendid advantage could be best improved. It was the opinion of many at the time, and has been repeated since, and was, it is said, originally the predominant sentiment of Charles Edward himself, that the blow at Prestonpans should be followed up as speedily as possible by an irruption into England. This, it was said, would rouse the spirits of the English Jacobites, surprise the Government while in a state of doubt and want of preparation, and, in short, give the readiest prospect of completing a counterrevolution. On consideration, however, the Prince, from reasons of the most cogent nature, was compelled to renounce an enterprise which was, perhaps, not uncongenial to his daring temper. He could not but be sensible that his army, after the battle, was reduced nearly one-half, by the number of Highlanders who, according to their uniform custom, returned home to deposit with their families the booty which they had taken in the field. This was not all; he was as yet deprived of the assistance of Lovat, MacLeod, and Sir Alexander MacDonald, upon whom he had rested as main supports of his enterprise. These three chiefs might have augmented his forces to six or seven thousand men, with which strength he might have approached the English Borders, not without hopes of striking an important blow. But, besides the relics of Sir John Cope's dragoons, several British regiments, recalled from Flanders, had already reached England; and six thousand Dutch troops had, as in the insurrection in 1715, been supplied by the States of Holland, as an auxiliary contingent which they were bound to send over to England in case of invasion. These regiments, indeed, were chiefly Swiss and German troops in Dutch pay, who had been made prisoners by the French, and enjoyed their liberty under parole that they should not bear arms against his Most Christian Majesty or his allies. There was, therefore, some doubt whether they could regularly have taken a part in the British civil war. It was understood that the French Government had made a remonstrance against their being employed, founded on the terms of the capitulation. But the laws of war, as well as others, have their points of casuistry; and since the troops were sent to Britain, it can be little doubted that, being there, it must have been with the resolution of fighting although at a later period, when the Chevalier actually had in his camp a French force, they were withdrawn from the conflict.

It must be also remembered that, in advancing into England, the Chevalier, without being certain of any friends in the South, must have abandoned all chance of supplies from France, which he could only hope to receive in small quantities by means of Montrose, Dundee, and other ports on the north-eastern coast; while, at the same time, he must have withdrawn from a junction with all the recruits whom he expected from the Highlands, and from the great clans, which he still hoped might join him,

To conclude, the British and Dutch forces were drawing to a head at Newcastle, under Field-Marshal Wade, to a number already superior to that of the Highland army.

Having such a force in front, the advance of the Chevalier into England with 1800 or 2000 men would have been an act of positive insanity. There remained only another course—that he should endeavour to augment his army by every means in his power, and prepare himself for the prosecution of his adventure before he went farther.

With this purpose, the public money was levied in every direction, and parties were despatched as far as Glasgow, which city was subjected to payment of £5000 sterling. The utmost exertion was made to collect the arms which had been taken from the vanquished in the field of battle; and various gifts were received into the Prince's exchequer from individuals, who, too old or too timid to join him, took this mode of showing the interest which they felt in his cause.

The news of the victory, in the meantime, animated the Jacobites in every quarter of the kingdom, and decided many who had hitherto stood neutral. Officers were appointed to beat up for volunteers, and did so with success; many Lowland gentlemen joined the ranks of the rebels,—General Gordon of Glenbucket brought down 400 men from the upper part of Aberdeenshire; Lord Ogilvie led a body of 600 from Strathmore and the Mearns; Lord Pitsligo, a nobleman of the most irreproachable character, and already in an advanced stage of life, took the field at the head of a squadron of north-country gentlemen, amounting to 120 in number; Lord Lewis Gordon, brother of the Duke, undertook to levy considerable forces in his own country, though his brother, disgusted, perhaps, with the recollection of 1715, declined to join the Chevalier's standard.

The new forces were organised in all possible haste. Two troops of cavalry were formed as guards, one of which was placed under the command of Lord Elcho; the other, first destined to the son of Lord Kenmure, who declined to join, was finally conferred on the unfortunate Lord Balmerino. A troop of horse-grenadiers was placed under the command of the equally unfortunate Earl of Kilmarnock. This nobleman, if his early education is considered, could scarcely have been expected to have enrolled himself as an adherent of the cause which cost him so dear. In the 1715, being then only twelve years old, he appeared in arms with his father in behalf of the Government, at the head of 1000 men, whom the influence of the family had raised in Ayrshire. He had also enjoyed a pension from George II.'s Government. But his wife, Lady Ann Livingston, daughter of James, Earl of Linlithgow and Callander, was a zealous Jacobite, and it is supposed converted her husband to that unhappy faith. Lord Kilmarnock was also in embarrassed circumstances, and his ambition was awakened by the gleam of success which shone on the Prince's standard at Prestonpans, and which induced him to take the step which cost him his life. Mr. Murray, the secretary, desirous of a military as well as a civil command, made some progress in levying a regiment of hussars, designed for the light-cavalry duties, which were commanded under him by an Irish officer in the French service, named Lieutenant-Colonel Bagot.

While recruits of considerable rank were thus joining the standard, the camp at Duddingston assumed a more regular and military appearance—the Highlanders being, with some difficulty, prevailed upon to occupy the tents which had fallen into their possession, declaring, however, that they did so only out of respect to the Prince's orders, as these hardy people preferred the open air, even in the end of a Scottish autumn. The tents were very indifferently pitched, and only half inhabited, so that the appearance of the camp was extremely irregular.

It may here be noticed that the behaviour of the Highlanders was, upon the whole, exemplary. Some robberies were, indeed, committed in the vicinity of Edinburgh by persons in Highland dresses and wearing white cockades, but they were considered as having been perpetrated by ordinary thieves, who had used the Prince's uniform as a disguise. On some occasions the Highlanders forgot themselves, and presented their pieces at the citizens to extort money, but the moderation of the demand bore a strange disproportion to the menacing manner in which it was enforced. It was generally limited to a penny, a circumstance strongly expressive of the simplicity of this singular people.

The court at Holyrood was in those halcyon days of Jacobitism so much frequented by persons of distinction that it might almost have been supposed the restoration had already taken place. The fair sex, in particular, were dazzled with the gallant undertaking of a young and handsome Prince so unexpectedly successful, and the young men, of course, if in the least biassed in favour of the politics of the softer sex, found it difficult to differ from their opinions. In the eyes of the public, the young Chevalier, whether from policy or a natural good disposition, showed no sentiments but such as were honourable and generous; and many anecdotes were circulated tending to exalt his character in the general opinion. It was said, for example, as Charles rode through the field of battle at Prestonpans, that an officer describing the bodies with which it was covered as being those of his enemies, he replied, that he only beheld with regret the corpses of his father's misguided subjects. It was more certain, that when the Chevalier proposed to the court of London to settle a cartel for prisoners, and when that proposal was refused, he was strongly advised to consider those English captives who were in his hands as hostages for the lives of such of his own party as might become prisoners to the enemy. But Charles Edward uniformly rejected this proposal, declaring that it was beneath him as a Prince to make threats which he did not intend to execute, and that he would never, on any account, or under any provocation, take away the lives of unoffending men in cold blood, after having spared them in the heat of action.

Another opportunity occurred in which Charles had means of exhibiting the same tone of generosity after his return from Prestonpans. He had established a blockade around the castle of Edinburgh; this could, in fact, do little more than occasion inconvenience to the garrison, by depriving them of fresh provisions, for of salted stores they had an abundant supply; there was no great prospect, therefore, of reducing so strong a place by the effects of famine, nor did the Governor take much notice of a proclamation forbidding any one to carry provisions to the castle under pain of death. A few shots fired on the Highland guards were the only acknowledgment of the insult; but after this had lasted a few days General Preston, the Governor of the fortress, sent a message to the Lord Provost and magistrates, declaring that unless the communication with the city was opened he would cannonade the town, and lay it in ashes. When this threat was communicated to the Chevalier, to whom the affrighted citizens naturally carried their appeal, he observed, that nothing could be more unjust than to make the city responsible for the actions of an armed force which was not under their control; that he might, by a parity of reasoning, be summoned to evacuate the capital, or yield up any other advantage, by the same threat of destroying the city; and that, therefore, he would not permit his feelings, on the present occasion, to interrupt the plain course which his interest recommended. But to intimidate General Preston, the Chevalier caused him to be informed, that if he fired on the city of Edinburgh, he would, in retaliation, cause the General's house, at Valleyfield, in Fife, to be burnt to the ground. The stout veteran received the threat with scorn, declaring that if Valleyfield were injured, the English vessels of war in the firth should in revenge receive instructions to burn down Wemyss Castle, which is built on a rock overhanging the sea. This castle was the property of the Earl of Wemyss, whose eldest son, Lord Elcho, was in the Prince's camp. Fortunately this exasperating species of warfare was practised on neither side. General Preston, in pity to the entreaty of the inhabitants, consented to suspend the cannonade until he should receive orders from St. James's.

Some misapprehension, however, having taken place about the terms of this kind of armistice, General Preston, according to his threat, opened a fire upon the city. The confusion was great; the garrison made a sally to dislodge the rebels from some posts near the castle; the streets were swept with cartridge-shot, and several of the inhabitants as well as Highlanders were slain. It is said that the Governor engaged in this sort of warfare, in order to induce the rebel army to remain before the fortress; and that he caused letters to fall into the hands of their council, expressing fears of a scarcity of provisions, so as to determine them to adopt the course of continuing the blockade. Charles, however, feeling, or affecting, to feel, much interest for the distress of the inhabitants, gave orders to open the communication with the castle, and the cannonade in consequence ceased.

All this conduct on the part of the Adventurer was so far politic, as well as generous. But there were at the bottom of this apparent lenity and liberality private feuds, which rendered the Chevalier's opinions and doctrines less acceptable to some of those who immediately approached his person than to the adherents who only beheld events at a distance. For this purpose I will transcribe the manner in which his councils were conducted, as it is given by Lord Elcho.

"The Prince formed a council which met regularly every morning in his drawing-room. The gentlemen whom he called to it were the Duke of Perth, Lord Lewis Gordon, Lord George Murray, Lord Elcho, Lord Ogilvie, Lord Pitsligo, Lord Nairne, Lochiel, Keppoch, Clanranald, Glencoe, Lochgarry, Ardshiel, Sir Thomas Sheridan, Colonel O'Sullivan, Glenbucket, and Secretary Murray. The Prince, in this council, used always first to declare what he himself was for, and then he asked everybody's opinion in their turn. There was one-third of the council whose principles were, that kings and princes can never either act or think wrong; so, in consequence, they always confirmed whatever the Prince said. The other two-thirds thought that kings and princes thought sometimes like other men, and were not altogether infallible, and that this Prince was no more so than others, and therefore begged leave to differ from him when they could give sufficient reasons for their difference of opinion. This very often was no hard matter to do; for as the Prince and his old governor, Sir Thomas Sheridan, were altogether ignorant of the ways and customs of Great Britain, and both much for the doctrine of absolute monarchy, they would very often, had they not been prevented, have fallen into blunders which might have hurt the cause. The Prince could not bear to hear anybody differ in sentiment from him, and took a dislike to everybody that did; for he had a notion of commanding this army as any general does a body of mercenaries, and so let them know only what he pleased, and expected them to obey without inquiring further about the matter. This might have done better had his favourites been people of the country; but as they were Irish, and had nothing to risk, the people of fashion that had their all at stake, and consequently ought to be supposed prepared to give the best advice of which they were capable, thought they had a title to know and be consulted in what was for the good of the cause in which they had so much concern; and if it had not been for their insisting strongly upon it, the Prince, when he found that his sentiments were not always approved of, would have abolished this council long ere he did.

"There was a very good paper sent one day by a gentleman in Edinburgh, to be perused by this council. The Prince, when he heard it read, said that it was below his dignity to enter into such a reasoning with subjects, and ordered the paper to be laid aside. The paper afterwards was printed, under the title of The Prince's Declaration to the People of England, and is esteemed the best manifesto published in those times, for those that were printed at Rome and Paris were reckoned not well calculated for the present age.

"The Prince created a committee for providing the army with forage. It was composed of Lord Elcho, President;—Graham of Duntroon, whom they called Lord Dundee; Sir William Gordon of Park, Hunter of Burnside, Haldane of Lanark, and his son; Mr. Smith, and Mr. Hamilton. They issued out orders in the Prince's name to all the gentlemen's houses who had employments under the Government, to send in certain quantities of hay, straw, and corn, upon such a day, under the penalty of military execution if not complied with, but their orders were very punctually obeyed.

"There were courts-martial sat every day for the discipline of the army, and some delinquents were punished with death."

Charles Edward, while he exercised at Holyrood the dignified hospitality of a Prince, and gave entertainments to his most distinguished followers, and balls and concerts to the ladies of the party, of whom the Duchess of Perth and Lady Ogilvy formed conspicuous persons, omitted not the attention that might become a prudent general. He visited the camp almost every day, exercised and reviewed his troops frequently, and often slept in the camp without throwing off his clothes.

While the internal management of the Prince's affairs, civil and military, was thus regulated, no time was lost in applying to every quarter from which the insurgents might expect assistance. Immediately after the battle of Prestonpans, the Prince had despatched a confidential agent to France; the person entrusted with this mission was Mr. Kelly, already mentioned as an accomplice in the Bishop of Rochester's plot. He had instructions to magnify the victory as much as possible in the eyes of the French King and Ministry, and to represent how fair the Prince's enterprise bade for success, if it should now receive the effective support of his Most Christian Majesty. This mission was not entirely useless, though it may be doubted whether the French Ministers considered the opportunity as being so favourable as was represented. Vessels were despatched from time to time with money and supplies, although only in small quantities. One of these vessels arrived at Montrose with £5000 in money, and two thousand five hundred stand of arms. There came over in this vessel Monsieur de Boyer, called Marquis D'Eguilles, son of a president of the Parliament of Aix, with one or two officers connected with those already engaged in the undertaking.

The Prince received the Marquis D'Eguilles with much studied ceremony, affecting to regard him as the accredited agent of the King his master. The Chevalier also gave out that the Marquis had brought him letters from the King of France in which he promised his assistance, and asserted more specifically that his brother, Henry Benedict, calling himself the Duke of York, was to be despatched to Britain immediately at the head of a French army. This news raised the spirits of the insurgents to a very high pitch; for an attempt at invasion was so obviously the policy of the French court at this period that nobody had the least difficulty in believing it.

Three more ships arrived from France at Montrose and Stonehaven. A train of six brass four-pounders, and in each vessel two thousand five hundred stand of arms and £1000 in money were received on this occasion. Some Irish officers also came by these vessels. To intercept such communications, Rear-Admiral Byng entered the Firth of Forth with four or five ships of war, which obliged the cavalry of the insurgents to scour the coast by nightly patrols.

Neither was the Prince remiss in endeavouring to extend the insurrection in Scotland. We have mentioned already that MacPherson of Cluny had been taken prisoner in his house by the Prince's soldiers and carried to Perth as a captive. While in that city he had been released upon coming under the same engagement as the clans already in arms. On returning, therefore, to his house in Badenoch, he had called his men together and led three hundred MacPhersons to join the Chevalier's standard at Edinburgh.

But though Cluny, the son-in-law of Lovat, had thus chosen his part, the crafty old chief himself continued to hesitate and to retain the mask of pretended loyalty to George the Second. Charles Edward corresponded with him, both by means of his secretary Hugh Fraser and by that of MacDonald of Barrisdale, a partisan, who affected in a peculiar manner the ancient Highland character, and was, therefore, supposed to be acceptable to Lord Lovat. Through the medium of these agents Charles stimulated the chief's ambition by every object which he could suggest; and while he pretended to receive as current coin the apologies which the old man made for delaying his declaration, he eagerly urged him to redeem the time which had been lost by instantly raising his clan.

Lovat still hesitated. President Forbes possessed over him that species of ascendency which men of decided and honest principles usually have over such as are crafty and unconscientious. Lovat was driven, therefore, upon a course of doubtful politics by which he endeavoured to give the Chevalier such underhand assistance as he could manage without, as he hoped, incurring the guilt of rebellion. Whilst, therefore, he made to the President empty protestations of zeal and loyalty to the Government, he maintained a private correspondence, expressing equally inefficient devotion to the Prince; and without joining either party, endeavoured to keep fair terms with both till he should make himself of such importance as to cast the balance between them by his own force.

The vacillation and duplicity of Lord Lovat was the more unhappy for the cause which he finally adopted, because his example lost all the weight which a decisive resolution would have given it in the eyes of those who looked upon him as a model of cautious wisdom. It is generally allowed in the Highlands that had Lovat taken arms in the beginning of the affair the two great chiefs, Sir Alexander MacDonald of Sleat and MacLeod of MacLeod, would certainly have done the same. The power of these three chiefs would have nearly doubled the numbers which the Chevalier collected from other quarters; nor would it be too much to assert that with so great a force the Chevalier might have ventured upon an instant march to England after the battle of Prestonpans and made a fair experiment of what impression he could have effected in that country while the full freshness of victory shone upon his arms. But Lovat had proposed to himself to exercise the influence which he possessed over these island chiefs in a very different manner. He had formed a plan of uniting their men from the island of Skye and elsewhere with the MacPhersons, under the command of Cluny; the MacIntoshes, the Farquharsons, and other branches of the Clan Chattan, over whom he possessed considerable influence; with these he proposed to form a northern army at the pass of Corryarrack, which would, as he calculated, probably have amounted to five or six thousand men, and might, at his own option, have been employed in a decided manner, either for the purpose of effecting a restoration of the Stewarts, or for that of putting down the unnatural rebellion against King George, as might happen eventually best to suit the interests of Simon, Lord Lovat.

This plan was too obviously selfish to succeed. The two chiefs of MacLeod and MacDonald of Sleat became aware of Lovat's desire to profit by their feudal power and following, and thought it as reasonable to secure to themselves the price of their own services. The ambiguous conduct and delays of Lord Lovat inclined the two chiefs to listen to the more sincere and profitable counsel of Lord President Forbes, who exhorted them by all means to keep their dependents from joining in the rebellion; and, finally, persuaded them to raise their vassals in behalf of the reigning sovereign.

The President was furnished with means of conviction more powerful than mere words. Government having, as already noticed, placed a hundred commissions of companies at the disposal of this active and intelligent judge, he was enabled still further to improve his influence among the Highlanders, by distributing them among such clans as were disposed to take arms in behalf of the Government. Both Sir Alexander MacDonald and MacLeod were prevailed upon to accept some of these commissions; and when Alexander MacLeod of Muiravonside, a sincere adherent of the Chevalier, went to Skye for the purpose of inducing them to join the Prince, he found that they had committed themselves to the opposite degree far more active than the political principles which they had hitherto professed gave the slightest reason to expect. The other chiefs among whom commissions were distributed, were the Lord Seaforth, the Earl of Sutherland, Lord Reay, Sir Robert Monro of Foulis, the Master of Ross, and the Laird of Grant. The companies which were raised under these commissions, were ordered to assemble at Inverness, and thus a northern army of loyalists was on foot about the end of October, in the rear of the rebels, while the increasing forces under Marshal Wade threatened to prevent the possibility of any attempt upon England.

The defection of MacDonald and MacLeod rendered altogether abortive Lovat's plan of a northern army of Highlanders assembling at Corryarrack, and it might have been expected that he would now have been forced openly to adopt either one side or the other. But, ingenious in overreaching himself, the wily old man imagined he had invented a scheme by which he could render Charles Edward such assistance as would greatly forward his enterprise, while, at the same time, he might himself avoid all personal responsibility.

This plan, which he finally adopted, was, that his eldest son, the Master of Lovat, should join the Adventurer with seven or eight hundred of his best-armed and most warlike followers, and take upon himself the whole guilt of the rebellion;[1] while he, the father, should remain at home, affecting a neutrality between the contending parties, and avoiding all visible accession to the insurrection. Even when be adopted the unnatural scheme of saving himself from personal danger by making a cat's-paw of his eldest son, the old lord interposed so many doubts and delays, that the Master of Lovat, who was a noble and gallant gentleman, shed tears of rage and indignation at the train of dark and treacherous intrigue in which he was involved, and flung into the fire the white cockade which his father had commanded him to assume, yet refused for a time to let him display in the field.[2]

When Lovat finally took the resolution of despatching his son, with the best part of his clan, to the assistance of Charles Edward, a resolution which was not adopted without much hesitation and many misgivings, he feigned, with characteristic finesse, an apology for his march. It was pretended that some of the rebel clans had driven a great prey of cattle from the country of Lovat, and that the Master was obliged to march with his clan for the purpose of recovering them. It was even averred, that, advancing too near the insurgent army, the Frasers were obliged to join them by actual compulsion.

It is singular to remark how the craft of Lovat disappointed his own expectations. He had doubtless desired to give real assistance to the insurrection, for he could hardly suppose that his neighbour, the Lord President, was imposed on by his pretext of neutrality; and he must have feared being called to a severe account, if tranquillity was restored under the old government. And yet, notwithstanding the

---

[1] The victory obtained by the Chevalier determined his sentiments; and in presence of many of his vassals, being urged by an emissary of the Prince to "throw off the mask," he flung down his hat and drank success to the young adventurer by the title which be claimed, and confusion to the White Horse and all his adherents. But with the Machiavelism inherent in his nature he resolved that his own personal interest in the insurrection should be as little evident as possible, and determined that his son, whose safety he was bound by the laws of God and man to prefer to his own, should be his stalking-horse, and in case of need, his scapegoat.

[2] It appears from the evidence of Fraser of Dumballoch and others, upon Lord Lovat's trial, that all this while the threats and arguments of the father were urging the son (afterwards the highly-esteemed General Fraser) to a step of which he disapproved, and that he was still more disgusted by the duplicity and versatility with which his father qualified it.

interest he took in Charles's success, he delayed his son's junction with the rebel forces so late as to deprive that Prince of the assistance of the Frasers in his march into England, which was begun before the Master of Lovat commenced his journey southward. This delay induced the young nobleman to halt at Perth, where he united his corps with other reinforcements designed for the Prince's army. Thus, the indirect policy of Lord Lovat, while it led him to contribute aid to Charles's cause, in such a manner as to ruin himself with Government, induced him, at the same time, to delay and postpone his assistance until the period was past when it might have been essentially useful.

The Chevalier was aware of the difficulties of his situation, and not inclining to remain at Edinburgh, like Mar at Perth, while they thickened around him, was disposed to supply by activity his want of numerical force. Having, therefore, received all such supplies as he seemed likely to bring together, he informed his council abruptly that he designed to march for Newcastle, and give battle to Marshal Wade, who, he was convinced, would fly before him. This proposal seems to have been exclusively the suggestion of the sanguine temper which originally dictated his enterprise. His father's courtiers, who endeavoured to outvie each other in professing doctrines of unlimited obedience, had impressed the young man with an early belief that his father's cause, as that of an injured and banished monarch, was that of Heaven itself, and that Heaven would not fail to befriend him, if he boldly asserted those rights with which Providence had invested him. He believed the opinions of his English subjects to be the same in which he himself had been brought up. The manner in which the populace of Edinburgh had received him, and the unexpected and decisive victory at Prestonpans, both confirmed him in his sanguine confidence of success; and he was strongly persuaded, that even the paid soldiers of the English would hesitate to lift their weapons against their rightful Prince.

These sentiments, though they might well suit a Prince born and educated like Charles Edward, were too vague and visionary to gain the approbation of his council.

To his proposal of marching into England, it was replied that the Scottish army which he now commanded, consisting only after every augmentation of upwards of 5500 men, was far beneath the number necessary to compel the English to accept him as their sovereign; that, therefore, it would be time enough for him to march into that country when he should be invited by his friends there, either to join them or to favour their rising in arms. Secondly, it was urged, that as Marshal Wade had assembled most of the troops in England, or lately arrived from Flanders, at Newcastle, with a view to a march into Scotland, it would be better to let him advance than to go forward to meet him, because in the former case he must of necessity leave England undefended, and exposed to any insurrection of the Jacobites, or to the landing of the French armament, which the Marquis D'Eguilles and the Prince himself seemed daily to expect.

The council also observed that it was the Prince's interest, as it was understood to be the King of France's advice and opinion, to postpone a decisive action as long as possible, because, in case of his sustaining a defeat, the French ministers would send no troops to support him, and the loss would be irretrievable; whereas the longer the insurgents remained unbroken and in force, the greater would be the interest and encouragement which their allies would have in affording them effectual assistance. To those arguments the Prince only replied by again asserting that he was confident the French auxiliary force would be landed by the time he could cross the Border; and that he possessed a strong party in London and elsewhere, who would receive him as the people of Edinburgh had done. To which the members of his council could only answer that they hoped it might prove so. They then dispersed for the night.

The next morning the debate was renewed, and the Prince again proposed to march into England and fight Marshal Wade. As he found the council in no more complacent a humour than they had been the day before, he was induced for the time to be silent upon the main proposition in debate, and limit his proposal to a march to the Borders, in order that the troops might be kept in activity, and make some progress in learning their duty. This was agreed to, and orders were given out that the army should be ready to rendezvous at Dalkeith, and to march forward at the word of command.

On the evening of that same day, the Chevalier, for the third time laid before his officers, then assembled in his own apartment, the proposal for a march upon Newcastle. To the objections which had been formerly offered, he replied, by saying, in a positive manner, "I see, gentlemen, you are determined to stay in Scotland and defend your country; but I am not less resolved to try my fate in England, though I should go alone."

It being at length clear that the Prince's determination was taken, and that they could not separate themselves from his project without endangering his person, and ruining the expedition irretrievably, Lord George Murray and the other counsellors thought of obtaining some middle conclusion betwixt their own plan of remaining in Scotland, and that of the Prince for marching directly to fight Marshal Wade. Lord George Murray, therefore, proposed, that since the army must needs enter England, it should be on the western frontier; they would thus, he calculated, avoid a hasty collision with the English army, which it was their obvious interest to defer, and would, at the same time, afford the English an opportunity to rise, or the French to land their troops, if either were disposed to act upon it. If, on the contrary, Marshal Wade should march across the country towards Carlisle, in order to give them battle, he would be compelled to do so at the expense of a fatiguing march over a mountainous country, while the Highlanders would fight to advantage among hills not dissimilar to their own. This plan of the western march was not instantly adopted, but the Chevalier at length came into it, rather than abandon his favourite scheme of moving southward.

On the 31st of October 1745 Charles Edward marched out of Edinburgh at the head of his guards, and of Lord Pitsligo's horse; they rendezvoused at Dalkeith, where they were joined by other corps of their army from the camp at Duddingston, and different quarters. Here the Adventurer's army was separated into two divisions.

One of these consisted of the Athole Brigade, Perth's, Ogilvie's, Roy Stewart's, and Glenbucket's of foot regiments; Kilmarnock's and the hussars, of horse; with all the baggage and the artillery. This division was commanded by the Duke of Perth, and took the western road towards Carlisle. At Ecclefechan they were compelled, by the badness of the roads, to leave a part of their baggage, which, after they had marched on, was taken possession of by the people of Dumfries.

The other column of the Highland army consisted chiefly of the three MacDonald regiments, Glengarry's, Clanranald's, and Keppoch's, with Elcho and Pitsligo's horse; this division was commanded by the Prince in person. On the 5th of November, after halting two days at Kelso, they marched to Jedburgh, thus taking a turn towards the west. Their original demonstration to the eastward was designed to alarm Marshal Wade, and to prevent his taking any measures for moving towards Carlisle, their real object of attack. On Monday, the 8th, the

Prince, marching by Hawick and Hagiehaugh, took post at the village of Brampton, in England, with the purpose of facing Wade, should he attempt to advance from Newcastle in the direction of Carlisle.

In the meantime, the column under the Duke of Perth, consisting chiefly of Lowland regiments, horse, and artillery, advanced more to the westward, and reached Carlisle. This town had long been the principal garrison of England upon the western frontier, and many a Scottish army had, in former days, besieged it in vain. The walls by which it was surrounded were of the period of Henry VIII., improved by additional defences in the time of Queen Elizabeth. The castle, situated upon an abrupt and steep eminence, and surrounded by deep ditches on the only accessible point, was very ancient, but strong from its situation and the thickness of its walls. Upon the whole, although Carlisle was in no respect qualified to stand a regular siege, yet it might have defied the efforts of an enemy who possessed no cannon of larger calibre than four-pounders.

It was a considerable discouragement to the Highland leaders that their men had deserted in great numbers. The march into England was by no means popular among the common soldiers, who attached to the movement some superstitious ideas of misfortune, which must necessarily attend their crossing the Border. When the army of the Prince marched off from Dalkeith, it was upwards of 5500 strong, and they were computed to have lost by desertion at least 1000 men before the one column arrived at Brampton, and the other in the vicinity of Carlisle.

The town of Carlisle showed a spirit of defence. The mayor, whose name was Pattison, was at the trouble to issue a proclamation to inform the citizens that he was not Paterson, a Scottishman, but Pattison, a true-born native of England, determined to hold out the town to the last. The commandant of the castle, whose name was Durand, and who had lately been sent down to that important situation, was equally vehement in his protestations of defence.

The Duke of Perth, who commanded the right column of the Prince's army, thought it necessary, notwithstanding these adverse circumstances, to attempt the reduction of this important place. He opened, therefore, a trench on the east side of the town, and in two days afterwards began to construct a battery. On seeing these operations, the town of Carlisle, and its valiant Mayor, desired to capitulate. The Duke of Perth refused to accept of their submission unless the castle surrendered, but allowed them a reasonable time for determination. The consequence was, that both town and citadel surrendered, on condition that the privileges of the community should be respected, and that the garrison, being chiefly militia, should be allowed to retire from the town, after delivering up their arms and horses, and engaging not to serve against the Chevalier for the space of twelve months. This capitulation was signed by the Duke of Perth and Colonel Durand, whose defence must have been but a sorry one, since during the short siege there was only one man killed and another wounded in the besieging army.

On the 17th of November the Prince himself made a triumphal entry into Carlisle. The inhabitants, who entertained no affection for his cause, received him coldly; yet they could not help expressing a sense of the gentleness with which they had been treated by the Duke of Perth, whose conduct towards them had been generous and liberal. Their expressions of gratitude, and those of favour which the Prince thought himself obliged to bestow upon the Duke, were productive of great injury to the cause, by fostering the jealousy which subsisted between Lord George Murray and his Grace. We have already noticed that this discord had its origin as early as the time when the Duke and Lord George first joined the Prince at Perth, and that the Secretary Murray had sought to gratify his own ambition by encouraging the pretensions of the Duke of Perth (whom he found an easy, practicable person, very willing to adopt his suggestions), in preference to those of Lord George Murray, who, though an officer of much higher military talents, was haughty, blunt, and not unwilling to combat the opinions of the Prince himself, far more those of his favourite secretary.

There being thus a sort of jealousy betwixt these eminent persons, Lord George considered the preference given to the Duke of Perth, to command the proceedings of the siege of Carlisle, as an encroachment upon his own pretensions; he regarded also, or seemed to regard, the Duke's religion, being a Catholic, as a disqualification to his holding such an ostensible character in the expedition. Under the influence of these feelings, he wrote a letter to the Prince, during the time of the siege, in which he observed he was sorry to see that he did not possess his Royal Highness's confidence, and that, although a Lieutenant-General, others were employed in preference to him; for these reasons, he perceived he was likely to be of more service as a volunteer than as a general officer; so that he begged his Royal Highness's acceptance of the resignation of his commission in the latter capacity. The Chevalier intimated to him, accordingly, that his resignation was accepted.

But, however acceptable the preference given to the Duke of Perth over Lord George Murray might be to Secretary Murray, and to the immediate personal favourites of the Prince, the Duke's principles and tenets being more acceptable to them than those of an uncompromising soldier of high rank, there was a general feeling of anxiety and apprehension spread through the bulk of the army, who had a much higher opinion of the military capacity of Lord George than of that of the Duke, though partial to the extreme good-nature, personal valour, and gentlemanlike conduct of the latter. The principal persons, therefore, in the army, chiefs, commanders of corps, and men who held similar situations of importance, united in a petition, which was delivered to the Prince at Carlisle, praying that he would be pleased to discharge all Roman Catholics from his councils. This request was grounded upon an allegation which had appeared in the newspapers, stating that the Prince was altogether guided by the advice of Roman Catholics, and comparing Sir Thomas Sheridan to his grandfather, James the Second's, father-confessor, the Jesuit Petre. In allusion to the surrender of Carlisle, the petition expressed an affected alarm upon the subject of Papists assuming the discussion and decision of articles of capitulation, in which the Church of England was intimately concerned. To mark the application of the whole, the Prince was entreated to request Lord George Murray might resume his command. To this last article of the petition the Prince returned a favourable answer; to the rest he waved making any reply. Thus the intrigue was for a period put a stop to, which, joined to his own rough and uncourtly style of remonstrance, had nearly deprived the insurgents of the invaluable services of Lord George Murray, who was undoubtedly the most able officer of their party.

The Prince might not have found it easy to extricate himself from this difficulty had the Duke of Perth remained tenacious of the advantage which he had gained. He could not, indeed, be supposed to admit the principle of a petition, which was founded on the idea that the religion which he professed was a bar to his holding high rank in the Prince's service, and accordingly repelled with spirit the objections to his precedence on this ground. But when it was pointed out to him that Charles could not at that moment adhere to his resolution in his favour, without losing, to the great disadvantage of his affairs, the benefit of Lord George Murray's services, he at once professed his willingness to serve in any capacity, and submit to anything by which the interest of Charles and the expedition might be most readily promoted.

While the Prince lay at Carlisle he received intelligence which showed that his successes in Scotland had been but momentary, and of a kind which had not made any serious impression upon the minds of the people. The populace of the towns of Perth and Dundee had already intimated their dislike of the Stewart cause, and their adherence to the House of Hanover. Upon the birth-day of King George, the populace in both places assembled to celebrate the festival with the customary demonstrations of joy, notwithstanding their Jacobite commandants, and the new magistracy which had been nominated in both towns by the prevailing party. At Perth, the mob had cooped up Mr. Oliphant of Gask, with his friends, in the council-house, and shots and blows had been exchanged betwixt the parties, At Dundee, Fotheringham, the Jacobite governor, had been driven from the town, and although both he and Gask had been able to reassert their authority on the succeeding day, yet the temporary success of the citizens of both places showed that the popular opinion was not on the side of Prince Charles.

A more marked expression of public feeling was now exhibited in the metropolis. The force which had restrained the general sentiment in Edinburgh was removed by the march of the Highland army towards England. The troops from the castle had resumed possession of the deserted city. The Lord Justice-Clerk, the Lords of Session, the Sheriffs of the three counties of Lothian, with many other Whig gentlemen who had left the town on the approach of the rebels, had reentered Edinburgh in a kind of solemn procession, and had given orders to prosecute the levy of 1000 men, formerly voted to Government. General Handyside also had marched into the capital on the 14th of November, with Price's and Ligonier's regiments, which had come from Newcastle; also the two regiments of dragoons who had behaved so indifferently at Prestonpans. The towns of Glasgow, Stirling, Paisley, and Dumfries, were also embodying their militia; and Colonel John Campbell, then heir of the Argyle family, had arrived at Inverary, and was raising the feudal interest of that powerful house, as well as the militia of the county of Argyle.

All these were symptoms that showed the frail tenure of the Chevalier's influence in Scotland, and that it was not, in the Lowlands at least, likely to survive long the absence of the Highland army.

Neither were the Highlands in a safe situation, so far as the Prince's interest was concerned. Lord Loudon was at Inverness with the MacLeods and MacDonalds of Skye, and overawed the Jacobites north of Inverness, as well as those of Nairn and Moray. It is true, Lord Lewis Gordon, who commanded in Banff and Aberdeenshire, had raised three battalions for the Prince, commanded by Moir of Stonywood, Gordon of Abachie, and Farquharson of Monaltry. The rest of Charles's reinforcements lay at Perth; they consisted of the Frasers, as already mentioned, MacGillivray of Drumnaglass, who commanded the MacIntoshes; the Farquharsons, the Earl of Cromarty, the Master of Lovat, with several detachments of MacDonalds of various tribes, and one hundred and fifty of the Stewarts of Appin. A large body of MacGregors lay at Doune, under the command of MacGregor of Glengyle, and kept the country in great awe. All these troops made a considerable force; those at Perth, in particular, together with Glengyle's people, amounted to between three and four thousand men, as good as any the Prince had in his army, and Colonel MacLauchlan was despatched to order them immediately to march and join their countrymen in England.

In those circumstances several of the Prince's followers were much surprised when, in a council at Carlisle, the sanguine young Adventurer proposed that they should without delay pursue their march to London, as if the kingdom of England had been wholly defenceless. It was objected that the Scottish gentlemen had consented to the invasion of England in the hope of being joined by the English friends of the Prince, or in expectation of a descent from France; without one or other of these events they had never, it was stated, undertaken to effect the restoration of the Stewart family. To this the Prince answered that he was confident in expecting the junction of a strong party in Lancashire, if the Scots would consent to march forward. D'Eguilles vehemently affirmed his immediate expectation of a French landing; and Mr. Murray, who was treasurer as well as secretary, assured them that it was impossible to stay longer at Carlisle for want of money. All these were urgent reasons for marching southward.

Whether the Prince had any stronger reasons than be avowed for believing in the actual probability of a Jacobite rising which he averred, will probably never be exactly known. It is certain that many families of distinction were understood to be engaged to join the Prince in 1740, provided he appeared at the head of a French force, and with a certain quantity of money and arms; but the same difficulties occurred in England which he had encountered on his first landing in Scotland. The persons who had come under an agreement to join, under certain conditions, in a perilous enterprise, considered themselves as under no obligation to do so when these conditions were not complied with. It is probable, nevertheless, that many of those zealous and fanatical partisans, which belong to every undertaking of the kind, and are usually as desperate in their plans as in their fortunes, might, since his entering England, have opened a communication with the Prince, and excited his own sanguine temper by their representations. But, at the same time, it is pretty clear that the Prince had no information of such credit as to be laid before his council; at least, if it were so, it was never seen by them; nor were there any indications of a formed plan of insurrection in his favour, although there seemed a strong disposition on the part of the gentry in Lancashire, Cheshire, and Wales to embrace his interest. As for Lord George Murray, and the counsellors who differed in opinion from Charles, they assented to the advance into England merely lest it might be said that, by their restiveness, the Prince had lost the chance of forming a union with his English friends, or profiting by a descent from France.

The army was now reduced to about 4400 men, out of which a garrison of two or three hundred were to be left in Carlisle; with the remainder it was now resolved to march to London by the Lancashire road, although, including the militia and newly-raised regiments, there were upwards of 6000 men under arms upon the side of the Government, who lay directly in their way. It would, therefore, seem that the better course would have been to have waited at Carlisle until the reinforcements arrived from Perth; but this proposal was made and overruled. On the 21st of November the Prince marched from Carlisle, and arrived that night at Penrith, Lord George Murray commanding the army as general under him. He halted a day at Penrith, with the purpose of fighting Field-Marshal Wade, who had made a demonstration towards Hexham, to raise the siege of Carlisle; but who had marched back, on account, as was alleged, of a heavy snowstorm. Wade was now an old man, and his military movements partook of the slowness and irresolution of advanced age. The Prince, neglecting the old marshal, pushed southward, resumed his adventurous march, and advanced through Lancaster to Preston, where the whole army arrived on the 26th. They marched in two divisions, of which the first, commanded by Lord George Murray, comprehended what were called the Lowland regiments, that is to say, the whole army except the clans; although the greater part so called Lowland, were Highlanders by language, and all of them by dress, the Highland garb being the uniform of all the infantry of the Jacobite army. The Prince himself at the head of the clans properly so called, each of which formed a regiment, led the way on foot, with his target on his shoulder, sharing the fatigues of his hardy followers. The little army was compelled, for convenience of quarters, to move, as we have said, in two divisions, which generally kept half a day's march separate from each other.

These adventurous movements, from the very audacity of their character,—for who could have supposed them to be hazarded on vague expectations?—struck a terror into the English nation, at which those who witnessed and shared it were afterwards surprised and ashamed. It was concluded that an enterprise so desperate would not have been undertaken without some private assurances of internal assistance, and every one expected some dreadful and widely-spread conspiracy to explode. In the meantime, the people remained wonderfully passive. "London," says a contemporary, writing on the spur of the moment, "lies open as a prize to the first comers, whether Scotch or Dutch;" and a letter from the poet Gray to Horace Walpole paints an indifference yet more ominous to the public cause than the general panic: "The common people in town at least know how to be afraid; but we are such uncommon people here" (at Cambridge) "as to have no more sense of danger than if the battle had been fought where and when the battle of Cannae was. I heard three sensible, middle-aged men, when the Scotch were said to be at Stamford, and actually were at Derby, talking of hiring a chaise to go to Caxton (a place in the highroad) to see the Pretender and Highlanders as they passed." A further evidence of the feelings under which the public laboured during this crisis is to be found in a letter from the well-known Sir Andrew Mitchell to the Lord President.[1] "If I had not," says the writer, "lived long enough in England to know the natural bravery of the people, particularly of the better sort, I should, from their behaviour of late, have had a very false opinion of them; for the least scrap of good news exalts them most absurdly, and the smallest reverse of fortune depresses them meanly."

---

[1] Culloden Papers.

In fact, the alarm was not groundless; not that the number of the Chevalier's individual followers ought to have been an object of serious, at least of permanent alarm, to so great a kingdom; but because, in many counties, a great proportion of the landed interest were Jacobitically disposed, although with the prudence which distinguished the opposite party in 1688, they declined joining the invaders until it should appear whether they could maintain their ground without them.

In the meantime, the unfortunate Prince marched on in full confidence in his stars, his fortunes, and his strength, like a daring gambler, encouraged by a run of luck which was hitherto extraordinary; but his English friends remained as much palsied as his enemies, nor did anything appear to announce that general declaration in his favour which he had asserted with so much confidence.

On arriving at Preston, in Lancashire, Lord George Murray had to combat the superstition of the soldiers whom he commanded. The defeat of the Duke of Hamilton in the great Civil War, with the subsequent misfortune of Brigadier MacIntosh in 1715, had given rise to a belief that Preston was to a Scottish army the fatal point, beyond which they were not to pass. To counteract this superstition, Lord George led a part of his troops across the Ribble Bridge, a mile beyond Preston, at which town the Chevalier arrived in the evening. The spell which arrested the progress of the Scottish troops was thus supposed to be broken, and their road to London was considered as laid open.

The people of Preston received Charles Edward with several cheers, which were the first he had heard since entering England but on officers being appointed to beat up for recruits, no one would enlist. When this was stated to the Prince, he continued, in reply, to assure his followers with unabated confidence, that he would be joined by all his English friends when they advanced as far as Manchester; and Monsieur D'Eguilles, with similar confidence, offered to lay considerable wagers that the French either had already landed or would land within a week. Thus the murmurers were once more reduced to silence.

During this long and fatiguing march, Charles, as we have already said, shared with alacrity the fatigues of his soldiers. He usually wore a Highland dress and marched on foot at the head of one of the columns, insisting that the infirm and aged Lord Pitsligo should occupy his carriage. He never took dinner, but, making a hearty meal at supper, threw himself upon his bed about eleven o'clock, without undressing, and rose by four the next morning and, as he had a very strong constitution, supported this severe labour day after day. In all the towns where the Highland army passed, they levied the public revenue with great accuracy; and where any subscriptions had been levied in behalf of Government, as was the case in most considerable places, they exacted an equivalent sum from each subscriber.

On the march between Preston and Wigan the road was thronged with people anxious to see the army pass by, who expressed their good wishes for the Prince's success; but when arms were offered to them, and they were invited to enroll themselves in his service, they unanimously declined, saying in excuse they did not understand fighting. On the 29th, when the Prince arrived at Manchester, there was a still stronger appearance of favour to his cause; bonfires, acclamations, the display of white cockades, solemnised his arrival, and a considerable number of persons came to kiss his hand and to offer their services. About two hundred men of the populace were here enlisted, and being embodied with the few who had before joined his standard, composed what was termed the Manchester regiment. The officers were in general respectable men, enthusiasts in the Jacobite cause; and Mr. Townley, a gentleman of good family and considerable literary accomplishments, was named colonel of the regiment. But the common soldiers were the very lowest of the populace. All this success was of a character very inferior to that which the Prince had promised and which his followers expected; yet it was welcome, and was regarded as the commencement of a rising in their favour, so that even Lord George Murray, when consulted by a friend whether they should not now renounce an expedition which promise so ill, gave it as his opinion that, before doing so, they should advance as far as Derby, undertaking that, if they were not joined by the English Jacobites in considerable numbers at that place, he would then propose a retreat.

The Highland army advanced accordingly to Derby; but in their road through Macclesfield, Leek, Congleton, and other places, were received with signs of greater aversion to their cause than they had yet experienced, so that all hopes founded on the encouragement they had received from the junction of the Manchester Regiment were quite obscured and forgotten.

They now also began to receive notice of the enemy. Colonel Ker of Gradon nearly surprised a party of English dragoons, and made prisoner one Weir, a principal spy of the Duke of Cumberland, whom the Highland officers were desirous of sending to instant execution. Lord

George Murray saved him from the gallows, and thus obtained some valuable information concerning the numbers and position of the enemy. Accuracy in these particulars was of the last consequence, for, having arrived at Derby, Charles might be said to be at the very crisis of his fate. He was within 127 miles of London, and at the same time less than a day's march of an army of 10,000 and upwards, which had been originally assembled under General Ligonier, and was now commanded by his Royal Highness the Duke of Cumberland, who had his headquarters at Litchfield, somewhat farther from the metropolis than those of Charles Edward. On the other hand, another English army, equal in numbers to their own, was moving up along the west side of Yorkshire, being about this time near Ferrybridge, two or three marches in the rear of the Scottish invaders, who were thus in danger of being placed between two fires.

Besides these two armies George the Second was himself preparing to take the field at the head of his own Guards. For this purpose they were marched out of London and encamped upon Finchley Common. Several regiments who had served abroad were destined to compose this third army, and form the defence of the capital, should its services be required.

The Prince showed no abatement of the high confidence which he had hitherto entertained of success. It seems to have been his idea to push forward at the head of his active troops, and, eluding the Duke of Cumberland (which, from their mutual position with respect, to London, he would not have found difficult, being the nearest to the capital by nearly a day's march), to press forward upon the metropolis, and dispute the pretensions of the reigning monarch beneath its very walls. He continued to entertain the belief that George the Second was a detested usurper, in whose favour no one would willingly draw his sword; that the people of England, as was their duty, still nourished that allegiance for the race of their native princes which they were bound to hold sacred; and that, if he did but persevere in his daring attempt, Heaven itself would fight in his cause. His discourse, therefore, when at table, at Derby, was entirely about the manner in which he should enter London, whether on foot or horseback, or whether in Lowland or Highland garb; without hinting at the possibility of his having to retreat without making the final experiment on the faith and fortitude of the English. He remained at Derby for nearly two days to refresh his forces.

On the morning of the 5th of December Lord George Murray, with all the commanders of battalions and squadrons, waited on the Prince and informed him that it was the opinion of all present that the Scots had now done everything that could be expected of them. They had marched into the heart of England, through the counties represented as most favourable to the cause, and had not been joined, except by a very insignificant number. They had been assured also of a descent from France to act in conjunction with them; but of this there had not been the slightest appearance nevertheless, Lord George stated that if the Prince could produce a letter from any English person of distinction, containing an invitation to the Scottish army either to march to London or elsewhere, they were ready to obey. If, however, no one was disposed to intermeddle with their affairs, he stated they must be under the necessity of caring for themselves, in which point of view their situation must be considered as critical. The army of the Duke of Cumberland, ten thousand strong, lay within a day's march in front, or nearly so; that of Marshal Wade was only two or three marches in their rear. Supposing that, nevertheless, they could give both armies the slip, a battle under the walls of London with George the second's army was inevitable. He urged that with whomsoever they fought they could not reckon even upon victory without such a loss as would make it impossible to gather in the fruits which ought to follow it; and that four or five thousand men were an army inadequate even to taking possession of the city of London, although undefended by regular troops, unless the populace were strongly in his favour, of which good disposition some friend would certainly have informed them if any such had existed.

Lord George Murray, to these causes for retreat, added a plan for a Scottish campaign, which he thought might be prosecuted to advantage. In retreating to that country the Prince had the advantage of retiring upon his reinforcements, which included the body of Highlanders lying at Perth, as well as a detachment of French troops which had been landed at Montrose under Lord John Drummond. He therefore requested, in the name of the persons present, that they should go back and join their friends in Scotland, and live or die with them.

After Lord George had spoken, many of the council expressed similar opinions. The Duke of Perth and Sir John Gordon only proposed penetrating into Wales, to give the people there an opportunity to join. To this was opposed the necessity of fighting with the Duke of

Cumberland with unequal numbers, and perhaps with Marshal Wade also, who was likely to strain every nerve to come up in their rear.

Charles Edward heard these arguments with the utmost impatience, expressed his determination to advance to London, having gained a day's march on the Duke of Cumberland, and plainly stigmatised as traitors all who should adhere to any other resolution. He broke up the council and used much argument with the members in private to alter their way of thinking. The Irish officers alone seemed convinced by his reasoning, for they were little accustomed to dispute his opinions; and besides, if made prisoners, they could only be subjected to a few months' imprisonment, as most of them had regular commissions in the French service. But at length the Chevalier, knowing that little weight would be given to their sanction, and finding that his own absolute commands were in danger of being disobeyed, was compelled to submit to the advice or remonstrance of the Scottish leaders.

On the 5th, therefore, in the evening, the council of war was again convoked, and the Chevalier told them, with sullen resignation, that he consented to return to Scotland, but at the same time informed them that in future he should call no more councils since he was accountable to nobody for his actions excepting to Heaven and to his Father, and would, therefore, no longer either ask or accept their advice.

Thus terminated the celebrated march to Derby, and with it every chance, however remote, of the Chevalier's success in his romantic expedition. Whether he ought ever to have entered England, at least without collecting all the forces which he could command, is a very disputable point; but it was clear that whatever influence he might for a time possess, arose from the boldness of his advance. The charm, however, was broken the moment he showed, by a movement in retreat, that he had undertaken an enterprise too difficult for him to achieve.

LXXX

The First Retreat

1745

U PON the 6th of December the Highland army began its retreat northward. As they marched in the gray of the morning the men did not at first perceive in what direction they were moving; but so soon as the daylight gave them the means of perceiving that they were in retreat, an expression of deep regret and lamentation was heard among the ranks—with such confidence had these brave men looked forward to a successful issue, even in the precarious situation in which they were placed.

It was also observed that from the time the retreat commenced the Highlanders became more reckless in their conduct. They had behaved with exemplary discipline while there remained any possibility of conciliating the inhabitants. The English might then stare with wonder on men speaking an unknown language, wearing a wild and unwonted dress, and bearing much of the external appearance of barbarians, but their behaviour was that of an orderly and civilised people. Now, when irritated by disappointment, they did not scruple to commit plunder in the towns and villages through which they passed; and several acts of violence induced the country people not only to fear them as outlandish strangers but to hate them as robbers. In the advance they

showed the sentiments of brave men, come, in their opinion, to liber-
ate their fellow-citizens;—in the retreat they were as caterans returning
from a creagh. They evinced no ferocity, however, and their rapine was
combined with singular simplicity. Iron being a scarce commodity in
their own country, some of them were observed, as they left Derby, to
load themselves with bars of it, which they proposed to carry down to
Scotland with them!

The behaviour of the Prince also tended to dishearten the soldiers.
He seemed to conduct himself on the retreat as if he were no longer
commander of the army. Instead of taking the vanguard on foot, at the
head of his people, with his target at his back, as had been his custom
during the advance, he now lingered behind his men, so as to retard
them, and then rode forward and regained his place in the column; he
showed, in short, obvious marks of being dejected and out of humour.

The few English insurgents by whom the Prince had been joined
were divided in opinion whether they should follow this retrogade
movement, which coincided so ill with their more sanguine hopes, or
remain behind, and desert the cause. Morgan, one of these English volunteers, came up to Vaughan, a gentleman of the same country, and
observed, in a tone of surprise, that the army were going to Scotland;
"Be it so," answered Vaughan, "I am determined to go with them wherever their course lies." Morgan replied, with an oath, it was better to be
hanged in England than starved in Scotland. He had the misfortune to
be hanged accordingly, while Vaughan escaped, and died an officer in
the Spanish service.

The people of the country, who had shown them little goodwill
upon their advance, appeared more actively malevolent when they
beheld the Scots in retreat and in the act of pillaging the places they
passed through. At a village near Stockport the inhabitants fired upon
the patrols of the Highlanders, who, in retaliation, set fire to the place.
Most of the country people were in arms and all stragglers were killed
or made prisoners. The sick men, also, of the Jacobite army, who were
necessarily left behind the march, were killed or treated with violence.
On the 9th of December the army approached Manchester; but in that
city which had lately appeared so friendly, they now encountered
opposition. A violent mob was in possession of the town, and
opposed the quartermasters of the Chevalier's army. Two battalions
and two squadrons were detached to support the quartermasters, by
whom the mob was dispersed. £2500 was demanded from the town

in consequence of this riot. On leaving the place the mob even pursued and fired upon the rear of the Chevalier's army, although they uniformly retreated so soon as the rearguard faced about. The temper of the people, however, served to show how little reliance could at any time have been placed upon their attachment.

The Duke of Cumberland, who, as I already said, was lying at Litchfield, while Prince Charles was at Derby, did not learn for two days that the Highlanders had left Derby for Ashburn on the 6th; and did not commence any pursuit until the 8th, when the Duke marched northward with all his cavalry, and a number of infantry mounted upon horses furnished by the neighbouring gentry. The troops, advanced with the utmost spirit. The retreat of the Scottish army, whose advance had been regarded with a vague apprehension of terror, was naturally considered as an avowal of their inability to execute their purpose; and it was concluded by the regular soldiery that they were pressing upon the flight of a disappointed and disheartened body of adventurers, who had failed in an attempt to execute a desperate object. The English troops also felt in spirits, as being under the command of a Prince of the blood, of undoubted experience and courage, who had arrived in Britain in time to assert the cause of his father, and to fix upon his head the crown which had been so boldly struck at. They anticipated little opposition from an enemy in full retreat, and whom, it might be supposed, a brisk attack would throw into utter disorder their cavalry, therefore, pressed forward in spirits and by forced marches.

On their part the Highlanders retreated with speed, regularity, and unabated courage. Lord George Murray, to vindicate the sincerity of his attachment to the cause he had embraced, undertook the charge of the rearguard, the post of danger and of honour. This frequently detained him a considerable time beyond the march of the main body, more especially for the purpose of bringing up the baggage and artillery of the army, which, from the bad weather and bad state of the roads, was perpetually breaking down, and detained the rearguard considerably.

Towards the evening of the 17th of December the Prince, with the main body of his army, had entered the town of Penrith, in the county of Cumberland. Lord George Murray had, in the meanwhile, been delayed so much by those various accidents, that he was forced to pass the night six miles in the rear, at the town of Shap. The Glengarry regiment of Highlanders were at that time in charge of the rearguard; and at Shap Lord George found Colonel Roy Stewart, with another small regiment of 200 men. In the meantime the Chevalier had determined to halt at Penrith until he was joined by his rearguard.

Next day, being the 18th of December, Lord George Murray marched with both the corps which we have mentioned. The march began, as usual, before daybreak; but when it became broad daylight he discovered the village of Clifton, which is within three or four miles south of Penrith, and the heights beyond it, crowned with several parties of cavalry, drawn up betwixt him and the village. The Highlanders, you must be reminded, had in former times an aversion to encounter the Lowland horse; but since their success at Prestonpans they had learned to despise the troops of whom they formerly stood in awe. They had been instructed, chiefly by the standing orders of Lord George Murray, that if they encountered the cavalry manfully, striking with their swords at the heads and limbs of the horses, they might be sure to throw them into disorder. The MacDonalds, therefore, of Glengarry, on receiving the word of command to attack those horsemen who appeared disposed to interrupt their passage, stript off their plaids without hesitation and rushed upon them sword in hand. The cavalry in question were not regulars but volunteers of the country, who had assembled themselves for the purpose of harassing the rear of the Highland army, and giving time for the Duke of Cumberland, who was in full pursuit, to advance and overtake them. On the fierce attack of Glengarry's men they immediately galloped off, but not before several prisoners were made,—among the rest a footman of the Duke of Cumberland, who told his captors that his Royal Highness was coming up in their rear with 4000 horse.

Lord George Murray despatched this information to the Chevalier at Penrith, requesting some support, which he limited to 1000 men. Colonel Roy Stewart, who was charged with the message, returned with orders that the rearguard should retreat upon Penrith. At the same time MacPherson of Cluny, with his clan, was sent back as far as Cliftonbridge with the Appin regiment, under command of Stewart of Ardshiel. With the assistance of these reinforcements, Lord George Murray was still far inferior in number to the enemy, yet he determined to make good his retreat.

The Duke of Cumberland's whole cavalry was now drawn up in the rear of the Highland army, upon the open moor of Clifton; beyond the moor, the rearguard of the Highlanders must necessarily pursue their retreat through large plantations of fir-trees, part of Lord

Lonsdale's enclosures. Lord George Murray foresaw an attack in this critical posture, and prepared to meet and repel it. He drew up the Glengarry regiment upon the highroad, within the fields, placed the Appin Stewarts in the enclosures on their left, and again the MacPherson regiment to the left of them. On the right he stationed Roy Stewart's men, covered by a wall.

The night was dark, with occasional glimpses of the moon. The English advanced about 1000 dismounted dragoons, with the intention of attacking the Highlanders on the flank, while the Duke of Cumberland and the rest of his cavalry kept their station on the moor, with the purpose of operating in the rear of their opponents. Lord George Murray perceived, by a glimpse of moonshine, this large body of men coming from the moor, and advancing towards the Clifton enclosures. The MacPherson and Stewart regiments which were under his immediate command were stationed behind a hedge; but Lord George, observing a second hedge in front, protected by a deep ditch, ordered his men to advance and gain possession of it. It was already lined on the opposite side by the enemy, who, as was then the custom of dragoons, acted as infantry when occasion required. Lord George asked Cluny his opinion of what was to be done: "I will attack the enemy sword in hand," replied the undaunted chief, "provided you order me." As they advanced, the MacPhersons, who were nearest to the hedge of which they wished to take possession, received a fire from the soldiers who had lined it on the opposite side. Cluny, surprised at receiving a discharge of musketry, when he conceived he was marching against a body of horse, exclaimed, "What the devil is this!" Lord George Murray replied, "There is no time to be lost—we must instantly charge!" and at the same time drawing his broadsword, exclaimed, "Claymore!" which was the word for attacking sword in hand. The MacPhersons rushed on, headed by their chief, with uncontrollable fury; they gave their fire, and then burst, sword in hand, through the hedge, and attacked the dragoons by whom it was lined. Lord George himself headed the assault, and in dashing through the hedge lost his bonnet and wig (the latter being then universally worn), and fought bare-headed, the foremost in the skirmish Colonel Honeywood, who commanded the dragoons, was left severely wounded on the spot, and his sword, of considerable value, fell into the hands of the chief of the MacPhersons. The dragoons on the right were compelled, with considerable loss, to retreat to their party on the moor. At the same moment, or nearly so, another body of dismounted dragoons pressed forward upon the high-road, and were repulsed by the Glengarry regiment, and that of John Roy Stewart. The Highlanders were with difficulty recalled from the pursuit, exclaiming that it was a shame to see so many of the King's enemies standing fast upon the moor without attacking them. A very few of the MacPhersons, not exceeding twelve, who ventured too far, were either killed or taken. But the loss of the English was much more considerable, nor did they feel disposed to renew the attack upon the rear of the Highlanders. Lord George Murray sent a second message to the Prince, to propose that he should detach a reinforcement from the main body, with which he offered to engage and defeat the cavalry opposed to him. The Prince, doubtful of the event, or jealous of his general, declined to comply with this request.

On receiving this answer, Lord George Murray retreated to Penrith, and united the rearguard with the main body; and it seems that the Duke of Cumberland became satisfied that a good deal of risk might be incurred by a precipitate attack on the Highland army, since he did not again repeat the experiment.[1] The next day Charles retreated to Carlisle, and arrived there with his army on the morning of the 19th of December.

It was thought desirable that the Highland garrison in that town should be reinforced, but it was not easy to find forces willing to be left behind in a place almost certain to be sacrificed. The men of the Manchester regiment, who were disheartened at the prospect of a retreat into Scotland, were pitched upon for this duty, together with a number of French and Irish. The last had little to fear, being generally engaged in the French service, and the English were probably of the mind of Captain Morgan, that hanging in England was preferable to starving in Scotland.

The skirmish at Clifton seems to have abated the speed of the English pursuers, who no longer attempted to annoy the retreat of their active enemy. The Scottish army left Carlisle upon the 20th of December, and effected their retreat into Scotland by crossing the Esk at Long-town; the river was swollen, but the men, wading in arm in arm,

---

[1] "Cumberland and his cavalry fled with precipitation, and in such great confusion, that if the Prince had been provided in a sufficient number of cavalry to have taken advantage of the disorder, it is beyond question that the Duke of Cumberland and the bulk of his cavalry had been taken prisoners."—M'PHERSON's *M.S. Memoirs, quoted in Notes to Waverley.*

supported each other against the force of the current, and got safely through, though with some difficulty. It is said that the Chevalier showed both dexterity and humanity on this occasion. He was crossing on horseback, beneath the place where some of his men were fording the river, one or two of whom drifted from the hold of their companions, and were carried down the stream in great danger of perishing. As one of them passed, the Chevalier caught him by the hair, called out in Gaelic, "*Cohear, cohear!*" that is, "Help, help!" supported the man till he was taken safely from the water, and thus gave himself an additional claim to the attachment of his followers.

The Highland army, marching in two divisions, arrived at Annan and Ecclefechan on the same day, and pursued their road through the west of Scotland.

While the Scottish rebels were advancing, the utmost alarm prevailed in London; there was a sharp run upon the Bank, which threatened the stability of that national establishment; the offers of support from public bodies showed the urgency of the crisis; the theatres, for example, proposed to raise armed corps of real not personated soldiers. There was the more alarm indicated in all this, because the Highlanders, who had not been at first sufficiently respected as soldiers, had acquired by their late actions credit for valour of a most romantic cast. There was something also in the audacity of the attempt which inclined men to give Charles credit for secret resources, until his retreat showed that he was possessed of none except a firm belief in the justice of his own cause, and a confidence that it was universally regarded in the same light by the English nation. The apathy of the English had dissipated this vision, few or none, excepting Catholics, and a handful of Jacobites of Manchester, having shown themselves disposed to acknowledge his cause. The retreat, therefore, from Derby was considered throughout England as the close of the rebellion; as a physician regards a distemper to be nearly overcome when he can drive it from the stomach and nobler parts into the extremities of the body.

LXXXI

Another Falkirk

1745-1746

THE state of Scotland had materially changed during the absence of the Prince and his army upon the expedition to Derby; and the nation was now in the situation of one who, having received a stunning blow, recovers at last from his stupor, and aims, though feebly and with uncertainty, at retaliating the injury which he has sustained.

Inverness was in the hands of Lord Loudon, commanding an army composed of the MacLeods, MacDonalds of Skye, and other northern clans, who, to the number of two thousand men, had associated against the insurgents. The Earl of Loudon even felt himself strong enough to lay hands on Lord Lovat in his own castle, named Castle Downie, and brought him to Inverness, where he detained him in a sort of honourable captivity. Fraser of Gortuleg, one of his clansmen, relieved Lovat by a stratagem. The old chief, having made his escape, lurked in the Highlands, keeping up his correspondence with Charles Edward. The house of Gortuleg was Lovat's chief residence. Matters in the north were, therefore, unfavourable to the Chevalier's cause.

The capital of Scotland was again in possession of the constituted authorities, garrisoned by a part of Marshal Wade's army, which had been sent down for the purpose, and preparing to redeem, by a more obstinate resistance to the Highlanders upon their return from England, the honour which they might be supposed to have lost by their surrender in the September preceding.

This spirit of resistance had reached the Western Border, where reports were generally disseminated that the Chevalier and his forces had been defeated in England, and were now flying across the Border in such extreme confusion that the militia and volunteers of the country would have little trouble in totally destroying them. For this purpose, many of the peasants of Dumfriesshire had assumed arms, but they showed little inclination to use them, when they saw the Chevalier's army return in complete order, and unbroken in strength or spirit.

The Highland army, after crossing the river Esk, was divided into three bodies. The first, consisting of the clans, moved with the Chevalier to Annan. Lord George Murray was ordered to Ecclefechan with the Athole brigade and Lowland regiments. Lord Elcho, with the cavalry, received orders to go to Dumfries, and to disarm and punish that refractory town. The Prince himself shortly followed with the infantry, which he commanded in person.

Dumfries's ancient contumacy to the Jacobite cause had been manifested, not only by their conduct in the year 1715, but by a recent attack upon the Chevalier's baggage, as he marched into England in the November preceding. The horse marched thither accordingly with purposes of vengeance, and were speedily followed by the Prince's own division. He laid a fine of £2000 upon the town, and demanded, for the use of the army, 1000 pairs of shoes. Some of the money required was instantly paid down, and for the rest hostages were granted. No violence was committed on the town or inhabitants, for the Highlanders, though they threatened hard, did not, in fact, commit any violence or pillage.[1]

The magistrates and community of Glasgow were yet more guilty in the eyes of the Prince than those of the smaller town of Dumfries.

---

[1] The provost of Dumfries, a gentleman of family named Corsan, who had shown himself a staunch adherent of the Government, was menaced with the destruction of his house and property. It is not very long since the late Mrs. MacCulloch of Ardwell, daughter of provost Corsan, told your Grandfather that she remembered well, when a child of six years old, being taken out of her father's house, as if it was to be instantly burnt. Too young to be sensible of the danger, she asked the Highland officer, who held her in his arms, to show her the Pretender, which the good-natured Gael did, under condition that little Miss Corsan was in future to call him the Prince. Neither did they carry their threats into exertion against the provost or his mansion.

That city had raised a body of 600 men, called the Glasgow regiment, many of them serving without pay, under the command of the Earls of Rome and Glencairn. This corps had been sent to Stirling to assist General Blakeney, the governor of the castle, to defend the passes of the Forth. From Stirling, the Glasgow regiment fell back with the other troops which had assembled there and took post at Edinburgh. This was with a view to the defence of the capital, since the Highlanders, having bent their march to the westward, were likely to pay Edinburgh the next visit.

While the citizens of the capital were suffering from the apprehension of the neighbourhood of the rebels, those of Glasgow were paying the actual penalty attached to their presence. Clothing for the troops, and stores, were demanded from the town to the extent of more than £10,000 sterling, which they were compelled to pay, under the threat of military execution.

At Glasgow, the Prince learned, for the first time with some accuracy, the extent of the interest which France had taken in his cause, and the supplies of every kind which she had sent to him; supplies which, in amount, remind us of those administered to a man perishing of famine, by a comrade, who dropt into his mouth, from time to time, a small shell-fish, affording nutriment enough to keep the sufferer from dying, but not sufficient to restore him to the power of active exertion.

The principal part of these succours came under Lord John Drummond, brother to the Duke of Perth, and a general officer in the army of France. They consisted of his own regiment in the French service, called the Royal Scots; the piquets of six Irish regiments; and Fitz-James's light horse. Of the latter, not more than two squadrons appear to have mustered. He also brought some money and military stores. Lord John Drummond had been entrusted with letters from France, giving an account how matters had been conducted there, and what was designed for the assistance of the Chevalier. Charles's brother, the titular Duke of York, had arrived at Paris in August 1745, and, on the news of the battle of Prestonpans, there had originated a sincere desire on the part of the French to assist the attempt of the House of Stewart effectually.

The original plan was, to put the Irish regiments in the French service under the command of the said Duke of York, and place them on board of fishing-boats, which should instantly transport them to

England. This scheme was laid aside, and a much greater expedition projected, under the command of the Duke of Richelieu, which, it was designed, should amount to 9000 foot and 1350 horse. The troops were assembled for this purpose at Dunkirk, Boulogne, and Calais, and a number of small vessels were collected for the embarkation. The French, however, were so dilatory in their preparations, that the design took air, and the English Government, to whom the expedition, had it sailed during the time of Charles's irruption into the west frontier, must have been highly dangerous, instantly ordered Admiral Vernon, with a strong fleet, into the Channel, and assembled an army on the coast of Kent and Essex. Upon this the French abandoned the expedition, the danger of which was greatly diminished by the retreat of the Highlanders from Derby.

The Prince did not, for a long time, either hear or believe that this scheme of a descent in favour of his family was ultimately abandoned; and his confidence that the French continued to persevere in it led him into more than one serious mistake. It was now agitated among the Prince and his adherents in which way his small body of forces could be best employed. Some were of opinion that they ought to direct their march upon the capital of Scotland. It is true, that part of the troops which had constituted Wade's army at Newcastle were now preparing to defend Edinburgh, and that the rest of those forces were advancing thither under the command of General Hawley. It was nevertheless alleged that the Highlanders, might, in this severe season, distress the English troops considerably, by preventing them from dividing in their winter march in quest of quarters, and by obliging to keep the field in a body, and undergo hardships which would be destructive to them, though little heeded by the hardy mountaineers. But although this scheme promised considerable advantages, Charles preferred another, which engaged him in the siege of Stirling Castle, although his best troops were very unequal to that species of service. The Prince was no doubt the rather inclined to this scheme, that Lord John Drummond had brought both battering guns and engineers from France; and, thus supplied, he probably imagined that his success in sieges would be equally distinguished with that which he had attained by open war.

Before leaving the west country, the Highlanders burnt and plundered the village of Lesmahagow, and particularly the clergyman's house, on account of the inhabitants having, under that reverend person's direction, attacked and made prisoner MacDonald of Kinloch-Moidart, who was traversing the country unattended, having been sent by the Prince on a mission to the Western Isles.[1]

On the 3d of January Prince Charles Edward evacuated Glasgow, and fixed his headquarters on the following day at the house of Bannockburn, while his troops occupied St. Ninian's, and other villages in the neighborhood of Stirling. The town was summoned, and not being effectually fortified, was surrendered by the magistrates, although there were about six hundred militia within it. Some of these left the place, and others retired to the castle, where there lay a good garrison under General Blakney, a brave and steady officer. Having summoned this fortress, and received a resolute refusal to surrender, the Chevalier resolved to open trenches without delay, and having brought him to this resolution, we will resume the narrative of what had happened in the north of Scotland, and also in England, that you may understand what new actors had now come upon this eventful stage.

The arrival of Lord John Drummond at Montrose, already noticed, with his French forces, gave additional courage to Lord Lewis Gordon, who was levying men and money in Aberdeenshire in behalf of Prince Charles. He was a brave and active young man, brother of the Duke of Gordon, but had in the beginning seemed uncertain which side to take in the civil turmoil. At first he is said to have offered his service to Sir John Cope on his way northward. But Lord Lewis received little encouragement; and affronted, it was supposed, with the neglect shown him by the commander-in-chief, he finally embraced the cause of the Chevalier, and acted for him in Aberdeenshire, where his family interest and the Jacobite propensity of the country gentlemen gave him much influence. Thus strengthened, Lord Lewis was now joined by one part of Lord John Drummond's auxiliaries, while the rest were sent to Perth to unite with Lord Strathallan, who, as we have seen, commanded in that city a considerable Highland reinforcement, destined to follow their countrymen into England had the Prince's command been obeyed.

Lord Loudon, who, on the part of the Government, commanded at Inverness, was desirous to put a stop to the progress of Lord Lewis Gordon. For this purpose he despatched MacLeod, with 450 of his own men, and 200 Monroes, and other volunteers, commanded by Monro of Culcairn. With these he advanced as far as Inverury, about ten miles

---

[1] This unfortunate gentleman, at whose house Prince Charles landed on his first arrival, and who held the office of his aide-de-camp, was after wards executed.

from Aberdeen, to dispute with the Jacobite leader the command of the north of Scotland. On receiving intelligence of their approach, Lord Lewis Gordon got 750 under arms, chiefly Lowland men of Aberdeenshire, under Moir of Stonywood, and Farquharson of Monaltry, with a proportion of the Royal Scots regiment, and hastened against the enemy. MacLeod was nearly surprised, having sent many of his men to billet at a distance from the little town of Inverury. He had, however, time to get those who remained with him under arms, and to take possession of the most defensible parts of the town, when Lord Lewis Gordon marched in at the other end of the place, and a sharp action of musketry commenced. It was remarkable on this occasion that the Islesmen who appeared on the part of Government were all Highlanders in their proper garb; and that the greater part of those who fought for the Stewarts wore the Lowland dress, being the reverse of what was usually the case in the civil war. Lord Lewis Gordon, however, made his attack with much spirit—the firing continued severe on both sides—at length the Aberdeenshire men made a show of rushing to close combat, and the MacLeods gave way and retreated or fled. As the battle was fought at night, the pursuit did not continue far, or cost much bloodshed. The MacLeods fled as far as Forres, having lost about forty of their men.

It was generally believed of that martial clan, that they would have behaved with more steadiness if they had been fighting on the other side.[1] Lord Lewis Gordon, after this success, which he obtained on the 23d of December, marched his men to join the general rendezvous of Charles Edward's reinforcements, which was held at Perth.

There were thus assembled at Perth the Frasers, the MacKenzies, the MacIntoshes, and the Farquharsons, all which clans had joined the cause since the Prince left Edinburgh; there were also the various forces

---

[1] Several of the MacLeods, although they thought their Laird justified in refusing to join Prince Charles, since he came without the stipulated supplies of forces and money, were yet displeased at his yielding to President Forbes's persuasions, and raising his clan on the side of Government. One gentleman, a subordinate chieftain of the clan, who was summoned to arms by MacLeod, sent to his chieftain the twenty men which composed his immediate followers, with a letter to this purpose:—"Dear Sir—I place at your disposal the twenty men of your tribe who are under my immediate command, and in any other quarrel would not fail to be at their head; but in the present I must go where a higher and more imperious duty calls me." Accordingly he joined the camp of Charles Edward. M'Leod of Raasa also took arms for the Prince, with one hundred men. But the MacGilliechallum, as that chief is called, had always asserted his independence of M'Leod of Dunvegan.

raised by Lord Lewis Gordon, together with the regiments of Royal Scots and French piquets, which had come over with Lord John Drummond: their number, taken altogether, might amount to 4000 men and upwards—of whom more than one-half were as good Highlanders as any in the Prince's service. These reinforcements had, you may remember, received an order from Prince Charles by the hand of Colonel MacLauchlan, to follow the army up to England. The Highlanders lying at Perth were unanimously disposed to follow their Prince and countrymen, and to share their fate. Lord Strathallan, on the other hand, supported by the Lowland and French officers, demurred to obeying this order. The parties were considerably irritated against each other on this occasion, and the dispute was not ended until the return of the Prince from England, when an order was transmitted from Dumfries, summoning the body of men in Perth to join the Prince at Stirling.

By this junction the Adventurer's force was augmented to about 9000 men, being the largest number which he ever united under his command. With this, as we have already said, Charles formed the siege of the castle of Stirling. He opened trenches before the fortress on the 10th of January 1746, but was soon interrupted in his operations by the approach of a formidable enemy.

We must now turn our eyes to a different quarter, and give an account of the measures the English Government were taking for putting an end to the present disturbances.

The Duke of Cumberland, whom we left after the skirmish at Clifton, did not, as already stated, renew his attempt upon the rear of the Highland army. But they had no sooner crossed the Esk than he formed the investment of Carlisle, in which the Highlanders had left a garrison of about 300 men. They refused to surrender to the Duke's summons, conceiving, probably, which seems to have been the idea of Charles himself, that the Duke of Cumberland had no battering cannon at his command; there were such, however, at Whitehaven, and he sent to obtain the use of them. They were placed on two batteries, the one commanding the English and the other the Scottish or North gate. The governor of the place, upon a breach being made, although not yet practicable, sent out a white flag, demanding what terms should be allowed to the garrison. They were informed in reply, that if they surrendered at discretion they would not be put to the sword. These were the only conditions, the garrison being understood to be reserved for the King's pleasure. Colonel Townley, the commander of the Manchester Regiment, was here made prisoner, with about twenty of his officers, and one Mr. Cappoch, a clergyman, who was designed by the Prince to be Bishop of Carlisle, Governor Hamilton, with about 100 Scottish men, also surrendered, as did Geohagan and other Irish officers in the French service. The melancholy fate of the gentlemen included in this surrender might have been so easily foreseen, that the Chevalier was severely censured for leaving so many faithful adherents in a situation which necessarily exposed them to fall into the power of the Government which they had offended so seriously. The defence of the measure is, that, conceiving he might be presently recalled to England to aid a descent of the French, he deemed it essential to hold Carlisle as a gate into that country. But to this it may be replied, that, by blowing up the fortifications of Carlisle, and dismantling the castle, he might have kept that entrance at all times open without leaving a garrison in so precarious a situation.

On December the 31st the Duke of Cumberland entered Carlisle on horseback, and presently after received the congratulations of deputies, not only from every place in the neighbourhood, but from Edinburgh itself, to congratulate him upon the advantages which he had obtained over the rebels.

In the meantime, the Duke's pursuit of the Highlanders in person was interrupted by despatches which called him to London, to be ready to take the command against the projected invasion from France. The greater part of the infantry, which had been lately under his command, when his headquarters were at Litchfield, was now marched to the coasts of Kent and Sussex, being the readiest force at hand in case the descent should actually take place. It was at the same time, however, resolved, that such part of the Duke's army (being chiefly cavalry) as had followed him to the neighbourhood of Carlisle, should continue their march northward, and unite themselves with the troops which had long lain at Newcastle under the command of Field-Marshal Wade. This aged officer had not been alert in his movements during the winter campaign, particularly in his march for the relief of Carlisle, and was therefore removed from his command.

General Henry Hawley was in the meantime named by the Duke of Cumberland to the command of the forces destined to follow the Highland army. Hawley was an officer of military experience, but dreaded and disliked by the soldiers as a man of a severe and even savage disposition; and although personally brave, yet of a temper more fitted to obey than to command. This general had been a lieutenant in Evans's dragoons at the battle of Sheriffmuir, and as he fought in the right wing of the Duke of Argyle's army, he had seen the success of the cavalry when engaged with Highlanders. This experience had given him a poor opinion of the latter force, and he had frequently been heard to impute the miscarriage of General Cope to that officer's cowardice and want of conduct, and to affirm that a very different result might be expected from an encounter betwixt Highlanders and dragoons, when the last were properly led on to action.

With these feelings of confidence in himself, and with that experience of the Highland mode of fighting which his campaign in 1715 was supposed to have given him, General Hawley marched into Scotland at the head of a force which, when joined by the troops already at Edinburgh, amounted to 8000 men, two-thirds of whom were veterans. The rest consisted of upwards of a thousand Argyleshire men, commanded by Colonel Campbell (afterwards Duke of Argyle), and of the Glasgow regiment, to the amount of 600 men. There also joined, from Yorkshire, a body of volunteer light horse, called the Yorkshire Hunters, who were in arms for the House of Hanover and the established government.

Hawley, on arriving in Edinburgh, gave a specimen of his disposition, by directing gibbets to be erected, as an indication of the fate of the rebels who should fall into his hands; a preparation designed to strike terror, but which rather inspired aversion and hatred. The time was speedily approaching when such vaunts were to be made good by action. General Hawley, at the head of such a gallant force as he now commanded, conceived himself fully able to march towards Stirling, and attack the rebels, who were engaged in the siege of the castle. Having accordingly directed his forces to move in two divisions, the first marched from Edinburgh on the 13th of January, under the orders of General Huske, Hawley's second in command. This gentleman was of sounder judgment and better temper than his superior officer; he had formerly been quartered in Scotland, and was well known and esteemed by many of the inhabitants.

The Highland army, lying before Stirling, were regularly apprised of the movements of the enemy. Upon the 13th of January Lord George Murray, who lay at Falkirk, obtained intelligence that the people of the neighbouring town of Linlithgow had received orders from Edinburgh to prepare provisions and forage for a body of troops who were instantly to advance in that direction. Lord George, made aware of Hawley's intention, resolved to move with a sufficient force and disappoint these measures, by destroying or carrying off the provisions which should be collected in obedience to the requisition.

The Jacobite general marched to Linlithgow, accordingly, with the three MacDonald regiments, those of Appin and of Cluny, and the horse commanded by Elcho and Pitsligo. Parties of the cavalry were despatched to patrol on the road to Edinburgh for intelligence. About noon, the patrolling party sent back information that they perceived a small body of dragoons, being the advance of General Huske's division, which, as I have stated, marched from Edinburgh that morning. Lord George sent orders to the patrol to drive the dragoons who had shown themselves back upon the main body, if they had one, and not retire until they saw themselves in danger of being overpowered. In the meantime he drew up the infantry in line of battle in front of the town of Linlithgow. Lord Elcho, according to his orders, drove back the advanced party of horse upon a detachment of sixty dragoons, and then forced the whole to retire upon a village in which there were masses both of horse and foot. Having thus reconnoitred close up to the main body of the enemy, Lord Elcho sent to acquaint Lord George Murray what force he had in his front, so far as he could discern, and received orders to retreat, leaving a small corps of observation. It was not Lord George's purpose to engage an enemy whose strength, obviously considerable, was unknown to him; he therefore determined to remain in Linlithgow until the enemy arrived very near the town, and then to make his retreat in good order. This object he accomplished accordingly; and, on his repassing the bridge, there was so little distance betwixt the advanced guard of General Huske's division and the rearguard of Lord George Murray's, that abusive language was exchanged between them, though without any actual violence. Lord George continued his retreat to Falkirk, where he halted for that night. On the next day he again retreated to the villages in the vicinity of Bannockburn, where he learned that General Huske, with half the Government army, had arrived at Falkirk, and that General Hawley had also arrived there on the 16th, with the second division; that besides his regular troops he was joined by 1000 Highlanders, followers of the Argyle family, and that they seemed determined upon battle.

Upon the 15th and 16th of January the Chevalier, leaving 1,000 or 1,200 men under Gordon of Glenbucket to protect the trenches and continue the blockade of Stirling Castle, drew up his men in a plain about a mile to the east of Bannockburn, expecting an attack. His horse reconnoitred close to the enemy's camp, but saw no appearance of advance. On the 17th the same manoeuvre was repeated, the Highland army being drawn up on the same open ground near Bannockburn, while that of the Government remained in Falkirk totally inactive.

The cause of this inactivity is stated to have been the contempt which General Hawley entertained for the enemy, and his unhesitating belief that, far from venturing on any offensive movement, the insurgents were upon the point of dispersing themselves from the dread of his approach. It is moreover said that General Hawley, having felt the influence of the wit and gaiety of the Countess of Kilmarnock (whose husband was in the Prince's army), had been unable to resist her ladyship's invitation to Callander House, and that he had resided there from the time of his arrival in Falkirk on the 16th until the afternoon of the 17th of January, old style, with less attention to the army which he commanded than became an old soldier. In the meantime rougher cheer was preparing for him than he probably experienced at Callander.

The Highlanders, holding a council of war on the field where they rendezvoused, had determined since the English General did not move forward to fight them that they would save him the trouble by an immediate advance on their side. There were only about seven miles between the two armies; and General Hawley, with a carelessness very unbecoming a veteran officer, appears to have sent out no patrols from his camp. This gave the insurgents an opportunity of trying a stratagem, which proved eminently successful. It was determined that Lord John Drummond, with his own regiment, the Irish piquets, and all the cavalry of the rebel army, should advance upon the direct road leading from Stirling and Bannockburn towards Falkirk. They were also to carry with them the royal standard and other colours, of which they were to make a display in front of the decayed forest called the Torwood. This march and position of Lord John Drummond was, however, only designed as a feint, to persuade the King's army that the whole rebel force was advancing in that quarter.

Meanwhile, Lord George Murray, making a circuit by the south side of the Torwood, had crossed the river Carron near Dunipace, and was advancing to the southward of the high ground called Falkirk Moor, then an open and unenclosed common, swelling into a considerable ridge or eminence which lay on the westward, and to the left of the royal camp. General Huske, who as we have said was second in command, was first aware of the approach of the enemy. About eleven o'clock Lord John Drummond's division was visible from the camp, and, as had been designed, attracted exclusive attention, till about two hours later, when General Huske, by information, and by the aid of spy-glasses, descried the approach of Lord George Murray's division, from which the real attack was to be apprehended.

But though Huske saw the danger, General Hawley, whose task it peculiarly was to apply the remedy, was still at Callander House. In this dilemma the second in command formed the line of battle in front of the camp, but in the absence of his superior officer he had it not in his power to direct any movement either towards the division of Highlanders which kept the road, under Lord John Drummond, or against that which was ascending the heights to the left, under the command of Lord George Murray. The regiments remained on their ground in wonder, impatience, and anxiety, waiting for orders, and receiving none.

Hawley, however, at length caught the alarm. He suddenly appeared in front of the camp, and ordering the whole line to advance, placed himself at the head of three regiments of dragoons, drew his sword, and led them at a rapid pace up the hill called Falkirk Moor, trusting by a rapid movement to anticipate the Highlanders, who were pressing on towards the same point from the opposite side of the eminence.

In the meantime that part of the Highland army which was designed to possess themselves of the heights, marched on in three divisions, keeping along the moor in such a manner that first the thickets of the Torwood, and afterwards the acclivity of the ground, hid them in some measure from Hawley's camp. In this movement they kept their columns parallel to the ridge and when they had proceeded as far in this direction as was necessary to gain room for their formation, each column wheeled up and formed in line of battle, in which they proceeded to ascend the eminence.

The first line consisted of the clans,—the MacDonalds having the right and the Camerons the left; in the second line, the Athole brigade had the right, Lord Lewis Gordon's Aberdeenshiremen the left, and Lord Ogilvie's regiment the centre; the third line, or reserve, was weak in numbers, chiefly consisting of cavalry, and the Irish piquets. It may be remarked that Lord John Drummond, who made the feint, remained with his troops on the highroad until the whole of the other division had passed the Carron, and then fell into the rear, and joined the cavalry who were with the Prince, thus reinforcing the third line of the army.

When Hawley set off with his three regiments of dragoons, the infantry of the King's army followed in line of battle, having six battalions in the first line, and the same number in the second. Howard's regiment marched in the rear, and formed a small body of reserve.

At the moment that the Highlanders were pressing up Falkirk Moor on the one side, the dragoons, who had advanced briskly, had gained the eminence, and displayed a line of horse occupying about as much ground as one-half of the first line of the Chevalier's army. The Highlanders, however, were in high spirits, and their natural ardour was still further increased at the sight of the enemy. They kept their ranks, and advanced at a prodigious rate towards the ridge occupied by Hawley's three regiments. The dragoons, having in vain endeavoured to stop this movement of the clans towards them by one or two feints, resolved at length to make a serious attack, while they still retained the advantage of the higher ground. Their first movement was to take the enemy in flank, but the MacDonalds, who were upon the right of the whole Highland line, inclined to a morass, which effectually disconcerted that scheme; the dragoons then came on in front at a full trot, with their sabres drawn, to charge the Highlanders, who were still advancing. The clans, seeing the menaced charge, reserved their fire as resolutely as could have been done by the steadiest troops in Europe, until Lord George Murray, who was in front, and in the centre of the line, presented his own fusee within about ten yards of the cavalry. On this signal they gave a general discharge, so close, and so well levelled, that the dragoons were completely broken. Some few made their way through the first line of the Highlanders, but were for the most part slain by those in the second line. About 400 fell, either man or horse being killed or wounded. The greater part went to the right in complete disorder, and fled along the front of the Highland line, who poured a destructive fire on them by which many fell.

This defeat of the cavalry began the battle bravely on the part of the insurgents, but they had nearly paid dear for their success. At the instant when the attack commenced a violent storm of wind and rain came on, which blew straight in the faces of the King's troops, and greatly disconcerted them. Lord George Murray called to the MacDonalds to stand fast, and not to regard the flying horsemen, but keep their ranks, and reload. It was in vain. The Highlanders, in their usual manner, rushed on sword in hand, and dropt their muskets. Their left wing, at the same moment, fell furiously sword in hand upon the right and centre of Hawley's foot, broke them, and put them to flight; but the lines of the contending armies not being exactly parallel, the extreme right of Hawley's first line stretched considerably beyond the left of the Highlanders. Three regiments, Price's, Ligonier's, and Burrell's, on the extreme flank, stood fast, with the greater advantage that they had a ravine in front, which prevented the Highlanders from attacking them sword in hand, according to their favourite mode of fighting. These corps gallantly maintained this natural fortification, and by repeated and steady firing repulsed the Highlanders from the opposite side of the ravine. One of the three routed regiments of dragoons, called Cobham's, rallied in the rear of this body of infantry who stood firm; the other two, being the same which had been at Prestonpans, did not behave better, and could not well behave worse, than they had done on that memorable occasion.

The battle was now in a singular state; "Both armies," says Mr. Home, "were in flight at the same time." Hawley's cavalry, and most of his infantry, excepting those on his extreme right, had been completely thrown into confusion and routed, but the three regiments which continued fighting had a decided advantage over the Prince's left, and many Highlanders fled under the impression that the day was lost.

The advantage, upon the whole, was undeniably with Charles Edward; but from the want of discipline among the troops he commanded, and the extreme severity of the tempest, it became difficult even to learn the extent of the victory, and impossible to follow it up. The Highlanders were in great disorder. Almost all the second line were mixed and in confusion,—the victorious right had no idea, from the darkness of the weather, what had befallen the left—nor were there any mounted generals or aides-de-camp, who might have discovered with certainty what was the position of affairs. In the meantime the English regiments which had been routed fled down the hill in great confusion, both cavalry and infantry, towards the camp and town of Falkirk. General Huske brought up the rear of a very disorderly retreat, or flight, with the regiments who had behaved so well on the right; this he effected in good order, with drums beating and colours flying. Cobham's dragoons, such at least who had rallied, also retreated in tolerable order. General Hawley felt no inclination to remain in the camp which he had taken possession of with such an affectation of anticipated triumph. He caused the tents to be set on fire, and withdrew his confused and dismayed followers to Linlithgow,[1] and from thence the next day retreated to Edinburgh, with his forces in a pitiable state of disarray and perturbation. The Glasgow regiment of volunteers fell into the power of the rebels upon this occasion, and were treated with considerable rigour; for the Highlanders were observed to be uniformly disposed to severity against those voluntary opponents who, in their opinion, were not, like the regular soldiers, called upon by duty to take part in the contention.[2]

Many valuable lives were lost in this battle; about twenty officers and four or five hundred privates were slain, on the part of General Hawley; and several prisoners were made, of whom the greater part were sent to Doune Castle.[3]

---

[1] On the night of the 17th, Hawley's disordered troops were quartered in the palace of Linlithgow, and began to make such great fires on the hearths as to endanger the safety of the edifice. A lady of the Livingston family, who had apartments there, remonstrated with General Hawley, who treated her fears with contempt. "I can run away from fire as fast as you can, General," answered the high-spirited dame, and with this sarcasm took horse for Edinburgh. Very soon after her departure her apprehensions were realised; the palace of Linlithgow caught fire, and was burned to the ground. The ruins alone remain to show its former splendour.

[2] Home, in his own History, is silent on the behaviour of the Glasgow regiment, but not so a metrical chronicler, who wrote a history of the insurrection, in doggrel verse indeed, but sufficiently accurate. This author, who is, indeed, no other than Dugald Grahame, bellman of Glasgow, says that the Highlanders, having beaten the horse—

> "The south side being fairly won,
> They faced north, as had been done;
> Where, next stood, to bide the crush,
> The volunteers, who zealous,
> Kept firing close, till near surrounded
> And by the flying horse confounded:
> They suffered sair into this place,
> No Highlander pitied their case:
> 'You cursed militia,' they did swear,
> What a devil did bring you here?'"
>
> *History of the Rebellion in 1745–1746.*

[3] "This noble ruin holds a commanding station on the banks of the river Teith, and has been one of the largest castles in Scotland. Murdock, Duke of Albany, the founder of this stately pile, was beheaded on the Castle-hill of Stirling, from which he might see

The loss of the rebels was not considerable; and they had only one made prisoner, but in a manner rather remarkable. A Highland officer, a brother of MacDonald of Keppoch, had seized upon a trooper's horse and mounted him, without accurately considering his own incapacity to manage the animal. When the horse heard the kettle-drums beat to rally the dragoons, the instinct of discipline prevailed, and in spite of the efforts of his rider he galloped with all speed to his own regiment. The Highlander, finding himself in this predicament, endeavoured to pass himself for an officer of the Campbell regiment, but being detected was secured; and although the ludicrous manner in which he was taken might have pleaded for some compassion, he was, afterwards executed as a traitor.

The defeat at Falkirk struck consternation and terror into all parts of Britain. The rebellion had been regarded as ended when the Highlanders left England, and Hawley's own assertion had prepared all the nation to expect tidings very different from those which were to be gathered from the disastrous appearance of his army, and the humiliating confession of his own looks and demeanour.

There were more visages rendered blank and dismayed by the unexpected event of the battle of Falkirk than that of the unfortunate general.

---

the towers of Doune, the monument of his fallen greatness. In 1745–6, a garrison on the part of the Chevalier was put into the castle, then less ruinous than at present. It was commanded by Mr. Stewart of Balloch, as governor for Prince Charles; he was a man of property near Callander. This castle became at that time the actual scene of a romantic escape made by John Home, the author of *Douglas*, and some other prisoners, who, having been taken at the battle of Falkirk, were confined there by the insurgents. The poet, who had in his own mind a large stock of that romantic and enthusiastic spirit of adventure which he has described as animating the youthful hero of his drama, devised and undertook the perilous enterprise of escaping from his prison. He inspired his companions with his sentiments, and when every attempt at open force was deemed hopeless, they resolved to twist their bedclothes into ropes, and thus to descend. Four persons, with Home himself, reached the ground in safety. But the rope broke with the fifth, who was a tall lusty man. The sixth was Thomas Barrow, a brave young Englishman, a particular friend of Home's. Determined to take the risk, even in such unfavourable circumstances, Barrow committed himself to the broken rope, slid down on it as far as it could assist him, and then let himself drop. His friends beneath succeeded in breaking his fall. Nevertheless, he dislocated his ankle, and had several of his ribs broken. His companions, however, were able to bear him off in safety. The Highlanders next morning sought for their prisoners with great activity. An old gentleman told the author, he remembered seeing the commander Stewart,

'Bloody with spurring, fiery red with haste.

riding furiously through the country in quest of the fugitives."—*Note to Waverley*.

Throughout the whole civil war, those of the better ranks in England had shown themselves more easily exalted and depressed than consisted with their usual reputation for steadiness. In the march upon Derby, they might have been said to be more afraid than the nature of the danger warranted, were it not that the peril chiefly consisted in the very stupor which it inspired. After the retreat had commenced, the hopes and spirit of the nation rose again to springtide, as if nothing further were to be apprehended from a band of men so desperately brave, who had already done so much with such little means. The news of the defeat at Falkirk, therefore, were received with general alarm; and at court, during a levee held immediately after the battle, only two persons appeared with countenances unmarked by signs of perturbation. These were, George the Second himself, who, whatever may have been his other foibles, had too much of the lion about him to be afraid; and Sir John Cope, who was radiant with joy at the idea that Hawley's misfortune or misconduct was likely to efface his own from the public recollection.[1]

No person was now thought of sufficient consequence to be placed at the head of the army but the Duke of Cumberland, who was, therefore, appointed to the chief command. His Royal Highness set off

---

[1] Hawley had not a better head, and certainly a much worse heart than Sir John Cope, who was a humane, good-tempered man. The new general ridiculed severely the conduct of his predecessor, and remembering that he had seen, in 1715, the left wing of the Highlanders broken by a charge of the Duke of Argyle's horse, which came upon them across a morass, he resolved to manoevre in the same manner. He forgot, however, a material circumstance—that the morass at Sheriffmuir was hard frozen, which made some difference in favour of the cavalry. Hawley's manoevre, as commanded and executed, plunged a great part of his dragoons up to the saddle laps in a bog, where the Highlanders cut them to pieces with so little trouble that, as one of the performers assured us, the feat was as easy as slicing *bacon*. The gallantry of some of the English regiments beat off the Highland charge on another point, and, amid a tempest of wind and rain which has been seldom equalled, the field presented the singular prospect of two armies flying different ways at the same moment. The King's troops, however, ran fastest and farthest, and were the last to recover their courage; indeed, they retreated that night to Falkirk, leaving their guns, burning their tents, and striking a new panic into the British nation, which was but just recovering from the flutter excited by what, in olden times, would have been called the Raid of Derby. In the drawing-rooms which took place at St. James's on the day the news arrived, all countenances were marked with doubt and apprehension, excepting those of George the Second, the Earl of Stair, and Sir John Cope, who was radiant with joy at Hawley's discomfiture. Indeed, the idea of the two generals was so closely connected, that a noble peer of Scotland, upon the same day, addressed Sir John Cope by the title of General Hawley, to the no small amusement of those who heard the *qui pro quo.*

from St. James's on the 25th of January 1746, attended by Lord Cathcart, Lord Bury, Colonel Conway, and Colonel York, his aides-de-
camp. His arrival at Holyrood House restored the drooping spirits of
the members of the Government. To the army, also, the arrival of the
commander-in-chief was very acceptable, not only from a reliance on
his talents, but as his presence put a stop to a course of cruel punishments instituted by General Hawley, who had invoked the assistance
of the gibbet and the scourage to rectify a disaster which had its principal source, perhaps, in how own want of military skill. The Duke's
timely arrival at Edinburgh saved the lives of two dragoons who were
under sentence of death, and rescued others who were destined to
inferior punishments, many of which had already taken place.

The army which the Duke commanded consisted of twelve
squadrons of horse and fourteen battalions of infantry; but several of
them had suffered much in the late action, and the whole were far from
being complete. Every effort had, however, been made, to repair the
losses which had taken place on Falkirk moor; and it may be said the
Duke of Cumberland was at the head of as gallant and well-furnished
an army as ever took the field. Hawley, who was a personal favourite
with the King, continued to act lieutenant-general under the Duke; and
Lord Albemarle held the same situation. The major-generals were
Bland, Huske, Lord Semple, and Brigadier Mordaunt.

In a council of war held at Edinburgh, it was resolved that the troops
should march the next morning towards Stirling, in order to raise the
siege of the castle, and give battle to the rebels, if they should dare to
accept of it under better auspices than that of Falkirk. Great pains had
been taken, in previous general orders, to explain to the common soldiers the mode in which the Highlanders fought,—a passage so curious,
that I shall extract it from the orderly book for your amusement. Perhaps
the most comfortable part of the instructions might be the assurance,
that there were but few *true* Highlanders in the Prince's army.[1]

---

1 "*Edinburgh, 12th January 1745–6, Sunday.*

        "Parole 1.—Derby

        "Field-officer for the day, to-morrow, Major Wilson. The manner of the
Highlanders' way of fighting, which there is nothing so easy to resist, if officers and
men are not prepossessed with the lyes and accounts which are told of them. They
commonly form their front rank of what they call their best men, or True Highlanders,
the number of which being always but few; when they form in battalions, they
commonly form four deep, and these Highlanders form the front of the four, the rest

being Lowlanders and arrant scum. When these battalions come within a large musket shott, or three score yards, this front rank gives their fire, and immediately throw down their firelocks, and come down in a cluster, with their swords and targets, making a noise, and endeavouring to pearce the body or battalion, before them, becoming 12 or 14 deep by the time they come up to the people they attack. The sure way to demolish them is at three deep to fire by ranks diagonally to the centre where they come, the rear rank first, and even that rank not to fire till they are within 10 or 12 paces; but if the fire is given at a distance, you probably will be broke, for you never get time to load a second cartridge; and if you give way, you may give yourselves for dead, for they,[1] being without a firelock or any load, no man with his arms, accoutrements, etc., can escape them, and they give no quarters; but if you will but observe the above directions, they are the most despicable enemy that are."

[1] The Highlanders.

LXXXII

Into the Highlands

1746

THE insurgents did not reap such advantages from the battle of Falkirk as might have been expected. The extreme confusion of their own forces, and their consequent ignorance respecting the condition of the enemy, prevented their pursuing Hawley's army, which might, in all probability, have been an easy prey. Had they done so, they might on the spur of the moment have again obtained possession of the capital, with all the eclât attendant on such success.

But the Chevalier, who had kept his word in convoking no councils since the retreat from Derby, saving that held on the field of battle, acted only by the advice of his secretary Mr. Murray, his quartermaster John Hay, Sir Thomas Sheridan, and the Irish officers, who were suspected of being less ready to give unbiassed advice to the young Prince than willing to echo back his own opinions. On this occasion he conceived that raising the siege of Stirling would be a disgrace to his arms, and resolved, therefore, to proceed with it at all events. This proved an unlucky determination.

M. Mirabelle de Gordon, the French engineer who conducted the siege, was imperfectly acquainted with his profession. He constructed a battery upon the Gowan Hill; but opening it when only three guns were mounted, they were speedily silenced by the superior fire of the castle. Some skirmishing took place at the same time between the English armed vessels, which endeavoured to force their way up the Forth, and the batteries which were established on the sides of the river; but these events were of little consequence. The progress of the siege seemed protracted, and was liable to interruption by the advance of the Duke of Cumberland and his army.

On the other hand, the Highland army had suffered great diminution since the battle of Falkirk, less from loss in the action than from the effects of the victory, which, as usual, occasioned a great desertion among the privates of the clans, who, according to their invariable practice, went home to store up their plunder. An accident also, which happened the day after the battle of Falkirk, cost the Chevalier the loss of a clan regiment of no small distinction. A private soldier, one of Clanranald's followers, was tampering with a loaded musket, when the piece went off, and by mishap killed a younger son of Glengarry, major of that chief's regiment. To prevent a quarrel between two powerful tribes, the unlucky fellow who had caused the mischief was condemned to death, though innocent of all intentional guilt, and was shot accordingly. This sacrifice did not, however, propitiate the tribe of Glengarry; they became disgusted with the service on the loss of their major, and most of them returned to their mountains without obtaining any leave, a desertion severely felt at this critical moment.

The chiefs of clans, and men of quality in the army, observing the diminution of their numbers, and disgusted at not being consulted upon the motions of the army, held a council by their own authority in the town of Falkirk, and drew up a paper addressed to the Prince, which was signed by them all, advising a retreat to the north. The purport of this document expressed that so many of their men had gone home since the last battle that they were in no condition to prosecute the siege of Stirling, or to repel the army of the Duke of Cumberland, which was advancing to raise it. They concluded by advising the Prince to retreat with his army to Inverness, there to annihilate the forces of Lord Loudon, with his other enemies in that country, and to take or demolish the Highland forts, thus making himself complete master of the north. This being effected, they assured him they would be ready to take the field next spring, with eight or ten thousand Highlanders, to follow him wherever he pleased.

This advice, which had, in the circumstances in which it was given, the effect of a command, came upon Charles like a clap of thunder. He had concluded that a battle was to be fought; and the sick and wounded, with the followers of the camp, had been sent to Dunblane with that view. Lord George Murray had also been at headquarters, and showed to Charles a plan which he had drawn of the proposed battle, which the Prince had approved of, and corrected with his own hand. When, therefore, this proposition for a retreat was presented to him, he was at first struck with a feeling of despair, exclaiming, "Good God! have I lived to see this?" He dashed his head with such violence against the wall, that he staggered, and then sent Sir Thomas Sheridan to Falkirk, to reason against the resolution which the chiefs had adopted. But it was found unalterable, and their number and importance were too great for Charles to contend with.[1]

The Prince, after yielding to the measure of retreating, concerted with Lord George Murray that on the 1st of February all the army should be ordered to cross the Forth at the fords of Frew very early in the morning; that the heavy cannon should be spiked; that the ammunition which could not be carried along with the army should be destroyed; and, finally, that a strong rearguard, composed of 1200 picked Highlanders, and Lord Elcho's body of horse, should protect the retreat of the army.

None of these precautions were, however, resorted to; and the retreat, attended with every species of haste and disorder resembled a flight so much, that there was nowhere one thousand men together. The army passed the river in small bodies, and in great confusion, leaving carts and cannon upon the road behind them. There was no rearguard, and Lord Elcho's troop, which had been commanded to wait at the bridge of Carron till further orders, was totally forgotten, and had nearly been intercepted by a body of troops from the town and castle of Stirling, ere they received orders to retreat. This confusion was supposed to have arisen from the recklessness with which the Prince altered the order of retreat, after it had been adjusted betwixt himself and Lord George Murray; a recklessness which seemed to show that he

---

[1] The address recommending the retreat was signed by Lord George Murray, Lochiel, Keppoch, Clanranald, Ardshiel, Lochgarry, Scothouse, and the Master of Lovat, all persons of importance and of considerable following, and unquestionably faithful to his cause.

was so much vexed at the measure, as to be indifferent with what degree of order or confusion it was carried into execution.

Accident added to the damage which attended this hasty movement. In destroying their magazine at St. Ninians, the Highlanders managed so awkwardly as to blow up at the same time the church itself, by which several lives were lost. This was represented, by the malice of party spirit, as having been an intentional act on the part of the Prince's army; a thing scarcely to be supposed, since some of themselves, and particularly the man who fired the train, were killed by the explosion.

The retreat from Stirling was, nevertheless, conducted without much loss, except from temporary dispersion. The march of the Highland army was by Dunblane and Crieff. On the 3d of February a council of war was held at a place called Fairnton, near the latter town. Here the argument concerning the necessity of the retreat from Stirling was renewed, and those officers who were hostile to Lord George Murray took care to throw on him the blame of a measure which, however necessary, was most unpalatable to the Prince, and had been in a great degree forced upon him. It was now said that the desertion was not half so great as apprehended, and did not exceed a thousand men, and that the Prince need not, on account of such a deficiency, have been forced into a measure resembling flight, which, in a contest where so much depended on opinion, must, it was said, lower his character both with friends and foes. But the resolution had been finally adopted, and it was now necessary to follow it out.

At Crieff the army of Charles separated. One division, chiefly consisting of west Highlanders, marched northward by the Highland road. Another, under Lord George Murray, took the coast road, by Montrose and Aberdeen, to Inverness. It consisted chiefly of the Lowland regiments and cavalry, the latter of whom suffered much, having lost many of their horses by forced marches at that inclement season of the year. The troopers being chiefly gentlemen, continued to adhere with fidelity to their ill-omened standards. A small part of the army, belonging to that part of the Highlands, went by Braemar.

The Duke of Cumberland followed the Highlanders as far as Perth, and found that, moving with rapidity and precision amid their disorder, they had accomplished their purpose of retreating to the Highlands, and carrying off their garrisons from Montrose and elsewhere. The presence of Charles in Inverness-shire, was likely to be attended with advantages which might protract the war. It is a mountainous province, giving access to those more western Highlands of which the Jacobite clans were chiefly inhabitants, and itself containing several tribes devoted to his cause. It was also thought the Prince would obtain recruits both in Caithness and Sutherland.

The Chevalier's only enemy in the north was the small army which Lord Loudon had raised by means of the Grants, Monroes, Rosses, and other northern clans, with whom had been united the MacDonalds of Skye and the MacLeods. Their number, however, was not such as to prevent the Prince's troops from spreading through the country; and, to indulge the humour of the Highlanders, as well as for their more easy subsistence, they were suffered to stroll up and down at pleasure, Prince Charles retaining only a few hundreds about his person. He appeared, indeed, to be everywhere master in the open country; and the little army of Lord Loudon, amounting at the utmost to 2000 men, remained cooped up in Inverness, which they had in some degree fortified with a ditch and palisade. In these circumstances, Charles found it easy to attack and take the barracks at Ruthven of Badenoch, which had resisted him on his descent from the Highlands; and after this success, he went to reside for two or three days at the castle of Moy, the chief seat of the Laird of MacIntosh, a distinction which was well deserved by the zealous attachment of the Lady MacIntosh to his cause. The husband of this lady Æneas or Angus MacIntosh of that Ilk, appears to have had no steady political attachments of his own; for at one time he seems to have nourished the purpose of raising his clan in behalf of the Chevalier,[1] notwithstanding which, he continued to hold a commission in Lord Loudon's army. Not so his lady, who, observing the indecision, perhaps we ought to say the imbecility, of her husband, gave vent to her own Jacobite feelings, and those of the clan of MacIntosh, by levying the fighting men of that ancient tribe, to the amount of

---

[1] There is in ancient dispute between the families of MacIntosh and MacPherson, concerning the leading of the confederated tribes forming the Clan Chattan. The Chevalier, it would seem, had assigned the right of leading the whole tribe to Cluny, who was his own adherent. In the subsequent letter, it will be seen that MacIntosh having, for the moment resolved to join the Prince, was desirous to assert his claim to the patriarchal following:—

"D^r· S^R·—As I am now fully determined to command my own people and run the same fate with them, having yesterday rece^d a letter from the Prince, and another from the Duke of Atholl, I hope, notwithstanding of the order you obtained from the Prince, you will not offer to middle with any of my men, as we are booth designed on the same

three hundred men, at whose head she rode, with a man's bonnet on her head, a tartan riding-habit richly laced, and pistols at her saddle bow. MacGillivray of Drumnaglass commanded this body in the field as colonel. The spirit excited by this gallant Amazon called at least for every civility which could be shown her by the Prince, and that of a visit at her castle was considered as the most flattering.

Charles Edward was living there in perfect security, and had not more than three hundred men about his person, when Lord Loudon made a bold attempt to end the civil war by making the Adventurer prisoner. For this purpose be proposed to employ chiefly the Highlanders of MacLeod's clan, as, well qualified to execute a swift and secret enterprise. They were accompanied by several volunteers. It is said that Lady MacIntosh had private intelligence of this intention; at any rate, she had employed the blacksmith of the clan, a person always of some importance in a Highland tribe, with a few followers, to patrol betwixt Inverness and Moy Castle. On the night of the 16th of February this able and intelligent partisan fell in with the vanguard of the MacLeods, bending their course in secrecy and silence towards Moy. The party thus advancing consisted of one thousand five hundred men. The smith and his followers, not above six or seven in all, divided into different parts of the wood, and fired upon the advancing columns, who could not discover the numbers by which they were opposed. The MacIntoshes, at the same time, cried the war-cries of Lochiel, Keppoch, and other well-known sounds of the most distinguished clans; and two or three bagpipers played most furiously the gathering tunes of the same tribes.

Those who are engaged in an attempt to surprise others are generally themselves most accessible to surprise. The sudden attack astonished the MacLeods, who conceived that they had fallen into an ambush consisting of the Chevalier's whole army. The consequence

---

errand. I am resolved to maintain the rank due to my family, and if you think proper to accept the nixt rank to me, youl be very wellcome. If you judge otherwise, act as you have a mind. But do not put me to the necessity of requiring my men of you in a more publick maner, the consequence of which may be disagreeable to booth. My kinde complements to Lady Cluny and Miss Fraser, and I am, D^r· S^{R,} your most humble servt and affectionat cousine,

(Signed) "Æneas MacIntosh.

"Inverness, 1st October."

Directed on the back,

"To Evan MacPherson, Younger of Cluny, Esq."

was, that they turned their backs, and fled back to Inverness in extreme confusion, incurring much danger and some loss, not from the fire of the enemy, but from throwing down and treading upon each other. The confusion was so great that the Master of Ross, a gallant officer, who was afterwards in many perils, informed Mr. Home that he had never been in a condition so grievous as what was called the *Rout of Moy.*

Some accounts state that the Prince was never disturbed from sleep during all the confusion attending this attack, which, but for the presence of mind of the lady, so admirably seconded by her retainer, might have put an end to his enterprise and to his life. It is at any rate certain, that early on the following day Charles assembled his army, or such part of it as could be immediately got together, and advanced upon Inverness with the purpose of repaying to Lord Loudon the unfriendly visit of the preceding night. Neither the strength of the place, nor the number of Lord Loudon's forces, entitled him to make any stand against an army so superior to his own. He was therefore compelled to retreat by the Kessoch ferry; and having carried the boats with him, he prevented for a time the pursuit of the rebels. But Lord Cromarty, having marched round the head of the ferry, dislodged Lord Loudon from the town of Cromarty, afterwards pursued him to Tain, and compelled him finally to cross the Great Ferry into Sutherland.

The Highland army took possession of Inverness on the 18th February, and on the 20th the citadel, called Fort George, was also yielded to them. By these movements it was proposed to follow up the plan of tactics recommended in the Address of the chiefs at Falkirk—that on retiring to the north they should employ the winter season in destroying Lord Loudon's power and reducing the forts held in the Highlands. With the latter purpose, the siege of Fort Augustus was formed by Lord John Drummond's regiment and the French piquets. The battering cannon proving too small for the purpose, conorns were employed to throw shells, by means of which the garrison, being only three companies, was compelled to surrender. It was determined by the Prince to send the officers to France, to remain as hostages for such of his own followers as had already fallen into the hands of the Government, or might have that fate in future. We have seen that such a scheme had been proposed after the battle of Prestonpans, and was refused by the Prince from motives of generosity; and that the prisoners were dismissed into Angusshire upon their parole of honour. At the time of

General Hawley's movement upon Stirling, some risings had taken place in support of Government in the county of Angus, of which the, prisoners of war had availed themselves, under the idea that they were thus liberated from their parole. The Highlanders were of a different opinion, and expressed their sentiments in a singular manner after the battle of Falkirk. General Hawley had, previous to that action, been pleased to foresee occasion for an extraordinary number of execution-ers in his camp. As some of these functionaries became prisoners to the insurgent army after the battle, they endeavoured to express their scorn of the behaviour of the regular officers who had, as they alleged, eluded their parole, by liberating these hangmen on their word of honour, as if equally worthy of trust with those who bore King George's commis-sion. The scheme of sending the captive officers to France might have operated as some check on the Government's judicial proceedings after the close of the rebellion, had it been adopted in the early part of the insurrection. As it was, the current of the insurgents' success had begun to turn, and there was no further prospect of succeeding by this method, which was adopted too late to be of service.

While the Highlanders were pushing their petty and unimportant advantages against the forts in the north, the Duke of Cumberland, advancing on their rear, and occupying successively the districts which they abandoned, was already bringing up important succours, by which he hoped to narrow their quarters, and, finally, to destroy their army. Following the track of the Highlanders, he had arrived at Perth on the 6th of February, and detached Sir Andrew Agnew, with 500 men, and 100 of the Campbells, to take possession of the castle of Blair-in-Atholl, while Lieutenant-Colonel Leighton, with a similar force, occupied Castle Menzies. These garrisons were designed to straiten the Highland army, and to prevent their drawing reinforce-ments from the countries in which their cause had most favour.

About the same time the Duke of Cumberland learned that a body of auxiliaries, consisting of 6000 Hessians, had disembarked at Leith, under the command of Prince Frederick of Hesse-Cassel. These troops had been sent for, because a dilemma had occurred which occasioned the withdrawing of the 6000 Dutch troops originally destined to assist the King of England. So soon as Lord John Drummond had arrived with the French auxiliaries a message had been despatched to the Dutch commandant, formally acquainting him that the colours of France were displayed in the Chevalier's camp, and that, troops upon their parole not to serve against that country, the Dutch were cited to withdraw themselves from the civil war of Britain. They recognised the summons, and withdrew their forces from Britain accordingly.

In order to replace these auxiliaries, the King of Great Britain concluded a subsidiary treaty with the Prince of Hesse-Cassel, which was confirmed in Parliament, and it was in consequence of this engagement that the Hessian troops had now arrived at Leith. The Duke of Cumberland made a hasty visit to Edinburgh, where he held a council with the Prince of Hesse and the principal officers. A general opinion was entertained and expressed, that the Highlanders would break up and disperse, and never venture a battle against the Duke of Cumberland and his army. Lord Milton, a Scottish judge, being asked to deliver his sentiments, was of a different opinion. He declared himself persuaded that the Highlanders would, according to their ready habits, again unite in a large body and make another struggle for the accomplishment of their enterprise.

This opinion of Lord Milton made a deep impression upon the Duke of Cumberland's mind, who resolved to proceed upon the probability that a battle would be necessary, and to move northwards slowly, but with an overpowering force. For this purpose he returned to Perth, and sending three regiments of infantry to Dundee, proceeded with the main body of his army to the north, and reached Aberdeen on the 27th of February. The Hessian troops, with their Prince, arrived at Perth after the Duke of Cumberland's departure. Their mustaches and blue dress occasioned some surprise to the Scottish people, who were greatly edified, however, by their quiet and civil behaviour, which formed a strong contrast to the profligate language and demeanour of the English soldiery. The country between Perth and Aberdeen, including Blair-in-Athole, and some posts still further north, were occupied by parties, both of the Campbells and of the regular troops. The Duke of Cumberland's headquarters were at Aberdeen, where it was generally believed by the rebels he intended to remain till summer.

In the meantime, the clans resolved to complete the subjection of the chain of forts, of which Fort William still remained in possession of the King's troops. General Campbell had taken care that it should be provided with everything necessary for a siege, and had reinforced the garrison with some companies of his own followers, so that it amounted to about six hundred men, under a commandant named

Campbell. Lochiel and Keppoch formed the blockade, but could not cut off the garrison's communications by sea, as two sloops of war supported them with their guns. General Stapleton soon after came up with the French piquets, and formed a regular battery against the fort; but, as we shall hereafter see, to little purpose.

About this time Charles heard news of the succours from France, which he had expected so anxiously. On the 23d of February he received a letter from Captain Shee of Fitz-James's dragoons, acquainting him that he made part of an armament commanded by the Marquis de Fimarion; that he had landed with a part of the above regiment; that the rest of the squadron conveyed about eight hundred men, and that each of the ships brought a certain sum of money.

In confirmation of this news, the Prince was informed that one of the squadron announced by Captain Shee, having appeared off Peterhead, had landed two thousand louis-d'or for his service, but had declined to land the soldiers who were on board, without an order from the Marquis D'Eguilles, called the ambassador of France. Prince Charles despatched Lord John Drummond and the Marquis D'Eguilles, with a strong body of troops to superintend the landing of this important reinforcement; but they came too late. The Duke of Cumberland, moving with all his forces, had arrived at Aberdeen on the 27th; and Moir of Stonywood, who commanded there for the Prince, was compelled to retreat to Fochabers, where he, and Captain Shee who accompanied him, met with Lord John Drummond, who had advanced so far to protect the disembarkation. A piquet of Berwick's regiment was also safely landed at Portsoy, but no other troops of this expedition afterwards reached the Prince's army. The remainder of Fitz-James's cavalry were taken by Commodore Knowles, and sent to the Thames. The Marquis de Fimarion, having held a council of war, thought it most prudent to return to France.

Thus unpitiably rigorous was fortune, from beginning to end, in all that might be considered as the *chances* from which Prince Charles might receive advantage. The miscarriage of the reinforcements was the greater, as the supplies of treasure were become almost indispensable. His money now began to run short, so that he was compelled to pay his soldiers partly in meal, which caused great discontent. Many threatened to abandon the enterprise; some actually deserted; and the army, under these adverse circumstances, became more refractory and unmanageable than heretofore.

Yet their spirit of military adventure was still shown in the instinctive ingenuity with which they carried on enterprises of irregular warfare. This was particularly evident from a series of attacks planned and executed by Lord George Murray, for delivering his native country of Athole from the small forts and military stations which had been established there by the Duke of Cumberland. This expedition was undertaken in the middle of March, and Lord George himself commanded the detachment destined for the service, which amounted to 700 men, one-half of these were natives of Athole, the other half were MacPhersons, under the command of Cluny, their chief. They marched from Dalwhinnie when daylight began to fail, and halted at Dalnaspidal about midnight, when it was explained to them that the purpose of the expedition was to surprise and cut off all the military posts in Athole, which were occupied either by the regular troops or by the Campbells.

These posts were very numerous, and it was necessary they should be all attacked about the same time. The most important were gentlemen's houses, such as Kinnachin, Blairfettie, Lude, Faskally, and the like, which, in the Highlands, and indeed throughout Scotland generally, were of a castellated form, and capable of defence. Other small posts were slightly fortified, and commanded by non-commissioned officers. Lord George Murray's force of 700 men was divided into as many small parties as there were posts to be carried; and in each were included an equal number of Athole men and MacPhersons. Each party was expected to perform the duty assigned to it before daybreak, and all were then to repair to the Bridge of Bruar, within two miles of the castle of Blair-in-Athole. The various detachments set out with eagerness upon an enterprise which promised to relieve their country or neighbourhood from invasion and military occupation; and Lord George and Cluny, with only 25 men, and a few elderly gentlemen, proceeded to the bridge of Bruar, being the rendezvous, there to await the success of their undertaking and the return of their companions.

It had nearly chanced that, in an enterprise designed to surprise others, they had been surprised themselves. For, in the gray of the morning, a man from the village of Blair came to inform Lord George Murray that Sir Andrew Agnew, who commanded at Blair Castle, had caught the alarm, from an attack on a neighbouring post; had got a great proportion of his garrison of 500 men under arms, and was advancing to the Bridge of Bruar, to see what enemies were in the neighbourhood. Lord George Murray and Cluny were in no condition to engage the veteran; and it was proposed, as the only mode of escape, to betake themselves to the neighbouring mountains. Lord George Murray rejected the proposition. "If," he said, "we leave the place of rendezvous, our parties, as they return in detail from discharging the duty entrusted to them, will be liable to be surprised by the enemy. This must not be. I will rather try what can be done to impose upon Sir Andrew Agnew's caution, by a fictitious display of strength." With this resolution Lord George took possession of a turf-dyke, or wall, which stretched along a neighbouring field, and disposed his followers behind it, at distant intervals from each other, so as to convey the idea of a very extended front. The colours of both regiments were placed in the centre of the pretended line, and every precaution used to give the appearance of a continued line of soldiers, to what was in reality only a few men placed at a distance from each other. The bag-pipers were not forgotten; they had orders to blow up a clamorous pibroch, so soon as the advance of the regulars should be observed, upon the road from Blair. The sun just arose when Sir Andrew's troops came in sight; the pipers struck up, and the men behind the turf wall brandished their broadswords, like officers at the head of their troops preparing to charge. Sir Andrew was deceived into the idea that he had before him a large body of Highlanders drawn up to attack him, and anxious for the safety of his post, he marched back his garrison to the castle of Blair-in-Athole.

Lord George Murray remained at the bridge to receive his detachments, who came in soon after sunrise: they had all succeeded more or less completely, and brought in upwards of 300 prisoners, taken at the various posts, which, great and small, amounted to thirty in number. Only one or two of the clansmen were killed, and but five or six of the King's troops; for the Highlanders, though in some respects a wild and fierce people, were seldom guilty of unnecessary bloodshed. Encouraged by this success, Lord George Murray was tempted to make an effort to possess himself of the castle of Blair, notwithstanding its natural strength, and that of its garrison. With this view he invested the place, which was a very large, strong old tower, long a principal residence of the Athole family. There was little hope from battering with two light field-pieces a castle whose walls were seven feet thick; the situation was so rocky as to put mining out of the question; but Lord George, as the garrison was numerous, and supposed to be indifferently provided for a siege, conceived the possibility of reducing the place by famine. For this purpose he formed a close blockade of the place, and fired with his

Highland marksmen upon all who showed themselves at the windows of the tower, or upon the battlements. And here, as in this motley world that which is ridiculous is often intermixed with what is deeply serious, I may tell you an anecdote of a ludicrous nature.

Sir Andrew Agnew, famous in Scottish tradition, was a soldier of the old military school, severe in discipline, stiff and formal in manners, brave to the last degree, but somewhat of a humorist, upon whom his young officers were occasionally tempted to play tricks not entirely consistent with the respect due to their commandant. At the siege of Blair some of the young wags had obtained an old uniform coat of the excellent Sir Andrew, which, having stuffed with straw, they placed in a small window of a turret, with a spy-glass in the hand, as if in the act of reconnoitring the besiegers. This apparition did not escape the hawk's eyes of the Highlanders, who continued to pour their fire upon the turret window, without producing any adequate effect. The best deer-stalkers of Athole and Badenoch persevered, nevertheless, and wasted, as will easily be believed, their ammunition in vain on this impassible commander. At length Sir Andrew himself became curious to know what could possibly induce so constant a fire upon that particular point of the castle. He made some inquiry, and discovered the trick which had been played. His own head being as insensible to a jest of any kind as his peruke had proved to the balls of the Highlanders, he placed the contumacious wags under arrest, and threatened to proceed against them still more seriously, and would certainly have done so, but, by good fortune for them, the blockade was raised after the garrison had suffered the extremity of famine.

The raising of the blockade was chiefly owing to the advance of a body of Hessians from Perth, together with some troops under the Earl of Crawford. Lord George Murray on this occasion sent an express to the Prince that, if he could spare him 1200 men, he would undertake to engage the Prince of Hesse and Lord Crawford. Charles returned for answer that he could not spare the men, being in the act of concentrating his army. Lord George Murray was therefore obliged to relinquish the blockade of Blair, and withdrew his forces into Strathspey, and from thence to Speyside. He himself went to the Chevalier's headquarters where he found that his exploits in the field had not been able to save him from enemies, who had made a bad use of their master's ear.

We have seen that, from the very first meeting at Perth, Mr. Murray, the secretary, had filled the Prince's mind with suspicions of

Lord George, as a person who, if disposed to serve him, was not inclined to do so upon the pure principles of unlimited monarchy. The self-will and obstinacy of this nobleman, a brave soldier, but an unskilful courtier, gave all the advantage which his enemies could desire; and in despite of his gallant achievements, the Prince was almost made to believe that the best officer in his army was capable of betraying him at least, if not actually engaged in a conspiracy to do so. Thus prepossessed, though usually eager for fighting, the Chevalier, both at Clifton, and on the present occasion, declined entrusting Lord George with a separate command of troops, to avail himself of a favourable opportunity for action.

On the present occasion, Charles entertained the opinion that Lord George might have taken the castle of Blair had he been so disposed; but that he abstained, lest by doing so he might injure the house of his brother, the Duke of Athole. Lord George was altogether undeserving of such a suspicion, there being perhaps no man in the Prince's army who had fewer indirect motives to decide his political creed than this nobleman. If the Prince succeeded in his enterprise, his eldest brother would recover the dukedom, now held by the second. But it does not appear that Lord George Murray could be thus personally benefited. It is no small merit to him, that, faithful while suspected, and honest though calumniated, he adhered to the tenor of his principles, and continued to serve with zeal and fidelity a master by whom he knew he was not beloved nor fully trusted. It is even said by Lord Elcho that the Prince told some of the French and Irish officers that he suspected Lord George; and it is added, that being requested to watch whether his conduct in battle authorised such a suspicion, they undertook to put him to death if such should appear to be the case.

LXXXIII

The Battle of Culloden

April 1746

THE final act of this great domestic tragedy was now about to begin, yet there remain some other incidents to notice ere we approach that catastrophe. The outposts of the principal armies were extended along the river Spey, and the Highlanders appeared disposed for a time to preserve the line of that river, although a defensive war is not that which Highlanders could be expected to wage with most success. It is probable they did not expect the Duke of Cumberland to make a serious advance from his headquarters at Aberdeen, until the summer was fairly commenced, when their own army would be reassembled. Several affairs of posts took place betwixt General Bland, who commanded the advance of the Duke's army, and Lord John Drummond, who was opposed to him on the side of the Chevalier. The Highlanders had rather the advantage in this irregular sort of warfare, and, in particular, a party of a hundred regulars were surprised at the village of Keith, and entirely slain or made prisoners by John Roy Stewart.

About the same time, Prince Charles sustained a heavy loss in the *Hazard* sloop of war, which made her appearance in the North Sea, having on board 150 troops for his service, and, what he needed still more, a sum of gold equal to £10,000 or £12,000. This vessel, with a cargo of so much importance, being chased by an English frigate, was run ashore by her crew in the bay of Tongue, in the shire of Sutherland, and the sailors and soldiers escaping ashore, carried the treasure along with them. They were, however, in a hostile, as well as a desolate country. The tribe of the MacKays assembled in arms, and, with some bands of Lord Loudon's army, pursued the strangers so closely as to oblige them to surrender themselves and the specie. It is said only £8000 of gold was found upon them; the rest having been embezzled, either by their captors or by others after they came ashore. This loss of the *Hazard*, which was productive of injurious consequences to the Highland army, was connected with a series of transactions in Sutherland, which I will here briefly tell you of.

Lord Loudon, you will recollect, had retreated from Inverness into Ross-shire, at the head of about 2000 men, composed of the Whig clans. In the beginning of March Lord Cromarty had been despatched by the Prince, with his own regiment, together with the MacKinnons, MacGregors, and Barrisdale's people, to dislodge Lord Loudon; this they effected by the temporary aid of Lord George Murray. Lord Loudon, retreating before an army which now consisted of the flower of the Highlanders, disposed his forces at various ferries upon the firth which divides the shire of Sutherland from that of Ross, in order to defend the passage.

On the 20th of March, however, the rebels, under Lord Cromarty, pushed across near a place called the Meikle Ferry, and nearly surprised a party that kept guard there. The Earl of Loudon, informed of this invasion, concluded that, as his forces were inferior in number, and much scattered, there was no possibility of drawing them together for the purpose of making a stand; he therefore sent orders to the officers commanding the different posts to provide for their safety by marching the men whom they commanded into their several districts. Loudon himself, with the Lord President, and other persons of rank, who might be supposed particularly obnoxious to the insurgents, embarked with the MacLeods and MacDonalds, and returned with them to the isle of Skye. The army, therefore, might be said to be dispersed and disbanded. Owing to this dispersion, it happened that some of Lord Loudon's soldiers were in the MacKays' country, and assisted in taking prisoners the crew of the *Hazard* sloop of war when they landed.

Lord Cromarty was now in full possession of the coast of Sutherland and of the castle of Dunrobin, which the Earl of Sutherland had

found it impossible to defend. The Jacobite general could not, however, exercise much influence in that country; the vassalage and tenantry not only declined to join the rebels, but kept possession of their
arms, and refused the most favourable terms of submission. The Earl
of Cromarty, indeed, collected some money, emptied the Earl of
Sutherland's stables of nineteen or twenty good horses, and cut his
carriage into pieces in order to convert the leather and brass mounting into targets; but the country itself being hostile to the Jacobite
cause, obliged the Earl, though a mild good-natured man, to use
some severity on this occasion. The houses and property of two of
the captains of the militia were plundered and burnt, in order to
strike terror into other recreants. This was alien to the inclinations of
some of the Highlanders, the gentleness of whose conduct had hitherto been the subject of surprise and panegyric. "I like not this raising
of fire," said an old Highlander, who looked on during the devastation; "hitherto five of us have put twenty to flight, but if we follow
this inhuman course, we may look for twenty of us to fly before five
of our enemies." In fact, the prophecy was not far from its accomplishment. The Earl of Cromarty extended his operations even into
the islands of Orkney, but received as little encouragement from the
inhabitants of that archipelago as from the people of Sutherland. In
Caithness a few gentlemen of the name of Sinclair adopted their
cause; but it is said that not above forty-three men in all from that
country joined the Chevalier's standard. The beginning of April was
now come, and the indications of the Duke of Cumberland's advance
in person made it plain that the insurgents would be no longer permitted to protract the campaign by a war of posts, but must either
fight or retire into the Highlands. The last measure, it was foreseen,
must totally break up Prince Charles's Lowland cavalry, many of
whom had already lost their horses in the retreat; it was necessary,
therefore, to form them into a body of foot-guards.

The Prince did not hesitate a moment which course to pursue. He
entertained, like others who play for deep stakes, a tendency to fatal-
ism, which had been fostered by his success at Prestonpans and
Falkirk, and he was determined, like a desperate gamester, to push his
luck to extremity. The kind of warfare which he had been waging for
some weeks past had necessarily led to a great dispersion of his forces,
and intent upon the impending contest, he now summoned his
detachments from every side to join his own standard at Inverness.

The powerful body of men under the Earl of Cromarty received similar orders. MacDonald of Barrisdale, in great haste to obey, set out on his march upon the 14th of April. On the 15th he was to have been followed by the Earl of Cromarty and his regiment. This projected evacuation of Sutherland, which ought to have been kept secret, was imprudently suffered to transpire; and the Sutherland men resolved to annoy the rear of their unwelcome visitants as they left the country. With this view, a great many of the armed militia collected from the hills, in which they had taken shelter, and prepared to take such advantage of the retreating insurgents as opportunity should permit. About two hundred men assembled for this purpose, and approached the coast. One John MacKay, a vintner in Golspie, had a division of about twenty to act under his own separate command. The Earl of Cromarty, for whom the militia were lying in ambush, was far from suspecting the danger he was in. He remained, with his son Lord MacLeod, and several other officers, at the castle of Dunrobin, witnessing, it is said, the tricks of a juggler, while his men, three hundred and fifty in number, were marched, under the command of subaltern officers, and with little precaution, to the ferry where they were to embark. The consequences were fatal. John MacKay, with his twenty men, threw himself between the rear of the main body and Lord Cromarty and his officers, who were following in imagined security, and suddenly firing, with considerable execution, upon the Earl and his attendants, forced them back to Dunrobin Castle, which they had just left. The same active partisan contrived to gain admittance into the castle without a single follower, and boldly summoned the Earl and his officers to surrender, which at length, under a false apprehension of the amount of force by which they were surrounded, they were induced to do. The Earl of Cromarty, Lord MacLeod, and the other officers of Lord Cromarty's regiment, who had not marched with their men, were thus made prisoners, and put on board the *Hound*, a British sloop of war. The rebellion, therefore, was thus extinguished in Sutherland on the 16th of April, the very day on which it was put an end to throughout Scotland by the great battle of Culloden.

Having given a short account of these distant operations, we must return to the motions of the main armies.

The Duke of Cumberland, with the last division of his army, left Aberdeen on the 8th of April, with the intention of moving upon Inverness, being Charles's headquarters, in the neighbourhood of

which it was understood that the Prince designed to make a stand. As
he advanced northward, the Duke was joined by Generals Bland and
Mordaunt, who commanded his advanced divisions, and the whole
army assembled at the town of Cullen, about ten miles from the banks
of the Spey.

An opinion had been entertained, to which we have already
alluded, that the Highlanders intended to defend the passage of this
deep and rapid river. A trench and some remains of works seemed to
show that such had been their original purpose, and a considerable
division of the Lowland troops were drawn up under Lord John Drummond, with the apparent purpose of maintaining these defences. The
Prince's ultimate orders, however, were, that Lord John should retreat to
Elgin as soon as the enemy should approach in force the south-eastern
bank of the river. He did so, and the Duke of Cumberland forded the
Spey with his army in three divisions, his music playing a tune calculated to insult his antagonists.[1] Several lives were lost, owing to the
strength of the stream; they were chiefly females, followers of the camp.

On the 13th of April the Duke of Cumberland's army marched to
the moor of Alves, and on the 14th advanced to Nairn, where there was
a slight skirmish between their advance and the rearguard of the Highlanders, who were just leaving the town. The last were unexpectedly
supported in their retreat, about five miles from Nairn, by the Chevalier
himself, who arrived suddenly at the head of his guards and the MacIntosh Regiment, at a place called the Loch of the Clans. On the appearance of this additional force, the vanguard of the Duke's army retreated
upon their main body, which was encamped near Nairn.

It is now necessary to examine the state of the contending armies,
who were soon to be called upon to decide the fate of the contest by a
bloody battle.

The Duke of Cumberland was at the head of an army of disciplined troops, completely organised, and supported by a fleet, which,
advancing along the coast, could supply them with provisions, artillery,
and every other material requisite for the carrying on of the campaign.
They were under the command of a Prince whose authority was
absolute, whose courage was undoubted, whose high birth was the
boast of his troops, and whose military skill and experience were, in

---

[1] Will you play me fair play,
    Bonnie laddie, Highland laddie?

the opinion of his followers, completely adequate to the successful termination of the war.

On the other hand, the army of Prince Charles lay widely dispersed, on account of the difficulty of procuring subsistence; so that there was great doubt of the possibility of assembling them in an united body within the short space afforded them for that purpose. The councils also of the adventurous Prince were unhappily divided; and those dissensions which had existed even in their days of prosperity, were increased in the present critical moment, even by the pressure of the emergency. The first difficulty might be in some degree surmounted, but the last was of a fatal character; and I must once more remind you of the causes in which it originated.

The aversion of the Prince to Lord George Murray has been already stated; and although the fact may seem surprising, the unwarranted suspicion with which this individual was regarded by the Chevalier is pretty well understood to have extended itself about this period to a great part of his other Scottish followers, more especially as the present state of the contest, joined to the private disaffection, or rather discontent, among the clans, tended to weaken the confidence of the commander. Such sparks of disagreement assume more importance in the time of adversity, as lights, little distinguished of themselves, are more visible on the approach of darkness. Since the council at Derby, the Prince had convoked or advised with no public assembly of his chiefs and followers of rank, as he had formerly been wont to do, if we except the council of war held near Crieff, which was in a manner forced on him by the retreat from Stirling. During all that time he had, in the fullest sense, commanded the army by his own authority. His trust and confidence had been chiefly reposed in Secretary Murray, in Sir Thomas Sheridan, his former tutor, and in the Irish officers, who made their way to his favour by assenting to all he proposed, and by subscribing, without hesitation, to the most unlimited doctrine of the monarch's absolute power. On the other hand, the Scottish nobility and gentry, who had engaged their lives and fortunes in the quarrel, naturally thought themselves entitled to be consulted concerning the manner in which the war was to be conducted, and were indignant at being excluded from offering their advice, where they themselves were not only principally interested, but best acquainted with the localities and manners of the country in which the war was waged.

They were also displeased that in his communication with the court of France, announcing his successes at Prestonpans and at Falkirk, the Prince had entrusted the negotiations with the court of France to Irishmen in the French service. They suspected, unjustly perhaps, that instead of pleading the cause of the insurgents fairly, and describing and insisting upon the amount and nature of the succours which were requisite, these gentlemen would be satisfied to make such representations as might give satisfaction to the French ministers, and insure to the messengers, their own advancement in the French service. Accordingly, all the officers sent to France by Charles received promotion. The Scots also suspected that the Irish and French officers, willing to maintain themselves in exclusive favour, endeavoured to impress the Prince with suspicions of the fidelity of the Scottish people, and invidiously recalled to his memory the conduct of the nation to Charles I. It is said that Charles was not entirely convinced of the falsehood of these suspicions till the faithful services of so many of that nation, during the various perils of his escape, would have rendered it base ingratitude to harbour them longer.

There was another subject of discontent in the Prince's army, arising, perhaps, from too high pretensions on the part of one class of his followers, and too little consideration on that of Charles. Many of the gentlemen who served as privates in the Prince's cavalry conceived that they were entitled to more personal notice than they received, and complained that they were regarded more in the light of ordinary troopers than as men of estate and birth, who were performing, at their own expense, the duty of private soldiers, to evince their loyalty to the cause of the Stewarts.

Notwithstanding these secret jealousies, Charles remained unaltered in the system which he had adopted. Neither did the discontent of his followers proceed further than murmurs, or in any case break out, as in Mar's insurrection, into mutiny, or even a desire on the part of the gentlemen engaged to make, by submission or otherwise, their separate peace with Government. Notwithstanding, however, what has been said, the gallant bravery and general deportment of the Prince secured him popularity with the common soldiers of his army, though those with higher pretensions were less easily satisfied, when mere civility was rendered instead of confidence.

The Chevalier had been unwell of a feverish complaint during several days of his residence at Elgin in the month of March. On his retreat to Inverness, he seemed perfectly recovered, and employed himself by hunting in the forenoon, and in the evening with balls, concerts, and parties of pleasure, in which he appeared in as good spirits, and as confident, as after the battle of Prestonpans. This exterior show of confidence would have been well had there been good grounds for its foundation; but those alleged by Charles rested upon a firm conviction that the army of the Duke of Cumberland would not seriously venture to oppose in battle their lawful Prince; an idea which he found it impossible to impress upon such of his followers as were in the least acquainted with the genius and temper of the English soldiery.

While the Prince was at Inverness, two gentlemen of the name of Haliburton arrived from France, with tidings of a cold description. They informed him that the court of that country had entirely laid aside the thoughts of an invasion upon a large scale, and that his brother, the Duke of York, who had been destined to be placed at the head of it, had left the coast, being recalled to Paris. This put a final end to the most reasonable hopes of the unfortunate Adventurer, which had always rested upon a grand exertion of France in his favour; although, indeed, he might have been convinced, that since they had made no such effort during the time of his inroad into England, when his affairs bore an aspect unexpectedly favourable, they would not undertake any considerable risk to redeem him from the destruction which seemed now to be impending.

Besides the discords in the Prince's camp, which, like a mutiny among the crew of a sinking vessel, prevented an unanimous exertion to provide for the common safety, the separation of his forces, and the pecuniary difficulties which now pressed hard upon him, were material obstacles to any probability of success in an action with the Duke of Cumberland. Charles endeavoured, indeed, to concentrate all his army near Inverness, but without entire success. General Stapleton, who had been engaged in attempting to reduce Fort William, abandoned that enterprise and returned to the Prince's camp, together with Lochiel and the other Highlanders by whom that irregular siege had been supported. But the Master of Fraser, who was employed in levying the full strength of his clan, together with Barrisdale and Cromarty, engaged as we have seen in Sutherland, were absent from the main army. Cluny and his MacPhersons had been despatched into Badenoch, with a view to their more easy subsistence in their own country, and were wanting in the hour when their services were most absolutely necessary. There were besides 800 or 1000 men of different Highland clans who were dispersed in visiting their own several glens, and would certainly have returned to the army if space had been allowed them for so doing.

It is also proper to mention that, as already hinted, the cavalry of the Prince had suffered greatly. That of Lord Pitsligo might be said to have been entirely destroyed by their hard duty on the retreat from Stirling, and was in fact converted into a company of foot-guards. Now, although these horsemen, consisting of gentlemen and their servants, might have been unable to stand the shock of heavy and regular regiments of horse, yet from their spirit and intelligence, they had been of the greatest service as light cavalry, and their loss to Charles Edward's army was a great misfortune.

The force which remained with the Prince was discontented from want of pay, and in a state of considerable disorganisation. The troops were not duly supplied with provisions and, like more regular soldiers under such circumstances, were guilty of repeated mutiny and disobedience of orders. For all these evils Charles Edward saw no remedy but in a general action, to which he was the more disposed that hitherto, by a variety of chances in his favour, as well as by the native courage of his followers, he had come off victorious, though against all ordinary expectation, in every action in which he had been engaged. On such an alternative then, and with troops mutinous for want of pay, half starved for want of provisions, and diminished in numbers from the absence of 3000 or 4000 men, he determined to risk an action with the Duke of Cumberland, at the head of an army considerably outnumbering his own, and possessed of all those advantages of which he himself at the moment was so completely deprived.

The preparations for the engagement were not made with more prudence than that which was shown in the resolution to give instant battle. Charles drew out his forces upon an extensive moor, about five miles distant from Inverness, called Drummossie, but more frequently known by the name of Culloden, to which it is adjacent. The Highlanders lay upon their arms all the night of the 14th; on the next morning they were drawn up in order of battle, in the position which the Chevalier proposed they should maintain during the action. On their right there were some park walls, on their left a descent which slopes down upon Culloden House; their front was directly east. They were drawn up in two lines, of which the Athole brigade held the right of the whole, next to them Lochiel. The clans of Appin, Fraser, and MacIntosh, with those of MacLauchlan, MacLean, and Farquhar-son, composed the centre; and on the left were the three regiments of MacDonalds, styled, from their chiefs, Clanranald, Keppoch, and Glengarry.

As if a fate had hung over the councils of Charles, the disposition of this order of battle involved the decision of a point of honour, esteemed of the utmost importance in this singular army, though in any other a mere question of idle precedence. The MacDonalds, as the most powerful and numerous of the clans, had claimed from the beginning of the expedition the privilege of holding the right of the whole army. Lochiel and Appin had waived any dispute of this claim at the battle of Prestonpans; the MacDonalds had also led the right at Falkirk; and now the left was assigned to this proud surname, which they regarded not only as an affront but as an evil omen. The Prince's second line, or reserve, was divided into three bodies, with an interval between each. On the right were Elcho's, Fitz-James's, and Lord Strathallan's horse, with Abachie's and Lord Ogilvie's regiments of infantry. The centre division was formed of the Irish piquets, Lord John Drummond's regiment, and that of the Earl of Kilmarnock. The left wing of the second line consisted of the hussars, with Sir Alexander Bannerman's and Moir of Stonywood's Lowland battalions. The number of the whole first line might be about 4700 men; that, of the second line 2300, of which 250 were cavalry; but, as I will presently show you, the numbers which appeared at the review were very considerably diminished before the action.

A great error on the part of the commissaries, or such as acted in that capacity in the Highland army, was exhibited in the almost total want of provisions; a deficiency the more inexcusable as it was said there was plenty of meal at Inverness. The soldiers, however, received no victuals, except a single biscuit per man during the whole day of the 15th, and this dearth of provisions was such, that whether the army had been victorious or vanquished, upon the day of the 16th, they must have dispersed to distant quarters for the mere purpose of obtaining subsistence.

Early on the 15th of April Lord Elcho was despatched to reconnoitre the camp of the Duke of Cumberland, situated near the little town of Nairn. It was the anniversary of the royal Duke's birthday, which was apparently dedicated to festivity and indulgence on the part of the soldiers whom he commanded. Lord Elcho remained within view of the enemy until high noon, and then retired to announce that, to all appearance, the English army did not mean to move that day.

Upon this report the Prince assembled the chief officers of his army, being the first council of war which he had held since that in which the retreat from Derby was resolved upon, excepting the meeting at Fairnton, near Crieff. Charles opened the business by asking the opinion of the council what was best to be done. There was a diversity of opinions. The want of provisions, alone rendered a battle inevitable, but the place and mode of giving that battle were matter of discussion. Lord George Murray, as usual, was the first to give his opinion, and enlarged much on the advantage which a Highland army was sure to possess in taking the enemy by surprise, and in darkness rather than in daylight. Regular soldiers, he said, depend entirely on their discipline, an advantage of which they are deprived by darkness and confusion. Highlanders, on the contrary, had, he observed, little discipline but what was of an intuitive nature, independent either of light or regularity. He concluded by giving his opinion that the first line should march in two divisions at the dusk of the evening; he himself offered to lead that composed of the right wing of the first line, with which he designed to march round the town of Nairn, and attack the Duke of Cumberland's camp in the rear; at the same time he proposed that the Duke of Perth, with the left division of the first line, should attack the camp in front, when he did not doubt that the confusion occasioned by the sudden onset on two points, joined to the effects of the past day's festivity, would throw the regulars into total confusion, and afford the Prince a complete victory. This plan also included a march of the whole second line, or body of reserve, under the command of the Prince himself, to support the front attack.

To this proposal several objections were made; one was, that it was a pity to hazard anything until the MacPhersons, a great part of the Frasers, MacDonald of Barrisdale, Glengyle, with his MacGregors, the Earl of Cromarty, whose misfortune was not known, and other reinforcements at present absent, should have joined the army. It was also stated, that in all probability the Duke would receive notice of the intended movement, either by his spies or his patrols; that in either case it would be difficult to provide against the necessary consequences of such discovery; and that, if the Highlanders were once thrown into confusion in a night attack, there would be no possibility of rallying them. The principal answer to these objections was founded on the exigency of the moment, which required a considerable hazard to be incurred in one shape or other, and that the plan of the night attack was as feasible as any which could be proposed.

Another objection, strongly urged, was the impossibility of marching twelve miles, being the distance between Culloden and the enemy's camp, between nightfall and dawn. To this Lord George Murray returned for answer that he would pledge himself for the success of the project, provided secrecy was observed. Other plans were proposed, but the night march was finally resolved upon.

Between seven and eight o'clock the Chevalier ordered the heath to be set on fire, that the light might convey the idea of his troops being still in the same position there, and got all his men under arms, as had been agreed upon.

It was explained by the Prince's aide-de-camp, Colonel Ker of Gradon, that during the attack on the camp the Highlanders were not to employ their firearms, but only broadswords, dirks, and Lochaber axes, with which they were instructed to beat down the tent-poles, and to cut the ropes, taking care at the same moment to strike or stab with force wherever they observed any swelling or bulge in the fallen canvas of the tent. They were also instructed to observe, the profoundest silence luring the time of the march, and the watchword assigned to them was "King James the VIII."

Thus far all was well; and for resolute men, an attempt so desperate presented, from its very desperation, a considerable chance of success. But an inconvenience occurred on the march, for which, and the confusion which it was sure to occasion, due allowance seems scarcely to have been made in the original project. It had been proposed by Lord George Murray that the army should march in three columns, consisting of the first line in two divisions, and the whole reserve, or second line, under the Prince himself. But from the necessity of the three columns keeping the same road as far as the house of Kilravock, where the first division was to diverge from the others, and cross the river Nairn, in order to get in the rear of the enemy's camp, it followed that the army, instead of forming three distinct columns of march, each on its own ground, composed only one long one, the second line following the first, and the third the second, upon the same track, which greatly diminished the power of moving with rapidity. The night, besides, was very dark, which made the progress of the whole column extremely slow, especially as there was a frequent necessity for turning out of the straight road, in order to avoid all inhabited places, from which news of their motions might have been sent to the Duke of Cumberland.

Slow as the march was, the van considerably outmarched the rear. A gap, or interval, was left in the centre of the whole, and messages were sent repeatedly to Lochiel, who was in front, and to Lord George Murray, who commanded the head of the line, requesting them to halt until the rear of the columns should come up. Fifty of these messages were brought to the van of the column before they had marched above eight miles, by which time they had reached Kilravock, or Kilraick House, within four miles of the Duke of Cumberland's camp.

Hitherto Lord George Murray had not halted upon his line of march; but had only obeyed the aides-de-camp by marching more slowly, in the hope that the rear might come up. But at this place the Duke of Perth himself, who commanded the second division, came up to Lord George Murray, and putting his horse across the road, insisted that the rear could not advance unless the van was halted. Lord George Murray halted accordingly, and many of the principal officers came to the head of the column to consult what was to be done. They reported that many of the Highlanders had straggled from the ranks, and lain down to sleep in the wood of Kilravock; which must have been owing to faintness, or want of food, since an eight miles' march could not be supposed to have fatigued these hardy mountaineers to such an excess. It was also said that more gaps were left in the line than one, and that there was no possibility of the rear keeping pace with the head of the column. Watches were next consulted. It had been proposed to make the attack before two o'clock in the morning; but that hour was now come, and the head of the column was still four miles distant from the English camp. The object of the expedition, therefore, was frustrated. Some of the gentlemen volunteers were of opinion that they ought to proceed at all risks; but as they must have marched for at least two miles in broad light, all hopes of a surprise must have been ended. In these doubtful circumstances Mr. O'Sullivan found the officers at the head of the column, when he came to Lord George Murray with orders from the Prince, expressing it to be his desire, if possible, that the attack should proceed; yet referring to Lord George, as nearest to the head of the column, to form his own judgment whether the attempt could be made with advantage or not. At this moment the distant roll of the drums from the Duke of Cumberland's camp announced that his army was upon the alert, and that the moment was gone by when the camp might have been taken by surprise. "They are awake," said Lord George. "I never expected to have found them otherwise," said Mr. Hepburn of Keith, who had joined the van as a volunteer; "but we may yet find them unprepared." Lord George applauded Hepburn's courage, but considered that, from the lateness of the hour, and the great diminution of the strength of the attacking column, the plan could not be persevered in with any hope of success. He therefore ordered the troops to march back with as much expedition as possible.

As this retreat, though apparently unavoidable, was executed by Lord George Murray without the express orders of the Prince, though in execution of an optional power reposed in Lord George himself, it was at the time, and has been since, used as a handle by those who were inclined to accuse that nobleman of treachery to a cause which he had served with so much valour and talent.[1]

It may be here remarked that the Duke of Cumberland's army took no alarm either from the march or countermarch of the enemy, and that, but for the inauspicious circumstances which delayed the movement, the attacking column had a great chance of success.

The retreat was executed with much more rapidity than the advance, it being unnecessary to take any precautions for concealing their motions; so that the whole army had regained the heights of Culloden moor before five o'clock in the morning. The disadvantages of the night march, and of the preceding day's abstinence, became now visible. The men went off from their colours in great numbers,

---

[1] I have taken Lord George Murray's account of this night march as he, himself gave it, for vindication of his own conduct. The Chevalier himself, then called Comte D'Albanie, returned a different answer to some inquiries on the part of Mr. John Home. It is singular enough that his reply acquits Lord George Murray of the alleged crime of commanding the retreat without orders, even more completely than Lord George's own account acquits himself. The Chevalier says that he rode up in person to the head of the column, and was at first anxious for advancing but when he heard Lord George's reasoning against it, he himself gave orders for the retreat. This striking difference between the evidence of two persons deeply interested in a subject of such importance to both, proves the uncertainty of human evidence. But it is natural to suppose Lord George Murray's account the more correct, because it was given as early as 1749. Besides, it is not likely he should make his own case worse than it really was, by resting his defence on the option transmitted to him by O'Sullivan, if, in fact, it was the Prince himself who gave the order for retreat, which Lord George was censured for having issued contrary to his intentions.

to seek food at Inverness and the neighbouring villages. They were unpaid, unfed, exhausted with famine and want of sleep, and replied with indifference to the officers who endeavoured to force them to return to their colours, that they might shoot them if they chose, but that they would not return till they had procured some food. The principal officers themselves were exhausted from want of rest and sustenance. They went, as if instinctively, to the house of Culloden, where they had previously assembled, but were so worn out, that, instead of holding a council of war, each laid himself down to sleep on beds or tables, or on the floor where such conveniences were not to be bad.

The time was now arrived for putting into execution the alternative proposed in the council of war of the preceding day, which was only postponed to the proposed march to Nairn. This was, that the Highland army should retire and take up a strong position beyond the river Nairn, inaccessible to cavalry. Such a movement would have been no difficult matter, had the confused state of the Chevalier's army, and the total want of provisions,[1] permitted them to take any steps for their preservation. All, however, which looked either like foresight or common sense seemed to be abandoned on this occasion, under the physical exhaustion of fatigue and famine. The army remained on the upper part of the open moor, having their flank covered on the right by the park walls which we have mentioned, their only protection from cavalry, and as it proved a very slight one.

About two hours after the Prince had again reached Culloden, that is, about seven or eight o'clock, a patrol of horse brought in notice that a party of the Duke of Cumberland's cavalry was within two miles, and the whole of his army not above four miles distant. Upon this alarm the Prince and the Duke of Perth, Lord George Murray and Lord John Drummond, mounted their horses, and ordered the drums to beat, and the pipes to play their respective gatherings. This sudden summons to arms caused much hurry and confusion amongst men half dead with fatigue, and roused from the sleep of which they had so much need. The chiefs and officers did what was possible to get them together; but, as they were dispersed in every direction, as far as Inverness itself,

---

[1] This might have been remedied, in so far as the simple wants of a Highland army were concerned, if a part of the troops had been employed on the night of the 15th April to bring meal from Inverness, and cattle from the neighbourhood.

nearly two thousand of the Highlanders who were at the review of the preceding day were absent from the battle of the 16th.

It would have been yet time to retreat by the right of their line, to cross the water of Nairn, and to draw up on ground inaccessible to the Duke of Cumberland's army, when they might, after sunset, have renewed, if it was thought advisable, the attempt to surprise his camp; for it was believed that the Duke was not, till some time afterwards, made aware of their purpose of the previous night. No motion, however, was made to this effect. The Chevalier talked confidently of a battle and a victory; and those who did not share his hopes were prepared to die, if they did not expect to conquer.

The Duke of Cumberland's army now appeared about two miles off, advancing straight in front of the Prince's line of battle. His Royal Highness's force consisted of fifteen battalions of foot, viz.—Pulteney's, 500; The Royals, 500; Cholmondely's, 500; Price's, 500; Scots Fusiliers, 500; Dejean's, 500; Burrell's, 500; Battereau's, 500; Blakeney's, 500; Howard's, 500; Fleming's, 500; Sackville's, 500; Sempill's, 500; Conway's, 500; Wolfe's, 500; and 600 Campbells; which with Lord Mark Ker's dragoons, 300, Cobham's, 300, and Kingston's horse, 300, made 8100 foot, and 900 horse. The day of the battle they were drawn up in two lines, seven battalions in the first, and eight in the second line, supported by the two squadrons of horse on the right, and four squadrons of dragoons on the left. The Campbells were on the left with the dragoons. There were two pieces of cannon betwixt every battalion in the first line, three on the right, and three on the left of the second. The army was commanded in chief by the Duke of Cumberland, and under him by Lieutenant-Generals Earl of Albemarle, Hawley, and Bland, Major-General Huske, Brigadiers Lord Sempill, Cholmondely, and Mordaunt

Had the whole Highland army been collected, there would have been very little, if any difference in numbers between the contending parties, each of which amounted to about 9000 men; but we have already shown that the Prince was deprived of about 2000 of his troops who had never come up, and the stragglers who left his standard between the time of the review and the battle amounted to at least 2000 more; so that, upon the great and decisive battle of Culloden, only 5000 of the insurgent army were opposed to 9000 of the King's troops. The men who were absent, also, were chiefly Highlanders, who formed the peculiar strength of the Chevalier's army.

There was no appearance of discouragement on either side; the troops on both sides huzzaed repeatedly as they came within sight of each other, and it seemed as if the Highlanders had lost all sense of fatigue at sight of the enemy. The MacDonalds alone had a sullen and discontented look, arising from their having taken offence at the post which had been assigned them.

As the lines approached each other, the artillery opened their fire, by which the Duke of Cumberland's army suffered very little, and that of the Highlanders a great deal; for the English guns, being well served, made lanes through the ranks of the enemy, while the French artillery scarcely killed a man. To remain steady and inactive under this galling fire, would have been a trial to the best disciplined troops, and it is no wonder that the Highlanders showed great impatience under an annoyance peculiarly irksome to their character. Some threw themselves down to escape the artillery, some called out to advance, and a very few broke their ranks and fled. The cannonade lasted for about an hour; at length the clans became so impatient that Lord George Murray was about to give the order to advance, when the Highlanders, from the centre and right wing, rushed without orders furiously down, after their usual manner of attacking sword in hand. Being received with a heavy fire, both of cannonade and grape-shot, they became so much confused that they got huddled together in their onset, without any interval or distinction of clans or regiments. Notwithstanding this disorder, the fury of their charge broke through Monro's and Burrell's regiments, which formed the left of the Duke of Cumberland's line. But that General had anticipated the possibility of such an event, and had strengthened his second line so as to form a steady support in case any part of his first should give way. The Highlanders, partly victorious, continued to advance with fury, and although much disordered by their own success, and partly disarmed by having thrown away their guns on the very first charge, they rushed on Sempill's regiment in the second line with unabated fury. That steady corps was drawn up three deep, the first rank kneeling and the third standing upright. The reserved their fire until the fugitives of Burrell's and Monro's broken regiments had escaped round the flanks, and through the intervals of the second line. By this time the Highlanders were within a yard of the bayonet point, when Sempill's battalion poured in their fire with so much accuracy that it brought down a great many of the assailants and forced the rest to turn back. A few pressed on, but, unable to break through Sempill's regiment, were bayoneted by the first rank. The attack of the Highlanders was the less efficient, that on this occasion most of them had laid aside their targets, expecting a march rather than a battle. While the right of the Highland line sustained their national character, though not with their usual success, the MacDonalds on the left seemed uncertain whether they would attack or not. It was in vain the Duke of Perth called out to them, "Claymore!" telling the murmurers of this haughty tribe, "That if they behaved with their usual valour they would convert the left into the right, and that he would in future call himself MacDonald." It was equally in vain that the gallant Keppoch charged with a few of his near relations, while his clan, a thing before unheard of, remained stationary. The chief was near the front of the enemy, and was, exclaiming with feelings which cannot be appreciated, "My God, have the children of my tribe forsaken me!" At this instant he received several shots, which closed his earthly account, leaving him only time to advise his favourite nephew to shift for himself. The three regiments of MacDonalds were by this time aware of the route of their right wing, and retreated in good order upon the second line. A body of cavalry, from the right of the King's army, was commanded to attack them on their retreat, but was checked by a fire from the French piquets, who advanced to support the MacDonalds. But at the same moment another decisive advantage was gained by the Duke's army over the Highland right wing. A body of horse, making 600 cavalry, with three companies of Argyleshire Highlanders, had been detached to take possession of the park walls, repeatedly mentioned as covering the right, of the Highlanders. The three companies of infantry had pulled down the east wall of the enclosure, and put to the sword about a hundred of the insurgents, to whom the defence had been assigned; they then demolished the western wall, which permitted the dragoons, by whom they were accompanied, to ride through the enclosure, and get out upon the open moor, to the westward, and form, so as to threaten the rear and flank of the Prince's second line. Gordon of Abachie, with his Lowland Aberdeenshire regiment, was ordered to fire upon these cavalry, which he did with some effect. The Campbells then lined the north wall of the enclosure so often mentioned, and commenced a fire upon the right flank of the Highlanders' second line. That line, increased by the MacDonalds, who retired upon it, still showed a great number of men keeping their ground, many of whom had not fired a shot. Lord Elcho rode up to the Prince, and eagerly exhorted him to put himself at the head of those troops who yet remained, make a last exertion to recover the day, and at least die like one worthy of having contended for a crown. Receiving a doubtful or hesitating answer, Lord Elcho turned from him with a bitter execration, and declared he would never see his face again.[1] On the other hand, more than one of the Prince's officers declared, and attested Heaven and their own eyes as witnesses, that the unfortunate Adventurer was forced from the field by Sir Thomas Sheridan, and others of the Irish officers who were about his person.

That Lord Elcho and others, who lost rank and fortune in this disastrous adventure, were desirous that the Chevalier should have fought it out to the very last can easily be imagined; nor is it difficult to conceive why many of the public were of the same opinion, since a fatal tragedy can hardly conclude so effectively as with the death of the hero. But there are many reasons besides a selfish desire of safety, which may dictate to a defeated chieftain the task of preserving himself for a better day. This is particularly the case with those in the rank of Kings and Princes, who, assured by the unanimous opinion of those around them that their safety is of the last importance to the world, cannot easily resist the flattering and peculiar reasons which may be assigned in support of the natural principle of self-preservation, common to them with all mankind.

Besides, although the Chevalier, if determined on seeking it, might certainly have found death on the field where he lost all hopes of empire, there does not appear a possibility that his most desperate exertions could have altered the fortune of the day. The second line, united with a part of the first, stood, it is true, for some short time after the disaster of the left wing, but they were surrounded with enemies. In their front was the Duke of Cumberland, dressing and renewing the ranks of his first line, which had been engaged, bringing up to their support his second, which was yet entire, and on the point of leading both to a new attack in front. On the flank of the second line of the Chevalier's army were the Campbells, lining the northern wall of the enclosure. In the rear of the whole Highland army was a body of horse, which could be greatly increased in number by the same access

---

[1] This vow he kept to his dying day, avoiding every place where he might have met the prince, for whose sake he had lost his rank, his estate, and his native country. His relentless anger was not, perhaps, just, but it must be allowed to be natural.

through the park wall which had been opened by the Campbells. The Highlanders, of the Prince's army, in fact, were sullen, dejected, and dispirited, dissatisfied with their officers and generals, and not in perfect good humour with themselves. It was no wonder that, after remaining a few minutes in this situation, they should at last leave the field to the enemy, and go off in quest of safety wherever it was to be found. A part of the second line left the field with tolerable regularity, with their pipes playing and banners displayed. General Stapleton also, and the French auxiliaries, when they saw the day lost, retreated in a soldier-like manner to Inverness, where they surrendered to the Duke of Cumberland on honourable terms. Many of the Highland army fled in the direction of Inverness, but the greater part towards Badenoch and the Highlands. Some of these never stopped till they had reached their own distant homes; and the alarm was so great, that one very gallant gentleman told your Grandfather, that he himself had partaken in the night march, and that, though he had tasted nothing for twenty-four hours, he ran near twenty miles ere he took leisure to sit down and eat a biscuit which had been served out to him at the moment the battle was to begin, and which he had put into his sporran, or purse, to eat when it should be ended.

The Duke of Cumberland proceeded with caution. He did not permit his first line to advance on the repulsed Highlanders till he had restored their ranks to perfect order, nor to pursue till the dispersion of the Highland army seemed complete. When that was certain, Kingston's horse, and the dragoons from each wing of the Duke's army, were detached in pursuit, and did great execution, Kingston's horse followed the chase along the Inverness road. They did not charge such of the enemy, whether French or Highlanders, as kept in a body, but dogged and watched them closely on their retreat, moving more or less speedily as they moved, and halting once or twice when they halted. On the stragglers they made great havoc, till within a mile of Inverness.

It was in general remarked that the English horse, whose reputation had been blemished in previous actions with the Highlanders, took a cruel pleasure in slaughtering the fugitives, giving quarter to none, except a few who were reserved for public execution, and treating those who were disabled with cruelty unknown in modern war. Even the day after the battle, there were instances of parties of wounded men being dragged from the thickets and huts in which they had found refuge, for the purpose of being drawn up and despatched by platoon-firing; while those who did not die under this fusilade, were knocked on the head by the soldiers with the stocks of their muskets. In a word, the savageness of the regulars on this occasion formed such a contrast to the more gentle conduct of the insurgents, as to remind men of the old Latin proverb, that the most cruel enemy is a coward who has obtained success.[1] It was early found necessary to make some averment which might seem to justify this unheard-of cruelty; and, accordingly, a story was circulated, concerning an order said to have been issued by Lord George Murray, commanding the Highlanders to give no quarter if victorious. But not one of the insurgent party ever saw such an order; nor did any of them hear of it till after the battle.

In this decisive action, the victors did not lose much above 300 men, in killed and wounded. Lord Robert Ker, captain of grenadiers, was slain at the head of his company.

The loss of the vanquished army was upwards of 1000 men. The Highlanders on the right wing who charged sword in hand, suffered most severely. These were the MacLeans, and MacLauchlans, the MacIntoshes, the Frasers, the Stewarts, and the Camerons. The chief of MacLauchlan was slain in the action, together with MacLean of Drimnin, MacGillivray of Drumnaglass, several of the Frasers, and other persons of distinction. Lochiel was wounded, but borne from the field by his two henchmen. In short, the blow was equally severe and decisive, and the more so, that the heaviest of the loss fell on the high chief's and gentlemen, who were the soul of the Highland army.

---

[1] Crudelis semper timidus, si vicerit unquam.

LXXXIV

Escape of the Prince

1746

IT was not to be expected that the defeat of Culloden should pass over without fatal consequences to those who had been principally concerned in the insurrection. A handful of men had disturbed the tranquillity of a peaceful people, who were demanding no change of their condition, had inflicted a deep wound upon the national strength, and, what is seldom forgotten in the moment when revenge becomes possible, had inspired universal terror. It was to be expected, therefore, that those who had been most active in such rebellious and violent proceedings should be called to answer with their lives for the bloodshed and disorder to which they had given occasion. They themselves well knew at what bloody risk they had played the deadly game of insurrection, and expected no less forfeit than their lives. But as all concerned in the rebellion had in strictness forfeited their lives to the law, it became fitting that Justice should so select her victims as might, if possible, reconcile her claims with the feelings of humanity, instead of outraging them by a general and undistinguishing effusion of blood. Treason upon political accounts, though one of the highest crimes that can be committed against a state, does not necessarily infer anything like the detestation which attends offences of much less general guilt and danger. He who engages in conspiracy or rebellion is very often, as an individual, not only free from reproach, but highly estimable, in his private character; such men, for example, as Lord Pitsligo, or Cameron of Lochiel, might be said to commit the crime for which they were obnoxious to the law, from the purest, though at the same time the most mistaken motives—motives which they had sucked in with their mother's milk, and which urged them to take up arms by all the ties of duty and allegiance. The sense of such men's purity of principles and intention, though not to be admitted in defence, ought, both morally and politically, to have limited the proceedings against them within the narrowest bounds consistent with the ends of public justice, and the purpose of intimidating others from such desperate courses.

If so much could be said in favour of extending clemency even to several of the leaders of the insurrection, how much more might have been added in behalf of their simple and ignorant followers, who came out in ignorance of the laws of the civilised part of the nation, but in compliance with the unalienable tie by which they and their fathers had esteemed themselves bound to obey their chief.[1] It might have been thought that generosity would have overlooked such poor prey, and that justice would not have considered them as proper objects of punishment. Or, if a victorious general of subordinate rank had been desirous to display his own zeal in behalf of the reigning family at the expense of humanity, by an indiscriminate chastisement of the vanquished foe, of whatever degree of intellect and fortune, better things might have been expected from a Son of Britain—a Royal Prince, who, most of all might have remembered that the objects whom the fate of war had placed at his disposal were the misguided subjects of his own Royal house, and who might gracefully have pleaded their cause at the foot of a father's throne which his own victory had secured.

Unfortunately for the Duke of Cumberland's fame, he saw his duty in a different light. This Prince bore deservedly the character of a blunt, upright, sensible man, friendly and good-humoured in the ordinary

---

[1] This idea of patriarchal obedience was so absolute, that when some Lowland gentlemen were extolling with wonder the devotion of a clansman, who had sacrificed his own life to preserve that of his chief, a Highlander who was present coldly observed that he saw nothing wonderful in the matter—he only did his duty; had he acted otherwise, he would have been a poltroon and a traitor. To punish men who were bred in such principles, for following their chiefs into war, seems as unjust as it would be to hang a dog for the crime of following his master.

intercourse of life. He was a brave soldier, and acquainted with the duties of war; but, both before and after the battle of Culloden, his campaigns were unfortunate; nor does it appear from his proceedings upon that occasion that he merited better success. He had learned war in the rough school of Germany, where the severest infliction upon the inhabitants was never withheld, if it was supposed necessary, either to obtain an advantage or to preserve one already gained.

His Royal Highness understood, as well as any commander in Europe, the necessity, in the general case, of restraining that military license which, to use the words of a revered veteran, renders an army formidable to its friends alone. In the march from Perth, an officer was brought to a court-martial, and lost his commission, by the Duke's perfect approbation, because he had suffered a party under his command to plunder the house of Gask, belonging to Mr. Oliphant, then in arms, and with the Prince's army. This strict exercise of discipline renders us less prepared to expect the violences which followed the battle of Culloden. But unhappily the license which it was thought fit to check while the contest lasted, was freely indulged in when resistance was no more. The fugitives and wounded were necessarily the first to experience the consequences of this departure from the ordinary rules of war.

We have mentioned the merciless execution which was done upon the fugitives and on the wounded who remained on the field of battle. The first might be necessary to strike terror into an enemy so resolute and so capable of rallying as the Highlanders; the second might be the effect of the brutal rage of common soldiers flushed by victory, to which they had not been of late accustomed, and triumphant over an enemy before whom many of them had fled; but the excesses which followed, must, we fear, be imputed to the callous disposition of the commander-in-chief himself, under whose eye, and by whose command, a fearful train of ravages and executions took place.

The Duke proceeded, in military phrase, to improve his victory, by "laying waste" what was termed "the country of the enemy;" and his measures were taken slowly, that they might be attended with more certain success. Proclamations had been sent forth for the insurgent Highlanders to come in and surrender their arms, with which very few complied. Several of the chiefs, indeed, had made an agreement among themselves to meet together and defend their country; but although a considerable sum of money, designed for the Chevalier's use, reached Lochiel, and others his staunch adherents, the list of the slain and disabled chiefs had been so extensive, and the terror and dismay attending the dispersion so great, as to render the adoption of any general measures of defence altogether impossible.

The Duke of Cumberland—so much may be said in his justification—entered what was certainly still a hostile, but an unresisting country, and, fixing his own headquarters in a camp near Fort Augustus, extended his military ravages, by strong parties of soldiery, into the various glens which had been for ages the abode of the disaffected clans. The soldiers had orders to exercise towards the unfortunate natives the utmost extremities of war.

They shot, therefore, the male inhabitants as they fled at their approach; they plundered the houses of the chieftains; they burnt the cabins of the peasants; they were guilty of every kind of outrage towards women, old age, and infancy: and where the soldier fell short of these extremities, it was his own mildness of temper, or that of some officer of gentler mood, which restrained the license of his hand. There can be no pleasure in narrating more particularly such scenes as this devastation gave rise to. When the men were slain, the houses burnt, and the herds and flocks driven off, the women and children perished from famine in many instances, or followed the track of the plunderers, begging for the blood and offal of their own cattle, slain for the soldiers' use, as the miserable means of supporting a wretched life. Certainly, such instances lead us to join in the observation of Monluc, that those engaged in war have much occasion for the mercy of the Deity, since they are, in the exercise of their profession, led to become guilty of so much violence towards their fellow-creatures. One remarkable narrative of this melancholy time is worth telling you; and I willingly consign to silence many others which could only tend to recall hostile feelings better left to slumber.

A gamekeeper of MacDonald of Glengarry, returning from the forest to his home, found it had been visited by a party of the English troops, who had laid waste and burnt his house, and subjected his wife to the most infamous usage. The unfortunate husband vowed revenge. The principal author of the injury, who commanded the party, was described to him as riding upon a gray horse. The detachment had to pass by the side of Loch Arkaig, through the wild rocks of Lochaber; lurking in a thicket, the MacDonald, a marksman by profession, took aim at the person whom he saw mounted on the gray horse, and shot him dead. His revenge, however, was disappointed; the person who had perpetrated the crime happened to have committed his horse to the charge of a groom, or individual of inferior rank, who suffered the penalty of the officer's outrage. The avenger, having learned his mistake, again waylaid the line of march, and once more seeing an officer ride upon the fatal gray horse, between the advanced guard and the main body of the troops, he again took aim, and his bullet again proved fatal—but he had a second time mistaken his victim. The person whom he shot was not the author of the injury, but a gentleman generally esteemed in the Highlands, Captain George Monro of Culcairn (the same who escaped so remarkably at Glenshiel, by the fidelity of his foster brother). Upon learning this second mistake, the MacDonald broke his gun, and renounced further prosecution of his revenge. "It was not the will of Heaven," he said, "that the man who had injured him should perish by his hands; and he would spill no more innocent blood in the attempt."

During the prosecution of these severities, no man experienced more keen regret than President Forbes, whose active zeal had made such an important stand in favour of Government, and who, by determining the wavering purpose of Sir Alexander MacDonald of Sleat, and the Laird of MacLeod, must be considered as having contributed so materially to the suppression of the rebellion. It is said that in venturing to quote to the commander-in-chief the law of the country, he was repulsed with the reply, "That a brigade should give laws." He was deeply affected by the miseries which civil war had brought upon his country; nor had he any reason to congratulate himself individually on having obtained personal favour by the part he had acted. It is certain that at his death his estate was embarrassed by debts contracted in behalf of Government during 1745–46. All we can say on the subject is, that justice was not so profuse in its rewards on this remarkable occasion as in its punishments.

Other persons, who had given sufficient proof of their loyalty in the course of the rebellion, fell, nevertheless, into disgrace with the commander-in-chief, for expressing the slightest sympathy with the distress of the vanquished, or uttering any censure of the severities inflicted on them. The late Lord Forbes, than whom a man more loyal to the King's government was not to be found, had served in the field of Prestonpans, and done all that an officer could do to prevent the flight of the cavalry; notwithstanding this he found that his preferment in the military profession was so much impeded as to render his retirement advisable. The only reason which could be assigned was, that this nobleman, the Premier Baron of Scotland, had ventured to interfere with the course of ravage practised upon the offending districts.

A story is told, that after the battle of Culloden, the Grants of Glenmoriston, who had been in the rebellion, came into Inverness to surrender themselves to the chief of their own name. They were armed cap-a-pie. "Who are these men?" said the Duke of Cumberland. He was informed by the Laird of Grant that they were the Grants of Glenmoriston. "And to whom have they surrendered?" "To me," answered their chief; "and to no man in Britain but me would they have submitted." "No?" replied the Duke after a pause; "I will let them know that they are the King's subjects, and must likewise submit to me." He ordered the Grants of Glenmoriston to be instantly surrounded and disarmed; which might be a very proper check to the spirit of clanship. But when we learn that they were shipped off for the colonies, we cannot wonder that the example of submission afforded small encouragement to such surrenders as this.

On most occasions these proceedings by martial law would have attracted animadversion in England whoever were the sufferers. But the truth is, that the English nourished a very false idea respecting the political opinions of the Scots, and were much disposed to conceive that the whole inhabitants of that kingdom were at heart their enemies; or at least to entertain violent suspicions against such as expressed the least sympathy with the sufferings of a Jacobite, or supposed that his punishment might, by possibility, be more severe than the crime deserved. There was something of consolation in such an opinion, in so far as it seemed a justification for the extent of the alarm of which, by this time, the English people had become ashamed, since it sounded more respectable to have feared the whole force of Scotland, than that of a few Highland clans, much inferior in number to those of their own nation who embraced the side of the Government. Nor would it be just to blame the English alone for these severities. It must be confessed that Scottish officers were found willing to escape from the suspicion of Jacobitism, so fatal to preferment, at the expense of becoming the agents of the cruelties practised on their unfortunate countrymen. At length and slowly the military operations began to be relaxed. After residing at Fort Augustus from the 24th of May till the 18th of July, the Duke of Cumberland returned towards Edinburgh.

That town had, in the meantime, witnessed a procession of four-teen of the rebel standards, borne by as many chimneysweepers, to be publicly burnt by the hands of the common hangman. A Jacobite might have observed, like a captive who received a blow after he was bound, that there was little gallantry in this insult. The Duke was received with all the honours due to conquest, and all the incorporated bodies of the capital, from the guild brethren to the butchers, desired his acceptance of the freedom of their craft or corporation. From Edinburgh his Royal Highness proceeded to London, to reap the full harvest of honours and rewards, which would not have been less richly deserved if he had min-gled more clemency with a certain degree of severity.

After this period the military executions, slaughters, and ravages were in a great measure put an end to. The license of the soldiery was curbed; courts of civil justice asserted the wholesome superiority of the law over violence; the aggressions of the parties of soldiery were pun-ished with damages in the usual course of justice; and the ordinary rules of civilised society were in a great measure replaced. We now dis-miss the consideration of the calamitous consequences brought on the country by general military execution, and proceed to consider the fate of those chiefs whose insurrection had been the cause of so much evil.

The first in rank, in misfortune, and in the temerity which led to the civil war, was unquestionably Charles Edward himself. A reward of £30,000 was offered for the discovery and seizure of this last scion of a royal line. It was imagined, that in a country so poor as the Highlands, lawless in a sense, so far as the law of property was concerned, and where the people were supposed to be almost proverbially rapacious, a much smaller reward would have insured the capture of the Pretender to the throne. His escape, however, so long delayed, and effected through so many difficulties, has been often commemorated as a bril-liant instance of fidelity. I shall only here touch upon its general out-lines, leaving you to acquire further details from other authors.[1]

During the battle of Culloden Charles had his share of the dangers of the field. The cannon especially directed against his standard made

---

[1] Mr. John Home, in his *History of the Rebellion in 1745*, and Mr. James Boswell, in his *Journal of a Tour to the Hebrides*, have given each a minute account of the Prince's escape, more correct than those formerly published under the name of *Ascanius, Young Juba*, etc. They have been embodied in Mr. Robert Chambers's *History of the Rebellion in 1745–46*, a work which contains a great quantity of curious information, both histori-cal and traditional, respecting the rebellion.

some havoc among his guards, and killed one of his servants who held a
led horse near to his person. The Prince himself was covered with the
earth thrown up by the balls. He repeatedly endeavoured to rally his
troops, and in the opinion of most who saw him did the duties of a brave
and good commander. When he retreated from the field he was attended
by a large body of horse, from whom, being perhaps under some doubt
of their fidelity, he disengaged himself, by dismissing them on various
errands, but particularly with instructions to warn the fugitives that they
were to rendezvous at Ruthven, in Badenoch; for such had been the
reckless resolution to fight, and such perhaps the confidence in victory,
that no place of rendezvous had been announced to the army in case of
defeat. Having dismissed the greater part of his horsemen, Charles
retained around his person only a few of the Irish officers, who had been
his constant followers, and whose faith he considered as less doubtful
than that of the Scots, perhaps because they were themselves more loud
in asserting it. He directed his flight to Gortuleg, where he understood
Lord Lovat was residing. Perhaps he expected to find counsel in the
renowned sagacity of this celebrated nobleman; perhaps he expected
assistance from his power; for the Master of Lovat, and Cluny MacPherson, Lovat's son-in-law, were neither of them in the action of Culloden,
but both in the act of bringing up strong reinforcements to the Prince's
army, and on the march thither when the battle was lost.

Charles and Lovat met, for the first and last time, in mutual terror
and embarrassment. The Prince exclaimed upon the distresses of Scotland; Lord Lovat had a more immediate sense of his own downfall.[1]
Having speedily found that neither counsel nor aid was to be obtained
at Lovat's hands, the Prince only partook of some slight refreshment
and rode on. He thought Gortuleg dangerous, as too near the victorious army; perhaps also he suspected the faith of its principal inmate.
Invergarry, the castle of the Laird of Glengarry, was the next halt, where

---

[1] A lady, who, then a girl, was residing in Lord Lovat's family, described to us the unexpected appearance of Prince Charles and his flying attendants, at Castle Downie. The
wild and desolate vale, on which she was gazing with indolent composure, was at once
so suddenly filled with horsemen riding furiously towards the castle that, impressed
with the belief that they were fairies, who, according to Highland tradition, are visible
to men only from one twinkle of the eye-lid to another, she strove to refrain from the
vibration, which she believed would occasion the strange and magnificent apparition
to become invisible. To Lord Lovat it brought a certainty more dreadful than the presence of fairies, or even demons.

the chance success of a fisherman who had caught a brace of salmon afforded him a repast. The mansion-house suffered severely for the temporary reception of the Prince, being wasted and destroyed by the English soldiery with unusual rigour.[2] From Invergarry the fugitive Prince penetrated into the West Highlands, and took up his abode in a village called Glenboisdale, very near the place where he had first landed. By this time he had totally renounced the further prosecution of his enterprise, his sanguine hopes being totally extinguished in the despair which attended his defeat. Charles despatched a message to those chiefs and soldiers who should rendezvous at Ruthven in obedience to his order, to acquaint them that, entertaining deep gratitude for their faithful attention and gallant conduct on all occasions, he was now under the necessity of recommending to them to look after their own safety, as he was compelled by circumstances to retire to France, from whence he hoped soon to return with succours.

Although not above one thousand men had attended at the appointed rendezvous, a great many of these thought that there was still hopes of continuing the enterprise, and were disposed to remonstrate with the Prince on his resolution of abandoning it. Lord George Murray was of this opinion, and declared that, as for provisions, if he was entrusted with any direction, they should not want as long as there were cattle in the Highlands, or meal in the Lowlands. John Hay was despatched to wait upon the Prince, and entreat him even yet to resume his post at the head of his army.

It must be owned that these were the thoughts of desperate men; the enterprise had been despaired of by all sensible persons ever since the retreat from Stirling, if not since that, from Derby. It was not to be supposed that an army with little hope of supplies or reinforcement, and composed of clans each independent of the others, and deprived of a great many of the best and boldest chiefs, while others, like Lochiel, were disabled by wounds, should adhere to an alliance in which there was no common object; and it is much more likely that, divided as they were by jealousies, they would have broken up as on former occasions, by each clan endeavouring to make its separate peace.

---

[2] Two large chestnut-trees were blown up with gunpowder; one was destroyed totally, the other survived the explosion, one-half continuing to flourish though the other was torn off. Glengarry's plate fell into the hands of the soldiery; part of it was melted into a cup, long in the possession of Sir Adolphus Oughton, commander-in-chief in Scotland, bearing the motto, *Ex præda prædatoris.*

When John Hay, therefore, came to Charles at Glenboisdale, to convey Lord George Murray's expostulation and request, he received from the Prince a letter in answer, declaring, in stronger and plainer words, his determined intention to depart for France, from which he hoped soon to return with a powerful reinforcement. Each behaved according to his character. The stubborn resolution of Lord George Murray demonstrated the haughty obstinacy of his rough and indomitable character, which had long looked on the worst as an event likely to arrive, and was now ready to brave it; while the Prince, whose sanguine hopes could not be taught to anticipate a defeat, now regarded it with justice as an irretrievable evil.

From this time Charles must be regarded as providing for his own escape, and totally detached from the array which he lately commanded. With this view he embarked for the Long Island, on the coast of which he hoped to find a French vessel. Contrary winds, storms, disappointments of several sorts, attended with hardships to which he could be little accustomed, drove him from place to place in that island and its vicinity, till he gained South Uist, where he was received by Clanranald, who, one of the first who joined the unfortunate Prince, was faithful to him in his distresses. Here, for security's sake, Charles was lodged in a forester's hut of the most miserable kind, called Corradale, about the centre of the wild mountain so named.

But every lurking-place was now closely sought after, and the islands in particular were, strictly searched, for the purpose of securing the fugitive Prince, suspected of being concealed in their recesses. General Campbell sailed as far as the island of St. Kilda, which might well pass for the extremity of the habitable world. The simple inhabitants had but a very general idea of the war which had disturbed all Britain, except that it had arisen from some difference between their master, the Laird of MacLeod, and a female on the continent—probably some vague idea about the Queen of Hungary's concern in the war.

General Campbell, returning from Kilda, landed upon South Uist, with the purpose of searching the Long Island from south to north, and he found the MacDonalds of Skye, and MacLeod of MacLeod, as also a strong detachment of regular troops, engaged in the same service. While these forces, in number two thousand men, searched with eagerness the interior of the island, its shores were surrounded with small vessels of war, cutters, armed boats, and the like. It seemed as if the Prince's escape from a search so vigorously prosecuted was altogether impossible; but the high spirit of a noble-minded female rescued him, when probably every other means must have failed.

This person was the celebrated Flora MacDonald; she was related to the Clanranald family, and was on a visit to that chief's house at Ormaclade, in South Uist, during the emergency we speak of. Her stepfather was one of Sir Alexander MacDonald's clan, an enemy to the Prince of course, and in the immediate command of the militia of the name MacDonald, who were then in South Uist.

Notwithstanding her stepfather's hostility, Flora MacDonald readily engaged in a plan for rescuing the unfortunate Wanderer. With this purpose she procured from her stepfather a passport for herself, a man servant, and a female servant, who was termed Betty Burke—the part of Betty Burke being to be acted by the Chevalier in woman's attire. In this disguise, after being repeatedly in danger of being taken, Charles at length reached Kilbride, in the Isle of Skye; but they were still in the country of Sir Alexander MacDonald, and, devoted as that chief was to the service of the Government, the Prince was as much in danger as ever. Here the spirit and presence of mind of Miss Flora MacDonald were again displayed in behalf of the object, so strangely thrown under the protection of one of her sex and age. She resolved to confide the secret to Lady Margaret MacDonald, the wife of Sir Alexander, and trust to female compassion, and the secret reserve of Jacobitism which lurked in the heart of most Highland women.

The resolution to confide in Lady Margaret was particularly hardy, for Sir Alexander MacDonald, the husband of the lady to be trusted with the important secret, was, as you will recollect, originally believed to be engaged to join the Prince on his arrival, but had declined doing so, under the plea, that the stipulated support from France was not forthcoming; he was afterwards induced to levy his clan on the side of Government. His men had been at first added to Lord Loudon's army, in Inverness-shire, and now formed part of those troops from which the Chevalier had with difficulty just made his escape.

Flora MacDonald found herself under the necessity of communicating the fatal secret of her disguised attendant to the lady of a person thus situated. Lady Margaret MacDonald was much alarmed. Her husband was absent, and as the best mode for the unfortunate Prince's preservation, her house being filled with officers of the militia, she committed him to the charge of MacDonald of Kingsburgh, a man of courage and intelligence, who acted as factor or steward for her husband. Flora MacDonald accordingly conducted Charles to MacDonald of Kingsburgh's house; and he was fortunate enough to escape detection on the road, though the ungainly and awkward appearance of a man dressed in female apparel attracted suspicion on more than one occasion.

From Kingsburgh the Wanderer retired to Raasay, where he suffered great distress, that island having been plundered on account of the laird's accession to the rebellion. During this period of his wanderings he personated the servant of his guide, and the country of the Laird of MacKinnon became his temporary refuge; but notwithstanding the efforts of the chief in his favour, that portion of Skye could afford him neither a place of repose nor safety, so that he was compelled once more to take refuge on the mainland, and was by his own desire put ashore on Loch Nevis.

Here also he encountered imminent danger, and narrowly escaped being taken. There were a number of troops engaged in traversing this district, which being the country of Lochiel, Keppoch, Glengarry, and other Jacobite chiefs, was the very cradle of the rebellion. Thus the Wanderer and his guides soon found themselves included within a line of sentinels, who, crossing each other upon their posts, out them off from proceeding into the interior of the province. After remaining two days cooped up within this hostile circle, without daring to light a fire, or to dress any provisions, they at length escaped the impending danger by creeping down a narrow and dark defile, which divided the posts of two sentinels.

Proceeding in this precarious manner, his clothes reduced to tatters, often without food, fire, or shelter, the unfortunate Prince, upheld only by the hope of hearing of a French vessel on the coast, at length reached the mountains of Strathglass, and with Glenaladale, who was then in attendance upon him, was compelled to seek refuge in a cavern where seven robbers had taken up their abode—(by robbers you are not in the present case to understand thieves, but rather outlaws, who dared not show themselves on account of their accession to the rebellion)—and lived upon such sheep and cattle as fell into their hands. These men readily afforded refuge to the Wanderer, and recognising the Prince, for whom they had repeatedly ventured their lives, in the miserable suppliant before them, they vowed unalterable devotion to his cause. Among the flower of obedient and attached subjects, never did a Prince receive more ready, faithful, and effectual assistance, than he did from those who were foes to the world and its laws. Desirous of rendering him all the assistance in their power, the hardy freebooters undertook to procure him a change of dress, clean linen, refreshments, and intelligence. They proceeded in a manner which exhibited a mingled character of ferocity and simplicity. Two of the gang waylaid and killed the servant of an officer, who was going to Fort Augustus with his master's baggage. The portmanteau which he carried fell into the robbers' hands, and supplied the articles of dress which they wanted for the Chevalier's use. One of them, suitably disguised, ventured into Fort Augustus, and obtained valuable information concerning the movements of the troops; and desirous to fulfil his purpose in every particular, he brought back in the singleness of his heart, as a choice regale to the unhappy Prince, a pennyworth of gingerbread!

With these men Charles Edward remained for about three weeks, and it was with the utmost difficulty they would permit him to leave them. "Stay with us," said the generous robbers; "the mountains of gold which the Government have set upon your head may induce some gentleman to betray you, for he can go to a distant country and Eve on the price of his dishonour; but to us there exists no such temptation. We can speak no language but our own—we can live nowhere but in this country, where, were we to injure a hair of your head, the very mountains would fall down to crush us to death."

A singular instance of enthusiastic devotion happened about this time (August 2d), which served to aid the Prince's escape. A son of a goldsmith in Edinburgh, one Roderick MacKenzie, late an officer in the Prince's army, happened to be lurking in the braes of Glenmoriston. He was about the same size as the Prince, and was reckoned like him both in person and features. A party of soldiers set upon the young man in his hiding-place; he defended himself gallantly; and, anxious to render his death useful to the cause which he must no longer serve in life, he said in his mortal agony, "Ah, villains! you have slain your Prince!" His generous design succeeded. MacKenzie's head was cut off, passed for that of Charles Edward, and was sent as such up to London. It was some time ere the mistake was discovered, during which the rumour prevailed that Charles was slain; in consequence of which the search after him was very much relaxed. Owing to this favourable circumstance, Charles became anxious to see his adherents, Lochiel and Cluny MacPherson, who were understood to be lurking in Badenoch with some other fugitives; and in order to join these companions of his councils and dangers, he took leave of the faithful outlaws, retaining, however, two of them, to be his guard and guides.[1]

After many difficulties he effected a junction with his faithful adherents, Cluny and Lochiel, though not without great risk and danger on both sides. They took up for a time their residence in a hut called the cage, curiously constructed in a deep thicket on the side of a mountain called Benalder, under which name is included a great forest or chase, the property of Cluny. Here they lived in tolerable security, and enjoyed a rude plenty, which the Prince had not hitherto known during his wandering.

About the 18th of September Charles received intelligence that two French frigates had arrived at Lochnanuagh, to carry him and other fugitives of his party to France. Lochiel embarked along with him

---

[1] I am ashamed to tell that one of these poor men, who had showed such inflexible fidelity, was afterwards hanged at Inverness for stealing a cow. Another, by name Hugh Chisholm, resided at Edinburgh, and was well known to your Grandfather, then a young man at College, who subscribed with others to a small annuity, which was sufficient to render him comfortable. He retired to his native country, and died in Strathglass some time subsequent to 1812. He was a noble commanding figure, of six feet and upwards, had a very stately demeanour, and always wore the Highland garb. The author often questioned him about this remarkable period of his life. He always spoke as a high-minded man, who thought he had done no more than his duty, but was happy that it had fallen to his individual lot to discharge it. Of the death of the officer's servant he spoke with great composure. "It was too much honour for the like of him," he said, "to die for the relief of a Prince." Hugh had some peculiar customs and notions. He kept his right hand usually in his bosom, as if worthy of more care than the rest of his person, because Charles Edward had shaken hands with him when they separated. When he received his little dole (I am ashamed of the small amount, but I had not much to give), which he always did with the dignity of one collecting tribute rather than receiving alms, he extended his left hand with great courtesy, making an excuse for not offering the other, "that it was sick." But the true reason was, that he would not contaminate with a meaner touch the hand that had been grasped by his rightful Prince. If pressed on this topic, or offered money to employ the right hand, he would answer with passion, that if your hand were full of gold, and he might be owner of it all for touching it with his right hand, he would not comply with your request. He remained till the last day of his life a believer in the restoration of the Stewart family in the person of Charles Edward, as the Jews confide in the advent of the Messiah; nor could he ever be convinced of the death of his favourite Prince. A scheme, he believed, was formed, by which every fifth man in the Highlands was to rise—if that number was insufficient, every third man was to be called—"If that be not enough," said the old man, raising himself and waving his hand, "we will all gather and go together." Such delusions amused his last years; but when I knew him, he was quite sane in his intellects.

on the 20th, as did near one hundred others of the relics of his party, whom the tidings had brought to the spot where the vessel lay. Cluny MacPherson remained behind, and continued to skulk in his own country for several years, being the agent by means of whom Charles Edward long endeavoured to keep up a correspondence with his faithful Highlanders. A letter is in my possession, by which the Prince expressed his sense of the many services which he had received from this gentleman and his clan. I give it as a curiosity in the note below.[1]

The Prince landed near Morlaix, in Brittany, on the 29th of September. His short but brilliant expedition had attracted the attention and admiration of Europe, from his debarkation in Boradale, about the 26th of August 1745, until the day of his landing in France, a period of thirteen months and a few days, five months of which had been engaged in the most precarious, perilous, and fatiguing series of flight, concealment, and escape that has ever been narrated in history or romance. During his wanderings, the secret of the Adventurer's concealment was entrusted to hundreds of every sex, age, and condition; but no individual was found, in a high or low situation, or robbers even who procured their food at the risk of their lives, who thought for an instant of obtaining opulence at the expense of treachery to the proscribed and miserable fugitive. Such disinterested conduct will reflect honour[2] on the Highlands of Scotland while their mountains shall continue to exist.

---

[1] "Mr. MacPherson of Clunie,

"As we are sensible of your and clan's fidelity and integrity to us dureing our adventures in Scotland and England, in the year 1745 and 1746, in recovering our just rights from the Elector of Hanover, by which you have sustained very great losses both in your interest and person, I therefore promise, when it shall please God to put it in my power, to make a gretfull return, sutable to your sufferings.

(Signed)   "Charles, P. R."

"Diralagich in Glencamyier of Locharkaig,
      18th Sept. 1746."

It is dated two days before Charles left Scotland.

[2] When General Stewart was printing his *Sketches of the Highlanders*, he asked Sir Walter Scott to suggest a motto for the title-page—and he pointed out those lines of Shakspeare—

            "Tis wonderful
That an invisible instinct should frame them
To loyalty unlearned; honour untaught,
Civility not seen from others; valour,
That wildly grows in them, but yields a crop
As if it had been sowed."

LXXXV

The Great Suppression

1746

WE must now detail the consequences of the civil war to the Prince's most important adherents. Several had been taken prisoners on the field of battle, and many more had been seized in the various excursions made through the country of the rebels by the parties of soldiery. The gaols both in England and Scotland had been filled with these unfortunate persons, upon whom a severe doom was now to be inflicted. That such was legally incurred cannot be denied; and, on the other hand, it will hardly be now contradicted, that it was administered with an indiscriminate severity which counteracted the effects intended, by inspiring horror instead of awe.

The distinguished persons of the party were with good reason considered as most accountable for its proceedings. It was they who must have obtained power and wealth had the attempt succeeded, and they were justly held most responsible when they failed in their attempt at accomplishing a revolution.

Lord George Murray, who acted so prominent a part in the insurrection, effected his escape to the Continent, and died at Medenblinck in Holland in 1760.

The Earls of Kilmarnock and Cromarty, and Lords Balmerino and Lovat, in Scotland, with Mr. Charles Ratcliffe, in England (brother of the Earl of Derwentwater, attainted and executed in 1715), were the persons most distinguished by birth and title whom the Government had within their power. The Marquis of Tullibardine had also been made prisoner, but death, by a disease under which he had long languished, relieved his captivity in the Tower, and removed him from all earthly trial or punishment. There could have been no difficulty in obtaining evidence against Kilmarnock, Cromarty, and Balmerino, all three of whom had acted openly in the rebellion at the head of an armed force; but in Lovat's case, who had not been personally in arms, it was absolutely necessary that evidence should be brought of his accession to the secret councils of the conspiracy, which it was also desirable should be made known to the British public.

The Government were therefore desirous to get at the grounds, if possible, on which the conspiracy had been originally formed, and to obtain knowledge of such Jacobites of power and consequence in England as had been participant of the councils which had occasioned such an explosion in North Britain.

A disclosure so complete could only be attained by means of an accomplice deep in the secret intrigues of the insurgents. It was, therefore, necessary to discover among the late counsellors of the Chevalier some individual who loved life better than honour and fidelity to a ruined cause; and such a person was unhappily found in John Murray of Broughton, secretary to Charles Edward. This unfortunate gentleman, as we have already seen, was intimately acquainted with the circumstances in which the rebellion had originated, had been most active in advancing the Chevalier's interest, both in civil and military transactions; and though he considerably embroiled his master's affairs by fanning the discord between the Duke of Perth and Lord George Murray, and stimulating the Chevalier's dislike to the latter nobleman, yet it would be overloading the memory of the unfortunate to suppose that his conduct arose from any other motive than a desire to advance the objects of his own ambition, without a thought of betraying his master's interest. After the battle of Culloden, Murray fled to the Highlands; but, unable to endure the hardships which he incurred in these regions, he returned to his native country, and took refuge with a relation, whose seat is in the mountains at the head of Tweeddale. He was here discovered and made prisoner.

Being assailed by threats and promises, this unhappy gentleman was induced, by promise of a free pardon, to confess to Ministers the full detail of the original conspiracy in 1740, and the various modifications which it underwent subsequent to that period, until the landing of Prince Charles in the Hebrides. It has never been doubted that his details must have involved the names of many persons, both in England and Scotland, who did not take up arms in the insurrection of 1745, although, as the law of England requires two witnesses to every act of high treason, none such could have been brought to trial upon Murray's single evidence. He himself urged, in extenuation of his conduct, that although he preserved his own life, by bringing forward his evidence against such men as Government could have convicted without his assistance, yet he carefully concealed many facts, which, if disclosed, would either have borne more hard upon such complotters before the fact, or would have implicated others, against whom Government had no other information. It is not necessary to examine this species of logic; as, on the one hand, it is unlikely that Government would have been trifled with in this manner by a person in Murray's situation; and, on the other, it does not appear that the moral guilt of an approver, or King's evidence, is diminished because he discharges with infidelity the base bargain he has entered into.

The Government thus made fully acquainted, by Mr. Murray's means, with the original plan and extent of the conspiracy, proceeded to bring to trial those leading culprits by whom it had been carried on in arms.

The two Earls of Kilmarnock and Cromarty, with Lord Balmerino, were brought to the bar of the House of Lords, towards the end of July 1746, upon a charge of high treason, to which the two Earls pleaded guilty, and adhered to that plea. Lord Balmerino, when asked to plead declared, that he had been indicted as the Lord Balmerino "of the city of Carlisle," a title which did not belong to him, and that he even had not been at Carlisle on the day when he was charged by the indictment. He was answered, that the words, "late of Carlisle," were not made part of his title, but only an addition of place, which law required by way of description, of a person indicted like his lordship. Lord Balmerino then pleaded not guilty. Several witnesses appeared, who proved that the accused party had been seen clothed in the uniform of the rebel guards, heading and commanding them, and acting in every respect as a chief of the rebellion. Lord Balmerino only alleged that he had not been at the taking of Carlisle on the day mentioned in the indictment. This, he said, was an idea of his own adoption, and as he was now satisfied that it was not founded on law, he was sorry that he had given their lordships the trouble of hearing it. The three peers were then pronounced guilty by the voice of the House of Lords.

On the noblemen being brought up for sentence, on the 30th July, Lord Kilmarnock again confessed his offence, and pleaded guilty, urging that his father had bred him up in the strictest revolution principles, and pleading that he himself had imprinted the same so effectually on the mind of his own eldest son, that Lord Boyd bore, at the very time, a commission in the royal service, and had been in arms for King George at the battle of Culloden, when he himself fought on the other side. He pleaded likewise that he had, in the course of the insurrection, protected the persons and property of loyal subjects; and that he had surrendered after the battle of Culloden of his own accord, although he might have made his escape. Although this confession of offences was made at a time when its sincerity might be doubted, the grace and dignity of Lord Kilmarnock's appearance, together with the resignation and mildness of his address, melted all the spectators to tears; and so fantastic are human feelings, that a lady of fashion present, who had never seen his lordship before, contracted an extravagant passion for his person, which, in a less serious affair, would have been little less than a ludicrous frenzy.

Lord Cromarty also implored his Majesty's clemency, and declined to justify his crime. He threw his life and fortune on the compassion of the high court, and pleaded for mercy in the name of his innocent wife,—his eldest son who was a mere boy,—and eight helpless children, who must feel their parent's punishment before they knew his guilt.

Lord Balmerino being called upon to speak, why judgment of death should not pass upon him, at first objected to the act of Parliament under which he was tried; but withdrew his plea in arrest of judgment upon further consideration. Sentence of death was pronounced according to the terrible behest of the law, in cases of high treason.

The conduct of Balmerino was a striking and admirable contrast to that of the other two noblemen. He never either disowned or concealed his political principles. He stated, that he had, indeed, held an independent company of foot from Queen Anne, which he accounted an act of treason against his lawful Prince; but that he had atoned for this by joining in the insurrection in 1715; and willingly, and with his full heart, drew his sword in 1745, though his age might have excused him from taking arms. He therefore neither asked, nor seems to have wished, for either acquittal or pardon, and the bold and gallant manner in which he prepared for death attracted the admiration of all who witnessed it.

It was understood that one of the two Earls who had submitted themselves to the clemency of the sovereign was about to be spared. The friends of both solicited anxiously which should obtain preference on the occasion. The circumstance of his large family, and the situation of his lady, it is believed, influenced the decision which was made in Lord Cromarty's favour. When the Countess of Cromarty was delivered of the child which she had borne in her womb while the horrible doubt of her husband's fate was impending, it was found to be marked on the neck with an impression resembling a broad axe; a striking instance of one of those mysteries of nature which are beyond the knowledge of philosophy.

While King George the Second was perplexed and overwhelmed with personal applications for mercy, in behalf of Lords Cromarty and Kilmarnock, he is said to have exclaimed, with natural feeling, "Heaven help me, will no one say a word in behalf of Lord Balmerino? he, though a rebel, is at least an honest one!" The spirit of the time was, however, adverse to this generous sentiment; nor would it have been consistent to have spared a criminal who boldly avowed and vindicated his political offences, while exercising the severity of the law towards others, who expressed penitence for their guilt. The Earl of Cromarty being, as we have said, reprieved, the Earl of Kilmarnock and Lord Balmerino remained under sentence, with an intimation that they must prepare for death. The King, however, commuted the mode of execution into decapitation.

The behaviour of both noblemen, during the short interval they had now to live, was of a piece with their conduct on the trial. Lord Kilmarnock was composed, though penitent, and prepared himself with decency for the terrible exit. Balmerino, on the contrary, with a bold military frankness, seemed disposed to meet death on the scaffold with the same defiance as in a field of battle. His lady was with him at the moment the death-warrant arrived. They were at dinner: Lady Balmerino fainted at the awful tidings. "Do you not see," said her husband to the officer who had intimated the news, "you have spoiled my lady's dinner with your foolish warrant?"

On the 18th of August 1746 the prisoners were delivered over by the Governor of the Tower to the custody of the Sheriffs; on which occasion the officers closed the words of form by the emphatic prayer, "God save King George!" Kilmarnock answered with a deep "Amen." Lord Balmerino replied, in a loud and firm tone, "God save King James!"

Having been transported in a carriage to an apartment on Tower-hill provided for the purpose, the companions in suffering were allowed a momentary interview, in which Balmerino seemed chiefly anxious to vindicate the Prince from the report that there had been orders issued at the battle of Culloden to give no quarter. Kilmarnock confessed he had heard of such an order, signed George Murray, but it was only after he was made prisoner. They parted with mutual affection. "I would," said Lord Balmerino, "that I could pay this debt for us both." Lord Kilmarnock acknowledged his kindness. The Earl had the sad precedence in the execution. When he reached the spot, and beheld the fatal scaffold covered with black cloth; the executioner with his axe and his assistants; the sawdust which was soon to be drenched with his blood; the coffin prepared to receive the limbs which were yet warm with life; above all, the immense display of human countenances which surrounded the scaffold like a sea, all eyes being bent on the sad object of the preparation, his natural feelings broke forth in a whisper to the friend on whose arm he leaned, "Home, this is terrible!" No sign of indecent timidity, however, affected his behaviour; he prayed for the reigning King and family; knelt calmly to the block, and submitted to the fatal blow.

Lord Balmerino was next summoned to enter on the fatal scene. "I suppose," he said, "my Lord Kilmarnock is now no more; I will not detain you longer, for I desire not to protract my life." His Lordship then, taking a glass of wine, desired the bystanders to drink "*ain degrae ta haiven,*" that is, an ascent to Heaven. He took the axe out of the hand of the executioner, and ran his finger along the edge, while a momentary thrill went through the spectators, at seeing so daring a man in the possession of such a weapon. Balmerino did not, however, meditate such desperate folly as would have been implied in an attempt at resistance; he returned the axe to the executioner, and bid him strike boldly, "for in that," he said, "my friend, will consist thy mercy." "There may be some," he said, "who think my behaviour bold. Remember what I tell you," addressing a bystander, "it arises from a confidence in God and a clear conscience."

With the same intrepid countenance, Balmerino knelt to the block, prayed for King James and his family, entreated forgiveness of his own sins, petitioned for the welfare of his friends, and pardon to his enemies. These brief prayers finished, he gave the signal to the executioner; but the man was so surprised at the undaunted intrepidity of his victim, that he struck the first blow irresolutely, and it required two to despatch the bloody work.

The conclusion of Lord Lovat's eventful and mysterious career was the next important act of this eventful tragedy. That old conspirator, after making his escape from his vassal's house of Gortuleg, had fled to the Highlands, where he was afterwards taken in one of the Western Islands, by a detachment from the garrison of Fort William, who had disembarked from on board a bomb vessel, called the *Furnace*. The old man was brought to the Tower of London. On this occasion, using the words of the Latin poet,[1] he expressed himself prepared either to resort to his old stratagems, or to meet death like a man, if he should find it inevitable. Lovat's trial, which came on before the House of Lords on the 9th, and was finished on the 19th day of March, was very long and extremely curious. On the former occasions it had not been necessary to produce the evidence of Secretary Murray; but on the present, as Lovat had not been personally engaged in the insurrection, it was indispensable to prove his accession to the previous conspiracy. This was accomplished in the fullest manner; indeed he said of himself, probably with great truth, that he had been engaged in every insurrection in favour of the family of James the Seventh since he was fifteen years old; and he might have added, he had betrayed some of them to the opposite party. His guilt, thinly covered by a long train of fraud, evasion, and deceit, was clearly manifested, though he displayed very considerable skill and legal knowledge in his defence. Being found guilty by the House of Lords, the sentence of high treason was pronounced upon the old man in the usual horrible terms. He heard it with indifference, and replied, "I bid your Lordships an everlasting farewell. Sure I am, we shall never all meet again in the same place."

During the interval between the sentence and its execution, this singular personage employed himself at first in solicitations for life, expressed pretty much in the style of a fawning letter, which, when he was first taken prisoner, he had written to the Duke of Cumberland, pleading his high favour with George the First, and how he had carried his Royal Highness about, when a child, in the parks of Kensington

---

[1] Seu versare dolos seu certæ occumbere morti.

and Hampton Court. Finding these meannesses were in vain, he resolved to imitate in his death the animal he most resembled in his life, and die like the fox, without indulging his enemies by the utterance of a sigh or groan. It is remarkable, my dear boy, how the audacity of this daring man rendered him an object of wonder and awe at his death, although the whole course of his life had been spent in a manner calculated to excite very different feelings. Lovat had also, indeed, the advantage of the compassion due to extreme old age, still nourishing a dauntless spirit, even when a life beyond the usual date of humanity was about to be cut short by a public execution. Many circumstances are told of him in prison, from which we may infer that the careless spirit of levity was indulged by him to the last moment. On the evening before his execution, his warder expressed himself sorry that the morrow should be such a bad day with his Lordship. "Bad!" replied his Lordship; "for what? do you think I am afraid of an axe? It is a debt we must all pay, and better in this way than by a lingering disease."

When ascending the scaffold (in which he requested the assistance of two warders), he looked round on the multitude, and seeing so many people, said with a sneer, "God save us, why should there be such a bustle about taking off an old gray head from a man who cannot get up three steps without two assistants?" On the scaffold he repeated the line of Horace—

"Dulce et decorum est pro patria mori."

It was more in his true character, that when a scaffold fell, and he was informed that many persons had been killed and maimed, he replied in the words of the Scottish adage—"The more mischief the better sport!" He submitted to the fatal blow with unabated courage, and left a strong example of the truth of the observation, that it is easier to die well than to live well. The British government did not escape blame, for having selected as an example of punishment an old man on the very verge of life. Yet, of all the victims to justice, no one either deserved or received less compassion than Lovat.

While the blood of the nobility concerned in the insurrection of 1745 was flowing thus plentifully, the criminals of minor importance had no cause to think that justice was aristocratic in her selection of victims. The persons who earliest fell into the hands of the Government were the officers of the Manchester regiment, left, as we have seen, in Carlisle after the retreat from Derby. Of these the colonel and eight other persons who had held commissions were tried and condemned in London. Eight others were found guilty at the same time, but were reprieved. Those who were destined for execution underwent the doom of law in its most horrible shape, upon Kennington Common; where they avowed their political principles and died firmly. A melancholy and romantic incident took place amid the terrors of the executions. A young lady, of good family and handsome fortune, who had been contracted in marriage to James Dawson, one of the sufferers, had taken the desperate resolution of attending on the horrid ceremonial. She beheld her lover, after having been suspended for a few minutes, but not till death (for such was the barbarous sentence), cut down, embowelled, and mangled by the knife of the executioner. All this she supported with apparent fortitude; but when she saw the last scene finished, by throwing Dawson's heart into the fire, she drew her head within the carriage, repeated his name, and expired on the spot. This melancholy circumstance was made by Mr. Shenstone the theme of a tragic ballad.

The mob of London had hooted these unfortunate gentlemen as they passed to and from their trial, but they witnessed their last sufferings with decency. Three Scottish officers of the party taken at Carlisle were next condemned and executed in the same manner as the former; others were similarly tried, and five were ordered for execution; among these, Sir John Wedderburn, Baronet, was the most distinguished.

At Carlisle no less than 385 prisoners had been assembled, with the purpose of trying a select number of them at that place, where their guilt had been chiefly manifested. From this mass 119 were selected for indictment and trial at the principal towns in the north. At York the Grand Jury found bills against 75 insurgents. Upon this occasion, the Chaplain of the High Sheriff of Yorkshire preached before the judges on the very significant text (Numbers xxv. 5), "And Moses said unto the judges of Israel, slay ye every one his men that were joined unto Baalpeor."

At York and Carlisle seventy persons received sentence of death; some were acquitted on the plea of having been forced into the rebellion by their chiefs. This recognises a principle which might have been carried much further, when it is considered how much by education and principle these wretched kerne were at the disposal of their leaders. The law, which makes allowance for the influence of a husband over a wife, or a father over a son, even when it involves them in guilt, ought unquestionably to have had the same consideration for the clansmen, who were trained up in the most absolute ideas of obedience to their chief, and politically exerted no judgment of their own.

Nine persons were executed at Carlisle on the 18th of October. The list contained one or two names of distinction; Buchanan of Arnpryor, the chief of his name; MacDonald of Kinloch-Moidart, one of the first who received the Prince on his landing; MacDonald of Teindreich, who began the war by attacking Captain Scott's detachment when marching to Fort Augustus, and John MacNaughten, a person of little note, unless in so far as he was said, but it is believed erroneously, to have been the individual by whose hand Colonel Gardiner fell at Prestonpans. Six criminals suffered at Brampton; seven were executed at Penrith, and twenty-two at the city of York; eleven more were afterwards executed at Carlisle; nearly eighty in all were sacrificed to the terrors which the insurrection had inspired.

These unfortunate sufferers were of different ages, rank, and habits; they agreed, however, in their behaviour upon the scaffold. They prayed for the exiled family, expressed their devotion to the cause in which they died, and particularly their admiration of the princely leader whom they had followed, till their attachment conducted them to this dreadful fate. It may be justly questioned whether the lives of these men, supposing every one of them to have been an apostle of Jacobitism, could have done so much to prolong their doctrines as the horror and loathing inspired by so many bloody punishments. And when to these are added the merciless slaughter of the fugitives at Culloden, and the devastation committed in the Highland districts, it might have been expected that the sword of justice would have been weary with executions.

There were still, however, some individuals, upon whom, for personal reasons, vengeance was still desired. One of these was Charles Ratcliffe, brother to the Earl of Derwentwater. This gentleman had been partaker in the Earl's treason of 1715, and had been condemned for that crime, but escaped from Newgate. In the latter end of the year 1745, or beginning of 1746, he was taken on board a French ship of war, with other officers. The vessel was loaded with arms and warlike stores, bound for the coast of Scotland, for the use of the insurgents. Ratcliffe's case was, therefore, a simple one. He was broughtbefore the King's Bench, where evidence was adduced to show that he was the same Charles Ratcliffe who had been condemned for the earlier rebellion, and who had then made his escape. Upon this being found proved by a jury, he was condemned to die, although, appealing to his French commission, he pleaded that he was not a subject of Britain, and denied himself to be the Charles Ratcliffe to whom the indictment and conviction referred, alleging he was Charles Earl of Derwentwater.

On the 8th of December Ratcliffe appeared on the scaffold, where he was admitted, in respect of his birth, to the sad honours of the axe and block. He was richly dressed, and behaved with a mixture of grace and firmness which procured him universal sympathy. Lovat, whose tragedy I have already given, was, in point of time, the last person who suffered death for political causes in 1747.

An Act of Indemnity was passed in June 1747, granting a pardon to all persons who had committed treason,[1] but with an awful list of exceptions, amounting to about eighty names. I may here mention the fate of some of those persons who had displayed so much fidelity to Charles during the time of his escape. The Laird of MacKinnon, Mac-Donald of Kingsburgh, and others, ascertained to have been active in aiding the Prince's escape, were brought to London, and imprisoned for some time. Flora MacDonald, the heroine of this extraordinary drama, was also, for a time, detained in the Tower. As I have recorded several of the severities of Government, I ought to add, that nothing save a short imprisonment attended the generous interference of those individuals in behalf of the unfortunate Adventurer, during his dangers and distresses. After being liberated from the Tower, Flora MacDonald found refuge, or rather a scene of triumph, in the house of Lady Primrose, a determined Jacobite, where the Prince's Highland guardian was visited by all persons of rank, who entertained any bias to that unhappy cause. Neither did the English Jacobites limit their expressions of respect and admiration to empty compliments. Many who, perhaps, secretly regretted they had not given more effectual instances of their faith to the exiled family, were desirous to make some amends, by loading with kind attentions and valuable presents, the heroine who had played such a dauntless part in the drama. These donations supplied to the gallant Highland lady a fortune of nearly £1500. She bestowed this dowry, together with her hand, upon MacDonald of Kingsburgh, who had been her assistant in the action which had procured her so much fame. The applause due to her noble conduct was

---

[1] 20th George II. 1747.

not rendered by Jacobites alone; many of the Royal Family, and particularly the good-natured and generous Prince Frederick of Wales,[1] felt and expressed what was due to the worth of Flora MacDonald, though exerted for the safety of so dangerous a rival. The simplicity and dignity of her character was expressed in her remark, that she never thought she had done anything wonderful till she heard the world wondering at it. She afterwards went to America with her husband Kingsburgh, but both returned, in consequence of the civil war, and died in their native Isle of Skye.

I should make these volumes thrice as long as they ought to be, were I to tell you the stories which I have heard (sometimes from the lips of those who were themselves the sufferers) concerning the strange concealments and escapes which the Jacobites were reduced to for the safety of their lives after their cause was ruined. The severity of legal prosecution was not speedily relaxed, although the proceedings under martial law were put a stop to. Lord Pitsligo, who lurked on his own estate, and displayed a model of patience under unusual sufferings, continued to be an object of occasional search long after the year 1746; and was in some degree under concealment till his death in 1762,[2] at the age of eighty-five. Some other criminals peculiarly obnoxious to Government were not liberated from prison until the accession of George the Third.

---

[1] Frederick, grandfather of King George the Fourth. His Royal Highness gave a proof of this generous and liberal mode of thinking, when the Princess his wife informed him that Lady Margaret MacDonald, concerned with Flora in saving the Chevalier, had been presented to her Royal Highness, adding, with some concern, that she did not know her to be the person implicated in the escape of Charles Edward. "And would you not have done the like, madam," replied the high-minded Prince, "had the unfortunate man appeared before you in such calamitous circumstances? I know—I am sure—you would."

[2] Farquharson of Monaltry, lieutenant-colonel of one of Lord Lewis Gordon's Aberdeenshire battalions, was the last person who remained in confinement for the affair of 1745.

LXXXVI

The End of the Clans

1746

W E have hitherto only detailed the penal procedure taken against the principal actors in the rebellion of 1745. Before proceeding to narrate the legislative measures which Parliament thought proper to adopt to prevent the recurrence of such a calamity, it may be necessary, in this place, to take a review of the character of the insurrection, and the result which it actually did or might have produced.

Looking at the whole in a general point of view, there can be no doubt that it presents a dazzling picture to the imagination, being a romance of real life equal in splendour and interest to any which could be devised by fiction. A primitive people, residing in a remote quarter of the empire, and themselves but a small portion of the Scottish Highlanders, fearlessly attempted to place the British crown on the head of the last scion of those ancient kings, whose descent was traced to their own mountains. This gigantic task they undertook in favour of a youth of twenty-five, who landed on their shore without support of any kind, and threw himself on their generosity—they assembled an army in his behalf—their speech, their tactics, their arms, were alike unknown to their countrymen and to the English,—holding themselves free from the obligations imposed by common law or positive statute, they were yet governed by rules of their own, derived from a general sense of honour, extending from the chief to the lowest of his tribe.[1] With men unaccustomed to arms, the amount of the most efficient part of which never exceeded 2000, they defeated two disciplined armies commanded by officers of experience and reputation, penetrated deep into England, approached within a hundred miles of the capital, and made the crown tremble on the King's head; retreated with the like success, when they appeared on the point of being intercepted between three hostile armies; checked effectually the attack of a superior body detached in pursuit of them; reached the north in safety, and were only suppressed by a concurrence of disadvantages which it was impossible for human nature to surmount. All this has much that is splendid to the imagination, nor is it possible to regard without admiration the little band of determined men by whom such actions were achieved, or the interesting young Prince by whom their energies were directed. It is therefore natural that the civil strife of 1745 should have been long the chosen theme of the poet, the musician, and the novelist, and each has in turn found it possessed of an interest highly suitable to his purpose.

In a work founded on history, we must look more closely into the circumstances of the rebellion, and deprive it of some part of the show which pleases the fancy, in order to judge of it by the sound rules of reason. The best mode of doing this is to suppose that Charles had accomplished his romantic adventure, and seated himself in temporary security in the palace of St. James's; when common sense must admit that nothing could have been expected from such a counter-revolution

---

[1] A remarkable instance of this occurred when the Highland army advanced to Kirkliston, in their march on Edinburgh, 1745. It was recollected that the house of Newliston, lying near the camp of the Highlanders, had been built by the Secretary, Lord Stair, who was so deeply implicated in the massacre of Glencoe; it was also remembered that the grandson of the murdered Glencoe was in the Highland camp, at the head of his clan regiment; it was, therefore, to be apprehended that they would commit some violence on the house of Newliston, and as this would be highly prejudicial to the reputation of the Chevalier's army, it was proposed to place a guard for the purpose of preventing it. Glencoe heard this proposal, and demanded an audience of the Prince. "It is right," he said, "that a guard should be placed upon the house of Newliston, but that guard must be furnished by the MacDonalds of Glencoe; if they are not thought worthy of this trust, they cannot be fit to bear arms in your Royal Highness's cause, and I must, of course, withdraw them from your standard." The claim of the high-spirited chief was necessarily admitted, and the MacDonalds of Glencoe mounted guard on the house of Newliston; nor was there the least article deranged or destroyed.

excepting new strife and fiercer civil wars. The opinion and conduct of the whole British empire, with very few exceptions, had shown their disinclination to have this man to rule over them; nor were all the clans in his army numerous enough to furnish more than two battalions of guards to have defended his throne, had they been able to place him upon it. It was not to be supposed that England, so opulent, so populous, so high-spirited, could be held under a galling yoke by a few men of unknown language and manners, who could only be regarded as a sort of strelitzes or janissaries, and detested in that capacity. By far the greater part of Scotland itself was attached to the House of Hanover, and the principles which placed them on the throne; and its inhabitants were votaries of the Presbyterian religion, a form of church government which it had been long the object of the Stewart family to destroy. From that quarter, therefore, Charles, in his supposed state of perilous exaltation, could have drawn no support, but must have looked for opposition. The interference of a French force, had such taken place, could only have increased the danger of the restored dynasty, by rousing against them the ancient feelings of national hatred and emulation; nor is it likely that they could have offered successful resistance to the general opposition which such unpopular aid would have accumulated around them.

Neither is it probable that Charles Edward, educated as he had been in foreign courts, and in the antiquated principles of passive obedience and arbitrary power, would have endeavoured to conciliate the affections of the great mass of his subjects by disavowing those sentiments of despotic government which had cost his grandfather so dear. Even while his enterprise was in progress, there existed a great schism in his camp between Lord George Murray, Lord Elcho, and others, who, though engaged with the Prince and favouring his pretensions to the throne, conceived themselves entitled, as their lives and fortunes were depending on the issue, to remonstrate against measures of which they did not always approve. Charles Edward naturally, but fatally for himself and his family, preferred and followed the counsels of those who made it a point to coincide with him in opinion; so that, had the strength of this army been adequate to place him upon the throne, he must nevertheless have speedily been precipitated into civil war, the seeds of which existed even among his own followers, since they did not agree among themselves on what principles he was to govern, whether as a despotic or constitutional monarch.

From all this it would appear that, however severe upon the High-landers and their country at the moment when it happened, the defeat of Prince Charles at Culloden could alone have ended the internal divisions of Great Britain; and that any victory which he might have obtained would only have added to the protraction of civil strife, and the continuance and increase of national calamity.

Neither were the actions of the Highlanders under Prince Charles, though sufficiently glorious for their arms, altogether so wonderful as to be regarded as miraculous. Without detracting from their undoubted bravery, it must be said that the Chevalier was fortunate in meeting with two such antagonists as Cope and Hawley, neither of whom appears to have dreamed of maintaining a second line or effectual reserve, though rendered so necessary by the violence and precipitance of the Highland attack, which must always have thrown a certain degree of disorder into those troops who were first exposed to its fury, but at the same time have brought confusion among the assailants themselves. The two regiments of dragoons who fought, or rather fled, at Prestonpans, having previously lost their character by a succession of panics, must be also looked upon as affording to the Highlanders an advantage unusual to those who encounter an English army. Of the general plan of insurrection, it may be safely said to have been a rash scheme, devised by a very young man, who felt his hopes from France to be rendered absolutely desperate; and by piquing the honour of Lochiel and his friends, wrought them to such a height of feeling as to induce them to engage in what their common sense assured them was positive ruin.

We may also observe, that though the small number of this Prince's forces was in a great measure the cause of his ultimate defeat, yet the same circumstance contributed to his partial success.

This may appear paradoxical, but you are to remember that the imperfections of an undisciplined army increase in proportion to its numbers, as an ill-constructed machine becomes more unmanageable in proportion to its size. The powerful army of clans commanded by Mar in the year 1715 could not have acted with the same speed and decision as the comparatively small body which was arrayed under Charles. And if, on the latter occasion, the Prince wanted the aid of such large forces as were brought to Perth in 1715 by the Marquis of Huntly and the Earls of Breadalbane and Seaforth, his councils were also unembarrassed by the respect and deference claimed by these dignitaries, and by the discords which often arose between them, either

amongst themselves, or with the commander-in-chief. It is also worthy
of remark that, without derogating from the desire to maintain discipline, which was certainly entertained by the Highland chiefs during
the enterprise, the small number of the Prince's army must also have
occasioned among themselves a consciousness of weakness, and they
were perhaps the more disposed to attend to orders and abstain from
all unnecessary violence because they saw from the beginning that
their safety depended on mutual concord, and on preserving or acquiring the good opinion of the country.

Upon the whole, it was perhaps fortunate for the history of Highland clanship, that in point of effective and recognised influence, the
system may be considered as having closed with the gallant and generous display of its character which took place in 1745. We have said
already that the patriarchal spirit was gradually decaying, and that the
system had been insensibly innovated upon in each successive generation. In the beginning of the eighteenth century it probably would not
have existed if the chiefs had not sedulously nursed and kept it alive, to
maintain in their persons that peculiar military power which most of
them expected to render the means of distinguishing themselves in the
civil war that was yearly expected. If the country had remained in profound peace, the chiefs, like the Lowland barons, would have been
induced to exchange the command of their clansmen, whose services
they had no prospect of requiring, for other advantages, which
increased rents and improved possessions would have procured them.
The slow but certain operation of those changes would have finally dissolved, though perhaps at a later period, the connection between the
clan and the chief, and under circumstances perhaps less creditable to
the latter. It is therefore better, even for the fame of the Highlands, that
the spirit of the patriarchal system, like the light of a dying lamp,
should have collected itself into one bright flash before its final extinction, and in the short period of a few months, should have exhibited
itself in a purer and more brilliant character than it had displayed
during the course of ages.

It must also be remarked, that the period at which the patriarchal
system was totally broken up was that at which it presented the most
interesting appearance. The Highland chiefs of the eighteenth century,
at least those who were persons of consideration, were so much influenced by the general civilisation of Britain as to be not only averse to the
abuse of power over their clansmen, but disposed, as well from policy

as from higher motives to restrain their followers from predatory habits, and discouraging what was rude and fierce, to cultivate what was honourable and noble in their character. It is probable the patriarchal system was never exercised, generally speaking, in a mode so beneficial to humanity as at the time when it was remotely affected by the causes which must ultimately have dissolved it. In this respect it resembled the wood of certain trees, which never afford such beautiful materials for the cabinetmaker as when they have felt the touch of decay.

For these and other reasons the view which we cast upon the system of clanship, as it existed in the time of the last generation, is like looking back upon a Highland prospect, enlivened by the tints of a beautiful summer evening. On such an occasion the distant hills, lakes, woods, and precipices are touched by the brilliancy of the atmosphere with a glow of beauty which is not properly their own, and it requires an exertion to recall to our mind the desolate, barren, and wild character which properly belong to the objects we look upon. For the same reason, it requires an effort of the understanding to remind us that the system of society under which the Highland clans were governed, although having much in it which awakens both the heart and the fancy, was hostile to liberty, and to the progress both of religious and moral improvement, by placing the happiness, and indeed the whole existence of tribes at the disposal of individuals whose power of administration was influenced by no restraint saving their own pleasure. Like other men, the heads of the clans were liable to be seduced into the misuse of unlimited authority, and you have only to recall what I have said in these pages of Lovat and others, to be aware what a curse and a plague a violent or crafty chief might prove to his own clan, to the general government, to the peace of his neighbours, and indeed to the whole country in which he lived. The possession of such power by a few men made it always possible for them to erect the standard of civil war in a country otherwise disposed to peace; and their own bravery and that of their retainers only rendered the case more dangerous, the provocation more easily taken, and their powers of attack or resistance more bloody and desperate. Even in peace the power of ravaging the estates of a neighbour or of the Lowlands, by letting loose upon them troops of banditti, kennelled like blood-hounds in some obscure valley till their services were required, was giving to every petty chieftain the means of spreading robbery and desolation through the country at his pleasure.

With whatever sympathy, therefore, we may regard the immediate sufferers; with whatever general regret we may look upon the extinction by violence of a state of society which was so much connected with honour, fidelity, and the tenets of romantic chivalry; it is impossible in sober sense to wish that it should have continued, or to say that, in political wisdom, the government of Great Britain ought to have tolerated its longer existence.

The motives however of the legislature in destroying the character of the patriarchal system adopted in the Highland were more pressing than those arising out of general expedience and utility. The measures struck less at what was inexpedient in general principles than at the constant source of repeated rebellions against the Royal Family; and we cannot wonder that, being now completely masters of the disaffected districts by the fate of war, they aimed at totally eradicating all marks of distinction between the Highlander and Lowlander, and reducing the mountains to the quiet and peaceful state which the Lowlands of Scotland had presented for many years.

The system of disarming the Highlands had been repeatedly reported to upon former occasions, but the object had been only partially attained. It was now resolved, not only, to deprive the Highlanders of their arms, but of the ancient garb of their country; a picturesque habit, the custom of wearing which was peculiarly associated with the use of warlike weapons. The sword, the dirk, the pistol, were all as complete parts of the Highland dress as the plaid and the bonnet, and the habit of using the latter was sure to remind the wearer of the want of the former. It was proposed to destroy this association of ideas, by rendering the use of the Highland garb in any of its peculiar forms highly penal.[1]

Many objections, indeed some which appealed to compassion, and others founded upon utility, were urged against this interdiction of an ancient national costume. It was represented that the form of the dress, light, warm, and convenient for the use of those who were accustomed

---

[1] This was a very harsh regulation, affecting the feelings and the habits of many who had no accession to the rebellion, or who had taken arms to resist it. Yet there was a knowledge of mankind in the prohibition, since it divested the Highlanders of a dress which was closely associated with their habits of clanship and of war. In like manner, I am informed that in some provinces of Italy the peculiar dress of the banditti is prohibited to be worn even at masquerades, as it is found to excite by association a liking to the freebooting trade.

to it, was essentially necessary to men who had to perform long journeys through a wild and desolate country; or discharge the labours of
the shepherd or herdsman among extensive mountains and deserts,
which must necessarily be applied to pasture. The proscription also of
a national garb, to which the people had been long accustomed, and
were necessarily much attached, was complained of as a stretch of arbitrary power, especially as the law was declared to extend to large districts and tracts of country, the inhabitants of which had not only
refrained from aiding the rebellion, but had given ready and effectual
assistance in its suppression.

Notwithstanding these reasons, and notwithstanding the representation of the loyal chiefs that it was unjust to deprive them of the
swords which they had used in the Government's defence, it was
judged necessary to proceed with the proposed measure, as one which,
rigidly enforced by the proposed severity of Government, promised
completely to break the martial spirit of the Highlanders, so far as it
had been found inconsistent with the peace and safety of the country
at large. A law was accordingly passed forbidding the use of what is
called tartan, in all its various checkers and modifications, under
penalties which at that time might be necessary to overcome the reluctance of the Highlanders to part with their national dress, but which
certainly now appear disproportioned to the offence. The wearing any
part of what is called the Highland garb, that is, the plaid, philabeg,
trews, shoulder-belt, or any other distinctive part of the dress, or the
use of any garment composed of tartan, or parti-coloured cloth, made
the offender liable for the first offence to six months' imprisonment;
and for the second, to transportation to the colonies. At the same time,
the wearing or even possession of arms subjected a Highlander to serve
as a common soldier, if he should prove unable to pay a fine of fifteen
pounds. A second offence was to be punished with transportation for
seven years. The statute is 20th George II. cap. 51.

Whatever may be thought of these two statutes, not only restraining the use of arms under the highest penalties, but proscribing the
dress of a whole nation, no objection can be made to another Act of
Parliament passed in the year 1748, for abolishing the last effectual
remnant of the feudal system, viz. the hereditary jurisdictions throughout Scotland. These last remains of the feudal system I have repeatedly
alluded to, as contrary alike to common sense and to the free and
impartial administration of justice. In fact, they vested the power of

deciding all ordinary actions at law in the persons of great landholders, neither educated to the legal profession nor in the habit of separating their own interests and passions from the causes which they were to decide as judges. The statute appointed sums of money to be paid as a compensation to the possessors of those judicial rights, whose existence was inimical to the progress of a free country. The administration of justice was vested in professional persons, called sheriffs-depute (so called as deputed by the crown, in contradistinction to the sheriffs principal, formerly enjoying jurisdiction as attached to their patrimony). Such a sheriff-depute was named for each county, to discharge the judicial duties formerly exercised by hereditary judges.

This last Act was not intended for the Highlands alone, its influence being extended throughout Scotland. By the Act of 20th King Geo. II. cap. 5, all tenures by wardholding, that is, where the vassal held lands for the performance of military service, were declared unlawful, and those which existed were changed into holdings for feu, or for blanch tenures,—that is to say, either for payment of an annual sum of money, or some honorary acknowledgment of vassalage,—so that it became impossible for any superior or overlord in future to impose upon his vassals the fatal service of following him to battle, or to discharge the oppressive duties of what were called hunting, hosting, watching, and warding. Thus, although the feudal forms of investiture were retained, all the essential influence of the superior or overlord over the vassal or tenant, and especially the right which he had to bring him into the field of battle, in consequence of his own quarrels, was in future abrogated and disallowed. The consequence of these great alterations we reserve for the next chapter.

LXXXVII

The Last of the Stewarts

1746-1807

BEFORE giving a further account of the effect produced on Scotland and its inhabitants by the Disarming Act, the Jurisdiction Act, and other alterations adopted into the law of Scotland, in consequence of the insurrection of 1745, we may take some notice of the melancholy conclusion of Charles Edward's career, which had commenced with so much brilliancy. There are many persons like this unfortunate Prince, who, having failed in an effort boldly made and prosecuted with vigour, seem afterwards to have been dogged by misfortune, and deprived, by the premature decay of the faculties they once exhibited, of the power of keeping up the reputation gained at the beginning of their career.

On his first arrival in France, with all the eclât of his victories and his sufferings, the Chevalier was very favourably received at court, and obtained considerable advantages for some of his followers. Lochiel and Lord Ogilvie were made lieutenant-colonels in the French service, with means of appointing to commissions some of the most distinguished of the exiles who had participated in their fate. The court of France also granted 40,000 livres a year for the support of such Scottish fugitives as were not provided for in their military service.

This allowance, however liberal on the part of France, was totally insufficient for the maintenance of so many persons, accustomed not only to the necessaries but comforts of life; and it is not to be wondered at that many, reduced to exile and indigence in his cause, murmured, though perhaps with injustice, against the Prince, whose power of alleviating their distresses they might conclude to be greater than it really was.

An incident which followed evinced the same intractability of temper which seems to have characterised this young man in his attempt to regain the throne of his ancestors. When the French Government, in the winter of 1748, were disposed to accede to a peace with England, it an indispensable stipulation, that the young Pretender, as he was styled, should not be permitted to reside within the French territories. The King and ministers of France felt the necessity of acceding to this condition if they would obtain peace; but they were desirous to do so with all the attention possible to the interest and feelings of Charles Edward. With this purpose, they suggested to him that he should retire to Friburg, in Switzerland, where they proposed to assure him an asylum, with a company of guards, a large pension, and the nominal rank and title of Prince of Wales.

It is not easy to say with what possible views Charles rejected these offers, or from what motive, saving the impulse of momentary spleen, he positively refused to leave France. He was in a kingdom, however, where little ceremony was then used upon such occasions. One evening as he went to the opera, he was seized by a party of the French guards, bound hand and foot, and conveyed first to the state prison of Vincennes, and from thence to the town of Avignon, which belonged to the Pope, where he was set at liberty, never to enter France again.

To this unnecessary disgrace Charles appears to have subjected himself from feelings of obstinacy alone; and of course a line of conduct so irrational was little qualified to recommend him as a pleasant guest to other states.

He went first to Venice with a single attendant; but upon a warning from the Senate he returned to Flanders.

Here, about the year 1751, he admitted into his family a female, called Miss Walkinshaw. The person whom he thus received into his intimacy had connections of which his friends and adherents in Britain were extremely jealous. It was said that her sister was a housekeeper at Leicester House, then inhabited by the Prince of Wales; and such was the general suspicion of her betraying her lover, that the persons of distinction in England who continued to adhere to the Jacobite interest sent a special deputy, called Macnamara, to request, in the name of the whole party, that this lady might be removed from the Chevalier's residence, and sent into a convent, at least for a season. The Prince decidedly put a negative upon this proposal,— "Not," he said, "that he entertained any particular affection or even regard for Miss Walkinshaw, but because he would not be dictated to by his subjects in matters respecting his own habits or family." When Macnamara was finally repulsed, he took his leave with concern and indignation, saying, as he retired,—"By what crime, sir, can your family have drawn down the vengeance of Heaven, since it has visited every branch of them through so many ages?"

This haughty reply to a request, reasonable and respectful in itself, was the signal for almost all the Jacobite party in England to break up and dissolve itself; they were probably by this time only watching for an opportunity of deserting with honour a cause which was become hopeless.[1]

Before this general defection, some intrigues had been set on foot in behalf of Charles, but always without much consideration, and by persons of incompetent judgment. Thus the Duchess of Buckingham, a woman of an ambitious but flighty disposition, took it upon her at one time to figure as a patroness of the House of Stewart, and made several journeys from England to Paris, and also to Rome, with the affectation of making herself the heroine of a Jacobite Revolution. This intrigue, it is needless to say, could have no serious object or termination.

In 1750 the Jacobite intrigues continued to go on, and the Prince himself visited London in that year. Dr. King, then at the head of the Church of England Jacobites, received him in his house. He assures us that the scheme which Charles had formed was impracticable, and that he was soon prevailed upon to return to the Continent.[2] Dr. King at

---

[1] "From this anecdote, the general truth of which is indubitable, the principal fault of Charles Edward's temper is sufficiently obvious. It was a high sense of his own importance, and an obstinate adherence to what he had once determined on—qualities which, if he had succeeded in his bold attempt, gave the nation little room to hope that he would have been found free from the love of prerogative and desire of arbitrary power which characterised his unhappy grandfather."—*Introduction to Redgauntlet.*

[2] "September 1750—I received a note from my Lady Primrose, who desired to see me immediately. As soon as I waited on her, she led me into her dressing-room and

this time draws a harsh picture of the unfortunate Prince; he represents him as cold, interested, and avaricious, which is one frequent indication of a selfish character. This author's evidence, however, must be taken with some modification, since the Doctor wrote his anecdotes at a time when, after having long professed to be at the head of the nonjuring party, he had finally withdrawn from it, joined the Government, and paid his duty at court. He is therefore not likely to have formed an impartial judgment, or to have drawn a faithful picture of the Prince whose cause he had deserted. In 1752 the embers of Jacobitism threw out one or two sparks. Patrick, Lord Elibank, conducted at this time what remained of a Jacobite interest in Scotland; he was a man of great wit, shrewdness, and sagacity; but, like others who are conscious of great talent, often both in his conduct and conversation chose the most disadvantageous side of the question, in order to make a more marked display of his abilities.

The Honourable Alexander Murray, one of Lord Eubank's brothers, a very daring man, had devised a desperate scheme for seizing upon the palace of St. James's and the person of the King, by means of sixty determined men. There was a second branch of the conspiracy which should have exploded in Scotland, where there were no longer either men or means to accomplish an insurrection. MacDonell of Lochgarry, and Dr. Archibald Cameron, brother to Lochiel, were the agents employed in this northern part of the plot. The latter fell into the hands of the Government, being taken upon the banks of Loch Katrine, and sent prisoner to London. Dr. Cameron was brought to trial upon the Bill of

---

presented me to——" [the Chevalier, doubtless]. "If I was surprised to find him there, I was still more astonished when he acquainted me with the motives which had induced him to hazard a journey to England at this juncture. The impatience of his friends who were in exile had formed a scheme which was impracticable; but although it had been as feasible as they had represented it to him, yet no preparation had been made, nor was anything ready to carry it into execution. He was soon convinced that he had been deceived; and therefore, after a stay in London of five days only, he returned to the place from whence he came."—KING'S *Anecdotes of his own Times*. Sir Walter Scott adds, "Dr. King was in 1750 a keen Jacobite, as may be inferred from the visit made by him to the Prince under such circumstances, and from his being one of that unfortunate person's chosen correspondents. He, as well as other men of sense and observation, began to despair of making their fortune in the party which they had chosen. It was indeed sufficiently dangerous; for during the short visit just described one of Dr. King's servants remarked the stranger's likeness to Prince Charles, whom he recognised from the common busts."—*Introduction to Redgauntlet*.

Attainder, passed against him on account of his concern in the Rebellion of 1745, and upon that charge be was arraigned, condemned, and put to death at Tyburn, June 1753. His execution for this old offence, after the date of hostilities had been so long past, threw much reproach upon the Government, and even upon the personal character of George the Second, as sullen, relentless, and unforgiving. These aspersions were the more credited, that Dr. Cameron was a man of a mild and gentle disposition, had taken no military share in the Rebellion, and had uniformly exercised his skill as a medical man in behalf of the wounded of both armies. Yet since, as is now well known, he returned to Scotland with the purpose of again awakening the flames of rebellion, it must be owned that whatever his private character might be, he only encountered the fate which his enterprise merited and justified.

The Honourable Alexander Murray ventured to London about the same period, where a proclamation was speedily issued for his arrest. Having discovered that the persons on whose assistance he had relied for the execution of his scheme had lost courage, he renounced the enterprise. Other wild or inefficient intrigues were carried on in behalf of Charles down to about 1760; but they have all the character of being formed by mere projectors, desirous of obtaining money from the exiled Prince, without any reasonable prospect, perhaps without any serious purpose, of rendering him effectual service.

A few years later than the period last mentioned, a person seems to have been desirous to obtain Charles's commission to form some interest for him among the North American colonists, who had then commenced their quarrels with the mother country. It was proposed by the Adventurer alluded to, to make a party for the Prince among the insurgents in a country which contained many Highlanders. But that scheme also was entirely without solid foundation, for the Scottish colonists in general joined the party of King George.

Amidst these vain intrigues, excited by new hopes, which were always succeeded by fresh disappointment, Charles, who had supported so much real distress and fatigue with fortitude and firmness, gave way both in mind and body. His domestic uneasiness was increased by an unhappy union with Louisa of Stohlberg, a German princess, which produced happiness to neither party, and some discredit to both. Latterly, after long retaining the title of Prince of Wales, he laid it aside, because, after his father's death in 1766, the courts of Europe would not recognise him as King of Great Britain.

He afterwards lived incognito under the title of Count D'Albany.[1] Finally, he died at Rome upon the 31st of January 1788, in his 68th year, and was royally interred in the cathedral church of Frescati, of which his brother was bishop.

The merits of this unhappy Prince appear to have consisted in a degree of dauntless resolution and enterprise bordering upon temerity; the power of supporting fatigues and misfortunes, and extremity of every kind, with firmness and magnanimity; and a natural courtesy of manner highly gratifying to his followers, which he could exchange for reserve at his pleasure. Nor, when his campaign in Scotland is considered, can he be denied respectable talents in military affairs. Some of his partisans of higher rank conceived he evinced less gratitude for their services than he ought to have rendered them; but by far the greater part of those who approached his person were unable to mention him without tears of sorrow, to which your Grandfather has been frequently a witness.

His faults or errors arose from a course of tuition totally unfit for the situation to which he conceived himself born. His education, entrusted to narrow-minded priests and soldiers of fortune, had been singularly limited and imperfect; so that, instead of being taught to disown or greatly modify the tenets which had made his fathers exiles from their throne and country, he was instructed to cling to those errors as sacred maxims, to which he was bound in honour and conscience to adhere. He left a natural daughter, called Countess of Albany, who died only a few years since.

---

[1] "Family discord came to add its sting to those of disappointed ambition; and, though a humiliating circumstance, it is generally acknowledged that Charles Edward, the adventurous, the gallant, and the handsome, the leader of a race of pristine valour, whose romantic qualities may be said to have died along with him, had, in his latter days, yielded to those humiliating habits of intoxication in which the meanest mortals seek to drown the recollection of their disappointments and miseries. Under such circumstances, the unhappy Prince lost the friendship even of those faithful followers who had most devoted themselves to his misfortunes, and was surrounded, with some honourable exceptions, by men of a lower description, regardless of the character which he was himself no longer able to protect. It is a fact consistent with the author's knowledge, that persons totally unentitled to, and unfitted for such a distinction, were presented to the unfortunate Prince in moments unfit for presentation of any kind. Amid these clouds was at length extinguished the torch which once shook itself over Britain with such terrific glare, and at last sunk in its own ashes, scarce remembered, and scarce noted."—*Introduction to Redgauntlet.*

The last direct male heir of the line of Stewart, on the death of Charles, was his younger brother, Henry Benedict, whom the Pope had created a Cardinal. This Prince took no other step for asserting his claim to the British kingdoms than by striking a beautiful medal, in which he is represented in his cardinal's robes, with the crown, sceptre, and regalia in the background, bearing the motto, *Voluntate dei non desiderio populi*, implying a tacit relinquishment of the claims to which, by birth, he might have pretended. He was a Prince of a mild and beneficent character, and generally beloved. After the innovations of the French Revolution had destroyed, or greatly diminished, the revenues he derived from the church, he subsisted, singular to tell, on an annuity of £4000 a year assigned to him by the generosity of the late King George the Third, and continued by that of his royal successor. In requital of their bounty, and as if acknowledging the House of Hanover to be the legitimate successors of his claims to the crown of Britain, this, the last of the Stewarts, bequeathed to his Majesty George IV. all the crown jewels, some of them of great value, which King James the Second had carried along with him on his retreat to the Continent in 1688, together with a mass of papers, tending to throw much light on British history. He died at Rome, June 1807, in the 83d year of his age.

Having now finished my account of the House of Stewart extinguished in the person of its last direct male heir, I return to notice the general effects produced in Scotland, by the laws adopted for the abolition of the hereditary jurisdictions, and prohibition of the Highland dress and arms. On the first point, no dissatisfaction was expressed, and little was probably felt, excepting by a few landed proprietors, who might conceive their dignity diminished by their power over their tenants being abridged and limited. But it was different with the Disarming Act, which was resented by the Highlanders as a deadly insult, and. which seemed for a considerable time rather to increase than allay the discontent which it was the desire of the Government to appease.

Indeed, when the state of the Highlands is considered, we cannot be surprised, that for the space of ten years at least, it should have been wilder than it was before, the insurrection. The country was filled with desperate men, whom their education to the use of arms, as well as the recent scenes of civil war, had familiarised to rapine and violence, and the check, such as it was, which the authority of the chiefs extended over malefactors, was entirely dissolved by the downfall of their power. Accordingly, the criminal records of that period are full of atrocities of various kinds, perpetrated in the Highlands, which give a strange idea of the disorderly state of the country.

Tradition also delights to enumerate, among the sons of vulgar rapine, the names of Sergeant Mor Cameron, and others, depredators of milder mood, and whose fame might rank with that of Robin Hood and his merry archers, as friends and benefactors to the poor, though plunderers of the rich. The sword of justice was employed in weeding them out; and if frequent examples of punishment did not correct the old depredators, it warned the young from following their footsteps. But the race of *Forty-five* men, as they were called, who supplied this generation of heroes, became in time old, and accustomed to peaceful habits.

Government also had, by the Act of Attainder, which forfeited the lands of those engaged in the rebellion, acquired very large estates in the Highlands, which had previously belonged to the Jacobite chiefs. More wise than their predecessors in 1715, instead of bringing this property to sale, they retained it under the management of a Board of Commissioners, by whom, after the necessary expenses were defrayed, the surplus revenue was applied to the improvement of Scottish arts and manufactures, and especially to the amelioration of the Highlands. The example of agriculture and successful industry, which was set on foot under the patronage of these commissioners, was initiated by those Highlanders who, excluded from the rough trade of arms, began to turn a late and unwilling eye to such pursuits. The character of the natives, as well as the face of the country, underwent a gradual change; the ideas of clanship, which long clung to the heart of a Scottish Highlander, gradu-ally gave way under the absence of many chiefs and the impoverishment of others. The genius of the Earl of Chatham, about the same time also, opened a fresh career to the martial spirit of the Highlanders, by levying regiments for the service of Government in Canada, where they behaved themselves in a distinguished manner; while, in the meantime, the absence of the most inflammable part of a superabundant population greatly diminished the risk of fresh disturbances. Many persons also, who had served in their youth in the campaigns of Prince Charles, now entered this new levy, and drew the sword for the reigning monarch, whose generosity readily opened every rank of military service to his ancient enemies. I will give you one instance among many:

The commission of a field officer, in one of these new regiments, being about to be bestowed on a gentleman of Athole, a courtier, who had some desire to change the destination of the appointment, told his late Majesty (George III.) of some bold and desperate actions which the candidate for military preferment had performed on the side of Charles Edward, during the insurrection of 1745. "Has this gentleman really fought so well against me?" said the good-natured and well-judging monarch; "then, believe me, he will fight as well in my cause." So the commission kept its original destination.

Such instances of generosity, on the part of the sovereign, could not but make proselytes among a warm-hearted people like the Jacobites, with whom George the Third became personally popular at an early period of his reign. With an amiable inconsistency, many of those who had fought against the grandfather would have spent the last drop of their blood for the grandchild, and those who even yet refused to abjure the right of the Pretender, showed themselves ready to lay down their lives for the reigning monarch.

While a good understanding was gradually increasing between the Highlanders and the Government, which they had opposed so long and with so much obstinacy, the management of the forfeited estates in the Highlands was so conducted as to afford the cultivators a happy and easy existence; and though old men might turn back with fondness to the recollection of their younger days, when every Highlander walked the heath with his weapons rattling around him, the preference must, upon the whole, have been given to a period in which a man's right needed nothing else to secure it than the equal defence of the law. In process of time, it was conceived by Government that the period of punishment by forfeiture ought, in equity as well as policy, to be brought to a close, and that the descendants of the original insurgents of the year 1745, holding different tenets from their unfortunate ancestors, might be safely restored to the enjoyment of their patrimonial fortunes. By an Act of Grace accordingly, dated 24th George III. cap. 37, the estates forfeited for treason, in the year 1745, were restored to the descendants of those by whom they had been forfeited. A long train of honourable names was thus restored to Scottish history, and a debt of gratitude imposed upon their representatives to the memory of the then reigning monarch. To complete this Act of Grace, His Majesty King George IV., in addition to the forfeited property returned by his father, restored, in blood, such persons descended of attainted individuals as would have been heirs to Peerages had it not been for the attainder—a step well chosen to mark the favour entertained by his Majesty for his Scottish subjects, and his desire to obliterate all recollection that discord had ever existed between his royal house and any of their ancestors.[1]

Another feature of the same lenient and healing measures was the restoring the complete liberty of wearing the Highland dress, without incurring penalty or prosecution, by 22d George III. cap. 63. This boon was accepted with great apparent joy by the natives of the Highlands; but an effectual change of customs having been introduced during the years in which it was proscribed, and the existing generation having become accustomed to the Lowland dress, the ancient garb is seldom to be seen, excepting when assumed upon festive occasions.

A change of a different kind is very deeply connected with the principles of political economy, but I can here do little more than name it. Clanship, I have said, was abolished, or subsisted only as the shadow of a shade; the generality of Highland proprietors, therefore, were unwilling to support, upon their own estates, in the capacity of poor kindred, a number of men whom they no longer had the means of employing in military service. They were desirous, like a nation in profound peace, to discharge the soldiers for whom they had no longer use, and who, indeed, could no longer legally remain under their authority. The country was, therefore, exposed to all the inconveniences of an over population, while the proprietors were, by the same circumstance, encumbered by the number of persons whom, under the old system, they would have been glad to have enrolled in their clan-following.

Another circumstance greatly increased the multitude of Highlanders whom this new state of things threw out of employment.

The mountainous region of the north of Scotland contained large tracts of moorland, which was anciently employed, chiefly if not

---

[1] "While the life of Charles Edward was gradually wasting in disappointed solitude, the number of those who had shared his misfortunes and dangers had shrunk into a small handful of veterans, the heroes of a tale which had been told. Most Scottish readers who can count the number of sixty years, must recollect many respected acquaintances of their youth, who, as the established phrase gently worded it, had been *out in the Forty-five*. It may be said, that their political principles and plans no longer either gained proselytes or attracted terror,—those who held them had ceased to be the subjects either of fear or opposition. Jacobites were looked upon in society as men who had proved their sincerity by sacrificing their interest to their principles; and in well-regulated companies it was held a piece of ill-breeding to injure their feelings, or ridicule the compromises by which they endeavoured to keep themselves abreast of the current of the day."—*Introduction to Redgauntlet*.

entirely, for the rearing of black cattle. It was, however, found at a later period, that these extensive pastures might, with much better advantage, be engaged in the feeding of sheep; but to this latter mode of employing them the Highlanders are by nature and education decidedly averse and ill qualified, being as unfit for the cares of a shepherd as they are eminently well acquainted with those of the rearer of cattle. The consequence was, that as the Highlands began to be opened to inhabitants from the Lowlands, the sheep farmers of the southland mountains made offers of large rents to the proprietors of these storefarms, with which the Highland tenant was unable to enter into competition; and the latter, deprived at once of their lands and their occupation, left the country in numbers, and emigrated to North America and other foreign settlements.

The author can well recollect the indignation with which these agricultural innovations were regarded by the ancient Highlanders. He remembers hearing a chief of the old school say, in sorrow and indignation, the words following: "When I was a young man, the point upon which every Highland gentleman rested his importance was the number of MEN whom his estate could support; the question next rested on the amount of his stock of BLACK CATTLE; it is now come to respect the number of *sheep*; and I suppose our posterity will inquire how many *rats* or *mice* an estate will produce."

It must be allowed that, in a general point of view, this change was a necessary consequence of the great alteration in the system of manners, and that, therefore, it was an inevitable evil. It is no less true, that the humanity of individual proprietors bestowed much trouble and expense in providing means to enable those inhabitants who were necessarily ejected from their ancient pastures and possessions, to obtain new occupation in the fisheries, and other modes of employment, to which their energies might be profitably turned. Upon the great estate of Sutherland in particular, the Marquis of Stafford incurred an outlay of more than £100,000 in providing various modes of employment for Highland tenants who might be unfit to engage in the new system of improved farming, while two years' free possession of their old farms without rent, in order to furnish funds for their voyage, was allowed to those who might prefer emigration.

But many other Highland proprietors neither possessed the means nor the disposition to await with patience the result of such experiments, and the necessary emigration of their followers was attended with circumstances of great hardship.[1]

It is, however, a change which has taken place, and has had its crisis. The modern Highlanders, trained from their youth to the improved mode of agriculture, may be expected to maintain their place in their native country, without experiencing the oppressive rivalry of the south country farmers, which a change of times has done much to put a stop to. The late introduction of steam navigation, by facilitating the communications with the best markets, presents an important stimulus to the encouragement of industry, in a country almost every-where indented by creeks and salt-water lakes, suitable to the access of steam vessels. We may therefore hope, in terms of the Highland Society's motto, that a race always renowned in arms will henceforward be equally distinguished by industry.

With the Highlands we have now done, nor are their inhabitants now much distinguished from those of the rest of Scotland, except in the use of the Gaelic language, and that they still retain some vestiges of their ancient feelings and manners.

Neither has anything occurred in Scotland at large to furnish matter for the continuation of these narratives. She has since 1746 regularly felt her share in the elevation or abasement of the rest of the empire. The civil war, a cruelly severe, yet a most effectual remedy, had destroyed the seeds of disunion which existed in the bosom of Scotland; her commerce gradually increased, and, though checked for a time by the American war, revived after the peace of 1780, with a

---

[1] A Reviewer in 1816 says—"In many instances, Highland proprietors have laboured with laudable and humane precaution to render the change introduced by a new mode of cultivation gentle and gradual, and to provide, as far as possible, employ-ment and protection for those families who were thereby dispossessed of their ancient habitations. But in other, and in too many instances, the glens of the Highlands have been drained, not of their superfluity of population, but of the whole mass of the inhabitants, dispossessed by an unrelenting avarice, which will be one day found to have been as shortsighted as it is unjust and selfish. Meanwhile, the Highlands may become the fairy ground for romance and poetry, or subject of experiment for the pro-fessors of speculation, political and economical. But if the hour of need should come—and it may not, perhaps, be far distant—the pibroch may sound through the deserted region, but the summons will remain unanswered. The children who have left her will re-echo from a distant shore the sounds with which they took leave of their own—*Ha til, ha til, ha til, mi tulidh!*—'We return—we return—we return—no more!'" —*Review of Culloden Papers.*

brilliancy of success hitherto unexampled. The useful arts, agriculture, navigation, and all the aids which natural philosophy affords to industry, came in the train of commerce. The shocks which the country sustained after the peace of 1815 arose out of causes general to the imperial kingdoms and not peculiar to Scotland. It may be added also, that she did not bear more than her own share of the burden, and looked forward with confidence to be relieved from it as early as any of the sister kingdoms.

KINGS OF SCOTLAND

Dep. indicates *deposed*—Ab. *abdicated*—Res. *resigned*—d. *daughter*

Name	Parentage	Marriage	Accession (A.D.)	Death (A.D.)	Reign (Yrs.)	Children
Duncan I.	Crinan, Abbot of Dunkeld, and Beatrice, d. of Malcolm II.	With the sister of Seward, Earl of Northumberland.	1034	1039	6	1. Malcolm Canmore; 2. Donald Bane.
Macbeth.	Finlegh, Thane of Ross and Doada, d. of Malcolm II.	The Lady Gruach, granddaughter of Kenneth IV.	1039	1056	17	
Malcolm III. (Canmore.)	Duncan I.	Margaret of England.	1057	1093	36	1. Edward; 2. Ethelred; 3. Edmund; 4. EDGAR; 5. ALEXANDER; 6. DAVID; 7. Matilda; 8. Mary.
Donald Bane.	Duncan I.		1093	1094	1	
Duncan II.	Grandson of Malcolm III.	Ethreda, daughter of Gosspatric.	1094	1095	1	William.
Donald (restored).			1095	Dep 1097	2	Madach, 1st Earl of Athole.
Edgar.	Malcolm III.		1097	1107	10	
Alexander I.	Malcolm III.	Sibilla, natural d. of Henry I. of England.	1107	1124	18	
David I.	Malcolm III.	Matilda, d. of Waltheof, Earl of Northumberland.	1124	1153	30	Henry[1].
Malcolm IV.	Henry, son of David I. and Ada, d. of the Earl of Warrne and Surrey.		1153	1165	13	
William the Lion.	The same.	Ermengarde, d. of Viscount Beaumont.	1165	1214	49	1. ALEXANDER; 2. Margaret; 3. Isabella; 4. Marjory.
Alexander II.	William.	I. Joan, d. of King John of England, no issue; II. Mary of Picardy.	1214	1249	35	ALEXANDER.

[1] Prince Henry who died before his father, 12th June 1152, married Ada, d. of Earl of Warrene and Surrey. Issue: 1. Malcolm; 2. William, afterwards Kings; 3. David, Earl of Huntington, and three daughters.

Name	Parentage	Marriage	Accession (A.D.)	Death (A.D.)	Reign (Yrs.)	Children
Alexander III.	Alexander II.	I. Margaret, d. of King Henry III. of England, issue; II. Joleta, d. of the Count de Dreux, no issue.	1249	1286	37	1. Alexander; 2. David; 3. Margaret.
Margaret.	Eric, King of Norway, and Margaret, d. of Alexander III.		1286	1290	5	
Interregnum.					2	
John Baliol.	John Baliol of Barnard Castle, and Devorgoil, gr. d. of David, Earl of Huntington, gr. son of David I. Marriage: Isabella, d. of John de Warren, Earl of Surrey.	Isabella, d. of John de Warren, Earl of Surrey.	1292	Res. 1296 died 1314	4	1. Edward; 2. Henry.
Interregnum.					10	
Robert I. The Bruce.	The grandson of Bruce, Baliol's competitor.	I. Isabella, d. of Donald, tenth Earl of Mar; II. Elizabeth, d. of the Earl of Ulster.	1306	1329	24	I. Marjory. II. 1. DAVID; 2. Margaret; 3. Matilda; 4. Elizabeth.
David II.	Robert Bruce.	I. Johanna, d. of King Edward II. of England; II. Margaret, d. of Sir J. Logie.	1329	1371	42	

HOUSE OF STEWART

Name	Parentage	Marriage	Accession (A.D.)	Death (A.D.)	Reign (Yrs.)	Children
Robert II.	Walter, Steward of Scotland, and Marjory, d. of Robert Bruce.	I. Elizabeth, d. of Sir Adam More of Rowallan; II. Euphemia, d. of the Earl of Ross.	1371	1390	19	I. 1. John, afterwards named ROBERT; 2. Walter; 3. Robert; 4. Alexander; and six daughters. II. 1. David; 2. Walter; and four daughters.
Robert III.	Robert II.	Annabella, d. of Sir John Drummond of Stobhall.	1390	1406	17	1. David, Duke of Rothsay; 2. James; and three daughters.
Regencies of the Dukes of Albany, 1406 to 1424			1406	1424	18	
James I.	Robert III.	Joanna, d. of John, Duke of Somerset, gr. Grandson of King Edward III.	1424	1437	13	1. JAMES; and five daughters.
James II.	James I.	Mary, d. of Arnold, Duke of Guelderland.	1437	1460	24	1. JAMES; 2. Alexander; 3. John; 4. Mary; 5. Margaret.

Name	Parentage	Marriage	Accession (A.D.)	Death (A.D.)	Reign (Yrs.)	Children
James III.	James II.	Margaret of Denmark.	1460	1488	28	1. JAMES; 2. James, Marquis of Ormond; 3. John, Earl of Mar.
James IV.	James III.	Margaret, d. of King Henry VII. of England.	1488	1513	26	1. JAMES; 2. Alexander.
James V.	James IV.	I. Magdalen, d. of King Francis I. of France; II. Mary, d. of the Duke of Guise.	1513	1542	29	MARY.
Regency.			1542	1561	19	
Mary.	James V.	I. Francis, son of King Henry II. of France; II. Henry, Lord Darnley; III. Hepburn, E. of Bothwell.	1561 Res. 1567	1587	6	JAMES.
James VI.	Mary.	Anne of Denmark.	1567		36	
Union of the Crowns. James VI. now James. I. of England.			1603	1625	22	1. Henry; 2. CHARLES; 3. Elizabeth.
Charles I.	James VI.	Henrietta of France.	1625	1649	24	1. CHARLES; 2. JAMES; 3. Henry; 4. Mary; 5. Elizabeth; 6. Henrietta.
Charles II.	Charles I.	Catherine of Portugal.	1649		2	
The Commonwealth			1651	1660	9	
Charles II. restored.			1660	1685	25	
James VII. and II. of England[1].	Charles I.	I. Anne Hyde, d. of the Earl of Clarendon; II. Mary of Este.	1685	Abd. 1688	4	I. 1. MARY; 2. ANNE. II. James, afterwards known as the Pretender.
William III. and	Prince of Orange	Mary, d. of King James VII.	1689	M. 1694	6	
Mary	James VII.	William, Prince of Orange.	—	W. 1701	13	
Anne.	James VII.	Prince George of Denmark.	1701	1714	14	

[1] The last Sovereign of the House of Stewart, in the male line.

Name	Parentage	Marriage	Accession (A.D.)	Death (A.D.)	Reign (Yrs.)	Children
Union of Parliaments (1707)						
George I.	Sophia, grand d. of James VI.	Sophia, d. of the Duke of Zell.	1714	1727	13	1. GEORGE; 2. Sophia.
George II.	George I.	Caroline of Anspach.	1727	1760	34	1. Frederick, father of George III.; 2. William, Duke of Cumberland; and five daughters.

INDEX

Printed in the USA
CPSIA information can be obtained
at www.ICGtesting.com
JSHW082149140824
68134JS00014B/147